BEYOND BRATWURST

FOODS AND NATIONS is a new series from Reaktion that explores the history – and geography – of food. Books in the series reveal the hidden history behind the food eaten today in different countries and regions of the world, telling the story of how food production and consumption developed, and how they were influenced by the culinary practices of other places and peoples. Each book in the Foods and Nations series offers fascinating insights into the distinct flavours of a country and its culture.

Already published

Al Dente: A History of Food in Italy
Fabio Parasecoli

Beyond Bratwurst: A History of Food in Germany
Ursula Heinzelmann

Beyond Bratwurst

A History of Food
in Germany

Ursula Heinzelmann

REAKTION BOOKS

To Barbara, Darra and Elisabeth –
strongholds of encouragement
and wisdom

Published by Reaktion Books Ltd
33 Great Sutton Street
London EC1V 0DX, UK
www.reaktionbooks.co.uk

First published 2014
Copyright © Ursula Heinzelmann 2014

Printed and bound in China
by Toppan Printing Co. Ltd

A catalogue record for this book is available from the British Library
ISBN 978 1 78023 272 0

CONTENTS

German Food: A Complex Dish

What is German about the way Germans eat, what they eat and why? Following renewed discussion in recent years about what makes Germans German, this book tries to answer that question through looking at the country's food and its evolution through history. It is a complex question to which there is no one definitive answer. But as a German food writer, a food historian and a passionate cook, I strongly believe that even an incomplete answer has much to offer. In our pots and pans, on our plates and in our glasses, just as in other areas of life, the past can help us to understand the present, and ideally could serve as a guide for the future.

From the earliest beginnings, food and cooking in Germany have been marked by the geographic and climatic differences between north and south as well as the continuous cultural influences from all sides. I argue that the openness and receptiveness Germans have shown towards those influences mark them right up to the present day. Instead of clinging desperately to something static that must at all costs be preserved, such as an haute cuisine that is cut in stone, new layers of cuisine have again and again been added from all sides, leading to frequent rejuvenation and a food culture with a remarkable flexibility. I further argue that Germany's decentralized structure, so often quoted as being to its disadvantage, actually promoted this receptiveness and plurality.

Instead of being uniform, German food has always been extremely complex. The regional variations of today are based as much on political, cultural and socio-economic history as on geography. This process has by no means always been easy or smooth. Different social groups often reacted quite differently to changes. One only needs to think of coffee (very rapidly found highly desirable by all social strata but quickly deemed dangerously expensive and wasteful, and only appropriate for a select few) or potatoes (which eventually proved to be life-saving nourishment, but were first thought of by most as animal fodder at best). Both eventually gained wide acceptance as vital elements of German food culture.

Food and Germany is a combination that makes most people think of beer and sausage, pretzels and Limburger cheese. However, the 82 million inhabitants of contemporary Germany do not all exclusively live on Oktoberfest fare. If they did, a food historian's job would quickly be done. In fact the opposite is the case, as in most modern cultures: the far-reaching effects of globalization have made it difficult to trace the complex roots of the many traditions that together form German food.

Looked at on a geo-historical level, Germany is a country in the middle of the European continent, situated between the Slavs and the Romans, cold and heat, sea and mountains. In the course of history it has seen an enormous number of influences from all sides. To understand the past – the background of all this meeting and melding – is to understand the reasons why people in Germany eat how they do today. Unlike its neighbour France, for instance, Germany has no single national, overarching 'haute' cuisine, nor even a national dish, such as Brazil's *feijoada*. Although it is not a particularly large country (in terms of land area, it is slightly larger than half the size of France, with a population that outnumbers its western neighbour by one-third), its culture is remarkably complex.

Aside from geographic and climatic reasons, this is mainly due to four factors. First, in the past as now, populations were not static, and when people moved they took some of their food preferences with them. In a similar manner German emigrants took their foodways with them over the Atlantic to the Americas. Second, the disintegration of the (albeit not very tightly joined) nation into countless small political units following the decline of Charlemagne's kingdom in the course of the ninth century (a process that did not go into reverse until Napoleon's restructuring of the European map in the early 1800s) was the basis for a variety of regional cuisines, each itself a complex system of socio-economic and cultural layers. Third, the Reformation movement instigated by Martin Luther and many like-minded innovators set an example for the wider populace that it was possible to be different and act differently from each other. Last, the late but far-reaching and intense industrialization which turned a patchwork of agrarian states into one

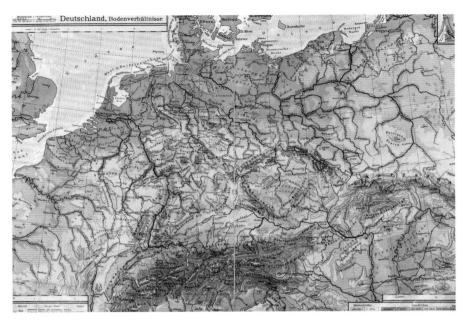

The topography of Germany (within the borders of 1930).

thoroughly urbanized industrial one led to a surge of irrational fears as well as longings for paradise lost, that is, a supposedly perfect past of naturalness. In some respects the origins of contemporary organic food stores go back to this.

How far can one trace German foodways back in time? One of the first written records comes from the Roman historian Tacitus in the first century AD. In his *Germania* he described the food habits of the 'wild' German tribes. According to him they survived on wild fruits, game meat that was fresh and had not been hung (a serious indication of lack of civilization, from a Roman point of view) and *lac concretum* (curdled milk or quark). Tacitus also mentioned a beverage he described as wine-like, made from fermented barley or other grain. Although he seems partly to have been interested in showing his effeminate, degenerate compatriots an unspoilt, naturally strong people (and his description must therefore be taken with a pinch of salt), it is striking that beer, meat and cheese, three of the usual Oktoberfest suspects, were already big favourites of the Germans nearly 2,000 years ago.

Of course, the history of food in Germany starts much earlier than the first century. I will use the term 'Germany' throughout the book to avoid too much entanglement with political geography. Germania, the Roman Empire, the Holy Roman Empire, the Holy Roman Empire of the German Nation, Imperial Germany . . . as designations changed, frontiers moved back and forth again and again. The further one goes back in time, the more difficult it is to separate the specific area that is Germany today from the development of Central Europe in general. For instance, it was only over a long period of time that Austria and Switzerland became clearly separate places on the culinary map. Nevertheless, as far as possible my focus will be on the area contiguous with contemporary Germany.

Food is more tangible than any abstract historical theory. Food history not only shines a light on who eats what, how, where and when, but also illuminates the production, selection, preparation and presentation of food as well as all practicalities surrounding it. The absence of food – famine and hunger – is very much part of the story, as it shaped the Germans just as much as what they did and do still consume. Although this quickly leads to larger political questions, I will refrain from telling Germany's general history. For this many and more competent sources are available, not least in English.

As we progress through time, different periods make for radically different situations for the historian. Generally speaking sources become more abundant and the emerging picture more complex, up to the point when we reach what is currently filling our larder, cooking on our stoves and steaming on our plates. On our way through the centuries, whenever possible, I will suggest and describe culinary places in time – that is, places in Germany where the historical layers that form the present incarnation of German food can be directly experienced, be it in kitchens, restaurants or farms. And now, to quote the great American food writer M.F.K. Fisher, let's set out 'with bold knife and fork' and dig deep into German food.

ONE

From Gruel to Sourdough Bread: The Neolithic, Bronze and Iron Ages

The smell of gruel filled the hut. The coarsely ground emmer simmered gently in a round earthen pot whose pointed bottom was stuck into the glowing embers at the edge of the open fire. The finely cut pieces of pork in it gave it a special aroma, as did the roughly chopped wild garlic and the fresh, soft hazelnuts. The wooden spoons were all ready for everybody to dig in. The next day, there would be simple flat bread instead of gruel, accompanied with boiled lentils and a bit more of the pork. That was a rather special meal, because the grain had to be ground finer, and the women would have to heat the dome-shaped oven in order to make the bread. But it also meant they would be able to dry the crabapples they had gathered while the men slaughtered the pig. This would not only take away the halved apples' tannic sharpness, but would help them to keep until well into the winter. It took experience and a lot of work to stock the larder well and make it through the long, cold, dark months.

It is certainly tempting to imagine our Neolithic ancestors's meals in this way, and more than a little vexing that we have no clue about their favoured recipes. Ever so often, while writing this book, I wished I could travel back in time and smell, taste and see for myself. Even if some archaeological miracle suddenly presented us with something like a recipe, our modern ingredients would make it very difficult to get any meaningful results from 'reconstructing' it. However, archaeologists have been coming up with increasingly detailed information, and in fact we know rather a lot about the foodstuffs early Germans chose to gather and collect, hunt or raise, and how they slaughtered, harvested, stored and cooked them.

Grain is undoubtedly one of the keys to our civilization. It is extremely difficult to survive on meat alone, especially lean meat, as the body also needs fat and/or carbohydrates. Even if you use all the fat a wild beast's carcass offers, you wouldn't put on much yourself. Grains – first gathered from the wild, then encouraged to grow more intensively – offer easily digestible and storeable energy. This budding agriculture seems to have been as flexible as the first nomadic herding, since fields were moved frequently. With time, both tended to become more sedentary, possibly at especially convenient spots. In the Near East agriculture and animal husbandry began as early as 12,000 BC, but these practices took several millennia to reach Central Europe.

Up in the cooler northern regions of Europe, our earliest ancestors only survived the many ice ages because they learnt to control fire. Cooked food, especially meat, proved to be much more easily digestible than raw, and the range of food on offer became much more varied – and tasty. But you had to adapt as best you could to what nature offered in order to live well. Hunting, nomadic herding and animal husbandry on one hand, and gathering, selective cropping and an agriculture that frequently moved fields on the other, presented a wide choice of possibilities. If you wanted to eat well – that is, to survive – you needed to figure out the right mix that suited your location. Around 5,500 BC a more sedentary lifestyle with permanent settlements as well as domesticated plants and animals began to appear in Germany. Experts are divided as to whether these changes indicate the migration and resettlement of peasants or a general adoption of this new way of life. Seeing that the new trend came from the southeast and that in Germany the south and centre took to it much more quickly and widely, one would be tempted to argue for the former. A recent study of ceramic containers from immediately before and after the first evidence of domesticated animals and plants on the Western Baltic has shown that the so-called Neolithic Revolution happened very gradually indeed. In those cooking pots domestic cattle and sheep (or goat, as these are extremely difficult to tell apart) are mixed with red deer and mussels.[1] The former tundra and later forest hunters of the north were also skilled fishermen who built elaborate dug-out canoes. Like their contemporaries all around the Baltic, they hunted seals with harpoons and caught fish such as cod, turbot and flatfish with the help of various nets and traps. They might well have found this much easier than working the soil. But even they succumbed to the trend and became more settled as they gradually got used to the new additions to their diet. Eventually all of them could be called 'proto-farmers'.[2]

Neolithic spoons.

Crops obviously varied from region to region, but they generally included einkorn and above all emmer, ancient kinds of husked wheat. Both these grains are seeing a revival today within the organic movement. Besides these, barley, millet and spelt were harvested, some as winter, some as summer crops. Rye and oat were still very rare and probably just wild invaders. All these grains were supplemented by peas and in some cases lentils. Linseed was valued for its oil content (and later also for its fibre), as were poppyseeds and other seeds gathered from wild plants. Whereas all other domesticated plants came from the Near East, it is interesting to note that the poppy seems to originate in the western Mediterranean.

Initially fields were moved whenever the soil was exhausted, but became more permanent when more manure was available from domestic animals. In these early days of organized agricultural activity, something more akin to horticulture was practised on small plots protected by fences and hedges. Around or near houses, they might have been used for plants considered especially useful and therefore precious, or crops such as peas and lentils which might be threatened by wild animals, or plants that provided a household with everyday supplies. Wooden spades and hoes were used to work the early gardens; as these were extended to become fields, the ard, a simple scratching plough, gradually replaced the hoe. It had the advantage that it could be pulled by draft animals, as evidenced by the earliest example of a yoke dating from around 3,380 BC found close to Lake Constance. Recent archaeological findings in eastern Germany have shown that even before the introduction of metal, these first farmers were accomplished carpenters who excelled in complex timber constructions.[3]

Except for dogs, all domestic animals were introduced in their tame form and came from the Near East. Sheep (much like today's moufflon or moorland breeds) were closely followed by goats, pigs and cattle. Any cross-breeding with wild species was actively avoided. As palaeogenetic studies have shown, the native European aurochs was never domesticated, so that all present-day cattle in fact go back to a small herd in the Near East.[4] Our early animal keepers clearly preferred smaller, tamer beasts, just as they frequently castrated working animals to make them more manageable. Hunting, practised to varying degrees, made for more culinary variety, and provided useful raw material for clothing, tools and so on, but also sought to protect humans and domestic animals from predators such as bears, wolves and wild cats. Hunters had a wide range of efficient weapons: bows and precisely shaped arrowheads fashioned from flint (which were also used for harpooning fish and wild birds) and the javelin, slingshot and spear. Red deer was the most popular prey, followed by fallow deer, wild boar, aurochs and bison, as well as beaver, badger, fox, otter, lynx and (occasionally) hare. Dogs, though valuable for hunting, might on occasion also be eaten or killed for their fur. Molluscs – both fresh and seawater bivalves and snails – were included in the menu, as were pond turtles in some areas during the summer. As for river fish, pike seems to have been particularly sought after, as well as eel, catfish, tench, trout, perch, carp, sturgeon (on occasion), and various smaller varieties. Fish seems to have been popular: in the south fishing was undertaken in lakes situated at significant distances from the relevant settlements.

Berries, fruit, vegetables and herbs mostly added flavour to the food rather than caloric energy: they provided 2.8 per cent of the total on average. Depending on region and season, women (whom archaeologists assume were responsible for the gathering and collecting as well as the cooking) would know to find strawberries, raspberries, blackberries, dewberries, elderberries, hawthorn, rosehips, cornelian cherries, wild grapes, sour cherries, pears, sloes, plums and the very popular crabapples. Hazelnuts were equally sought after and frequently grew around settlements. Wild vegetables such as carrots and parsnips were collected, probably others as well, but evidence of these is difficult to trace as these plants did not set seed before they were cropped and therefore have left no traces behind. Herbs such as nipplewort (lapsana, possibly culti-vated), wild garlic (*Allium ursinum*), several kinds of field lettuce and turnips, orach, bistort, sorrel, stinging nettle and various kinds of fat hen (goosefoot) were soon joined by imports from the Mediterranean littoral, most notably parsley, celery, dill and lemon balm. It is very likely that mistletoe, marjoram, verbena, juniper berries, caraway and mugwort were used for culinary as well as medicinal purposes in the form of spicings or herbal infusions.

Fertile loess soils in the regions of the central uplands were generally the preferred locations for settlements, mostly on gentle slopes along rivers and streams. Settlements ranged from isolated farms at considerable distances from each other, and protected by hedges and fences, to structured villages surrounded by fortifications. Large rectangular half-timbered houses (in wet areas on stilts) were constructed using wood, clay and chalk. They were 5–7 m wide and 10–40 m long and included fireplaces. These large-scale constructions are evidence of extensive, far-reaching resources and a high degree of co-operation. Families or clans of up to three generations (approximately seven to 30 people) shared them, occasionally with animals, though these were usually kept all year round on forest pastures or kraal-like enclosures to protect them from predators. The one-house farms were also used for storing crops, above all grain, and other suitable foodstuffs. Pots for storage were strong and egg-shaped, although those used to store liquids were shaped like big bottles. As with similiar containers made from birch bark, these pots often had handles to which string could be attached, so that they could be hung up to protect them from pests. For longer storage periods, earth-pits up to 2 m deep were used. In these the grain would germinate and form a strong, thick, protective layer that kept the content dry and protected it, as in a silo. Grain was also dried and sometimes roasted before being threshed and winnowed. Threshing was done with wooden flails; grind-ing in hand mills between two stones. Grain varieties with unusually stubborn husks, such as spelt, required arduous pounding in wooden mortars before the kernels could be ground. All these lengthy processes and the tools needed for them were only efficient when carried out in bulk, thus turning grain almost by necessity into a basic food. It has been estimated that a family of seven would have needed to harvest

3,300 kg of grain per year, requiring the cultivation of 1.8 hectares of land.[5]

As animal husbandry developed, separate stable buildings began to appear, though it was only those animals needed for breeding which were kept in the houses and fed through the winter, often with ashtree foliage. Each settlement supplied itself with its own meat, though with noticeable regional preferences. Pork consumption was high in the southwest while it was of lesser importance in the northeast, where red deer hunting was more intense than in any other region. Slaughtering was more frequent during the autumn months. Archaeologists know that it was done by stunning the animal with a hard blow on the head, then cutting the main artery, but unfortunately we can only guess what happened to the blood. The meat of large animals was generally deboned, whereas smaller ones were prepared on the bone, roasted or boiled. Large bones and skulls were often smashed to allow access to marrow and brains, choice parts because of their high fat content.

A wide range of instruments served to produce and prepare food, including shafted hatchets and axes and sickles for cutting grass and harvesting grain. Firestone was knapped into knives and handaxes, and wood, bone, sinews, claws, hides, antlers and vegetable fibres were all used to make other tools and weapons. Earthen containers had been made even before the 'modern' influences from the south and again, styles, methods and decor depended on region and personal preferences. Bowls and flat plates were often polished and decorated. Three-legged pots served for cooking, complemented by a wide variety of wooden utensils in the form of spoons, ladles, mortars and baskets. Wicked lamps served as light sources and might have burned tallow or oil produced from linseed.

Coming back to our initial musing about possible recipes and looking at the wide range of possible ingredients and tools, it is important to keep in mind that they were obviously never found together in one single spot. However, a coherent trading network did stretch all over Central Europe from the Paris basin to the Black Sea, as evidenced by the travels of so-called ribbonware, ceramic containers of a very particular pattern and design that appear throughout Central Europe. Carts were used for transport on roads which in some areas were made up with wooden boards, especially in the wetlands of the northwest. Dug-out canoes and boats made from hides carried people and goods on rivers and streams. Traded goods included grinding stones, usually made from quarried volcanic rock. If our gruel dish was salted, the salt would have been another luxury traded over long distances. Salt, a flavour enhancer as well as a preservative, was increasingly distributed throughout Europe, creating wealth and power for the leading elite of entire regions; as an indication of this, place names that include the word *sal* (Latin) or *hals* (Greek) survive up to the present, such as Schwäbisch Hall or Salzgitter.

As ore started to be mined and worked into copper, yet another import from the Near East, wood became ever more important. Serial production of tools became technically possible through casting, unlike the earlier stone tools which could only be made one at a time. As various groups moved across Europe from the Iberian peninsula up through Bohemia in search of new sources of ore, the spread of copper technology was a catalyst for a new cultural uniformity, not unlike contemporary globalization. This new mobility can be traced though beakers of various styles – pottery as well as gold – generally associated with drinking rituals. Again, we can only speculate as to what kind of liquids these would have involved – mead from precious honey (bees were encouraged to settle in wickerwork beehives) and perhaps some berries? A kind of ale made from more liquid fermented gruel? A mixture of the two? In any case these beakers, found at funeral sites and in other ritual contexts, certainly served as indicators of social importance and high status. They bear witness to the emergence of an elite class who controlled mining and smelting activities and were buried with a great many precious possessions.

However, copper served prestige and vanity rather than being very practical, since it is much softer than stone. As far as food production and preparation were concerned, the next step, copper alloys such as bronze and pewter, usually with tin added, were much more significant, as they enabled different grades of hardness and elasticity. At this time some people might well have cooked gruel in a metal cauldron and served it with a metal ladle. Although stone tools continued to be used in many areas, early small metal sickles and other utensils were made of metal. As a result of more efficient tools, cultivation became a little easier and less labour intensive, enabling higher crop yields and in turn the division of labour among peasants, miners, bronze-casters (resident or travelling), weavers, dyers, tanners and other specialist craftsmen. This increased productivity even further. The result was a store of readily available carbohydrates that provided security and a surplus that could be traded. This led to rapid population growth. Areas away from rivers and on less fertile soils, where some hunters and gatherers were still living the old way, gradually came under cultivation.

Less productive grains such as einkorn became rarer, while spelt, millet, oats and rye were cultivated more widely. Increased grain production furthered the development of mills. For turning mill stones, harder stone was needed, mostly granite, basalt or porphyr. Again these were traded over long distances. Gruel continued to be the main staple food, and was mostly made from barley and millet. Bread was still rare and was usually made from millet, wheat or a combination of both. Bread was a strong indicator of social differentiation: the milling time for a 250 g loaf of fine flour during this period has been estimated at 2½ to 3 hours, which can be taken as a sign of its rarity. Nevertheless it was technically possible to produce finely ground flour from wheat or barley. It could also be used to prepare small, *Spätzle*-like pasta, which required a pot for boiling rather than a bread oven (which in some places had developed into a separate building).

Milk became an additional advantage of animal husbandry as adult humans gradually overcame their inherent lactose intolerance. Early milk drinkers would certainly have known of the benefits of natural curdling as a way of adding a little extra 'shelf life' to a perishable source of protein. The latest archaeological findings confirm the existence of this early cheesemaking: the evidence is ceramic vessels riddled with holes, visually reminiscent of cheese strainers and with traces of milk fat still on them.[6]

Agricultural improvements included the introduction of new oilseed plants such as camelina and hemp, the latter of which was used for fibres as well as oil. In mountainous regions legumes (members of the vetch family) became more important as a food source and possibly also for their usefulness as an indirect source of nitrogen fertilizer. Since legumes were also valued as fodder for domestic animals, the appearance of the fava or broad bean in funerary rituals may well be linked to the gradual domestication of the horse – as indicated by the bean's secondary name in German as in English, *Pferdebohne* or horsebean. Horses joined the domestic menagerie from around 2,500 BC, with the addition shortly thereafter of chickens and, somewhat later, geese. Horsemeat seems rarely to have been eaten, but the animals were used for ritual sacrifice, travelling or riding into battle. Hunting for meat ceased to play an important role in the provision of everyday food, and the hunting of larger animals in particular gradually took on a more ritual and/or social meaning.

Much of Central Europe was still covered with dense forest composed of alder, linden, ash, maple, elm and – somewhat later – beech, with pine trees dominating the woodlands towards the east. But the forest was increasingly cleared for fields by felling or the slash-and-burn method, or cut down to provide material for building, work and fuel. Thus in places where farming became the norm the natural landscape was gradually transformed. Different soils formed, from the original post-glacial loess and black chernozem to brown, gradually decalcified cambisols and different grades of loam. The latter accumulated in stretches along rivers through loess originating from high-lying land that had been deforested. You shaped the place where you lived, but the place you lived also strongly shaped the food you could produce and therefore what you ate. It was important to find out more about it if one was not to go hungry. Astronomical data was collected over a very long period of time and used for agricultural planning. A 'sky disc' found in Nebra/Saxony from around 2,000 BC represents the sun, moon and stars, including the seven Pleiades, used to determine the dates for sowing and harvest. This knowledge and the diversification of varieties minimized the risk of crop failure, but annual variations in climate persisted and it is highly unlikely that seed stocks of more than a year were available.

With the spread of iron, even more effective tools could be produced. As ard-ploughs were reinforced with iron tips, cultivation became easier and efficiency in food production rose a little further. At the same time a marked cultural division took place between Germanic tribes in the north and the Celts in the south. Celtic settlements in alpine regions were founded on copper mining and were mainly supported by cattle, pigs and grain. The Greek historian Strabo described the diet of the Celts as consisting mainly of milk and several kinds of meat, but above all pork, some fresh and some salted. Trade in rare metals such as pewter increased economic and cultural contacts. Salt mining was now flourishing and Celtic salt pork was even exported in barrels to Rome. The Celts had a knack for shopping and, tired of bartering, introduced coinage, a method of payment they had encountered on their migrations in Asia Minor. Prior to that, objects with systematized weights – gold rings, hatchets, scythes and bracelets – had been used in the exchange of goods. Contact with the Etruscans and Greek colonies in southern Italy resulted in 'oriental' cultural influences. Powerful Celtic princes started to import fine drinking and eating vessels, which might well have been filled with imported foods and wines. Evidence for this can be found in a tumulus burial site in Hochdorf/Baden-Württemberg, dated to around 525 BC, where a Celtic prince was buried with a massive cauldron and vessels for drinking and eating. Feasting and fine dining, it can be assumed, were powerful social and political elements then as now.

Once again, we can dream up a menu. The luxurious meal would certainly include lighter sourdough bread and salt pork, perhaps in the form of air-dried sausages or smoked ham. But then? Possibly some form of cheese? Sweet pears, plums or cherries traded from more southern orchards? Walnuts or sweet chestnuts, new and very rare arrivals from the Mediterranean? Some highly luxurious, exotic spices that had travelled from Rome in exchange for salted meat? We don't know. We do know though that differences in foodways became more marked with the increase in trading activities. Then as now, people tended to move to places where life seemed easier and their plates were fuller. Towards the end of the so-called Iron Age, overpopulation and failed crops made for much upheaval in Central Europe. The Celts were pushed west by expansive, migrating Germanic groups while at the same time the Romans advanced onto the Rhine and Danube.

TWO

Fresh Meat and *Lac Concretum*: The Roman Age, 1st Century BC to 5th Century AD

When the Romans began to take an interest in the lands of the north, they started to write about Germans' lifestyle and foodways. Here is the Roman historian Tacitus in his *Germania* from AD 98:

> As soon as they wake up, which is often well after sunrise . . . they take a meal, each one having a separate seat and table. Then they go out, with their weapons, to business, or often enough to a feast. No one thinks it disgraceful to carry on drinking all day and all night. As is natural among men who are drunk there are frequent quarrels, which are occasionally settled by violent words, more often by killing and wounding. All the same, they also frequently deliberate at feasts . . . At no other time, they think, is the heart so open to frank thoughts or so warm towards noble sentiments . . . For drink they have a liquid made out of barley or other grain, fermented into a certain resemblance to wine. Those who live nearest to the river-bank [the Rhine] buy wine as well. Their food is plain: wild fruit, fresh game, or *lac concretum*, curdled milk. They satisfy their hunger without elaborate preparation or seasonings. But as far as thirst is concerned they are less restrained: if you indulge their intemperance by supplying as much as they crave, they will be as easily defeated by their vices as by force of arms.[1]

Tacitus probably never travelled to Germany, but relied mostly on the reports of Pliny the Elder. He described Germany's climate as raw. Its landscape held little appeal for him since it was covered by forests and marshes; it was suitable for grain crops but not for the planting of orchards. Germans, he observed, took pride in the quantity of their cattle, by which they counted their wealth, and made no fuss about their food. Mothers breastfed their own children as a matter of principle. The idea that the simpler diet of more primitive cultures was healthier would be reiterated by later physicians and would spring up again in the writings of Jean-Jacques Rousseau and the Romantics.

Ever since the arrival of the first professional cooks and bakers from Greece at the end of the third century BC, the Romans had developed an enthusiastic interest in good food and wine and become experts in related food production and processing technologies. The elaborate road and transport systems introduced in all Roman provinces enabled the exchange of culinary knowledge and products across the whole empire. Spices were an important part of the intensely flavoured Roman cuisine, although the substantial sums spent on them were severely critized by Tacitus, Pliny and some of their colleagues as decadent and unnatural – an idea which later came into its own in the Christian disapproval of gluttony. Reading this early report about German ways, we should keep in mind that Tacitus had an agenda: he wanted to demonstrate an unspoilt, naturally strong people as a reprimand to his effeminate, degenerate compatriots (he was a young boy at the time of Nero's debauchery and the great fire of Rome). In Roman eyes the diet he described was truly wild: Romans did not eat meat before it had been hung, so failure to do this was a serious sign of lack of civilization, as was hunting instead of growing your own produce. *Lac concretum*, curdled milk or quark, must also have sounded primitive, since the Romans were well accustomed to the use of rennet to produce large storable cheeses.

The Romans did their best to spread their culture as far as possible, pushing the frontiers of their empire further and further into barbarian territories. With the Roman army came their foodways. It was a major task to feed the soldiers and those following them and Roman commanders had to stock a year's worth of food at all times. Figs, rice, olives and chickpeas were imported, but for grain, meat and wine, local production was essential. It was inevitable that the Germans would sooner or later become familiar with and involved in the Roman ways and habits, and there can be no doubt that the Roman influence improved German provender.

The introduction of Mediterranean-style agriculture initiated an agrarian revolution on German soil, with Roman culture reaching its peak in the new provinces in the second century AD, when the military

Germany during Roman times.

administration was replaced by a free and private economy. The Germanic Roman provinces became quite densely inhabited, with a cross-cultural mix of Celtic, Celtic-Germanic, Germanic, Gallic and Italic people and lifestyles. Food production for the army as well as the larger settlements relied on *villae rusticae*, Roman-style farms whose location was carefully chosen according to topography, soil type and infrastructure. They were often placed between fields on high dry areas on one side and lower areas along a stream on the other. Isolated from other settlements and surrounded by fields, woods, grasslands and pastures, holdings ranged from 50 to 250 hectares. *Villae rusticae* consisted of buildings of varying levels of comfort and included stables, barns, storage buildings and workshops for the purposes of iron smelting, pottery making and glass production. Food surpluses were traded by some, while others developed specialized products through milling, drying or sawing. New agricultural technology, possibly triggered by the different climate, made for faster and more efficient working processes without the need for slave labour. A more sophisticated kind of plough using coulters and mouldboards, larger scythes and a grain harvesting 'machine' came into common use. Rye was introduced from the Germanic east, and naked wheat arrived from the Gallic west, to join local varieties which kept longer and better in a moderate, humid climate, since they were covered by husks. As with all husked grain varieties, they needed to be dried in kilns, which may well also have been used for flax or malt in beer production.

The daily grain ration for the Roman military was 650 g, supplemented by meat (mostly bacon), cheese, vegetables, salt, olive oil and simple wine. Soldiers' daily staple was the familiar gruel, which they called *puls*. It was made from millet, oats and barley and was comparable to a very rough polenta. Bread was also produced in considerable quantity and thought of as more nourishing and indispensable in times of war. And, since Roman cuisine needs plenty of oil, local production from linseed, poppyseed and camelina augmented imported olive oil from the Mediterranean, as did locally grown herbs as additions or replacements for imported spices. Roman agriculturalists were adept at developing new varieties suited to different climatic conditions. Orchards thrived and vegetable production became much more efficient under their care. They brought into cultivation new or previously rare food plants such as amaranth, chard, turnip, purslane, garlic, dill, coriander, savory, thyme, celery, apricots, almonds, peaches, quinces, walnuts, chestnuts and medlars, as well as *Vitis vinifera*, the wine grape.

Viticulture flourished: wine was an intrinsic part of the Roman lifestyle. In his poem *Mosella*, Decimus Magnus Ausonius described late fourth-century wineries in the region around Trier on the banks of the Mosel (also a useful source of river fish) with up to 60 hectares of vines planted on terraced slopes. But in contrast to the Germanic excess (at least according to Tacitus), Romans frowned upon drunkenness. Wine, and for lesser occasions (or social groups) vinegar, was usually mixed with water, the latter mixture called *posca*. *Lora* was made by soaking the skins and seeds left in the press after winemaking in water to produce a drink that was only slightly alcoholic, but less contaminated with germs. The Germans had developed excellent coopering skills that were taken over by the Romans, who found that transporting wine in wooden barrels was much easier than it was in amphorae.

Roman *convivia* consisted mostly of three courses, with the food cut in small pieces and eaten with a spoon. The meat of choice was pork, but venison, boar, hare, dormice, all kinds of birds, farmed snails, fish, oysters and mussels featured as well. Breeding improved cattle by crossing larger Roman bulls with the smaller local animals, and the proportion of cattle to pigs and goats rose substantially. While pigs were only useful as meat, cattle, in addition to producing milk, supplied by-products such as hides and, even more importantly, worked in the fields. In late summer cattle were also moved from their pastures to glean in the grain fields after they were harvested and improve the next year's yield by producing manure in situ. It can reasonably be assumed, too, that the Romans introduced rennetting, an essential prelude to the preparation of storeable cheese.

At times the complete standing Roman army was deployed along the Rhine. Agricultural productivity increased and the economy boomed, fuelled in addition by the development of related industries such as the production of *terra sigillata* or Samian ware, a glazed, bright orange earthenware popular throughout Germania. In larger settlements trading took place on fixed days in covered markets, with all kinds of specialists operating from nearby workshops. There were drying kilns for husking grain, bakeries and smokeries, usually combined with a cooking facility. Professional butchers slaughtered the traded livestock as required. As a general rule, one-third of young animals were kept for work and breeding while the rest were slaughtered for immediate consumption, either at home or in taverns equipped with street kitchens.

The economic boom, however, had its drawbacks. Exhausted soils required either fallow periods or the regular application of large amounts of manure. Plentiful supplies of wood were needed by various industries,

Wineship found in Neumagen am Mosel, 3rd century AD, as part of a funeral monument.

including shipbuilding, and overcropping of woodland led to soil erosion and the need to procure wood over ever-increasing distances. For the same reasons, pottery and brick-making workshops, originally conveniently located in or immediately around cities, followed the supply of wood and moved further away. Nevertheless the Roman system worked well enough for most of the population and offered some the chance of social mobility.

By no means all of Germany was under Roman occupation. In fact, a much larger part than just one small, indomitable village resisted the invaders and stopped Julius Caesar's troops halfway. The Romans were able to establish themselves in the so-called *Agri Decumates*, roughly today's states of Baden-Württemberg and Bavaria. Even there they felt constantly threatened by incursions from outsiders. Eventually, in spite of the protective *Limes*, the Alamans forced the Romans out of the *Agri Decumates* and back behind the Rhine and the Danube in around AD 260. But their culinary ways didn't disappear with them. What we call Alemannic food today in southwest Germany, the Romans' so-called Lesser Germania (as well as Alsace and the northwest of Switzerland), is based on the legacy of the erstwhile invaders. Northwest of the Rhine,

---

A culinary place in time: The Isis temple in Mainz

What might be regarded as Germany's oldest-known restaurant was excavated in 2001 (www.roemisches-mainz.de). It formed part of a temple consecrated to the goddesses Isis and Kybele at the Roman legionnaires' post of Mogontiacum, now Mainz. The meat offerings made here were a public affair. Gods and goddesses savoured the smoke and lesser parts while the choice cuts were cooked to be sold at the market or savoured in the small dining rooms where temple benefactors were permitted to entertain their friends. Since there were neither serving staff nor cooks, the arrangement could be considered much the same as a self-service restaurant. The expectation that the temple gods would join the meal, especially Isis's husband Serapis, seems to anticipate the Christian Communion (although in the Eucharist meat was replaced by bread and wine).

Market stall and wine transport found in Trier, 2nd or 3rd century AD. The shop is selling something from an open barrel, possibly fish or pickles (with measuring jugs hanging from the ceiling), as well as wild birds or poultry.

the imperialists hung on for some two centuries longer. Trier on the Mosel was the largest city north of the Alps, and Cologne, also a real metropolis at the time (which boasted one of the longest Roman-built aqueducts, linking the city to the Eifel mountain range) became deeply ingrained with a southern temperament and food culture.

In the free part of Germany Roman culture was obviously much less influential. The remains of Germanic settlements and graves at several sites in Berlin and far into the Germanic and Slavic east tell a different story from those in the southwest. Direct contact with Romans was unlikely for the inhabitants of the small farmsteads at such a great distance from the border, but some exchange took place through German legionnaires serving in the Roman army as well as through trade. Bronze vessels were in demand and, to a lesser degree, so was silver and glassware, as well as high-quality Samian ware. Native-born Germans such as the Cheruscan Arminius were permitted to enlist and could attain high rank in the

Roman army, returning home more or less assimilated and bringing with them elaborate tools, ceramic vases and tureens, drinking horns made of silver and horn, dainty silver cups, scissors, casseroles, jugs, bronze buckets and glass bowls. Goods traded from Germany to the Roman Empire, though less archaeologically visible, are mentioned in writings of the time; of particular note were cattle, horses, hides, furs, down feathers, slaves and amber.

The Roman poet Seneca shared Tacitus' gloomy view about the barbarians' unfortunate fate: 'Everlasting winter, a grey sky, the barren soil nourishing them meagrely.'[2] But in general agricultural standards were on the rise, though the improvements were much less pronounced than in the Roman-dominated provinces and far removed from the larger and highly professional Roman farming estates in the occupied provinces. During the milder periods of the early centuries AD, the marshes and islands along the coast were settled, often behind artificial banks of earth (*Wurten*) that provided extra space and safety. Tacitus wasn't far off the mark: animal husbandry more or less directly shaped everybody's life. People and animals (besides cattle, sheep were popular for their wool) lived alongside one another in large houses. In the inland regions, more spacious pens for livestock and additional pit-houses for the storage of hay were used. Chicken, geese and ducks provided meat and eggs. Pigs were often fattened in oak woods.

Hunting (with hounds and hawks) was increasingly seen as a sign of status and was reserved for the elite; the carcass was valued less for its meat than its feathers or furs, bones and antlers. Horses were still rarer than cattle and were rarely used for fieldwork; instead, they were hunting companions and warhorses. As in pre-Roman times, they were the sacrifical animal of choice. Sacrifices took place at fixed locations, often involving wooden sculptures of idols, and appear to have been related to significant agricultural events such as sowing, harvest or transhumance in spring and autumn.

Farms were rarely larger than 20 hectares, and settlements were generally self-sufficent. Field crops changed little during the period, although flax and hemp (grown for oil and fibre) saw a noticeable rise. Barley, both huskless and husked, was the most popular grain, followed by oats and rye, with millet and wheat, both huskless and as husked emmer, not far behind. Blocks of fields which formed an irregular mosaic were ard-ploughed in a crisscross pattern. Very gradually longer strip-shaped fields appeared because of the increasing use of the single-sided plough, which turned the soil in one direction, creating characteristic ridges and furrows. To the agricultural armoury were added harrows, harks and large sickles and scythes, all of which delivered faster and more efficient ways of cutting of straw and hay. Fertilizers such as limestone marl, seaweed, household waste and hearth-ash produced a slight improvement in yield.

Thus our imagined meal of gruel and boiled meat from the Neolithic period still held true. But while wild fruit and berries as well as herbs and nuts continued to be gathered, cultivated broad (fava) beans and onions were now a regular feature. Bread had become a more viable alternative, made from barley as the basic staple for ordinary people and wheat for the better-off. In the north, quark (without any doubt the *lac concretum* mentioned by Tacitus) was made by letting sour milk curdle and separating the liquid from the solids through an earthenware sieve. It might sometimes have been sweetened with honey: apiculture gradually became more sophisticated as wild forest bees were offered nesting opportunities in hollowed-out tree trunks equipped with entrance holes, frames for the combs and a lid to give beekeepers access to the contents. Wooden barrels helped to turn milk into butter, although there is no certainty that the butter was consumed as a foodstuff, since recorded uses are medicinal or cosmetic. As reported by Tacitus, beer (or rather a form of ale or kwass) was very popular, and besides that there were mead and possibly cider, whereas grape wine almost certainly remained an imported luxury. Thanks to low population numbers clean drinking water was abundant, even without aqueducts: large areas of free Germany remained covered with dense forests and were barely inhabited. Altogether their larders might have been stocked in less varied and sophisticated ways than those of the Romans, but there seems to have been a reliable surplus. As witnessed by the settlements on the coast, the area under cultivation slowly extended and the population gradually increased. Specialist craftsmen such as potters and glassblowers could ply their trade without the need for direct involvement in food production.

When the Franks drove the invaders out for good, the more prosperous of the Romans went with them, especially the owners of large estates. But many of the ordinary people – labourers and workers – stayed behind, maintaining the Roman agricultural system in Lesser Germania throughout the fifth century. Then the infrastructure of the distribution system gradually collapsed, roads fell into disrepair and trade became less efficient. Germanic settlements slowly absorbed the remaining Roman population (explaining the dark eyes and hair of many a Mosel winegrower today) and *villae rusticae* began to disappear. For roughly four centuries, though, agricultural and culinary developments in Germany had experienced new influences, reinforcing and augmenting the regional differences initiated earlier by the Celtic dominance in the south.

THREE

Christianity, Social Stratification and Medicine: The Early Middle Ages, 5th to 11th Century

Mentioning the Middle Ages invariably brings up stereotypes. In particular the early centuries of this period are often perceived as 'dark ages' when the sophistication and knowledge accrued during classical times were destroyed by barbarian tribes, a horde of savages who loved nothing more than to sink their teeth into raw meat and get drunk on beer, as opposed to the refined and well-informed gourmets and wine lovers of Roman times. Another stereotype of the high Middle Ages is that of courtly knights and gracious damsels dining in castle halls at tables covered with heavily spiced, 'exotic' dishes such as stuffed peacock and spit roasted ibex. There is truth in both of these extremes, but they are from different points in time – with at least five centuries between them – and represent extreme social differentiation. Where you lived continued to strongly influence your larder and menu, but so did the circles in which you moved and the social group to which you belonged. If you were born a peasant, you ate gruel, just as a noble's son learnt to hunt.

When the Roman Empire's influence in Central Europe came to an end in the first years of the fifth century, everybody seemed to be on the move, pushing west and south, some from sheer belligerence, but most out of hunger for food and the land to produce it. With the people came their food preferences, such as the Slavic habit for rye and buckwheat. In other cases existing food landscapes acquired the labels we are now familiar with; the Friesian, Saxon, Frank, Alaman, Swabian and Bavarian tribes settled down roughly in the areas we associate with them today. The population went into sharp decline, not least as a result of devastating pandemics and less favourable climate conditions. Larger cities like Cologne, Trier, Mainz and Augsburg continued to exist, but on a much more basic level. When migration subsided, more land was once again brought into cultivation, with animal husbandry now of equal importance to grain cropping.

At the time, another important influence on how Germans cooked and ate was gaining in strength: Christianity, the new religion that had developed out of Judaism and spread through the Roman Empire. Although early Christians had been severely persecuted, their faith proved extremely resilient, producing an extraordinary missionary zeal. By the turn of the millennium almost all of northern Europe was converted, if not necessarily always of their own free will, though the Slavic east could not be persuaded to accept the new religion until well into the thirteenth century. Based on the general virtues of thrift, modesty and honesty, Christianity had a strong influence on the diet and in retrospect proved to be quite pragmatic when confronted with economic and social problems. In some cases the church adapted pagan traditions to comply with the new religion; in others it prescribed abstinence from them (though it often turned a blind eye to non-compliance). When a series of severe famines threatened the stability of sixth-century Rome, the pope declared gluttony one of the Seven Deadly Sins. Two centuries later one of his successors denounced horsemeat consumption as ungodly and impure, intervening against erstwhile pagan rituals.

As Catholic Christian faith became the official German state religion, the hierarchical structure of the Christian church furthered social stratification. Tribal leaders developed into territorial princes, and the particularism that is one of Germany's defining characteristics in food, as well as other areas of life, began to take shape. Charlemagne's Holy Roman Empire provided a counterbalancing unifying element. With the offical blessing of the pope, as shown by his coronation in Rome at Christmas of the year 800, Charlemagne set out to renovate the former Roman Empire throughout western Europe, embarking on a programme of strict and aggressive Christianization (above all, of the stubbornly pagan Saxons). Based on a standardized administration and unifying system of laws, he established the Franks as the new European superpower.

Charlemagne is reported to have been physically impressive, at least in part because of his decidedly imperial appetite (which wasn't limited to food, as his five official wives, Frankish, Lombardian, Swabian, East Francian and Alemannian, indicate). His daily meal, admiring reports say, contained little bread but invariably included the spit roasted game his hunters brought to the table in person. Despite repeated warnings

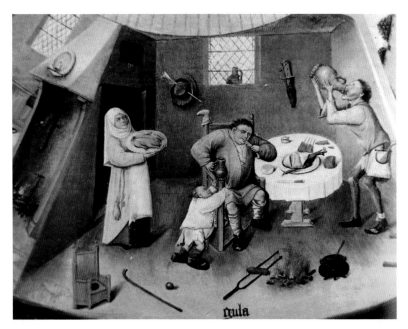

Hieronymus Bosch, detail of 'Gluttony', from *The Seven Deadly Sins*, *c.* 1480.

Schloss Johannisberg Wine estate label from 1904 (as usual, signed by the cellarmaster). This is the hillside where Charlemagne noticed the snow melting exceptionally early on and ordered it to be planted with vines.

from his doctors, the emperor resolutely refused to cut back on his meat consumption, complaining that he had problems eating less. Meat, Romans' erstwhile offering to the gods, was considered power-food in a 'magical' sense. As such it was undoubtedly essential for an emperor who asserted his authority through his personal presence by constantly travelling and staying mostly at church and royal properties. The symbolic importance of these reports becomes even more clear when we read about the Byzantine emperor who, at the end of the tenth century, was disparagingly described by an Italian diplomat as living on a diet of garlic, onions and leeks while drinking his own bathwater.[1]

Charlemagne not only needed food for himself, but for cities that were newly founded or had begun to grow again around existing settlements. He worked hard to produce an agricultural surplus because he knew that food shortages endangered political stability and would thereby undermine his position. He depended on local leaders' loyalty and sought to organize food production more stringently. Roman knowledge and craftsmanship had survived on some large estates and in the monasteries. Charlemagne issued the *Capitulare de villis vel curtis imperii*, an inventory of detailed directives for the management of the royal estates. They prescribed the more efficient, higher-yielding three-field-system under which summer and winter grain were rotated with root crops and fallow periods; included a list of recommended cultivars; and established hunting, Charlemagne's passion, as a permanent royal privilege. It went without saying that Charlemagne's ideas of the culinary world included wine, and directives for its production, such as the use of wooden barrels instead of skins to store it, were included in the *Capitulare*. The first record of viticulture in the Rheingau region, on the hillside that today belongs to the Schloss Johannisberg estate, dates back to 817. Legend has it that the emperor, staying in his palace in Ingelheim on the Rhine early in the year, looked over to the river at the Rheingau. Noticing that the snow had already melted on the hillside which today is Schloss Johannisberg, he ordered that vines be planted there, declaring it a particularly warm and therefore suitable spot. He was right!

Feudal manorialism, the organizing principle of the rural economy which had its origin in the Roman villa system, was well suited to maintaining order on the emperor's extensive territories. The peasantry had to pay rent or church-imposed tithes and provide labour, military service and haulage to obtain the right to use land; otherwise labourers could be reduced to serfs or bondsmen. In return the lord of the manor provided legal and military protection. The ultimate goal of manorialism was agricultural efficiency, as landlords could impose on a frequently reluctant workforce innovations such as the three-field system, the use of watermills and the systematic use of manure.

Sharing food was strongly loaded with social significance. In reports from Carolingian times meetings are often described in terms of how people met and spoke, ate and drank together, and then departed in peace. Such early medieval conviviality had little to do with personal friendship; rather the communal feast guaranteed and reinforced peaceful alliances among its participants. As a ritual, communal eating had a quasi-legal character. During his visit to the monastery of St Gall in 912 King Konrad made a point of dining with the monks and even spiced up their meal with pepper from his own provisions.[2] Treason and aggression were especially to be condemned when related to meals; the misuse of hospitality was a sign of extreme evil and treachery. After the feuding King Henry IV and Pope Gregory VII met in 1077 in Canossa, Henry was said in numerous reports not to have touched his food and to have barely talked during the communal meal, indicating how reluctant he was to admit defeat in this battle for ultimate power.[3]

From a political point of view, one could argue that Charlemagne's grandiose vision of a united western Europe was short-lived. His system was not strong enough to make it last, as his empire was divided into three after his death in 814. But food-wise it worked rather well. Charlemagne knew that national strength required population growth and that this was only possible with a grain-based diet, which in turn required solid organization of production. In this respect (though keeping in mind that the system had a lot of not so agreeable aspects for some of those involved in it) his legacy was a positive one. On top of that the Holy Roman Emperor and the Christian Church together continued to represent a unifying idea, without whose influence Europe might have fragmented even further.

Vikings, Arab tribes and nomadic Hungarian horsemen represented a continuing threat of invasion throughout the ninth and early part of the tenth century, but they also made for additional cultural impulses. The Vikings, called *nortmanni* or northern men by the Franks, in particular played an important role as merchants, explorers and colonists. In fact they probably did much more trading than the plundering legend attributes to them. Their seaworthy ships, while capable of making repeated Atlantic crossings, were sufficiently shallow of keel to allow them to be sailed or rowed upriver, maintaining trade routes which reached all over Europe and into northern Africa and the Black Sea, and extending the old Roman trade route along the Rhine that linked the Nordic countries with northwestern Germany. It is easy to imagine how they brought along exotic foodstuffs and spices which made for surprising and inspiring aromas and colours; great exceptions to the local cuisine.

Back then only the aristocracy travelled any distance from home. The average life expectancy was slightly over 30 years and infant mortality was very high. Most Germans lived in very small villages, hamlets or isolated farmsteads surrounded by small agricultural clearings amid vast forests. Labour division by gender meant that domestic economy was women's duty. For peasant women this included grain milling, beer brewing, cooking and cleaning, but also working in the lord's vineyards, collecting wild berries in the forest and helping with the grain harvest – not to mention making their own family's and the lord's garments from vegetable fibres and wool. While noble families tended to be large, peasants lived in small 'nuclear' families with three to four children on average, occasionally sharing houses or forming an estate with other families in which each household cultivated between 2.5 and 3.4 hectares.[4] At this time Córdoba, capital of the Muslim caliphate of Al-Andalus on the Iberian peninsula and the largest metropolis in Europe, counted some 300,000 inhabitants, 1,600 mosques and 900 bathhouses – which gives us an idea of what the kitchens must have been like.

It is difficult to know what was actually cooking in the early medieval pots and pans of Germany, as relevant written sources are sparse. Some historians maintain that high culture and refined cuisine were destroyed at the end of Roman era to be replaced by pagan gluttony. The graves containing food shared with the dead in funeral feasts are cited as evidence. While grave offerings became less complex during the following centuries, two fifth-century graves found under a church in Cologne contain chicken and eggs cooked with honey, along with other meats prepared with mustard and sage. Beef ribs and a large roasting spit were unearthed in a sixth-century grave in Krefeld.[5] Other historians support the idea that there was a more gradual transition from the dominance of Roman-style cuisine to local styles of cooking. This begs the question of whether essential ingredients of the Roman kitchen such as *liquamen* (a kind of fish sauce) and asafoetida continued to be imported. There is evidence from the early eighth century of the use of imported *garum* in a monastery in northern France, l'Abbaye de Corbie, along with other imported groceries such as olive oil, pepper, cumin, cloves, cinnamon, spikenard, costus, dates, figs, almonds, pistachios, olives, chickpeas and rice.[6] On the one hand, this might well have been the case in Germany as well. On the other, local herbs, vinegar and verjus might have replaced Roman condiments. The *Capitulare* lists some 70 herbs and vegetables as being cultivated in the imperial gardens. From the tenth century onwards, however, spices began to arrive once more from Asia, this time through Venetian merchants who dealt in pepper, ginger, cardamom, cinnamon, nutmeg, mace, cloves, galangal and sugar. Almonds were also a new luxury.[7] Saffron, among the most expensive and most valued of spices, was frequently mentioned as an imported spice, even though it was widely planted throughout Italy, Spain and France (and, from the beginning of the fifteenth century, in southern Germany and Austria).

Ibrāhīm ibn Ya'qūb, a tenth-century travelling physician, geographer and merchant from Arab Spain, provided us with a rare window on German habits of the time. When describing 'the very big city' of Mainz on the Rhine, he was amazed at finding 'in the utmost west of the Occident spices that only grow at the very end of the Orient, like pepper, ginger, cloves, spikenard, costus, and galangal; these plants are imported from India where they are growing abundantly.' There were two possible routes between Asia and Europe; one on the Mediterranean, from France or Spain through Alexandria or Antioch, the other across Central Europe, to Constantinople or the areas on the lower Volga. Mention of a well-stocked spice chest at this time confirms that these mysterious symbols of other worlds – possibly paradise – did not, as widely suggested, require re-introduction as Crusaders' souvenirs to European kitchens.

Ya'qūb's notes make fascinating reading. In the course of his travels Ya'qūb made a clear distinction between the Frankish (today Franconia and southern Germany) and Slavic (northern Germany) realms, confirming yet another cultural borderline along the Rhine and midway through Germany towards the east that can still be observed today. Travelling to Soest in Westphalia, he mentioned a source of salted water which the inhabitants of the fortified city boiled in large kettles on a big fire in a stone oven, a process which yielded a hard white salt. This method, he said, was employed in all of the Slavic countries. In fact Lüneburg was officially recognized for its saltworks in 956. Schleswig, an immediate neighbour of Haithabu, was described as a very big city on the ocean, poor in grain but surviving on abundant fish. Quoting the work of another Islamic author of the period, Ya'qūb wrote about 'strange' trading habits in Augsburg:

> When a merchant acquires merchandise, he writes the price on it and leaves it exposed in his shop. If a customer agrees with the price, he pays it and takes it with him in exchange for the money he is leaving. The shops are guarded and any disappearance of merchandise for the guardian leads to a fine equivalent to the loss.[8]

Ya'qūb mentioned wheat, barley, rye and vines, as well as fruit in abundance. As Charlemagne had envisaged, from the ninth century onwards a three-field crop rotation system had developed that distributed work more evenly through the year because of the more balanced use of winter and summer crops. This rotating system of cropping and fallow periods did not by itself lead to higher yields, but primarily served to restore soil fertility, though this was by no means understood in anything resembling a scientific manner. Such a system needed a close-knit village community and careful organization to regroup the small parcels of earlier times into larger, more efficient fields, a process which also limited individual decision-taking. Once again Germany gradually switched its diet to cereals, seen as nutritionally most efficient, with smaller supplements of meat and dairy products. Grain came in many different forms, from the thin, dark gruel eaten by the poor to fine white bread for the rich, reflecting the diversity of breads still found in present-day Germany (although today the social classification is almost reversed). Undemanding rye saw a very quick expansion from the eighth century. By the late Middle Ages it was to be by far the most important of Germany's grain crops, even on more fertile soils. Grain cultivars of lesser importance were huskless wheat (a winter crop), barley (a winter and a summer crop), oat, millet, spelt, emmer and very rarely einkorn. These were cultivated together with oil seeds and legumes – typical summer crops. All these crops, particularly grains, were in all probability a mix of different varieties, the genetic diversity a kind of insurance policy against pests and diseases.

However, famines were a regular feature, since regional redistribution was limited and the surplus from good harvests quickly turned into a shortage in bad years. Also, systematic cultivation gradually began to exhaust the soil, a problem exacerbated by earth-turning ploughs which exposed the subsoil and led to greater soil erosion. Lower numbers of animals also meant less manure, with sheep and cattle murrains such as rinderpest frequently reducing them even further. Manure became a commodity much in demand, and tithes could actually include 'a pot of dung', with pigeon droppings considered the most valuable kind.[9] Marl was one of the few known alternatives to manure, though it added no new minerals but simply activated those already present in the soil, and, if overused, resulted in even poorer soils. In the northwest, where rye cultivation was especially intense on compact soils, the much more efficient *Plaggen* system developed. This required overlaying the surface of the soil with a mixture of animal dung and heather turf along with other organic and non-organic matter such as grass, leaf mould, peat, clay and sand.

Our imagined gruel-centred meal starts to be more limited in popularity and reputation, turning into a marker for non-urban lower social groups. Archaeological finds from small rural settlements indicate that the early medieval rural diet in the northwest was very much dictated by local conditions, with a notable lack of exchange or trading activity even between neighbouring communities. At one particular site only four crops were grown: fava beans were by far the most important (and might have been partially fed to the horses these peasants kept), while the other three were barley, oats and flax for oil, without any evidence of any fruit gathered from the wild; besides horses there were sheep and cattle, along with smaller numbers of pigs. At another site where winter floods made for more fertile soils, those four crops were supplemented by wild fruits, apples, camelina, common vetch (a legume and again possibly fed to livestock) and emmer, a rare throwback to earlier times, perhaps because rye dislikes wet soil. On a third site nearby, with poor sandy soils, three-quarters of all available land was planted with rye, with subsidiary crops of barley, oats, flax, a little wheat, fava beans, vetch and peas.

The urban diet was much more varied and refined than that of the countryside. The best-documented example of urban plenty, a result of favourable natural conditions and trading, was found in the Viking settlement of Haithabu (near modern Schleswig). The town was founded around 800, and we can assume similar conditions in other early medieval towns. Foodstuffs cultivated or gathered from the immediate surroundings of Haithabu included barley, rye, oat, wheat, millet, fava beans and flax. Evidence of plums and peaches was found, as well as eight varieties of wild berries, cherries, beechnuts and hazelnuts, with only wine and walnuts imported from a significant distance.[10]

Viticulture was practised throughout Germany but tended to disappear in unfavourable areas as trade increased. Wine was barrelled up for export to other regions, travelling from the Upper Rhine as far as Stockholm. In northern Germany the preference was for beer or ale and (less frequently) mead. Weak beer was produced and consumed in large quantities, and (at 2 per cent alcohol) was often safer than water. All grain varieties were used in its manufacture. With hops slowly replacing gruit (which could include all kinds of preservative or flavouring herbs such as bog myrtle and sweet gale), beer improved greatly in both palatability and keeping-qualities, and evidence from Haithabu tells us that hopped beer was not restricted to monasteries.

Detailed plans drawn up in the early years of the ninth century for a monastery garden, known as the Plan of St Gall, were probably never fully realized but still supply us with abundant information about what cooks of the time might have had at their disposal. The vegetables to be grown in the *hortus* were onions, leeks, celery, coriander, dill, opium and field poppies, radishes, chard, garlic, shallots, parsley, chervil, lettuce, savory, parsnips or carrots, cabbage and nigella. The *herbularius* was reserved for medicinal herbs: sage, rue, iris, pennyroyal, spearmint, cumin, lovage, fennel, lilies, roses, beans, savory, costmary, fenugreek, rosemary and mint. The orchard included apples, pears, plums, pine nuts, sorb, medlar, laurel, chestnuts, figs, quinces, peaches, hazelnuts, almonds, mulberries and walnuts (it also served as a graveyard).

Archaeological records confirm that many of the plants listed for St Gall (although the list was actually drawn up on the Reichenau island) were available from castle gardens in the lower Rhine area in the eleventh and twelfth century. There fruits included cherries (selected for the largest fruits with the smallest stones), but also sloes, quetsches, elder- berries, blackberries, raspberries, dewberries, strawberries, grapes and whitethorn. Archaeologists found also amaranth, hemp, peas, mustard, lamb's lettuce, purslane, cress, spinach, lentils, chickpeas, centaurium, henbane, physalis, dyers' rocket, acorns and beechnuts. This demon- strates that a varied supply of fruit, vegetables and medicinal plants could be on offer, at least in some privileged places.[11]

Cultivated sweet fruit was undoubtedly regarded as a great luxury and reserved for those of high social standing, as an episode recorded by a tenth-century scribe in St Gall shows. He tells of a noblewoman who – unable to resist her sugar cravings in spite of having joined the monastery and chosen the simple life – asked for sweet apples. When given 'poor people's sour crabapples', being well-educated, she understood the reprimand immediately.[12]

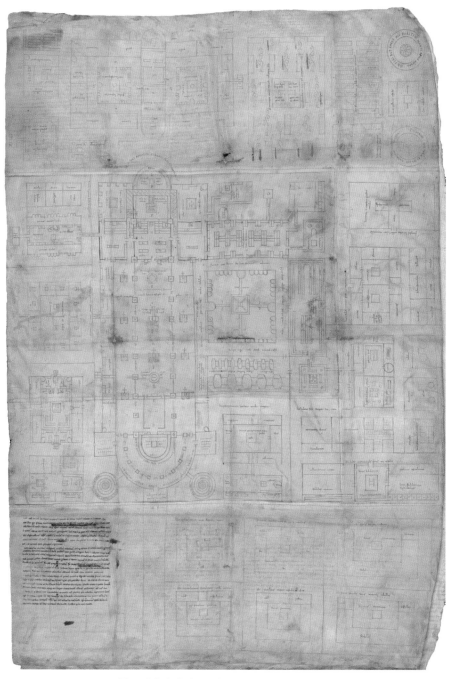

Plan of St Gall, 819–26, Reichenau, parchment.

Meat, especially the roasted choicer cuts, was another aristocratic privilege. Bone debris recovered from the castle mentioned earlier in the western Rhineland indicates a regular diet of meat from pigs, cattle, sheep, goats, domestic or wild geese, as well as duck, chicken, hare, wild rabbit, deer and boar.[13] Pigs, of no use as draught animals and offering no secondary products such as wool, were killed at optimum size for culinary use, typically in late autumn after fattening in oak or beech woods. Forests and pastures had by then become separate entities and manorial forests' use had to be paid for. Because of Charlemagne's hunting restrictions, game had been removed from the peasantry's regular diet for good. Charlemagne's *Capitulare* also addressed the *Forestarii*, the royal civil servants who were the predecessors of modern foresters. The common folk were required to provide hunting services to the king, such as maintaining the royal grounds and keeping dogs. The rural population was often forbidden even to trap game and was severely punished for poaching. Not only were their crops damaged by hunters on horseback, but they had no effective means of protecting their crops from being damaged by their quarry – their dogs either had to wear heavy sticks attached to their necks or have their front legs lamed so that they could not chase game.

Hunting rights emphasized a ruler's territorial claims, with organized hunts serving as a practice for wartime as well as a theatrical performance for the purpose of self-aggrandizement. As meat it became less and less important: by the thirteenth century even the aristocracy consumed less than 5 per cent of their meat as game.[14] As a mark of favour, the king could confer hunting rights on his most important loyal vassals, who could in turn pass them on to subordinates. Usually, though, the right to hunt 'higher game' was reserved for the king or aristocrats of elevated standing. Thus arose a distinction between *Hochwild* and *Niederwild*, higher and lower game (reflecting the Bible's permissible and impermissible animals). At the top of this hierarchy were the stag (red and fallow deer) and the wild boar, along with bear, elk, ibex, chamois, capercaillie and pheasant. To the category of lower game belonged roe deer, hare, partridge, fox, badger, marten and duck. However, the exact makeup of these categories varied depending on royal preferences and regional differences.

Meanwhile the Christian church preached a simpler life. Fasting was presented as the link between diet and virtue. From at least the fourth century on, Christianity had promoted culinary abstinence for its spiritual benefits. The association of meat, eggs and dairy fats with the vices of gluttony and lechery led to a complex pattern of eating. The 40 days of Lent from Ash Wednesday to Easter Sunday (not counting Sundays), the three Rogation days before Ascension Day and the four Ember days (or even weeks), as well as Advent (the four weeks before Christmas), altogether about one-third of the year, were fast days. The evenings pre-ceding all major saints' days, Fridays (in memory of the Cruxification) and Saturdays (the Sabbath's eve) were lean days. Although regional variations undoubtedly occurred, on fast days all parts of warm-blooded animals, milk, dairy products and eggs were prohibited and only one meal could be taken. On lean days the rules were less strict and mostly concerned with the exclusion of meat; a certain amount of intellectual acrobatics was involved, such as the arguments that made the beaver into a fish, citing its amphibious lifestyle and the scales on its tail. Decrees concerning Christian fasting laws flowed freely, the most severe being the *Capitulatio de partibus Saxoniae* of 782, in which Charlemagne imposed the death penalty on anyone who practised any form of pagan-ism, including the consumption of meat during Lent. Fasting could also be imposed as a penance, standing in for prayers, the giving of alms or celibacy. Prohibitions were imposed on certain foods and drink: not only meat and eggs, but fat, oil and wine too. Alternatively redemp-tion could be had by direct payments to the Church and penances could be performed by a stand-in. Carolingian kings tended to use the same measures to punish secular offences, mingling secular and ecclesiastical power.[15]

The asceticism of nuns and monks – in theory at least – was indi-cated by modesty in eating as well as clothing. Repeated warnings were issued for priests and bishops not to wear secular clothes, indirectly implying that they had to renounce the possession of weapons and hun-ting. As we have seen, clerical aristocrats in the early Middle Ages clearly found it difficult to shed the aristocratic lifestyle. Walahfrid Strabo, abbot of the Benedictine monastery on the Reichenau island in Lake Constance in the early ninth century, cultivated and described his sophis-ticated vegetable garden (possibly the model for the Plan of St Gall) while recommending a simple diet of salt, bread, leeks, fish and wine. He had studied with Hrabanus Maurus, abbot of Fulda, who advised what would now be judged a vegan diet as supposedly recommended in the Bible. Strabo really cherished the products of his garden. The monastery had been founded in the eighth century by Irish and Anglo-Saxon

The Hunters' Lunch, c. 1420, tapestry from Alsace. The dogs also get their share.

missionaries and benefited from an extensive library. In his writings Strabo referred to the works of natural historians of classical times, such as Pliny the Elder, Cato, Columella and Palladius. He stressed the importance of soil quality and the use of dung as fertilizer, recommended adequate watering and was aware of the moon's influence on growing plants. He clearly favoured regional cultivars such as the bottle-gourd, describing it as being delicious as a dessert when fried in lard (an early example of a recipe!). The garden produced peaches and white-fleshed melons as well as lovage, a newcomer to the monastic herbarium (it is notable that Strabo compared the price paid for pennyroyal in India with that of black pepper in Gaul – another indication that oriental spices did not disappear with the Romans).

Admittedly, in contrast to the Mediterranean regions, which enjoyed an abundance of fruit, vegetables, fish and olive oil, such a diet was more difficult to realize the further north you lived. In response to the regional shortcomings, from the eleventh century onwards manors and monasteries stocked their own fishponds and bought in salted herring and stockfish.

In practice abstinence was not always strictly enforced. The chronicler Ekkehard IV, writing of the Benedictine monastery of St Gall, went to great lengths in the early eleventh century to defend the monks' failures in this respect, concluding that it was possible to be true to Benedict's spirit even when indulging in good food and wine.[16] Fasting periods were preceded and followed by feasting: Easter eggs ritually blessed in church together with the first lamb's meat, and the twelve traditional dishes standing for the twelve days of Christmas, are the most prominent examples. The excesses of Carnival before the restrictions of Lent can be observed in Germany to this day, especially along the Rhine valley. In many cases pagan habits were incorporated into Christian traditions, as in the case of the Carnival parade in Cologne, first recorded in 1341: this originates in Saturnalia, in connection with the worship of a Roman goddess of shipping and fertility. Other examples include the winter solstice and Christmas, for which the German word *Weihnachten* (or back then *wihe nacht*) was first recorded in 1178.

Besides the Christian food rules, medicinal teachings were another, somewhat less obvious factor in determining the composition of early medieval meals. In fact ingredients and spices as well as preparations 'trickled' from the pharmacy into the kitchen, since culinary recipes developed out of medicinal prescriptions – the German word for both is still *Rezept*. It was thanks to Benedict, sixth-century founder of the Benedictine order in Monte Cassino in southern Italy, that classical medical knowledge was preserved and, as a result, disseminated throughout religious establishments in the rest of Europe. Benedictine rules required monks to read at least one religious book a year, thereby furthering literacy, and set the care for the sick above all other duties. Benedictine monasteries were required to provide a separate room and a special 'servant'

A culinary place in time: Strabo's Reichenau

Up to the present day the small fertile island at the western end of Lake Constance is renowned for its vegetables and since 2000 a UNESCO world heritage site. The old monastery buildings sit among gardens and vineyards and form a heaven of tranquillity that makes it easy to be transported back to Strabo's times. His garden has been recreated on old monastery ground. Don't forget to try the delicious local fish, *Felchen* (*Coregonus wartmanni*), which the abbot certainly appreciated as much as contemporary Germans do.

45

for the purpose of caring for the sick, thus establishing the tradition of monastic hospitals staffed by specialist physicians and pharmacists.

In Germany medieval medicine was significantly improved with the publication of the *Lorscher Arzneibuch*, a medical and pharmaceutical handbook written in the monastery of Lorsch near Worms around 795. The introduction included a robust defence of the physician's work against those Christians who thought medical intervention was performed in defiance of the divine will, interpreting illness as a punishment from the Almighty for sins committed. The Lorsch text, in contrast, recommended illness as an opportunity of exercising Christian compassion. The text integrated ancient knowledge with Christian ideals, thus making it part of the Caroligian Renaissance, a process of educational reform which promoted the study of 'science'.

The Lorsch text also included a great many medicinal recipes based on the works of the Roman natural historian Pliny the Elder and recommended that medical treatment be accessible for everybody. Physicians were required to adapt to the patient's means and acquaint themselves with suitable drugs and herbs available locally. This was a bold defence and valorization of regional products; it might be seen as a medical equivalent to all the vegetables and fruit enumerated in Charlemagne's *Capitulare*.

The ideas of the ancient Greeks also flowed back into Germany via the alumni of the medical school of Salerno. Salerno first attracted scholars to what was to all intents and purposes a teaching hospital for the monks of Monte Cassino. It was in eleventh-century Salerno that Constantin, a spice merchant from North Africa, translated medicinal texts from Greek and Arabic into Latin. By this time the Arabs, culturally superior (and more advanced in mathematics and science) and with a far higher standard of living than that of most Europeans, were established in southern Spain, from where they were driven out in 1492, and Sicily, from whence they were expelled by the Normans in 1091. During their ascendancy they introduced a great many innovative ideas to the apothecaries and kitchens of Europe. These included pasta and ice cream as well as the secrets of food preservation and the art of distilling. Perhaps most importantly, they started to cultivate sugar cane in the western Mediterranean region, from where it was exported to northern Europe.

All these elements, disseminated through the close connection between preventative medicine and cookery, made their way slowly northwards and spread throughout Germany. Improved medical treatment led to an understanding of dietetics and, finally, the recording of culinary recipes which were directed at the wealthy classes (since only they were able to read them) – a great leap from the rural labourer's gruel.

Wolfram von Eschenbach, *Parzival*, Schwaben, *c.* 1240–50. Last page, upper third: the banquet on the occasion of Parzival's return. Note the sumptuous tablecloth and the symbolic difference in size between diners (all seated on one side) and servants.

FOUR

Luxurious Feasts and Terrible Famine: The High Middle Ages, 11th to 14th Century

If you had the choice between the somewhat harsh climate of Germany and the balmy air of Sicily, wouldn't you choose the latter? That's exactly what some of Charlemagne's successors did when the Mediterranean island became part of the Holy Roman Empire. What a luxury to have all that fruit growing at your doorstep! The imperial palace was surrounded by citrus and mulberry orchards, pistachio plantations, groves of date palms and fields in which cotton and melons grew. Like apricot and peaches, they were Arab introductions, their cultivation made possible through elaborate irrigation systems.

But even back home in Germany, as we have seen, oriental spices and the dishes in which they were included were certainly known and available. Goods from the trade between Christian Italian merchants from Venice, Genoa and Pisa with the Muslim cities of the eastern Mediterranean started to cross the Alps into southern Germany on a more regular base, and the Crusades reinforced this exchange through continuous contact with the East by diverse social groups over a long period of time, including the occupation of various eastern Mediterranean ports.

Among the select few in Germany with access to aromatic spices and other imported luxuries were the local rulers. Many of them resided in the proverbial castles, *Burgen*, which had often developed out of former Roman border fortifications (*burgi*), or were purpose-built solid houses on raised locations that included a keep. During the twelfth and thirteenth centuries most of them evolved into small fortified stone-built towns that issued their own coinage, exercised local jurisdiction and collected their own taxes. In times of war enemies would try to starve out these settlements after laying waste to the surrounding area necessary for their subsistence. Castles therefore tended to be permanently well stocked against sieges.

Just as the castle towered over the rest of the surrounding settlements, their lords demonstrated their superiority by indulging in conspicuous consumption of the kind of food indicated by their social status: banquets with enormous roasts in the vast halls of their imposing abodes. According to the somewhat over-romanticized popular view of these times, the aristocracy in their castles practised a chivalric code centred on weapon skills and the mastery of horses; the world of knights, damsels and Minne singers. Aristocratic etiquette required hosts to wine and dine visitors graciously, as depicted by singers and poets such as Walther von der Vogelweide, Hartmann von Aue, Gottfried von Strassburg and Wolfram von Eschenbach. Meals were an occasion for hosts to demonstrate power and superiority, along with music and other entertainment, followed by tournaments, which were watched by ladies from the windows above.

The *palas*, the main building where guests were entertained, consisted mostly of a large hall with a fireplace or open chimney on the ground floor. Furniture was simple, sparse and flexible. For banquets, walls would be covered with tapestries and carpets laid out, and long tables would be set up with loose planks on trestles (an important change from the Roman tradition of eating food in a reclining position), so that at the end of the meal the table would literally be lifted, in German *die Tafel aufheben*. The table was covered with a cloth which could also serve as a communal napkin. Before and after the meal handwashing was a ritual with special water jugs and basins. Beakers and bowls were often shared, whereas (at least in noble households) everybody had their personal spoon. Plates were rare and consisted of flat wooden boards, though trenchers made of stale bread cut in thick slices were more usual. These weren't necessarily eaten, or at least not by those who used them as plates, but were frequently passed on to the lower folks in the servant quarters or as alms to the poor. In these elite circles grain consumption took the form of bread or dainty rolls made with white flour that were freshly baked every day. The oldest German manual on table manners from the mid-thirteenth century confirmed that a good meal wasn't complete without good bread and wine.[1]

Not only the tableware but the composition and extensiveness of meals depended on social rank and means. The Church ate well. When in 1303 a bishop visited the town of Weissenfels near Leipzig for a church inauguration, he did not go hungry. The menu he enjoyed was festive, luxurious and well spiced:

> Egg soup with saffron, peppercorns and honey – mutton with onions – roast chicken with plums – stockfish with oil and raisins – bream baked in oil – boiled eel with pepper – smoked herring (*bückling*), roasted, with Leipzig mustard – boiled fish, made sour – a baked barbel – small birds fried in lard – a pig's leg with cucumbers.[2]

Around the same time as the bishop's feast, the menu served to the canons of the Hildesheim convent was somewhat more sober but still not exactly a pauper's meal, with plenty of meat.

> They were seated at three long tables, provided with two bowls with warm or cold water according to the season and towels, and a bell was rung three times. The Bishop's vicar said the Benedictate and each of them was presented with a bread roll of which they each cut a two finger thick slice for alms and put them on one heap. A pupil handed each one cup of wine and one of beer. The meat dishes consisted of a roast, lamb meat, *Magenwurst* [stomach stuffed like a sausage] and headcheese. If pork was served, a bowl of mustard was set between every two covers, and for mutton, a salt cellar. Cabbage was usually served for vegetables, and the leftovers were distributed among the pupils and servants.[3]

It is something of a literary cliché that the aspirations of richer peasants were symbolized by their lust for chicken and white bread instead of their forefathers' gruel. When the son in the late thirteenth-century poem *Helmbrecht* declared that he would eat nothing but bread made from fine white flour and leave the father to eat oats, he was revolting against the *ordo*, the God-given social order which applied to all; the reader understands that he will come to grief. Many of our modern prejudices about crude medieval table manners might indeed be based on those derogatory stories in which culinary (and therefore social) transgressions were ridiculed or severely punished.

Until the middle of the twelfth century, serving enormous amounts of food and entertaining large groups was an indication of elevated social rank. Thereafter, possibly because the lower classes could increasingly afford enough to satisfy their hunger, overly hearty eating was frowned upon by the aristocracy as suitable only for the common man. An educational epic from around 1300 urged to avoid '*herr frass und herr schlund*', Sir Greedy and Sir Gulp.[4] What might possibly be the first attempt in the Western world to deal with the effects of gluttony with the help of a surgeon's knife took place at the end of the twelfth century, though the unfortunate object of medical intervention, the Markgraf Dedo of Wettin, did not survive the procedure.[5] In a countertrend many a merry folk song praised gluttony as an alternative to the restrained Minnesang ideal, naming individual dishes and including peasant food such as offal and garlic sausages.

For the aristocracy more refined means of social distinction were needed than ostentatious consumption. Among these were table manners; meals became more regulated and ritualized. In Wolfram von Eschenbach's early thirteenth-century romance *Parzival*, the hero's bad table manners and inability to control his appetite had to be slowly tamed, symbolizing his lack of education. In time Parzival learned to share food and distribute it evenly in a more civilized manner. Besides a sumptuous and highly ritualized table setting, the ceremonial meal in front of the Grail was depicted as including many beautiful maidens, precious stones and metals, with scribes assigned to prevent their theft by checking quantities.

Plates and beakers made from precious metals were a vital part of a rich castle's equipment and were displayed on buffet tables as status symbols. The oldest German inventory of such tableware dates from the twelfth century and had the Neuenburg castle boasting of 'six silver gobelets with lids and five silver tumblers without lids, three cups with lids and four without, a silver knife and two silver spoons. Altogether there were sixteen silver containers.'[6]

So what was served from these sumptuous vessels placed 'before the Grail'? 'I will be quick in brevity,' the poet said, much to the food historian's frustration, 'with courtesy they took from before the Grail dishes wild and tame, this man his mead, that man his wine, as his custom would have it – mulberry wine, sinopel, claret.'[7] With the sum total of the information delivered, it is worth noting that *Sinôpel* and *klâret* were white and red spiced wine and the 'dishes' (*spîse*) have been interpreted as meat from both domesticated and wild animals (Chrétien de Troyes, on whose unfinished earlier *Perceval* Wolfram undoubtedly based his work, had those present eating a peppered leg of venison).[8]

From the thirteenth century onwards personal knives were carried as 'cutlery', but a *trancheur* or carver would cut up the larger meat pieces following a highly elaborate technique, working within view of the guests at the table. The *trancheur* was also in charge of passing special bread or pastries around on a flat, square knife. The service of food developed into an increasingly complex procedure, with servants sometimes kneeling or even working from horseback, and guests seated only on one side of the long table. Service was overseen by the *Truchsess* (senechal or master of ceremonies), himself a high-ranking noble who entered bearing a mace, followed by the highest steward and the highest *Mundschenk*, or cupbearer, who in turn each commanded a whole regiment of servants. This order of precedence (the rigmarole of which lives on in high-class restaurants up to the present day) was mirrored behind the scenes by the *Küchenmeister*, kitchen master, a position established at the imperial German court around 1200, a century and a half after its first appearance in France.[9] In castles the kitchen was often located opposite the great hall, making food service one long procession across the courtyard.

One of the earliest European recipe collections from the twelfth century in northern Germany implies that cooking (baking and brewing were usually done in a separate building) generally involved a griddle, gridiron, pots and pans. The kitchen equipment, besides dishes, further included cloths, casks for storage, mortar and pestle, knives, spoons and a spit. In the thirteenth to fifteenth centuries pokers, wooden tongs, bellows, tripods, kettle hooks and large cooking vessels made from bronze, brass and copper tin were added, as well as iron frying pans and earthen hoods to cover embers during the night as a precaution against fire. Most dishes and pots for storing, serving and cooking directly on embers, as well as in ovens, were of earthenware. This could lend an earthen taste to food, which new studies suggest might have been considered desirable and actively sought after. Glazed stoneware was produced in Germany from the beginning of the fourteenth century. It required much higher temperatures for kiln firing and hence more wood to produce, making it more expensive.

Manuals on how to behave at table were first directed at children but soon became popular among adults as well. Many of the rules were concerned with basic hygiene. Here is the poet Tannhäuser in Germany's oldest such manual: do not drink too much, don't complain about the food, don't make any noise while eating, don't put the bones back into the serving bowl, don't use your fingers for the mustard or sauce, don't blow your nose into the tablecloth or your hand, don't blow into a hot drink and don't throw yourself over the table during the meal.[10] The necessity of such advice seems to reinforce the prejudice that medieval Germans lacked refinement. But it is worth remembering that forks did not yet exist, that knives and spoons were mostly used for serving and that bowls and beakers were often shared. The elaborate table rituals could also be extremely confusing for ambitious social climbers, since there was much more for them to keep in mind. It was considered important to arrange tables and chairs in the appropriate way, just as the seating plan had to reflect the guests' social rank. This was particularly difficult to achieve, as several criteria had to be balanced. The round table of King Arthur was a tactical decision designed to avoid what could easily be the cause of feuding. Some accounts of the time describe men and women as seated separately; others in pairs. At some point small tables were considered more elegant than large ones: *Parzival*, for instance, mentioned 100 small tables, each accommodating four knights. A work from the mid-thirteenth century listed thirteen guidelines for a successful table arrangement (all perfectly reasonable from a contemporary point of view), of which only three are concerned with food, advising diversity and tastiness, with no fatty or ordinary dishes but something choice, light and delicious. There should also be a good variety of wines. Besides this, the location, the time and length of the meal, the servants' manners, the abundance of candles and the musicians' accomplishment were considered decisive. Additional advice made clear that it was unacceptable to ask one's guests for a financial contribution to the banquet and declared it the host's duty to show a smiling face throughout the occasion.[11]

It is tempting to imagine that a peasant's meal was in complete contrast to the splendours enjoyed by the wealthy. The diet of the peasantry would certainly have been based on cereals – indeed, in some regions our Neolithic gruel would remain a staple dish until well into the twentieth century. But besides that, it now involved a stew, with mainly cabbage, occasionally a little meat, turnips and *kumpost* – salt-cured vegetables, usually sauerkraut. Depending on the region, millet might have been included, along with sour beer, hemp, lentils and beans. Coarse dark bread made from oats, barley or rye might have been on the table as well. The exact composition is uncertain, since written evidence is sparse and what there is has to be taken with a good pinch of salt, as food in poems and songs of the time often served to define social standing and the associated prejudices towards the lower classes. Aristocrats were stereotypically presented as enjoying dainty feasts of game, fish and white bread with imported, expensive delicacies such as rice, spices and/ or sugar, while peasants ate whatever there was – the rough fuel-food of the field worker. But just as nobles were a very complex social group, peasants could be rich or poor, free or bonded. On top of that, it is easy to forget that rural life was strongly dependent on the natural cycle of the seasons as well as logistic and economic constraints. On farms and in villages, rain and sunshine, ploughing and harvesting made for fasting and feasting, quite apart from dietary rules instigated by the Church. Sunday was not only for churchgoing but was as much for catching up with urgent tasks as it was for socializing or merrymaking.

Throughout the high Middle Ages, as the economy in general prospered, regional food preferences began to emerge much more clearly. While rye was favoured in the north and east, the west was dominated by wheat growing and the southwest specialized in spelt, also harvested green and dried as *Grünkern* (which has currently seen a revival). Field

Wolf Helmhardt von Hohberg, *Georgica Curiosa* (Nuremberg, 1682–1716), Book 7: *Agriculture*. Fenced cabbage gardens beyond the city walls.

crops and fruits came into more extensive cultivation and vineyards crept up hillsides, especially along the Rhine and the Neckar. Different forms and levels of cultivation could be found within short distances according to natural conditions. One example from around 1300 is a very basic form of slash-and-burn agriculture surviving in the higher Eifel region, whereas not far down in the Rhine valley, the Rheingau produced fruit, grain, grapes and nuts with 'wondrous fertility and speed'.[12] But even the Eifel region was not a uniformly structured landscape. The abbot of Prüm in the Eifel chronicled conditions in his region in 1222: '329 years have passed . . . many woods have been cleared, many villages been built, the tithes been increased . . . many mills have been erected, many vineyards been installed as well as endless lands cultivated.'[13]

Besides structural organization, many other factors combined to make agricultural food production more efficient. The amount of iron used for agricultural equipment vastly increased, particularly iron parts on ploughs and shoes for horses. The harness, generally used from the eleventh century onwards, was a vital innovation since it allowed the use of horsepower. A single horse had the same strength as a pair of oxen, although a horse was more expensive both to acquire and keep, requiring oats for feed. In addition, when too old to work, oxen were prized as a source of food. They were less liable to diseases and less temperamental than horses. They were yoked up in pairs, up to four in front of one plough. However, for small farmers and in areas where dairy farming, pastoral agriculture and husbandry were mixed, the harnessed horse was more versatile, being used for traction as well as personal travel. Horses also fetched a good price from the army in times of war.

By 1300 in some water-rich regions almost every village had its own water mill. This also influenced freshwater fish supplies. Contrary to common belief, aquaculture in Germany was not a Roman legacy and there is no evidence for fish culture in the early Middle Ages, even in monasteries. But mills regulated streams with dammed-in lakes as power reservoirs and this created new habitats of warm, standing water, often with high nutrient-content because of the disposal of human and animal waste. As Christian fasting laws combined with population growth, fish was in strong demand. With no refrigeration, fresh marine fish could only be transported up to 150 km inland. This led to an important market for salted herring and stockfish, dried cod, but both were regarded as less desirable than fresh fish. Prices for local wild fish rose and they became

So-called 'blue' carp
(prepared with vinegar),
a popular dish to the
present day, from the
GDR cookbook *Kochen*
(Leipzig, 1983).

an elite foodstuff – in fifteenth-century towns fish was three to five times more expensive than beef. Artificial fishponds (instead of just holding tanks) were built from 1150, with lay landowners following the monastic example. In particular the common carp, though not a native, was very well suited to the newly created habitat. An omnivore and bottom-feeder, it prospered in warm, turbid, slow or still waters, growing faster than the native bream, tolerating low oxygen levels and capable of surviving for a few days out of water if kept cool and damp during transport. From then on aquaculture in ponds steadily moved west and north, and with it the carp. It is still traditionally served on Good Friday or New Year's Eve.[14]

It is estimated that the German population grew from eight to fourteen million between 1200 and 1320 (reflecting the general development in Europe). This was made possible by the significant land area under cultivation, with all the best soils cleared by about 1200.[15] Along the coast, marshes were drained to create new land. In 1106 the archbishop of Hamburg brought in Dutch settlers for this purpose, just as Dutch engineers in the seventeenth century in Bordeaux would expand the region's vineyards. The newcomers were promised land in return for one-eleventh of all field crops raised and one-tenth of the sheep, pigs, goats and geese, as well as honey and flax. They were, however, required to pay a sum on St Martin's day for keeping a foal and a calf.[16]

In the Slavic east of Germany colonialization was undertaken by Cistercian monks and the peasantry, mostly from the Rhineland, followed by craftsmen and merchants. Among the first of these new Christian peasants were Franks who established themselves near Merseburg in 1104.[17] Many Slavic rulers converted to Christianity, often intermarrying with the German nobility and adopting their culture, whereas the Lausitz region near Cottbus remains a Slavic enclave to this day. Assarting – clearing forest land for cultivation – was hard work and the cultural leap from the Rhineland to Slavic surroundings certainly not without problems, but the attraction was great since it offered peasants the chance to work their own land. As on the coast, the new settlers were given privileges to encourage loyalty. They were also rewarded by the initial fertility and ensuing high yields of the new land, thanks to the 'virgin' soils enriched by ashes from burned woodland. Spandau, today a district of Berlin, together with Brandenburg represented the most important Slavic strongholds before and after the German conquest in the tenth century, situated at an intersection of important waterways and trade routes. In the twelfth century Spandau came under German rule, the Slavic upper class east of the Elbe was partly assimilated and the eastern regions rapidly incorporated into international trade networks, with rye from the Berlin region becoming available in Hamburg and Flanders (although at the start volumes were not very high).

Slavic influences added another facet to the landscape of German food. In contrast to the generous attention given to French and Italian culinary influences, these have often been neglected. Buckwheat, a fast-growing pseudocereal used for making pancakes and gruel rather than bread (since it lacks gluten), was probably introduced by the Slavs. First mentioned in Germany in the late fourteenth century, buckwheat is thought to have travelled west from its central Asian origins with the Mongols in the thirteenth century along with another modest member of the knotweed family, rhubarb, whose root was highly valued in classical medicine and traded from China. Buckwheat's virtues are that it does well on poor, acidic soils and is useful for bees as a source of nectar. Once established in the Slavic regions, it spread west through lower Saxony, Westphalia and into the Eifel region. The Alsace physician Melchior

Sebizius in his major dietary work *De Alimentorum facultatibus*, published in 1650, mentioned buckwheat 150 times, testament to its widespread popularity at the time (in the eighteenth century it would be largely replaced by the equally undemanding but more productive and nourishing potato).[18] The Slavic influence is also noticeable linguistically in words such as *Bemme*, bread spread with butter; *Graupen*, pearl barley; *Gurke*, cucumber; and *Jause*, snack, all going back to the fifteenth or sixteenth century.

As the population grew rapidly, towns multiplied in the patchwork of sovereign princely states of various size and structure. Being aristocratic and living in a castle made for more sumptuous meals, and urban folks also generally tended to live better than country people. But just as not everybody who lived in a castle was sitting at the high table with the knights, social differences among the urban population were considerable. In many cases a few prominent and wealthy families came to dominate urban societies in a patriarchy with distinct privileges and responsibilities. Just like castles, towns were continually under threat from invaders. Local rulers were responsible for keeping the peace within their own territories, but it was considered both normal and morally acceptable to wage war on each other. Whoever had the will, the weaponry and the power was entitled to proclaim war against another for the flimsiest of reasons, mostly for personal gain in wealth and power. Against this background large towns surrounded by walls and fortifications represented places of safety in potentially hostile surroundings. As a result, townsfolk built up substantial food reserves. Underground wooden pipes outside the city's walls were used for water supplies, their exact location kept strictly secret for security reasons. Many households dug their own wells; others shared them.

Contaminated drinking water was a serious health hazard. The problem was mainly inadequate garbage disposal, a duty devolved to each individual household according to strict principles: rubbish had to be dealt with without irritating the neighbours and, if at all possible, on the household's own land. Most houses had their own latrines and rubbish pits. These had to be emptied regularly by specialized workmen and the contents removed into rivers, preferably during the cold months. At the time this was thought to be a perfectly good solution, since it was believed that illness was transferred through the air in the form of what was known as miasma, a theory dating back to classical times. Latrines were insulated but mostly situated at the same level as the wells. From the late twelfth century on, public disposal trenches for used waters (excluding human waste) were managed by city employees. Two centuries later, as more and more city streets were paved and water provision and garbage disposal had to function on limited space, councils started to organize refuse disposal at separate sites.[19]

Vegetable gardens played an important role in adding to a town's supplies. Lübeck's *Vergartung* was first mentioned in the thirteenth century, likewise Hamburg and the *Altes Land*, Cologne, Bonn and the *Vorgebirge*, Breslau and the *Kräuterei*. As trade between towns increased, urban dwellers tended to be less self-sufficient. However, the *Ackerbürger*, citizens who made their living working fields just outside the town walls, were still active until the eighteenth century, and urban gardeners included the young Goethe's grandparents in Frankfurt.

Open fireplaces were gradually being replaced by ovens, adding to general comfort. An increasingly common innovation was an early central heating system in the form of a *Kachelofen*, tiled stove, often with green glazed bowl-shaped tiles that spread the heat more efficiently through the room. But the fire risk in towns was still high due to the building density. Houses were commonly built from wood and were often half-timbered, with wooden shingles for roofs. Towards the end of the thirteenth century, town councils increasingly issued decrees that any houses not built entirely of stone should at least have the ground floors made of stone. Firewood was mostly of lesser quality, emitting quite a lot of smoke, which herbs such as thyme were supposed to counteract. In urban houses the simple hearths that served as light and heat sources as well as for cooking tended to disappear around 1200, whereas in rural areas multifunctional central fireplaces were common until about 1500. In these the smoke escaped through a skylight in the roof, which often served the dual purpose of smoking meat and other food (although kitchen design and equipment varied regionally, and archaeological finds are often difficult to interpret).

As the infrastucture improved, long-distance travel became easier, encouraging business activities (followed inevitably by taxes, customs and tolls). Bridges and supporting walls on steep slopes were built, roads were mended and surfaces were improved with wood, gravel or paving. Shoed horses could draw four-wheeled carts as well as barges along cleared riverbanks. The concentrated demand of towns and cities for food led in time to networks of market-driven agricultural production and trade in the surrounding country, systems which were in a constant state

A culinary place in time: *Wurstkuchl* and *Bratwurstglöcklein*

In towns street food was common. The Wurstkuchl in Regensburg, directly on the Danube, competes with the Bratwurstglöcklein in Nuremberg for the title of the oldest bratwurst eatery. The Wurstkuchl (www.wurstkuchl.de) goes back to the 1130s. During the building of the city's old stone bridge, a Garküche or hot food stall was attached to the city's wall to provide food for the workers. After the bridge was finished, the stall stayed on to serve the dock workers around the big riverbank crane, as well as the stone masons and their colleagues who were building the Regensburg cathedral (started in the 1260s). Back then it probably served all kinds of simmered and boiled dishes, with its specialization on bratwurst being documented only at the end of the eighteenth century.

However, roasted sausages were very popular during the Middle Ages. A council decree in Regensburg in 1406 had meat inspectors checking on sausage making; only fresh and cleaned casings were to be used, and only pork, mixed with chopped pork fat, for the filling.[20] It appears that at the time,

Postcard from 1933 showing a fantasy of the historic *Bratwurstglöcklein* stall. The card was part of a promotional series issued by the gingerbread company Haeberlein-Metzger, an early example of marketing regional products.

as today, sausages were less expensive than fresh meat. Although sausage makers formed a separate guild, butchers seem to have produced sausages too, and on special occasions immense ones were proudly presented to the public. A report from Königsberg from 1650 described one made from 81 pork hams for Christmas 1601 (with numerous beer barrels emptied by the butchers involved in its making).[21]

Although the slim homemade sausages roasted on a charcoal grill and served on homemade sauerkraut at the Wurstkuchl are delicious, 'Regensburger' designates a scalded pork sausage the locals call Knacker, which is much thicker and can be traced back to the nineteenth century. The term 'Rostbratwurst', sausage roasted on a griddle, is mostly associated with Nuremberg, where the Bratwurst-glöcklein claims the year 1313 as its origin (die-nuern-berger-bratwurst.de). A publication from 1754 declared that the best bratwurst was to be had in Nuremberg, Franconia and Swabia, because elsewhere too much meat from old animals was used. The author recommended that suckling pigs destined for sausages should be fed with sour milk for twelve to sixteen weeks.[22]

Another legitimate claim to a considerable historical past in terms of sausages comes from Thuringia. Larger than both those from Nuremberg or Regensburg, Thüringer sausages were first mentioned in a monastery bill in 1404, and the oldest recipe for them dates back to 1613.

of expansion or contraction, not least in response to changes in climate. This explains the proliferation of intense pasture zones on the Marschen, the marshlands on the North Sea, and on the foothills of the Alps in the south of Germany where in the twelfth and thirteenth century numerous *Schwaigen* (an old term for dairy estates) were established. Market rights were usually granted to towns within half a day's travel of each other. While larger fairs were held only on special occasions (the first such trade fair was recorded in 1240 in Frankfurt am Main), more regular markets were held weekly. On market day towns were packed with traffic, with vendors and buyers streaming in from the countryside on foot and with

Peasant woman and market crier selling milk, butter milk and butter fat in Nuremberg. Undated, probably late 18th century.

hand carts, pack animals or oxen-drawn carts as well as on horseback, overwhelming the town centre with noises, smells and the cries of hawkers selling their wares. The peasantry generally confined themselves to short journeys to market by cart or on foot, with two days' travel the greatest distance covered, while hawkers were prepared to travel much greater distances. For accomodation everybody stuck to their own social group: merchants often stayed with their business partners, although *Herbergen* or public inns became more common, with certain trade guilds establishing their own inns.[23]

The Christian Crusades certainly weren't a holiday trip, even for those nobles leading them in full attire with flags flying. It is amazing how many people this international project, which went on for two centuries starting in the 1090s, attracted and from how wide a social spectrum. Provisions were scant and plundering was regarded as a lifesaving necessity. There are reports of famines in the army which obliged Christians to eat 'the putrid bodies of the Saracens'. There is much discussion among historians on cannibalism, which crept up again and again in reports on the hardships endured during the Crusades – was it just a literary hyperbole or could it actually have happened?[24] Just to add a footnote, the terms *heidnisch* (literally pagan) and *Saracen* in Germany, as in other countries, were applied to food with the meaning 'exotic' or 'foreign'. However, the dishes they denominated often had little in common with the originals, but acquired their titles through the inclusion of ingredients imported from the Islamic world or because they were for some reason considered foreign.

The most tangible target of the Crusaders' religious zealotry even before distant shores were reached were the Jews, perceived forever as 'the

Hildegard von Bingen, *Book of Divine Works,* Part One, Vision Four: Symmetries: World, Body and Soul, 1165.

others' and heretics, in spite of all the convenience they offered through moneylending. Whereas Christian food laws centred on lean and fast days, the more general Jewish kashrut laws were about right and wrong foods. Instead of the Christian Eucharist, Jews went on to celebrate Pessach, remembering the liberation and exodus from Egypt. This ran against the deep symbolism of communal meals and offered excuses enough to persecute this minority. Cologne, Worms and Mainz saw especially heinous behaviour in spite of well-documented attempts by local bishops to protect their own populations of Jews. In 1074 the Church Council of Rouen extended the prohibition of communal meals to Jewish wet nurses in Christian households, although the bishop of Speyer, obviously either a much more tolerant or perhaps just a more realistic man, explicitly allowed this in his 1090 declaration of privileges for the Jewish community of his town. During the following centuries, official church doctrine ruled against Christian wet nurses in Jewish households, and Jews were not allowed to run food stalls, nor to sell food to Christians.

Medieval texts often use the Latin verb *reficere* for eating (which explains the use of the word *Refektorium*, refectory, for the monks' dining hall): eating was considered a restorative act. Religious and medical ideas at the time were intricately linked and it is almost impossible to underestimate the influence medical thinking of the time had on what and how people ate. One of the key figures in early medicine was Hildegard von Bingen, the most influential German nun of the Middle Ages. A twelfth-century Benedictine abbess and mystic from a noble family in Bermersheim near Alzey, she lived in a convent from an early age and went on to found two monasteries on the Rhine and Nahe. Her books, letters and sermons were based on intensely spiritual visions inspired by a profound knowledge of religious, medical, botanical, musical and cosmological matters. She corresponded with many of the leading figures of her time and took several long trips along the Rhine to preach in public, thereby disseminating her strong convictions on spirituality, politics, ethics and medicine. In all her works Hildegard addressed many of the everyday questions women asked, touching on little-discussed subjects such as sexuality and illness. Her medical works *Physica* and *Causae et Curae* represent the high point of what is known as *Klostermedizin* or monastic medicine, setting the important precedent of describing plants by using their vernacular names. Hildegard's approach combined popular medical knowledge with the humoral theory spread by the medical teachings in Salerno, Paris, Bologna, Montpellier and Perugia.

The ideas of humoral theory are not only essential in order to understand medieval cuisine but can be traced in Germans' foodways right up to the present day. In this system the microcosm was held to mirror the macrocosm. The four humours – melancholic, sanguine, phlegmatic and choleric – matched the four elements: fire (hot and dry), water (cold and wet), earth (cold and dry) and air (hot and wet). These in turn corresponded to the four bodily fluids: yellow bile, phlegm, black bile and blood. With these elements and humours being present in all things to varying degrees, human well-being (spiritual and bodily) depended on a balanced, temperate state roughly defined as warm and moist. Any imbalance could lead to illness. As with Ayurvedic medicine, the system focused almost entirely on the prevention of imbalance and the belief that an excessive 'temperament' could be tempered through diet. While chopping or puréeing guaranteed a good blend and digestibility, it was understood that cooking changed the nature of a foodstuff, with colouring an additional option to render something more suitable for a certain person or occasion. Some ingredients were inherently imbalanced and needed tempering. If this sounds absurdly superstitious to contemporary ears, it suddenly turns into perfectly familiar culinary wisdom when we hear Hildegard's advice on lettuce, which was considered excessively 'cold' but was tempered – that is, rendered more wholesome – by a vinegar dressing.

Pregnant women, wet nurses and infants were considered as belonging to the same category as the elderly and convalescents. All were considered 'neutral', by which is meant that they were between health and illness, a condition which required the strengthening, appetizing foods thought to increase the substance of the body without altering its humoral composition. Thus light and delicate, 'tempered' food was recommended during pregnancy, such as kid, chicken, partridge or soft-boiled eggs, while bitter or pungent foods, such as capers, lupins (a legume) or sesame seeds, were to be avoided. Pregnant women should not eat too much at a time, and were instructed to drink only a little white wine diluted with water, or clear red wine. Wet nurses, it was written, should avoid sharp, constipating or pungent foods such as onions, garlic, vinegar and pepper, and were likewise instructed not to drink strong, undiluted wine. Their diet should be moderate in quantity, but of good-quality ingredients, such as lamb, capon, hen, chicken, partridge, pheasant and veal, mixed with egg yolk, warm goat's milk and sugar. Children of half a year to a year old should be given mild food such as rice cooked in milk, breadcrumbs soaked in chicken broth or the soft breast meat of birds and chicken. Children, it was instructed, were not to be breastfed for longer than two years and were to be weaned slowly when they began walking. Between the ages of six and ten, children were considered mature enough to progress to coarser food.[25]

Hildegard recommended fasting and the eating of green things, *viriditas*, for vitality. Her favoured grain was spelt, and she strongly advised against the consumption of pork, eel, duck, eggs, plums and strawberries (on the grounds that these last fruits grow too low and capture too much harmful morning dew – something that admittedly does not sound too plausible to modern readers). Although Hildegard didn't write what might be described as an actual cookbook, she included many preparations for numerous ingredients in her works, such as the one on lettuce. Some were copied and thus further disseminated in following centuries by compilers such as Meister Eberhard, a court chef in fifteenth-century Bavaria, who incorporated long passages from Hildegard's *Physica* into his own popular cookbook.[26]

Thus the first written recipes in German appear in medical texts, *Regimen sanitatis*, and to this day, as mentioned earlier, the word *Rezept* is used in German for a culinary instruction as well as a medical prescription. Besides Hildegard, one of the earliest dietetic manuals in German is the twelfth-century *Breslauer Arzneibuch*, which relied heavily on Constantin Africanus' Salerno translations and contained several culinary recipes for lentils, bean soup and poached eggs. Konrad von Eichstätt and Arnold von Bamberg wrote two other very influential *Regimen*, both published first in Latin and circulated widely for 200 years among members of the medical profession as well as an educated lay audience. They exerted a Mediterranean influence on the culinary ideas of upper-class Germans. Arnold von Bamberg's work was probably written in 1317 near Avignon and was certainly heavily influenced by his time spent in Italy and France. He provided 40 somewhat international recipes, but interestingly enough listed fried or boiled apples, grapes boiled in almond milk and figs boiled in water or almond milk as popular German dishes, claiming that a cheese soup (actually cheese cooked in water and eaten with bread) was a dish 'frequently used in Germany'. Konrad von Eichstätt, a southern German physician trained in either France or northern Italy, clearly intended to address his own countrymen, explaining among other things that the truth of the statement 'one German drinks more than two Latins' could be attributed to the German love of alcohol caused by the harsh northern climate.[27] He included eleven recipes for

Mediterranean dishes adjusted to the requirements of northern palates and cooking habits, and, in a similar manner to Hildegard von Bingen, gave a lengthy classification of foodstuffs according to their suitability for certain sensitivities in order to achieve a harmonious balance of both body and spirit.

Although remaining closely connected to dietetics and medicine, written recipes began to take on a life of their own. Finally we get a more thorough idea of what people were eating – or at least which preparations they thought important enough to keep a precise record of. The early material in this field is rare, as those who cooked were mostly illiterate and in any case many kinds of knowledge, including culinary knowhow, were usually transmitted orally. But as paper became more widely available and affordable, it was also used for recording recipes. They reinforce our earlier impressions and assumptions: whereas gluttony was one of the Seven Deadly Sins, fine cooking emerged as a means to social distinction.

Daz Buoch von guoter Spise (The Book of Good Food, long considered the oldest known German cookbook), written around 1350, was undoubtedly too precious to be used in the kitchen, living instead in the library of its owner, Michael de Leone. Leone was a patrician lawyer who served as the highest notary to the bishop of Würzburg and can thus be assumed to be a man of considerable wealth and status. The book gives a glimpse as to how the urban upper classes of Würzburg preferred to present themselves: the art of getting 'great meals from many small things' is the book's central message, with thrift praised as a virtue and the use of offal promoted; at the same time, the inclusion of such luxurious goods as white bread, saffron, rice and almonds demonstrated considerable wealth, with local vegetables such as beetroot, beans, cabbage, peas, leeks and turnips playing only a minor role. Frequent mention of chicken not only pointed to a comfortable social situation, but also to an urban setting in which barnyard fowl could be easily kept as a reliable source of fresh meat. Leone's recipes include a sophisticated well-spiced sweet-sour chicken dish with pears:

> Roast a chicken, and fry the crust of buns. Fry this in lard until it turns golden, and cut bite-sized pieces as you do for bread pudding. Cut the chicken up small, and roast six pears. Make a sauce of wine and honey, then grind spices in it, pepper and anise, and make a crêpe of five eggs. Break them into a pan, then

place each one in it separately, and fold the crêpe. Cover the pan
with a bowl, then turn the pan upside down, cut through the
top of the dough, pour in the sauce, and don't spill any on the
dough. These are called Chickens à la Rheingau. And serve.[28]

Early recipes such as this one often assumed a lot of technical
knowledge, making their logic somewhat difficult to disentangle for
twenty-first-century cooks. But even if we are not completely able to
imagine the dish in its finished form, it sounds intriguing and delicious.
It also confirms that the Rheingau stood for sweet fruit and wine. Another
noteworthy practice is the medieval habit of thickening sauces and dishes with bread (something worth experimenting with in one's own
cooking!). This is before the introduction of either the potato or corn
(maize), later on much used sources of starch, and dairy products like
cream were highly perishable due to the lack of refrigeration.

An alternative to dairy, and a real fad of the time since it was also
suitable for essentially vegan fast days, was 'milk' made from ground
almonds soaked in water. This preparation had the additional advantage
that it kept much better than animal milk and could also be turned into
a butter that did not need salt to preserve it. As with certain spices and
early imports of sugar, almonds were first seen in a medicinal context
before they could be accepted in the kitchen, and Konrad von Eichstätt
may have played an important part in introducing almonds and almond
milk to Germany by including them in his dietary advice. By the middle
of the fourteenth century, almonds and almond milk had become an inte-
gral part of upper-class cuisine in Germany and *Daz Buoch* gives nineteen
recipes involving almond milk. Arnold von Bamberg was the first German
writer to mention blancmanger, one of the most frequently recurring
medieval dishes. It was usually white, hence its name – literally white food.
According to humoral theory, white was a colour that was particularly
suited to infants and invalids, but sometimes could be coloured with
saffron or violets. It always involved almond milk and rice, but the variations were endless, using chicken on feast days and fish, especially pike,
on fast days. Blancmanger's exact definition is the subject of endless
discussions among food historians, throwing a light on the difficulty of
their often painstaking toil to reconstruct food accurately. Medieval
recipes were often copied by scribes who were ignorant of culinary matters and misread and subsequently misspelled dishes' names or ingredients.
Arnold called it *alba comestio sive blantmaser*; in *Daz Buoch* it appeared

as *blamensir*. Historians debate whether the *brouet d'Allemagne* in Taillevent's Le Viandier and the *brouès d'Allemaigne* in the *Ménagier de Paris* (from *c.* 1300 and the late fourteenth century respectively) were, in spite of their differences, actually based on the *blamensir* in *Daz Buoch*, or whether they represent imaginative linguistic deviations.[29]

The question becomes even more complex in the context of one of the oldest known collections of European culinary recipes written in a vernacular language. The small collection of about 35 recipes survived in four slightly different versions, of which two are in Danish, one in Icelandic and one in Low German. It clearly goes back to an 'original', the *Libellus de arte coquinaria*, which may have been written down in Middle Low German as early as the twelfth century.[30] It could be the very earliest record of the recipes and culinary themes that were to flourish throughout the late Middle Ages. The recipes are certainly not by a single author but, as was usual at the time, a compilation or adaptation. The lost original has been reconstructed from surviving manuscripts, of which the German version resurfaced as part of the *Mittelniederdeutsches Kochbuch*, dated to the fifteenth century.[31] These recipes in many ways are further confirmation of international influences at the top of the social pyramid. Obviously meant for someone with substantial means, they are all northern European adaptations of recipes originating in the south. Although the list of ingredients includes neither rice, olive oil, chickpeas nor delicate vegetables such as chard or spinach, it includes various almond preparations, the majority of which were later to be found all over Europe. The exciting thing about the *Libellus* is the fact that it confirms German cuisine's link to the north, an essential, but often neglected perspective: the Icelandic version of the manuscript includes a recipe for almond milk curdled with wine or vinegar, pronounced to be 'as good as skyr'. *Skyr* is popular in Iceland up to the present day and is very similar to German quark, the *lac concretum* mentioned by Tacitus.[32]

Reading these recipes and getting excited about their intricacies, it is easy to forget how small the readership they were aimed at was. Even under regular circumstances, such recipes, with their long lists of luxurious ingredients, were unimaginably distant from the reality of most people's lives, which at best could be called precarious, with hardship and famine always lurking around the next corner. Hunger is closely woven into Germans' culinary DNA. For medieval chroniclers *fames*, or famines, were virtually interchangeable with *mortalitas*, mortality, or the subsequent epidemics. In addition to natural causes, wars could severely interrupt food production and distribution, as military strategy often involved devastating the agricultural production of the enemy. Periods of famine generally extended over two to three years, since the economy needed longer than a single year to recover, not least because grain production was interrupted as a result of total or partial consumption of seed grain. From 1100 onwards, during the so-called medieval warm period, the climate in Central Europe generally turned milder. Summers were warmer, sometimes extremely warm, and winters were occasionally very much colder than we experience them today. In very hot summers flour – hence bread – was very expensive because mills had no water.[33] At the same time, with the wage-earning labour force on the increase, particularly because of the expansion of mining, more and more people were buying their food instead of producing it. The result, in years of poor harvests and other adverse conditions, was a rapid inflation of prices followed by famine.

Though most famines were localized, from 1315 to 1320 a catastrophic subsistence crisis known as the Great Famine affected the whole of northern Europe, creating a situation so protracted and extensive that it was still invoked in chronicles more than a century later. Its impact was especially harsh because the disaster struck when Germany had only just achieved a certain balance of agricultural production and demand after a period of intense population growth.[34] The causes of the Great Famine were various. Severe local flooding occurred in 1312 and 1313, and the latter winter was exceptionally cold, leading to regional shortages. By 1314, when Bavaria went to war with Austria, armies were so hungry that a chronicler of the time reported that knights were selling their mounts in exchange for food and drink: 'And what a wonder! Some knights who were sitting on a magnificently outfitted horse gave the horse and their weapons away for cheap wine; and they did this because they were so terribly hungry.' The following year saw the start of one of the worst and most sustained periods of bad weather in the entire Middle Ages, a situation scarcely to be anticipated given the overall mildness of the period. Torrential rains and the ensuing floods meant that seedbeds were sodden, crops and pastures went under water, grain rotted, meadows were too wet to be mown, turf was too soggy to be cut, quarries were inundated, buildings and walls were undermined and transport was severely hindered. In regions with light soils severe erosion led to an 'unheard-of barrenness'. The rain, in addition, leeched nitrates from the soil, triggering plant diseases. A succession of severe winters which caused the Baltic to freeze over were followed by heavy rains in spring, summer and autumn. Skies were recorded as abnormally overcast and the weather unusually cool and windy. Malnutrition led to weakness and a general loss of energy and will: as early as 1316 a Bremen chronicler mentioned a great lethargy afflicting many of his countrymen. In 1317 in western Germany, torrential rains were followed by the harshest winter ever experienced. Thereafter a slight improvement set in, but the winter of 1321 was once again bitterly cold, with the Baltic and parts of the North Sea frozen over. Murrains affected draft and food animals, especially the highly contagious rinderpest. Because of the persistent dampness, hay wouldn't dry. Salt production, vital for the conservation of meat and fish, was hindered by insufficient sunshine and excessive dampness. Food prices – volatile at best, especially for grain and salt – soared throughout Europe. Wages failed to keep up. Apart from those few who profited from the salt and grain trades or speculated in property, people struggled to make a living and bankruptcies were common. An inscription on a pillar of St Catherine's church in Oppenheim on the Rhine reminded future generations that when the church was built in 1317, bread had cost four *Heller*, presumably a very high price.[35] Lords with small estates often retreated from direct exploitation and leased farms to richer peasants, a situation that was later reversed when it became obvious that only direct management could secure enough seed grain. There were reports of desperate people feeding on diseased cattle (normally a hygienic taboo) and 'grazing like cows on the growing grasses of the fields'. Even cannibalism was mentioned, and although this might be the chronicler's literary device to convey the events' enormity, we are almost inclined to take his word for it.

Monasteries tried as best they could to feed and care for the growing stream of the poor, orphans, beggars and the weak, increasing alms as far as possible. Hospitals were founded, most notably the Heilig-Geist-Spital in Würzburg in 1319 by a wealthy local patrician. In the northeast the Teutonic Order distributed their grain reserves; their castles, like all garrison towns and frontier villages, were well stocked for sieges. Many towns struggled, however, and made sure to keep their gates closed as rural indigents assembled nearby. Where charity failed, theft increased and riots loomed. Cities hired labourers to gather up corpses for mass burials. Homesteads and settlements were abandoned to what came to be known as *Wüstungen*, deserted settlements.

In the wake of the Great Famine came the Great Plague. Many of the surviving children had suffered severe malnutrition at a critical age, which might explain the immense toll on a whole generation taken by the plague when it reached Germany in 1349. Thought to have been imported by merchants arriving from the Far East, the Black Death is said to have killed between 10 and 30 per cent of the German population, and was particularly catastrophic in densely populated larger cities such as Hamburg and Cologne. There wasn't much one could do. Attempts at purifying the air through the use of spices and herbs were considered particularly efficient when the mix included saffron, the most precious of remedies – social status applied in hard times just as much as in good ones. The dramatic decline in the population was followed by an agricultural depression that lasted for about a century. The density of settlements and areas of cultivated land diminished by about one-quarter, with the smallest estates being hit the hardest. But unlike today, the population's general attitude to the disaster was somewhat similar to that towards famine: miseries were sent by God and you couldn't do much about them.

FIVE

Butterbrot and Saffron: The Late Middle Ages, 14th and 15th Centuries

With regional epidemics repeatedly flaring up until the end of the fifteenth century, the plague continued to create labour short-ages. Those who were spared found themselves in a better position than in earlier centuries, and in consequence their meals increased in quantity and quality. In addition to the two main meals, an early lunch in the middle of the day and an evening meal at dusk, up to three in-between meals such as a morning soup, bread at night and a nightcap were commonly expected. Judging from their contract, in 1465 carpenters in Hamburg were served rye bread, butter, gruel, eggs, beef, herring, cod and cheese as well as light beer. Food purchased for workers during the grape harvest in Heilbronn in Württemberg in 1483 included white bread, bread made from mixed grains, barley, peas, ground oats, millet (for porridge), salt, lard, drawn butter, boiling meat, roasting meat, cheese, milk, cabbage, oat kernels, turnips, eggs, semolina, fish, stockfish, herring, onions, apples, cooking pears and spices. Besides variety, argu-ably the most striking difference between those two lists is in the bread: rye in the north, white (that is, wheaten) and mixed in the south. The butter adds to the contrast. *Botterbroth*, sliced dark sourdough rye bread with firm salted butter, could almost fly as a symbolic flag over the north of late medieval Germany, whereas in the south even labourers now expected their bread to be somewhat lighter and made from wheat. Much like Mediterranean folks today, they ate it as it was, using soft drawn butter and lard for cooking.

At the time geographical and social differences were reinforced through trade, the dominant economic force of the period. Obviously merchants traded in all kinds of things, but the German food trade in par-ticular reached previously unseen dimensions. It highlighted the very

Butter production was women's work. Two different technologies are depicted:
an upright churn for smaller quantities and a larger horizontal one.

different priorities in the north and the south, reinforcing existing cultural
networks, and was reflected on merchants' plates. Patrician families like the
Fuggers and Welsers in Augsburg, who controlled the German trade with
the south, not only often rose to the ranks of the aristocracy through their
commercial acumen but emulated the Italian nobles' refined food culture.
No rye bread for them, and if there wasn't enough olive oil, at least the
local butter had to be soft and oil-like. Expensive spices and complex
preparations (much in the style of Leone's Chicken à la Rheingau) were
essential to demonstrate their achievements and elevated status.

In contrast the northern Hanseatic League was a much more egalitarian affair. Operating on the communal level of town and city councils,
it was in the hands of a much greater number of less wealthy people. In
Hamburg or Lübeck, possibly also due to the still intensely agrarian
structure of the whole region, dishes did not become significantly more
refined as you climbed the social ladder, but quantities certainly grew. Meat
consumption in northern towns and cities went up considerably on feast
days, just as herring and stockfish became common foodstuffs on fast days.
For everyday food a stew of vegetables and salted meat was commonly prepared in a big pot, with salt and pepper used in abundance. The rapidly
emerging middle-class *Bürger* households demonstrated their growing
wealth with cooking utensils and serving dishes in bronze, pewter and

silver, occasionally even gold. *Grapen*, three-legged cast iron or bronze roasting dishes similar to Dutch ovens, were a regular feature in their kitchens and gave rise to the *Grapenbraten*, a braised beef dish popular up to the present day. The dark sourdough rye bread which was northeners' staple foodstuff was baked in dome-shaped ovens and had been greatly improved by advances in milling techniques, so that the loaves could be cut in slices. It ranged from heavy wholemeal which included 80 per cent of the grain to lighter variants called *Schönbrot* and *Schönroggen* (literally nice bread and nice rye). The butter they put on it, stored and traded in wooden barrels, was salted, so that it remained fresh and firm for quite some time. On special feast days, particularly during the days before Lent, the bakers made *Heisswecken*, white buns from wheat flour, yeast and sometimes milk. Whereas in the south all bread could include some spice like coriander, aniseed or caraway, up in the north only these feast day treats were flavoured with cinnamon and sweetened with currants. Beer was the drink of choice in the north, undoubtedly considered more thirst-quenching in combination with a rather salty diet than wine, which was reserved for special occasions. Wine and beer were served in pewter tankards, stoneware beakers from the Rhineland and, on more exclusive occasions, silver beakers or drinking glasses.[1]

The Hanseatic League (commonly known as the Hanse) was an international traders' alliance active from the twelfth until the seventeenth century that evolved into the leading socio-economic influence in the north. At its peak, the Hanse comprised almost 300 towns and cities from the Zuidersee and Yssel in the west and the Lower Rhine in

Grapen (three-legged pots), 1200–1400, clay. These pots were put directly into the embers and lifted with a stick fitting into the hollow handle.

the south to Polish Krakau and Silesian Breslau in the east. It catered to a growing urban population that was no longer self-reliant or supplied by their hinterlands, as well as providing goods to less productive regions. Although the Hanse also dealt in more expensive foodstuffs and spices (along with other commodities), its most important food wares were salt, herring and stockfish, at that time all basic necessities of life. The *Hansekogge*, a wooden cog with an angled prow and stern, a flat bottom and high sides, was developed in the twelfth or thirteenth century and was well suited to carrying large loads with a comparatively small crew. The bill of loading for a shipment to Antwerp in 1431 listed beer, wine, spices, almonds, rice, oil, butter, honey, cheese, stockfish, bacon, grain (wheat, rye, barley and oats), vetches, peas, beans, flour, hops, gale (for grut beer), herring and salt. Other lists include figs, dates and raisins, millet, *Bückling* (smoked herring), eel, salmon, sturgeon and meat.

The Hanse's lingua franca was middle Low German, and its first interest was to guarantee the safety of its seafaring members as well as maintaining its own privileged market position and treaty rights. It repeatedly used economic measures such as embargos to achieve its ambitious political goals. The Hanse had originated in the rather loose structures and alliances of German merchants abroad in places like London or Wisby, and had a decentralized structure in spite of Lübeck's and Hamburg's predominance – in fact, confusingly, smaller alliances of towns and/or merchants at the time were also called Hanse. Major decisions were taken during the *Hansetage*, regular assemblies that took place in Lübeck.

The importance of Lübeck for members of the Hanse was due in part to the fact that unless one wanted to undertake the perilous and long journey from the Baltic to the North Sea around the Skagerak, Lübeck was an unavoidable stopover where all goods had to be unloaded and carried by land across the peninsula. Eventually this was one of the reasons for the building of Europe's first channel between two watershed systems, a channel linking the Trave with the Elbe (and thus the Baltic with the North Sea), finished in 1398 and avoiding the long detour by sea as well as the slow land route. The Hanse's most important trade commodity was salt, mostly from the Lüneburg saltworks. During the thirteenth century, production in Lüneburg more than tripled, reaching its peak of more than 20,000 tons per year at the end of the sixteenth century. More than half of the production was marketed through Lübeck as *Travesalz*. Cheaper salt from the French, Spanish and Portuguese Atlantic

A culinary place in time: the Schiffergesellschaft in Lübeck

The Schiffergesellschaft in Lübeck was founded in 1401 as a fraternity of seafaring men and their families (www. schiffergesellschaft.com). In 1535 it combined with the fishermen's guild and bought an imposing redbrick house in early Renaissance style opposite the Jakobi church, one of the stops on the pilgrimage from northern Europe to Santiago de Compostela. Spared from destruction during the Second World War, today it houses a restaurant where the Hanse spirit lives on, reinforced through memorabilia. Obviously the thing to eat here is marinated herring!

Interior of the Schiffergesellschaft restaurant in Lübeck.
Note the room's church-like character.

coast was imported into the Baltic regions from the late fourteenth century onwards and was commonly called *Baiensalz*. It was said to be less pure and less efficient for preserving than the *Travesalz*, which was produced from a 25 per cent brine solution. Preserving was the main reason for the high demand, as it turned highly perishable foodstuffs such as fish (most importantly herring), meat and butter into widely traded commodities. During the late Middle Ages, the average consumption per person in Germany has been calculated as between 15 and 16 kg of salt per year (as compared to around 3.65–5 kg today). From the thirteenth century onwards butter generally increased in importance, with Dutch, Friesian, Danish, Swedish and Norwegian butter traded in Westphalia, Saxony and the regions up the Rhine to Cologne.[2]

Lübeck goes back to a former Slavic settlement and initially had an open air market on the riverbank, similar to the one in London, documented in 898 as *ripa emtoralis*.[3] Riverbank markets were common even before urbanization in ancient cultures north of the Alps, and they provide an impressive example as to how food trade shaped urban landscapes. They have been traced archeologically to as early as 3,000 BC, when peasants from east of the Elbe exchanged goods with hunters living near Hamburg on small islands. The markets' appearance changed over time, but their fundamental structure remained the same: waterways were used for transport and the seller didn't want to leave his wares alone but preferred to cook and live in tents on land, as near as possible to potential customers and/or where interesting goods such as ore, salt or fish were on offer. For their part, the customers erected their tents next to those of the sellers.

In the early Middle Ages the latter had become merchants and built houses at the riverbank market to live there permanently, with landing places for potential trading partners and, at more important markets such as the one in Lübeck, even a church for the foreigners, documented as *forensis ecclesia* in 1163. For security reasons the fortifications on the towns' walls included the merchants' houses, whereas the public part of the market was outside, directly on the riverbank. Since this was rather inconvenient for the town people's shopping, the diverse market functions gradually separated, with daily supplies moving inside towns and the riverbank reserved for long-distance trade. The one exception was fish, which continued to be sold directly from fishing boats.

Due to the Hanse's 'corporate' structure, the merchants travelling inland from the lower Rhineland and Westphalia no longer waited at the riverbank for their seafaring colleagues to unload their wares, but travelled with them to inspect the goods in situ or placed orders for certain goods in advance, thus linking seafaring trade to inland demand. The riverbank markets subsequently lost their importance and came to be used only for the technicalities of loading, unloading and weighing, as well as the collection of tolls and taxes. Transactions, increasingly recorded in writing, moved into the merchants' houses and *Kontore* or offices. Visiting merchants stayed at their colleagues' homes, leaving only a guard on board ship, while goods already transferred to shore were stored in cellars or under the roof. As the volume of trade increased, ships became larger, so that small ports were abandoned in favour of larger ones, leaving only the fish markets at the previous location.

After salt, herring was the second most important commodity controlled by the Hanse. Herring had been widely caught all around the Baltic prior to the rise of the league, but in order to be traded over long distances to inland markets, the catch had to be treated with salt, a commodity controlled by the Hanse. To facilitate the process, during the fishing season from mid-July until early October, German merchants established their own salting and packing stations on the coast of Danish Scania (present-day southern Sweden) where the Danish fishing fleet landed their catch. This arrangement was later expanded to Norway. Annual exports of salted herring, the staple food of fast days, were estimated at 40,000 tons, distributed throughout Germany and beyond via the fairs held at Frankfurt and Cologne. From the early fifteenth century Dutch herring from the North Sea gained in commercial importance owing to improvements in fishing methods resulting from larger economic structures and more advanced technology. Since the Dutch salted and packed the partly gutted fish on board ship, the preservation process was speeded up. However, by mid-century the herring shoals began to move north, favouring the Hanse trade once more. The first of the young fat herring, *Matjeshering*, were caught and offered for sale either lightly salted or dried and packed in baskets on straw. A Cologne decree from 1467 prohibited any herring catch before 31 May, identifying the more mature fish caught from 25 July onwards as of more reliable quality. The decree also stipulated that immature and mature herring were not to be mixed in the barrels, as the more tender young fish disintegrated in the heavier salt brine required for the latter. Barrels began to be used in the fourteenth century, with those made from oak considered the best, and were marked with a series of brands designating quality and origin. The fish had to be salted at least ten days prior to being packed and dispatched.[4]

Herring prepared as *Brathering* (on the right, fried and marinated in vinegar)
and *Matjes* (lightly salted). The beer glass has the typical shape used for wheat
beer from Berlin, although it looks too dark for that. From the popular GDR
cookbook *Kochen* (Leipzig, 1983).

The Hanse cities first concentrated on the exchange of local wares
mostly on the Baltic sea, but by and by extended their trade abroad,
establishing *Kontore*, or offices, in major ports such as Bruges, London,
Bergen and Novgorod. These offices were small enclaves of Hanseatic
power within the respective cities, rather like modern embassies but with
a focus on trade. The Bruges office, for instance, established in 1323,
was the northern European trade centre for textiles, grain, fruit, wine, spices
and many other commodities from the Baltic, Atlantic and Mediterranean.

In due course the Hanse gained sufficient collective bargaining power to allow them to negotiate tax concessions and trading monopolies.

By the fifteenth century Hanse merchants were powerful enough to drive the English fishing fleet out of their cod fishing grounds off the coast of Norway by gaining exclusive export rights from the authorities in Bergen. The English fishing fleet then moved north to Iceland, only to be squeezed out again by the Hanse, so that they opened up a route to the coasts of Labrador and Newfoundland. Similar trade wars included Hanse blockades against Holland and Flanders, which deprived these countries of grain, beer and other foodstuffs.[5]

Stockfish production in northern Norway seems to have started with the Vikings, with the cod fishing season lasting from February until April. Whereas salted herring was considered a very ordinary food, stockfish, air-dried cod, was more highly esteemed and expensive. As Norway in particular depended heavily on imported food, in 1316 the Norwegian king decreed that nobody was allowed to export stockfish or butter without importing so-called 'heavy goods' – essentials such as grain, flour, malt and beer. Twice a year the fishermen's catch was carried down by Norwegian merchants from the Lofoten to Bergen where the Hanse merchants waited, prohibited by their agreements from sailing further north. In the fifteenth century the direct trade in stockfish with Iceland, previously exclusive to the Normans, became a rival for the Bergen monopoly. In 1530 Icelandic stockfish was documented in Cologne, though it was regarded as slightly inferior in quality. The best and most expensive was made from ling, followed by cod. At the end of the sixteenth century cod and ling were also salted in barrels and traded as *Laberdan*, supposedly a Basque method.

In spite of all their egalitarian northern modesty, the good Hanse merchants certainly could afford to and did indulge in some more exclusive culinary luxuries. At the end of long festive meals like the Bremen *Schafferrmahlzeit*, a ceremonious fundraising ritual in honour of captains and trade in general that has been held every February since 1545 (and up to the present day does not allow women to join the long, laden tables), the bread and butter would be supplemented by hard cheese. Renneted and therefore storable, the wheels came from Cheshire, Flanders, Frisia, southern France and northern Italy as well as Swiss Emmenthal and Gruyère, and were traded in Antwerp, Cologne, Strasbourg and Basel.

Even more exclusive was marzipan. Due to the Hanse trading activities, almonds were by now widely available to those who could afford them, and the first written record of marzipan in Germany is to be found in the rules of a Lübeck guild in 1530. Long a staple in Arab countries and thought to be highly nourishing, it was first made by apothecaries (cane sugar being another Arab introduction that began as medicine and was initially very expensive) and given to wealthy women in childbirth. When Thomas Aquinas confirmed the suitability of sugar-covered spices for fast days, the former medicine quickly became an expensive sweet offered to kings, the apothecaries replaced by confectioners. The thirteenth-century Catalan physician Arnaldus de Vilanova mentioned *mazapan*; it became *mazapán* in Toledo, *massapan* and *massepain* in France, the *calissons* of Provence and *marzapane* in Italy. Rose- or orange-flower water, candied fruit or eggs were added; the mixture was roasted in copper kettles over the fire or shaped and baked in the oven, then covered with chocolate or sugar icing. Along with other sugar confections, it would grace the tables of German nobles from the sixteenth century on and become an absolute must for demonstrating high social status.

In Germany two distinctive schools of marzipan developed, both originating on the northern coast. As a general rule today it is made from almonds and sugar at a ratio of two to one, with other aromatic ingredients like rosewater added. The precise amounts are kept secret by

Marzipan modelled into fruit at the Lübeck company Niederegger, mid-20th century.

most producers. Lübecker marzipan is generally covered in dark choco-late, whereas Königsberger marzipan is traditionally browned in the oven. Both cities started to establish themselves as marzipan strongholds from the early nineteenth century on. The most important German marzipan producer today is Niederegger, a family-run business in Lübeck with over 500 employees where the paste is shaped into almost everything from traditional loaves, eggs and Easter bunnies to all kinds of fruit and vegetables. In Königsberg (present-day Russian Kaliningrad) things started very similarly, with young dynamic confectioners establishing marzipan factories, although for historical reasons these specialists are now spread all over Germany. Good-quality Königsberg-style marzipan tastes quite different from Lübeck marzipan: it is somewhat juicier and less sweet, as demonstrated by the small artisan company Paul Wald in Berlin. *Frankfurter Bethmännchen* and *Brenten* as well as *Mannheimer Dreck* are local marzipan specialities, whereas during the Christmas season marzipan takes the shape of *Marzipankartoffeln*, small balls coated in cocoa powder and resembling potatoes.

The Hanse era came to an end with the rise of strong nation states, particularly England and Holland, whose rulers weren't particularly keen on an independent maritime confederacy operating within their accepted spheres of influence (a situation exacerbated by the Thirty Years War). The increase in piracy in the fifteenth century added to its undoing, although these problems had previously been overcome: during the Great Famine pirates had been active up and down the entire coast of Europe, with Gascon and Flemish raiders even preying upon anchored ships in major ports of call. The last official Hanse meeting took place in 1669, with only eight members putting in an appearance. However, to this day a number of German cities, including Lübeck, Hamburg, Bremen and Rostock, proudly call themselves *Hansestädte*.

Meanwhile southern German trade with Italy and beyond focused on luxury goods. Among the best known and most successful of the families involved in it were the Fuggers, descendants of a weaver from a rural background who came to the city of Augsburg in 1367. In a little over a century the Fuggers were granted their own office at the Fondaco dei Tedeschi, the German merchants' representation in Venice. As other medieval traders had, they recognized spices' potential as an easy way to make a great deal of money out of a commodity that was neither heavy nor bulky. The tightly woven network of political and finan-cial interdependancies that made them one of the most powerful economic and political players in Europe was based on transactions of enormous scale. They organized the pope's sale of indulgences, financed his Swiss guard and bankrolled imperial warfare for consecutive Habsburg rulers. (Their influence came to an end with the Reformation, when their reputation as dealers in luxury goods and financiers to both emperor and pope did them no favours.)

The entrepreneurial spirit of the Fuggers extended to financing Magellan's circumnavigation of the globe, a highly profitable undertaking that was to strongly influence the way spices were seen and used. When from 1500 the new route to India around the Cape of Good Hope lowered transport costs, the Venetians were forced to drop their prices and increased the volume of trade in response. Pepper above all became more affordable and ostentatious spice consumption a widely shared ideal among the upwardly mobile. Overall the use of spices was still a class marker; indeed the literature of the time described the lowly peasant as having to make do with onions, garlic, herbs and mustard. But almost anybody else could at least afford some imported spices occasionally and social rank now also manifested itself in how often one used them. Lower down the social ladder they marked special events, being consumed more heavily on lean days and more often in winter than in summer.

The notion that spices were used to keep meat from putrifying or to mask its offtaste has long been disproved. Likewise a thriving trade in spices did not necessarily indicate that consumption had become globalized, as is sometimes suggested. Medieval cooks did not use just any spice with any dish; rather they had exact ideas about compositions, and in spite of the international nature of the rich man's table at the time, regional and national preferences played an important role in their choices. Germans in that respect seem to have lagged somewhat behind the fashions. Recipes often mention spices in general terms, such as *stupp*, *gestupp* or *wurcz*. Pepper remained popular far longer than in neighbouring countries (although less so in the more 'modern' south and among aristocrats). In fourteenth-century France pepper was somewhat disparagingly thought of as appropriate for dishes involving blood and innards. In fact the thirteenth-century Catalan physician Arnaldus de Vilanova considered pepper sauce a peasants' condiment, just like garlic. The *Viandier*, a French recipe collection from about the same time, doesn't mention pepper at all while some Italian manuscripts openly declare it to be 'old-fashioned'. In France ginger was much more popular; according to humoral theory, it was regarded as well balanced, being neither too hot nor too cold, so that a pinch could be combined with almost everything. Ginger combined with cinnamon made the ubiquitous *sauce cameline*. As French cuisine became ever more influential, it made the cooking of Germany (and Poland) looked increasingly *démodé*.

In Germany ginger was comparatively unpopular. Local herbs continued to be widely used while more 'modern' spices such as cinnamon, cloves and nutmeg did not increase in popularity till the end of the fifteenth century. Far longer than elsewhere in western Europe, honey was the sweetener of choice. In the fourteenth century cane sugar imports from Egypt, Sicily, Rhodes and Cyprus became more important, but it was still very expensive and used sparingly, passing gradually from the medicine cupboard to the spice chest. However, when sugar cane cultivation started on the Canary Islands and Madeira in the 1450s, prices began to fall, tumbling further when competing imports from Brazil and the Caribbean entered the market about a century later. At this point the sweet-toothed English and Italians really went for it. The Italians ostentatiously sprinkled sugar mixed with cinnamon on finished dishes, a habit familiar to modern Germans, who like sugar and cinnamon on their rice pudding – a dish that originated as an early eighteenth-century festive northern German wedding dessert, replacing the earlier millet gruel. In England saffron, sugar, ginger and to a lesser degree cinnamon were favoured. It might well be that the English appetite for sweet-savoury dishes was linked to the fact that shortly after their conquest of England the Normans became rulers of Sicily, where the same culinary preference can be found to this day. In Germany the picture is much less clear. Did pepper's popularity result from the fact that it was the least expensive spice, or did its taste hit a particular nerve?[6]

Saffron, probably the most expensive of all spices, represents a rather different and special case.

Backe backe Kuchen, der Bäcker hat gerufen. Wer will guten Kuchen backen, der muss haben sieben Sachen: Eier und Schmalz, Butter und Salz, Milch und Mehl, Safran macht den Kuchen gehl.

Let's bake, let's bake cake, the baker has called. Who wants to have good cake, has to have seven things: eggs and lard, butter and salt, milk and flour, saffron makes the cake yellow.

Leonhart Fuchs, 'Saffron', in *Kreutterbuch* (Basel, 1543). Fuchs writes in his description: 'Right now the German Austrian saffron that grows around the city of Vienna is more expensive than that from the Orient and anywhere else. Saffron is also grown on many other locations in our German country.'

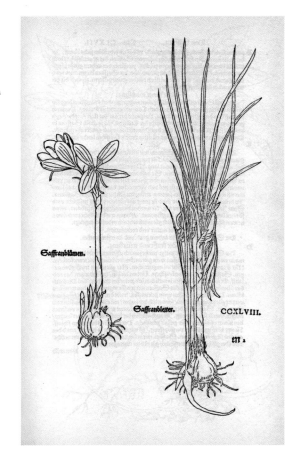

This popular German nursery rhyme about the seven ingredients needed for a good cake is commonly said to have its origin in early nineteenth-century Thuringia and Saxony. However the first written evidence for it actually dates back to 1460 and the recipe collection of Meister Hans, court chef to a Württemberg count. His version only differs in replacing *Kuchen* (cake) by *mus* (porridge):[7]

> *Wer ein gut mus will haben das mach von sibennler sachn du must haben milich, salcz, vnd schmalcz, zugker, ayer, vnd mel saffran dar zue so wirt es gell.*

Who wants to have a good sidedish should make it from seven things: you have to have milk, salt, and lard, sugar, eggs, and flour, with saffron added, thus it becomes yellow.

Mentioning saffron right at the start of his compendium made clear that his work was addressed to an elite audience – the deep orange threads were (and still are) the most expensive spice to be had. The Phoenicians, Alexander the Great and the Arabs had been responsible for spreading it from its Bronze Age origins in Crete eastward to Mesopotamia and India, and to ancient Greece and Egypt. The golden glow of saffron, possibly reinforced by egg yolks and honey, represented the most elevating, wonderful and glorious thing, be it on a modest lord's applecake or a whole roasted peacock for the imperial table. But saffron had more to offer. It was seen as hot and dry and therefore was frequently used in the preparation of certain cold, humid fish (humorally speaking). In times of pestilence whoever could afford it sought it out as an air cleanser, burning it like incense or covering their nose with little pouches. In middle high German it is first mentioned as *caferân* in a pharmacopoeia written in 1150.

But how did something as exotic and valuable as saffron make it from a fifteenth-century top chef's recipe book into a modern nursery rhyme? The answer lies in the fact that unlike all the other exotic and prestigious spices, saffron can be grown in central and western Europe. In fact from the tenth century on saffron cultivation spread from Spain to the south of France, Tuscany and the Abruzzo, and from around 1150 it was even exported from the west to the east. Today 'German-speaking' saffron is grown in the Swiss Alps (Mund/Valais) and in the Wachau region not far from Vienna as well as on the Austro-Hungarian border (Klingenbach/Burgenland). The surprising thing is that in spite of not coming from mystic distant places, it remained expensive and exclusive, because of its unbelievably small yields. That fact made it an attractive investment, and in the twelfth and thirteenth centuries saffron was frequently used as a security or payment, or as a bribe or reward. In Germany the main trading place for it was Nuremberg, where the city council in 1420 (some sources mention 1358) established a saffron fair. Police regulations insisted on clean and unmixed merchandise, threatening fraudsters with death by burning or by being buried alive, while getting rid of the fraudulent wares at the same time. This was directed not only at merchants but local peasants. In the southern German-speaking regions saffron cultivation developed into a rewarding additional source of income that fitted well into the rural work rhythm: after the main harvest at the end of October families joined in picking the crocus flowers and in the evening sat around the table separating the stigmas from the petals. As tedious as this task must have been, and as precious as every gram of it was, a tiny part of the crop probably went into some dish or a Sunday cake for the family, hence the nursery rhyme.[8]

Saffron was also on offer at the markets of Cologne, the third strong-hold of the German food trade between the *Botterbroth* of the north and the Italianate ways of the south, and with 40,000 inhabitants the largest city of medieval Germany. Here the Romans had never really left, but rather had been successfully assimilated by the Franks. Cologne's location predestined it for trade and in the heyday of the Hanse it was Lübeck's only serious rival as a trading centre, frequently pursuing its own interests. Here influences and wares from the north and south met to form one amazing and intricate mix that still seemed to have one foot in the Roman traditions, so that when we read about growing imports of olive oil and the first lemons and oranges, both recorded around 1500, this seems to reinforce an existing link.

While the power of feudal lords was founded on the exploitation of the peasantry to cultivate their lands, among the urban classes special-ized skills and money became the new basis for a social hierarchy. Towns and cities actively sought political independence, establishing their own town charters and offering more personal freedom and potential social mobility than in the country. Everyone – with the exception of appren-tice craftsmen, day labourers, beggars and servants – was able to participate in public affairs and considered equal before the muncipal court where all urban litigation took place. The saying *Stadtluft macht frei*, urban air makes you free, goes back to the fact that medieval serfs were considered free after spending one year and one day in a town. The urban upper class in general consisted of patrician families involved in long-distance trade, while the middle classes were made up of merchants and craftsmen, organized in guilds whose horizontal ties replaced both larger family structures and vertical feudal ones. When in 1272 the bakers' guild was founded in Berlin, it requested a test-baking from potential members and introduced fixed prices.

The towns as trading centres were responsible for quality control. The frequent complaints about food adulteration and fraud might well be an indication of increased expectations rather than lower standards. The food trade was highly regulated and well-policed. As we have seen for saffron, urban legal systems imposed draconian punishments ranging from confiscation and destruction of the merchandise under dispute to removal of limbs or even capital punishment for the wrongdoer.

Cologne's importance derived not only from its size, but from the fact that the Rhine was the most important European north–south trade route, linking Italy and Upper Germany with Holland and England. This is underlined by the three large trade fairs established there by the eleventh century. *Stapelrecht*, a privilege granted by the archbishop in 1259, required that all merchandise passing through the city had to be locally inspected and offered for sale for three days. This made for an extreme diversity of wares of the highest quality, which greatly contributed to the economic growth of Cologne, allowing it to become a feeder market for smaller towns in the area and establishing trade links reaching from the Iberian peninsula to the Danube regions and from the Baltic and Silesia to Rome.

Besides being known for its textiles, metalworks, leather and furs, the city dominated the food and wine trade, specializing above all in the exchange of wine from the Rhine valley upstream from the city for fish from the northern coasts. Retail and wholesale soon developed into separate activities. On the one hand, the city itself had to be supplied with fish; on the other, Cologne acted as an agent for the distribution of the catch to southern Germany. Trade in perishable merchandise was highly regulated in order to guarantee fair pricing and the transference of the wares in palatable condition. This demanded expert supervision: in 1421 Cologne is recorded as complaining to Lübeck about small herring barrels and asking for a correct standard measure to be introduced. The bulk of the city's fish trade was with Holland. Merchants frequently went to the coast to buy herrings, but also to southern German towns such as Nuremberg, Speyer and Strasbourg to sell them. They often had servants acting on their behalf, besides dealing with middlemen who acted as buyers for several clients, just as *Wirte*, hosts, did for the sellers. The latter housed their visiting trading partners when they were in town, but were not allowed to accomodate merchants from the north and south simultaneously, since guests were not allowed to trade directly. The overall tendency was to simplify and standardize in order to speed up the trading process and reduce costs, then as now the largest possible profit margin being the ultimate goal.

Besides salted herrings and stockfish and coastal fish like plaice, haddock, sturgeon, ray and smelt, there were freshwater fish from the Rhine, including salmon, pike and carp. Most were salted in an attempt to maintain the delicate balance between acceptable taste and rapid rotting. Transport was primarily on the Rhine, but could be delayed

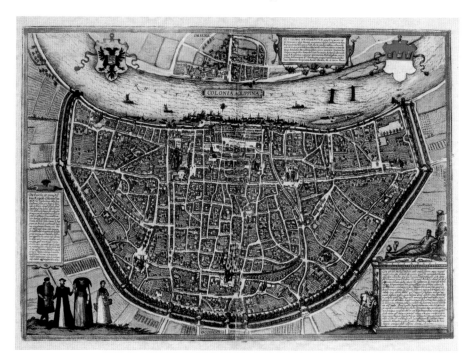

Map of Cologne, 1575.

by adverse winds or towpaths that were in bad condition. Occasionally floods forced goods onto the much slower roads. Haulage was in the hands of former peasants who offered their services to merchants, essentially doing the same job they had done for their feudal lords. Once they made it to Cologne, ships carrying fish docked at the harbour crane opposite the fishhall. Built in the 1420s, facilities here included a public scale and storage rooms wholesale merchants could rent. The retail sale of fresh fish was in the hands of the *Fischmenger*, or fishmongers (while the word is the same in both languages, only the English version survives). Among the sellers were fishermen themselves, selling their catch from the Rhine or the city's moat to the local market. Of the highly esteemed 'green' or fresh salmon, a proportion also went to non-local buyers, although the allocation was limited by the town council in order to guarantee adequate supplies for Cologne's citizens on lean days. Prices for fresh fish were usually fixed by the town council, and when in 1396 the fishmongers organized themselves into a political group the town council only permitted them to form a fraternity, as opposed to a more economically independent guild, in an effort to retain direct control (as with the bakers and butchers) of a vital foodstuff.

The fishmarket's activities are documented from the twelfth century onwards, with separate, officially regulated locations allotted to the sellers of fresh, dried, smoked and salted fish, and *Bückling*, dried or smoked herring, with the highly esteemed salmon given a separate location. It was mostly offered fresh from the river from as far down as Holland and transported in watercages attached to ships. The fish were slaughtered at the point of sale, cut in eight pieces and sold as *Krimpsalm*, freshly killed fish, which was considered a delicacy and favoured over 'dead' fish whose muscles had already been allowed to relax. Distinctions were also made between summer or autumn salmon and the darker, meatier winter salmon. In addition salted salmon in barrels (roughly corresponding to lox) was on offer. From the beginning of the sixteenth century onwards salmon that had previously been salted was also smoked, though this was a significantly more expensive preservation method.

Cologne also displayed significant muscle in the spice trade, as witnessed in 1335 when the merchants of Venice, Lombardy and Nuremberg prohibited retail selling to Cologne citizens. Ginger, pepper and cinnamon had to be sold in quantities over 50 lb, saffron not less than 3 lb; the only exceptions were even rarer spices such as cinnamon buds and nutmeg, on which no minimum quantities were imposed. Increased volume of sales from 1390 onwards led to the imposition of *octroi*, a tax on consumption, whereas in earlier times the spice trade was only indirectly taxed through high weighing costs. *Octroi* payments provide an indication of the diversity of spices traded, offering detailed information about the amounts of each spice and how many merchants were involved in each transaction. Throughout the mid-fifteenth century the highest number of merchants was involved in the ginger trade. Ginger was sold as dried whole roots as well as the (far rarer) fresh or 'green' ginger; in addition to this large quantities of cheaper varieties known as *Mackin/ maeckijn/metkin* and galangal were traded, reaching a total of 4.25 tons per year, though exact quantities are difficult to calculate due to diverse units of measurement such as bags, sacks, bales and so on. About 6.5 tons a year of pepper was sold, including aromatic long pepper and *Pfeffertuch*, pepper cloth, a rough muslin soaked with pepper used to flavour doughs, pottages and broths.

Sugar was sold in refined form as loaves, light molasses, jaggery and rock candy. At the end of the fourteenth century refined sugar was still more expensive than either ginger or pepper, with a pound of sugarloaf worth more than 16 litres of honey. In spite of this the quantity of sugar sold steadily rose throughout the fifteenth century and by the 1450s, with some of Cologne's merchants themselves commercially involved in refineries on the sugar island of Palma, sugar prices had fallen below those of ginger and pepper.

Other spices traded in Cologne included saffron, nutmeg, cloves, grains of paradise (occasionally misidentified as cardamom), coriander and almonds. Caraway seeds mostly came from southern Europe. Onion and garlic seeds (and later turnip seeds) were grown for use as spices in the Rheingau, around Worms, Speyer and Strasbourg, with Cologne supplying most of northwest Europe. Aniseed and bay leaf were needed for flavouring grut ale and were traded until around 1450, when they were widely replaced by hops. Liquorice was imported from Italy, Spain, southern France and southern Russia, and pepper-flour (possibly mustard powder, serving as a cheap pepper substitute) began to gain popularity.

After 1470 the Cologne spice trade was mostly run by local merchants, of whom a small circle specialized in the southern European trade, buying oriental goods directly in Mediterranean ports including Venice. They were involved in the risky business of shipping goods round the Iberian peninsula and their need for bank and insurance services furthered the evolution of both. The small circle of individuals and families who made up Cologne's political, social and economic elite consisted of people like the wealthy merchant Hermann von Goch. The expenses of this financier and businessman's extended household reveal a lot about prevailing food habits.

Over the period from January 1391 to October 1394 Hermann von Goch's Cologne household comprised between two and three dozen people, including the family's nine children and several grandchildren, staff and guests. Food purchases were undoubtedly supplemented by meat, dairy products and vegetables and fruit, as well as grain and beer from Goch's own garden and estates. Nevertheless, the cost of food and beverages was by far the highest of all household expenditures, slightly more than half of the total. The same amount was spent on meat as on fish, and only one-fifth of these sums were spent on bread, in spite of the fact that this was almost exclusively made from wheat, the most expensive of all grains.

The Goch kitchen was run by a cook, an undercook and a young apprentice, with the main meal served at midday. Leftovers following special feast days or banquets were put to good use. The kitchen was well equipped, judging from the expenses listing all kinds of earthenware pots, jars and jugs, along with barrels, spoons, knives and numerous pewter dishes. Food was bought fresh almost every day, including Sundays. Besides bread, the baker also provided *placentae* – cakes – and various kinds of pastries for special occasions, and was paid to bake the pies prepared in the Goch kitchen. Beef featured most prominently among household expenses for meat, with supplies bought throughout the whole year, anticipating what was to become the general trend in the fifteenth century. One-quarter of the family's meat expenditure was devoted to chickens and the capons reserved for feast days. Fish supplies varied and were clearly seen as much more than just a replacement for meat on lean days. Stockfish played a very minor role, while herring made up the bulk and was bought by the barrel, each of which contained approximately 1,000 fish and fed the household for just under two weeks during Lent. Fish from the Rhine such as pike and salmon (a popular gift) provided additional supplies, with five or six varieties frequently purchased on the same day. Slightly more than one-quarter of the amount spent on fish was spent on flavouring items, mostly salt, ginger, saffron, pepper and refined sugar, at the time just as luxurious as the small amounts of rice that featured on the list. Cinnamon, almonds, cloves, mace, nutmeg, caraway seeds, onions, dill, parsley, parsley root, leeks, molasses and honey were also purchased occasionally, while, in contrast, mustard was bought three or four times a week. On the other hand, the vegetables listed were more limited in variety. The explanation of this may be that many of the household's supplies came from the family's garden. Cabbage was purchased frequently (in this case this could indicate an important foodstuff that was consumed in larger quantities than the household was able to produce), fresh as well as salted. Dried peas, fresh turnips and beans were also mentioned. Fresh fruit from the garden was supplemented with imported dried fruits – raisins, figs and apples – as well as early strawberries and cherries, almost certainly imports from warmer areas on the Rhine or Mosel.

Wine was the main beverage, most of it of unspecified origin and variety, but there were some specialities such as spiced *Claret* and sweet *Strowin*, straw-wine, for which the grapes were dried on straw mats, thereby concentrating their sugar content prior to pressing. Expenses for beer were very low in comparison, but that could be explained in part by deliveries from Goch's own estates. Overall the household kept a very luxurious table that only the most wealthy Cologne burghers could afford. From the thirteenth century onwards the town council felt it was their duty to issue sumptuary laws to limit expenses on the occasion of weddings, baptisms, funerals and other family festivities. However, they seem to have been rarely implemented, with many wealthy families preferring to pay a fine instead.[9]

As a general rule, not only in Cologne, meals served on official or festive occasions were expected to be sumptuous. Etiquette demanded that more food be put on the table than could possibly be consumed, while guests were urged repeatedly to eat more – a concept Italian travellers found bewildering.[10] It is tempting to link this with the legendary *Schlaraffenland* or Land of Cockaigne first mentioned in the *Carmina Burana*, a collection of songs from the Tyrol found in a monastery in southern Germany and thought to date back to the eleventh to thirteenth centuries. The story of a mythical land of milk and honey (and wine) captured the wider public's imagination when Sebastian Brant's *Narrenschiff* (Ship of Fools) appeared in 1494. In it are descriptions of houses built from cake, cheese replacing cobblestones in the streets, roasted pigeons which fly into people's mouths and roasted pigs which come running with knives conveniently stuck in their backs. All in all, it is a land where enjoying the good times is regarded as the highest achievement and working and industriousness are the ultimate sins.

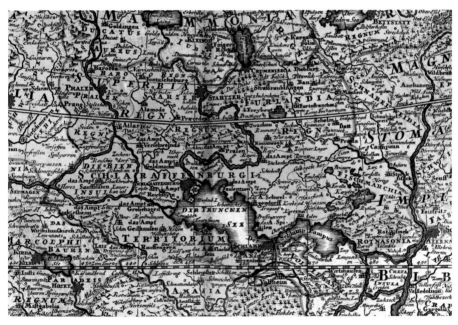

Johann Baptist Homann, *Accurate Map of Utopia* (Schlaraffenland), detail, published by Matthäus Seutter (Augsburg, 1730). All the names are comments or quotes relating to eating, drinking and indulging.

The story of *Schlaraffenland* became firmly embedded in German mythology. It was taken up by Hans Sachs, a poet and master singer of Nuremberg, in 1530, and appeared later in the Brothers Grimm's early nineteenth-century collection of fairy tales (which also took up the myth of the Grail in the form of *Tischlein deck dich*, or 'The Wishing-table'). The meaning behind the myth has variously been interpreted as wishful thinking during a time when hard physical labour, deprivation and famine seemed unavoidable, a social critique of the luxurious life in many of the monasteries or (as depicted in Pieter Breughel's *Schlaraffenland* painting of 1567), an exhortation against rustic gluttony which the picture, despite its culinary riches, certainly does not depict as a state of happiness.

Another version is given in *Reynke de Vos* (Reinecke/Reynard the Fox), a satirical and moralizing Middle Low German animal epic published in Lübeck in 1498 whose origins can be traced back to the Greek fables of Aesop. In it the fox (a gifted but mean liar and trickster) tries to tempt his wife into leaving their den and fleeing to the *Schwabenland* for a wonderful new life where all is there for the taking. 'Chicken, geese, hare and rabbits, dates, sugar, figs and raisins, and birds on top, large and small, there is bread baked with eggs and butter, the water is good, clean and clear. Oh, how delicious the air is there! They have fish . . . which taste better than raisins.' Mrs Fox, however, seems to know her mendacious husband well enough to refuse to be tempted by such illusive promises.[11]

Besides opulent menus, food gifts were another form of intricate social etiquette. Food of all kinds could be used for the purpose, but it could be tricky to get everything just right. The choice had to be appropriate to suit the occasion and status of both giver and receiver. When in 1472 Elector Albrecht travelled to the Margravate of Brandenburg, presented to him by his brother two years earlier, the regional aristocracy paid homage to their new ruler in Salzwedel with processions and presents. These consisted of oats, fish, four freshly slaughtered sheep and a substantial amount of local beer, all of which was obviously intended to cater to the visitors during their trip. However, the elector refused to accept the gifts, deeming them inappropriate, as they did not represent the luxurious fare to which he was accustomed but were everyday victuals and might have indicated that he was in real need. He even slighted the servants of the town who brought the gifts by not offering the tip they were normally due. Lesser recipients were easier to please: in January 1493 a mayor had no such problems on the occasion of his election in Hildesheim. Provisions supplied by fellow citizens included one *Schoppen* (about half a litre) of hippocras and seventeen of *Claret* (both spiced wine), five *Schoppen* of Malmsey, 105 *Schoppen* of regular wine and one barrel of Einbeck beer, besides half an ox, seven quarters of mutton, 33 chickens, two fallow deer, one part of a fallow deer, seven hares, £8 2*s.* worth of fish, fresh butter, 6*s.* worth of white bread, two English cheeses, two peacocks, 5 lb of ginger, 'quite some' almond sugar, some sugar confectionary, 1 lb of electuary (a medicine), gingerbread, a golden ring, a silver bowl and some money.[12] Food gifts could be highly symbolic: when the Cologne merchant Hermann von Goch was repeatedly given game (a meat he never consumed at home) during two short terms of imprisonment due to an accusation of misappropriation and conspiracy, these gifts were deliberate gestures of solidarity from well-meaning friends.

After the colonization of the eastern regions of Germany (started in the eleventh century), grain grown east of the Elbe fed much of Europe, including Norway, the Low Countries, Flanders, France and Britain. However, in contrast to earlier times, trade systems were now more flexible. When harvests failed, imports also occurred in the opposite direction: in 1389 Prussia bought grain from England. A significant proportion of all grain was used for brewing beer, indispensable in the German diet regardless of regional preferences. Beer consumption in non-wine regions has been estimated as 300 litres per person per year (as compared to the national average of about 111 litres today).[13] The Hanse might have adopted the cultivation and use of hops from the Slavs. For Wismar and Rostock on the Baltic, hop cultivation was documented in the towns' books as far back as the thirteenth century. Northern cities became renowned for their beer; Hamburg alone, around 1350, was thought to have produced 240,000 hectolitres of beer. Beer exports to places like London and Bruges initially were to keep German merchants well provided with their accustomed brew. Einbeck, another Hanse town in southern lower Saxony, was famous for a strong beer known as *ainpoickischen*. Often mentioned in the context of festivities, it is thought to have influenced the taste of southern German beer and to have been imitated as *Bockbier*, possibly by a brewer from Einbeck who established himself in Munich.[14]

While the *Reinheitsgebot* (literally purity decree), a Bavarian beer law of 1516 imposed in Ingolstadt, is often quoted as the oldest food law still in use in Germany, the reality is that there is not only uncertainty as to how consistently it was implemented, but there are also many earlier decrees concerning beer. Restricting beer-brewing ingredients to barley, hops and water (and regulating prices at the same time) made economic sense, as the medieval variety of beers was impressive and brewers used all kinds of cereals as well as a wide variety of fruit and herbs for addditional flavouring. Grut beer (whose potentially harmful side-effects, which could extend to blindness or even death, gradually became known) could be produced more or less everywhere, also at home, but unlike hopped beer was too unstable to represent a serious, tax-generating commodity. Thuringia and Saxony made a name for themselves growing hops from the late thirteenth century onwards, and by the sixteenth century many towns had their own breweries. Export opportunities expanded. A chronicler from Cologne recorded that in 1435, after severe frosts in May, wine became so expensive that it was on offer only in a single tavern in the city. At this point the Dutch started exporting their hopped beer to Cologne, introducing a city where grut beer was still the norm to a brew which seems to have tasted somewhat smoky due to the use of peat. Cologne people seem to have liked it and the former wine lovers transformed their city into the stronghold of beer it remains to the present day. Although the following vintage wine was much more abundant again, as an everyday beverage it was replaced to a significant degree by hopped beer. While the change from grut to hops was gradual, it eventually led to the special Cologne style of beer that is still named after its place of origin, *Kölsch* (from Köln, Cologne), today the Rhineland's most renowned brew. By the end of the fifteenth century, the city received more income from taxes on beer than it did from the wine trade.

The steep vineyards which are typical of certain regions of Germany today date back to the Romans and the early Middle Ages. The vineyards above Rüdesheim on the Rhine and the earlier mentioned Johannisberg estate instigated by Charlemagne are obvious examples. But the earliest documented German vineyards also include, in 996, the northernly Hildesheim, where there is no winegrowing today. Unlike today, vineyards were once to be found all over northern Germany from Westphalia to Prussia and Silesia, most having been planted by Cistercian monks and the landowning aristocracy. With Christianization vines travelled to Pomerania in the middle of the twelfth century, while in 1226 vineyards were mentioned at a monastery near Danzig. The difference – persisting to this day – was that in climatically more suitable regions where wine was abundant and had a historical record, it was drunk by all social classes, albeit of varying quality. In contrast, in these northern regions the fermented juice of the grape was deemed necessary for church rituals, but was otherwise considered something of a luxury reserved for the elite and special occasions, never replacing beer as the staple beverage.[15]

Following devastating frosts in 1437 viticulture receded south again. By the sixteenth century grape varieties began to be used for wine designations. Up to that time wines had been described by region, as *Elsässer*, *Rheinwein*, *Neckarwein* and so forth. Frequently wines were also designated as either Frankish or Hunnic (*huonicum* in Latin, which made for the ancient grape variety *Heunisch*) in order to distinguish good wine from bad. According to Hildegard von Bingen,

> Frankish and strong wine makes the blood boil up and that is why one has to mix it with water for drinking; but it is not necessary to mix the Hunnic wine with water, as it is watery by nature.

Frankish wines were clearly for the masters and Hunnic for the servants, but it is not clear if the description related to varieties, quality in general or something else. Records from the early fourteenth century offer an insight of the wine-consuming hierarchy, differentiating between knight's wine, good wine, old wine, good young wine, young wine, servant's wine, fill wine, good must, must and servant's must. To this could be added *Lurcke*, a beverage made from macerating grapeskins in water after pressing them for regular wine (the Roman *lora*, which was still made on the Mosel until quite recently under the name of *Bubel*); *Tropfwein*, drip-wine, which could either be the free-run juice – that is, the wine made from run-off without any pressing, considered very superior – or wine collected under a dripping bung (very inferior); and *Agrest*, verjus, which was made from unripe or half-ripe grapes of late ripening varieties or wild grapes. *Feuerwein*, firewine, was a speciality made in an insulated room on the ground floor of the winegrowers' dwelling. It earned its name from the preparation process, which included the burning of coals next to the barrels so that the must fermented very quickly and stopped fermenting earlier than usual. After about three days the wine retained a little residual sweetness as well as a refreshing acidity and some carbonic acid. *Feuerwein* required specialist winemakers and choice grapes and was made only in the Mosel, Rhine and Alsace regions. The practice continued until the eighteenth century in the Mittelrhein region around Bacharach. *Clarets* were made mostly using imported Spanish and Greek wines. They were spiced with saffron, cloves, sugar and honey, refermented and then filtered. *Claret* was drunk from large beakers with a perforated section to enable the infusion of the wine with even more spices.

The earliest record of a grape variety in Germany mentioned *Clävner*, today's *Spätburgunder* or Pinot Noir, said to have been introduced to Germany in the region of Lake Constance in 884 and in some parts of Baden known as *Klevner* or *Clevner* up to this day. In the fifteenth century it was joined by Riesling (first recorded, in Rüsselsheim, in 1435), Gänsfüsser, Muskateller and Traminer, all initally mentioned as planting material and only in the final decades of the sixteenth century in connection with a finished wine (the first record of a monovarietal Riesling vineyard, the Löhrer Berg in the Nahe region, then belonging to the bishop of Mainz, is from 1688). This change might well be due to the use of sulphur, which was legalized in 1497 by an official decree in Freiburg/Breisgau, the result of long lobbying, possibly to put a rubber stamp on a rather well established practice. Without sulphur wines tended to oxidize very quickly and were sometimes fermented for a second time with some fresh must or sugar added if they had not been consumed within the year. Sulphur seems not to have been used in antiquity, as it is not mentioned by Cato or Columella, the classical specialists on winemaking (one reason for this could be that in the presence of sulphuric acid, the calcium carbonate of earthen containers disintegrates into soluble gypsum). The practice of sulphuring young wines was first mentioned in a wine book in 1530, where it was said to keep wines white and fresh (and one might add, more expressive of the character of the grapes). Although the practice spread during this period, it was forbidden to use it more than once in any given wine to avoid excessive sulphur content – something Germans were concerned about even then.

In the early sixteenth century an account of the wealthy Tucher family's household, Nuremberg's equivalent of the Augsburg Fuggers, listed wines from the Tauber, Rhine and Neckar, from Erfurt, Wertheim, Heidelberg, Landau, St Martin, Seligenstadt, and Speyer as well as Franconia, Austria and Alsace (the first mention of single vineyard site on a German wine label would be the Marcobrunn of Erbach im Rheingau in 1726). There was also mention of more expensive imported wines such as Veltliner, Muskatel and Malvasia (all three of which might have been varietal wines). In more general terms wine included *virner*, the previous year's wine (*firn* in German winespeak today stands for mature or plain old), *essigwein*, vinegar wine and *süsser*, sweet wine.[16]

At the time wine was either bought by the barrel or fetched in jugs from a tavern, since glass bottles were only just starting to be used. Glass was gradually introduced during the thirteenth century, although glazed windows as well as drinking glasses did not become generally afford-able until the end of the fifteenth century, when glasses were explicitly mentioned in descriptions of table settings. Besides the glassworks estab-lished in monasteries, itinerant glassblowers took up the trade in areas where wood, the necessary heat source, was easy to come by. Italian glassmakers came to Prague and Bohemia in the fourteenth century and gradually moved westwards, with many different shapes of glasses and decanters developing over the centuries. Glassware was categorized by characteristics derived from the place or style of manufacture: *Waldglas*, or forest glass, was prized for its yellow-greenish colour, which resulted from impurities in the sand, the raw material used for glass production. One distinctive bottle shape used to this day for Franconian wines is the flat round *Bocksbeutel*, literally 'billy-goat's scrotum', thought to have evolved from spherical bottles to carry beverages on travels. However, another explanation is that the name derived from the similarly shaped *Buchbeutel*, girdle books, used from the fourteenth century in northern

Hans Rodlein, stone carving documenting the endowment of the Juliusspital in Würzburg with vineyards, including the earliest depiction of a *Bocksbeutel* wine bottle, 1576.

Germany. The first documentation of a *Bocksbeutel* bottle can be found on a stone carving dating from 1576 in the Juliusspital wine estate in Würzburg in Franconia.

By the late Middle Ages Cologne was said to be the *Weinhaus der Hanse*, the Hanse's wineshop. While wines from Franconia, Württemberg and Baden were mostly distributed to the south and southeast, Cologne dealt in Rhine wines, including those from the river's tributaries and from Alsace. A city's wine trade represented a very significant source of income in taxes, tolls and wine-related activities such as coopering, haulage, paid work by city servants and provision of shelter and food by landlords to those involved in the trade. At some point wine accounted for more than half of the goods exported downriver from Cologne. Along with Bordeaux, Cologne became the largest wine trading centre in western Europe, although considerable quantities were also traded in Bingen, Mainz, Speyer, Strasbourg and most particularly Frankfurt. Cologne-controlled brands on barrels were accepted everywhere in Europe; they were trusted enough to obviate the need for further checks. The city's merchants travelled to the winegrowing regions to procure the best wines in sufficient quantities and also acquired vineyards (sometimes directly trading them for herrings), which were then rented out to vintners. A description of a canonical estate near St Goar/Mittelrhein in the eleventh century gives an idea of the latter's duties:

> But if the wine turns out bad they still have to pay their rent, even if not always in full . . . From the start of the grape harvest until its end nobody should dare to break the ban [on entering the vineyards, to prevent theft] . . . To procure the wine barrels for the canons each day's work (*Tagewerk*) owes a penny for the hoops. When the wine is pressed, everybody has to bring a vat to the estate, another receptacle and a light. On the day they carry the wine to the lord's ship, they are each rightfully due one beaker and for each pair a penny-loaf. They also have to bring the wine themselves to the port in Trier where again they are rightfully due each two beakers of wine for each day they are working there, except for the guard who will have enough with one beaker daily. When they arrive at the port in Trier, the canons' messenger has to feed them once in sufficient quantities.[17]

Cologne's annual wine imports varied widely: in the period from 1379 to 1384 around twelve million litres of wine were imported per year. In 1391 more than twenty million litres were imported, but in 1393 this had shrunk to fewer than 7.5 million. Most of this was traded in *Fuder* barrels of 875 litres each, with upper German Rhine vessels carrying around 30 *Fuder* each. Imported quantities decreased in the fifteenth century because of the rising popularity of hopped beer, as previously mentioned. The main export markets were the southern Netherlands, where Cologne's merchants also sold their wine directly in taverns, and England, where the city's traders had been granted the same import rights as the French in 1175/76, although the quantities were never very impressive. In the fourteenth and fifteenth centuries 300–500 barrels per year crossed the Channel, and by the sixteenth century Rhine wine represented just 3–6 per cent of all wine imported into England.[18]

Wine prices are notoriously difficult to compare with other more perishable foods, since wine could be stored for considerable periods. Trading had a stabilizing effect on prices, although they rose sharply in consequence of the adverse weather pattern during the Great Famine of 1315 to 1322. Yields also varied considerably, even if vintages were not often as extreme as the year 1304 in Colmar, described in the chronicles of the town:

> The year was so hot that water mills stopped working and bread became very expensive and rare. The whole year was sunny, warm and without significant rain. On the hills wine was plentiful and of good quality although some vineyards on the plain yielded only poor and rather little wine. Good wine was to be had in large quantities and at low prices, as it could not be shipped on the Rhine. The river was so low that you could wade through it at several points between Strasbourg and Basel.[19]

Following the far reaching effects of the plague, many of the feudal lords turned from labour-intensive grain-growing back to the original source of their wealth: cattle farming. Meat consumption in Germany temporarily bounced back to an average annual consumption of 100 kg of meat per year per person, a figure which included the bones, as compared to today's figure, which as of 2009 of is 60 kg of pure meat.[20] As in earlier times, roasting was confined to the more prosperous households, since the process required not only choicer cuts but more firewood.

A stewpot hung over the fire was considerably more economical and allowed the use of a greater variety of cuts, including offal, which could be combined with cereals and vegetables, especially cabbage. The quality of the carcass and butchering were taken very seriously, with freshness, proper cutting and fair weight highly regulated by town decrees and subject to police regulation. Butchers were numerous; around 1450 Nuremberg had one for every 282 inhabitants.[21] Thus most city dwellers didn't need to resort to salted meat as they bought it fresh at the market, although even here some households (as in rural areas) butchered their own animals at home in the run-up to winter. Pork was popular in the cities, most pigs being shipped down the Rhine from the Saar and Lorraine regions to Cologne, while manorial lords in the southwest used their abandoned fields for rearing sheep. They pastured flocks of up to 1,000 animals for the production of wool and meat, making travelling shepherds a new introduction to the labour force. Even more impressive, however, is the scale and extent of the cattle trade, which from the fifteenth century covered very long distances, not unlike the American cattle trade in the ninteenth century. The animals were reared far from grain-growing regions, such as the northern tip of the Danish peninsula, Poland, Bohemia and Hungary, on occasions reaching as far afield as Russia and Romania. During spring the herds were driven from there along the so-called *Ochsenwege*, oxen trails through uncultivated areas, in order to avoid damage to crops. Beginning around 1600, specialized inns along these trails provided shelter and provisions for drovers. Herds generally consisted of 250–400 animals (mostly tame and fat oxen), although reports mentioned exceptional herds of well over 1,000. At certain market places, *Magerviehmärkte* or lean cattle markets, specialist herdsmen met the drovers, purchased the emaciated animals and took them to pastures to fatten them up again after the long trek from the north or east before selling them off. Transport on *Dickbäuche* (literally 'fat bellies'), special ships for carrying oxen, extended trade to the Netherlands and as far away as France.[22]

Like the oxen, people began to travel more widely. In fact travel became a mass phenomenon at the time, with many merchants and craftsmen moving to other regions and cities. Regular timetables were established and goods traffic and travel by coach were professionally organized, covering between 20 and 30 km a day – a distance the ICE express trains cover today in five to ten minutes. Differences in national preferences in the matter of food and drink were frequently mentioned

A culinary place in time: the Bremer Ratskeller

Northern Hanse towns always featured a Ratskeller, a tavern under the Rathaus, town hall, where burghers and council members could eat and drink. Each Ratskeller included a wine cellar well equipped with the wines traded by the Hanse members. The most famous of them today is the beautifully restored Bremer Ratskeller, with a huge list of over 650 German wines, although the Hanse in its time also imported French wines from Poitou, Gascogne and Bordeaux, Romania (from Aragona in Spain or from Greece) and Malvasia (originally from Crete and later called Malmsey in England). Since 1330 the Bremen town council had the monopoly on serving white wine in the city. When the old town hall was built in 1405 all wine merchants and tavern owners had to store their wine in its cellars so that prices and taxes could be controlled. Today the old barrel cellar, frequently extended over the centuries, is used for banquets and wine tastings, except for the so-called Apostel- and Rosekeller. The apostles' cellar holds twelve barrels filled with Rhine wines from the seventeenth and eighteenth centuries, whereas the Rose cellar stores the oldest surviving wine in a barrel in Germany, a vintage of 1653 from Rüdesheim that fills the air with its enveloping, mysterious and deliciously balsamic fragrance. Unfortunately only the cellarmaster and the mayor are allowed to taste it, and even then only very rarely.

Bremer Ratskeller, July 1955. The wine is served in stone jugs with the characteristic green-stemmed Römer glasses.

in records of the period. When, for instance, an elderly Parisian member of the bourgeoisie wrote a compendium of good advice for his very young wife in the 1390s entitled *Le Ménagier de Paris,* he included this warning:

> The Germans say that the French put themselves in great danger by eating their carp undercooked. And one has seen that if French and Germans have a French cook who cooks carp the way it is done in France, the Germans will take their part and will have it re-cooked longer than before, but not so the French.[23]

The Dutch humanist and theologian Erasmus of Rotterdam had an exceptionally low opinion of the German taverns and inns he encountered on his travels, finding them overheated and dirty, with the available food and drink of low or dubious quality. By contrast he raved about the hospitality he encountered at Lyons in France.[24] Although more favourable accounts were given by other travellers, German inns appear to have been considered a necessity rather than an indulgence, including the food, which came in the form of a fixed menu served at a common table. The fourteenth-century French poet Eustache Deschamps repeatedly complained of being obliged to consume disgusting dishes including rotten cabbage (he was obviously not a sauerkraut-lover), and of the excessive use of mustard, as well as the 'sickening, all-pervasive stench of beer'.[25] Germans were often depicted as drunkards. A court order ruling against alcohol consumption before bedtime in Brandenburg in 1470 could be seen as an attempt to address an acknowledged problem, though the ruling was never implemented. A second glance, however, reveals that the declaration was aimed at cutting expenses and running an efficient household.[26] Efficient organization in terms of economy and finance appears to have been a German strength, as reports from the council of Constance show. This was a huge event that took place from 1414 to 1418 in that city on Lake Constance and brought together church dignitaries from all over Europe. To avoid speculation and profiteering from visitors taking up temporary residence during the gathering, the town council set the maximum prices to be charged for accomodation, bread, grain, vegetables, wine, meat, game, fowl, fish, hay, straw and spices (though only pepper, ginger and saffron were specifically mentioned). The prices seem to have been relatively high at first, but dropped after three weeks. Apparently food was plentiful, with a weekly market held

Ulrich von Richental, *Chronicle of the Constance Council, c.* 1420.
Stalls selling fish, frogs and snails.

every Friday.[27] Illustrations to the historian Ulrich von Richental's
chronicles of the time show street food being sold by mobile bakers
offering everything from high-quality white bread to pretzels and pies,
butcher's shops displaying deer, rabbits, geese and other meats, and fish
shops selling fresh fish as well as salted fish in barrels. The presence of
snails and frogs on sale showed that much 'ethnic' food from the visitors'
homelands was imported for the occasion. Richental pointed out that
the snails and frogs were bought by the *Walhens* or Latins. The wines he

mentioned were mainly from Italy and Alsace, but also came from the vineyards around Lake Constance.

After the gathering the newly elected pope took two and a half years to reach Rome from Constance, possibly because he was unsure of the welcome that awaited him there. However, under his tutelage Rome became a thriving international community, with Germans representing the largest ethnic group in the city, according to contemporary accounts. The pope's kitchen during his journey, as well as for some time after it, was presided over by Johannes von Bockenheim, who preceded Maestro Martino and Bartolomeo Scappi as chef and scribe in the papal kitchens. Around 1430 he published *Registrum Coquine*, a short book written for his professional colleagues in Latin, the church's official language. This was unusual for the time, when such books were generally written in the vernacular. Perhaps typically of the German provenance of its author, the recipes appear to be somewhat old-fashioned: very little sugar is used, for example. Johannes certainly was concerned with hospitality, providing details as to which dishes were to be made for specific guests and assigning recipes based on national preferences as well as social standing. Although his recipes were Italianized by the inclusion of raisins, pine nuts and marjoram, they included ingredients such as honey, milk, stockfish and juniper, just as other German cookbooks of the time do. His *Torta pro Suenis et Bavaris*, a pie for Swabians and Bavarians, sounds familiar even to modern readers; a cross between a cheesecake and a strudel filled with quark and baked in milk, it is filled with thickened milk and fresh cheese and cooked in fat.

Johannes von Bockenheim reconfirmed the complexity of German cuisine: fourteen recipes out of a total of 74 were not only German, but for specific German groups: Bavarians, Swabians, Saxons, Thuringians and so on.[28] In spite of the abundance of cookbooks that started to appear in Germany around this time, or the new approach to time that was influenced by the first mechanical clocks appearing in monasteries during the late fourteenth century (which were to regulate the times for prayer, but soon enough crept into kitchens), German food remained marked by geographical, climatical and above all political diversity. At the end of the Middle Ages, in contrast to England or France, Germany still had no single capital. Instead it was a patchwork of dynastic and ecclesiastical territories dotted with imperial free cities and the castles of independent aristocrats. When the power of the Holy Roman Emperor began to decline from 1500 onwards due to social and financial pressures, regionality increased even further. The expansion of European influence in the world had a strong effect on national economies and politics elsewhere, but the effects of this reached Germany rather gradually and often indirectly. By 1600 Spain, Portugal, France, England and Holland were all expansive powers, but not Germany.

Traditional *Weihnachtsgebäck* (biscuits) and *Stollen* served at Christmas.

SIX

German Food Writing: The Early Modern Period, 1500 to 1648

Openly criticizing the Roman Church, which exploited fears of the afterlife through images of Hell and Purgatory to promote the sale of indulgences, Martin Luther, together with like-minded innovators in the early sixteenth century, kicked off a storm whose effects are clearly discernable to this day. At the time the scholarly language was still Latin, and the majority of the population of Europe was illiterate, although the fourteenth and fifteenth centuries saw a boom in university foundations. Studying, however, was still extremely expensive. During the three years of his son's university education in Vienna and Cologne in the 1390s, the wealthy Cologne businessman Hermann von Goch spent over half as much on his son's studies as he did on food for his large household.[1] Then as now, cookbooks weren't written by scholars, but the group they initially targeted and whose food habits they reflect was small. In Augsburg, for instance, the proud and well-off patrician families made up less than one-tenth of the city's population. Martin Luther not only insisted on a common German language, shaped by his translation of the Bible, but pushed the radical idea of elementary schooling. As Johann Gutenberg's printing technology made books more affordable, literacy became more common. With their own, Lutheran Protestant confession and language, Germans finally started to feel their way towards their own cultural identity, including the way they cooked and ate. Cookbooks were among the most popular reading material.

For Luther the Bible was the basis of holy authority: if God had made a world that included humble everyday work, good food, wine, beer and women, the duty of a good Christian was to show moderation in all things rather than indulge in extremes of fasting, or of abstinence and celibacy. The history of *Stollen*, the most traditional German Christmas cake (of which the *Bremer Klaben* is a close relative), contains the whole debate about religious food rules, sins and indulgences of that time. Looking at today's recipe, heavy with butter, almonds and dried fruit, it is hard to believe that it originally started as a cake for the Advent fasting period before Christmas. Its shape symbolizes the infant Jesus in swaddling clothes, and it was first recorded in 1329 in Naumburg on the Saale near Leipzig. At that time the strict fasting rules allowed it to be made only from water, oats and the local rapeseed oil. However, from the mid-fifteenth century on dispensations from fasting laws became more common all over Europe. In the north this was often based on the reasoning that olive oil (which German speakers called *Baumöl*, literally tree oil) as a replacement for butter or lard was very expensive. In 1475 Pope Sixtus IV authorized the use of butter in Germany, Hungary and Bohemia during Advent for the following five years, although most sources in connection with *Stollen* quote a dispensation given in a *Butterbrief* or butter letter sent by Pope Innocent VIII to the Duke of Saxony in 1491.[2] Both were by no means isolated cases but part of the regular sale of indulgences, often linked to the financing of concrete building projects, including the construction of the papal basilica of St Peter in Rome. Some historians think that this only put an official rubber stamp on everyday practice. Be that as it may, *Stollen*, the lean cake for the fasting period, developed into the familiar treat rich in fruit and almonds, and the most famous recipe today is undoubtedly the yeast-based one from Dresden/Saxony.[3]

True to form as an advocate for the secularization of monasteries, in 1525 Luther married the nun Katharina von Bora, and it was around their table that the famous *Tischgespräche*, table talks with students and colleagues, took place after plentiful but not overly luxurious meals. *Die Lutherin* Katharina, or Käthe as her husband affectionately called her, ran the household in the former Augustin monastery of Wittenberg like a business venture, taking in students to make ends meet. She was responsible for beer brewing, beekeeping, care of the wine barrels in the cellar, overseeing work in the gardens, fields, pastures and orchards and the husbandry of the household's cattle, pigs, goats and poultry. Käthe herself came from a moderately well-off local family of landed gentry. Contrary to common assumptions (and his own account), her husband had also been raised in a fairly affluent family. Luther's father owned a copper mine in nearby Mansfeld. Recent archaeological excavations of the refuse dump behind his parents' house shed fresh light on the family's culinary habits, delivering a great variety of freshwater fish bones, including debris from pike, perch, eel and bream, besides herring and cod, which presumably was consumed in the form of stockfish – all pointing to a family prepared to spend more than was absolutely necessary on their food. Their kitchen was representative of this era's households in small towns. A variety of pots and pans indicate that food preparation took many different forms. Implements include the characteristic northern German *Grapen*, a large three-legged Dutch oven which could be used to cook whole chickens or wild ducks, or closed with a pastry lid to thicken almond milk overnight in the embers. Shallow open pans of varying size made from iron or earthenware served to prepare different kinds of gruel, porridge, puréed vegetable or egg dishes. Smaller quantities of foodstuffs were baked in bowls; these, placed on a grid and covered with a large metal lid, were topped with glowing embers. A large metal kettle hung over the fire for boiling and stewing, and various spits were used for roasting, including small spits for the smaller varieties of wild bird.

Woodcuts used as illustrations in the earliest printed cookbooks show kitchens with a knee-high fireplace under a chimney: embers were moved to where they were needed according to the desired intensity of heat. Bellows were used to revive the fire in the morning. However, systems varied according to the region. In the southeast and in more modest houses open hearths were rarely used. Kitchens tended to be small, with a large stove in a separate soot-covered room next door forming the lower part of the chimney. This stove was used for cooking as well as heating the house, with pots and pans placed directly in the fire, and a separate warming compartment in the stove which could be accessed from the living room. Some stoves featured built-in water cisterns, which provided hot water as well as a boiling pot for cooking dumplings. The warmth of the stove was also useful for drying fruits and provided a warm place in which to rear chicks.[4]

Wooden tubs served to wash both dishes and foodstuffs in water fetched from a public well. Only wealthier households had their own wells and were sometimes equipped with elaborate pumping systems. Essential kitchen equipment included a bronze mortar for grinding salt, spices, almonds and so on, a finer consistency being achieved with a sieve and a cloth. Serving dishes, round and wide, were made of glazed earthenware, with separate smaller dishes for mustard and sauces. Small dessert plates were used to serve nuts and fruit after dinner. Earthen beakers and mugs, as well as glasses in similar shapes, served as drinking vessels.

Some of these stoves were still in use in the late 1960s in the Nuremberg area. The oven heats the living room, but is used for cooking from the kitchen side, with the smoke escaping into the open kitchen chimney.

In a middle-class household such as that of the Luthers, every dish was shared around the table. Serving was done quite literally by hand, as was eating, with the assistance of a personal knife and bits of bread for mopping up sauce. Spoons were only used for soup, stew or gruel and personal forks were still regarded as suspiciously close to the Devil's pitch-fork, with Luther ranting against the use of small forks, *Gäbelchen* (larger ones long having been accepted for serving purposes).

The Reformation and the subsequent Catholic Counter-Reformation reinforced the cultural diversity in Germany. The connection between confessions and economics was complex but, simply put, the Protestant work ethic suited the capitalist instincts of a sober bourgeoisie which re-invested its profits, whereas Catholicism seemed to provide dispensation for the enjoyment of worldly goods, feasting and extravagance. However, in both camps the sense of duty towards those who were poor, elderly or otherwise in need was strong, since social responsibility was shifted from the Church to society at large. A good example is the Magdalenen-hospital of Münster in Westphalia, the city's oldest. It was founded in the eleventh century, initially under the control of the bishop. By the early years of the fourteenth century, however, it was run by the staunchly Catholic city fathers. Typically for such an institution, it had been endowed with several estates around Münster and was thus supplied from its own fields, gardens and farmyards. It housed and fed eighteen elderly people who were charged a fee, with fifteen more poor people accomodated for free. Until 1636, when the communal kitchen was closed and replaced by the distribution of money and food, everybody, including labourers and servants, were fed from a single kitchen, although paying inmates received slightly higher fish, meat and beer rations in some cases.

The hospital's *Küchenbücher*, detailed kitchen accounts for the period from 1552 to 1636, give us a precise idea of daily provisions and

Lucas Cranach, altar for the Mönchskirche/Salzwedel, Johann-Friedrich-
Danneil-Museum Salzwedel. The painting shows a vineyard which
on the left-hand side is ruined by Catholic mismanagement
and overexploitation, while on the right-hand side the soberly
clad Protestants are repairing the damage.

> ## A culinary place in time: the Lutherhaus in Wittenberg
>
> For a glimpse of the period, the Lutherhaus in Wittenberg in Saxony-Anhalt (1½ hrs by car southwest of Berlin) houses a museum on the history of the Reformation. Its historic rooms offer the experience of a relatively well-off household of the first half of the sixteenth century, including the hall where the famous table talks took place. A special exhibition focuses on Luther's wife and her household management (www.martinluther.de/de/lutherhaus-wittenberg).

meals.[5] The diet followed the traditional Christian pattern of Friday as a designated lean day when less food was eaten, while every Monday, Wednesday and Saturday was meatless. Two main meals were served per day, with fish replacing meat on Fridays and on the eve of numerous holy days. Contrary to common assumption, most holy days required a reduction in quantity or in choice. Feasting only occurred at Easter, Pentecost, Christmas, Assumption, on two designated saints' days and (until 1570) on Shrove Tuesday. This meant additional fish on the days before and an additional roasted meat dish for midday on the day itself, with the occasional luxury of expensive saffron included in boiled meat dishes.

Quantities in general weren't meagre. Meat consumption was high at around 100 kg per head per year. Since meat was considered more nourishing than other ingredients, no extra dishes were provided on meat days – that is, between 125 and 133 days annually. Veal was served from April to June; beef and pork, the dominant meat sources, were available fresh from October to December. Mutton was on the menu from June to October. Goose, in season in September and October, was reserved for festive meals, along with chicken. Fresh meat was mostly consumed at the midday meal. Evening meals consisted of salted, smoked or otherwise preserved forms of beef and pork, with the famous Westphalian ham a highlight of Sunday evening meals. Fresh meat was usually boiled, with pepper added for a dish called *Potthast* (known today as Dortmund *Pfefferpotthast*), while roasted veal or chicken were reserved for the six highest feast days of the year.

Fish came on the table on 90 to 100 days per year on average, always at midday, and mostly in the form of salted herring or *Bückling*, the same fish smoked. Stockfish was reserved for feast days and Sundays. Fresh fish was even more expensive and only purchased for the councillors' annual banquets. Portions were 100 to 200 g – markedly smaller portions than meat. This was undoubtedly due to the fact that it had to be bought in, whereas most of the meat came from the hospital's own production. As fish prices began to rise from 1580 on, portions were reduced even further and were occasionally replaced by cheese. Side dishes, often based on pulses, were considered a necessity when fish was on the menu, as fish was deemed less nourishing than meat.

Midday meals on fast days consisted of bread, cheese and vegetables, the evening meal being limited to a small white loaf, *Pfennigswegge* or *Muiterwegge*, both of which were *schonebrot*, literally 'nice bread', that is, from more finely ground, sifted flour. Ordinary bread was unsalted wholemeal rye bread. More refined rye bread flavoured with caraway seeds and wheat bread made by a commercial baker using the hospital's own grain were both reserved for special occasions and fast days. Porridge and gruel played a lesser role and were made from barley.

Fasting rules relaxed with time and were officially lifted by the hospital in 1634, a move that is also documented for other institutions in Münster at the time. This might partly have been due to the rising prices of foodstuffs in the context of the Thirty Years War, but possibly also to the impact of Luther's ideas. Until then no animal products except eggs had been consumed during Lent, making for a monotonous diet consisting mainly of pulses and bread, with small amounts of dried figs as an occasional treat, along with vegetable oils, probably from rapeseed and local nuts. Cheese was dispensed twice a week on meatless and fishless days, with butter distributed in weekly rations. About half the cheese consumed came from the hospital's own production; the other half was Friesian hard cheese and had to be paid for. The weekly rations of

Bread baking in the city, 1716.

the latter alone were 340–600 g per person. As with fish, purchases of cheese dimished as prices rose and it was often replaced by the more affordable bread.

Münster belonged to the beer-drinking north: the everyday beverage at the hospital was a light hopped beer from the hospital's own brewery, made with barley malt, of which everybody drank between 2 and 3 litres a day. Purchased stronger *Vollbier* was distributed on festive days, whereas wine was reserved for the four highest religious feast days, and consumption averaged only 2.8 litres per person per year.

Meanwhile, Germans might have lagged behind their neighbours in terms of food trends, but they were still eager to write down culinary instructions. Culinary manuals were among the earliest printed books in Germany, and more have been preserved than in any other language. When evaluating their impact, it is useful to trace the evolution of the cookbook in Germany from the earliest times. As pointed out earlier, recipe collections initially reflected aristocratic and upper-bourgeois lifestyles and were produced by and intended for those who could afford a cook and a scribe. Professional cooks working in wealthy households appear to have been exclusively male. However, women joined the chorus relatively early in Germany, even though they were not supposed to deal with public affairs or become involved in decisions which did not directly concern the home.

In addition to *Daz Buoch* from around 1350 and its Low German predecessor examined earlier, there were a number of other manuscripts that included recipe collections, such as *Mondseer Kochbuch* and *Kochbuch des Dorotheenklosters*, both from the first half of the fifteenth century. Many were based on *Daz Buoch*, including *Reichenauer Kochbuch* and another version, probably copied some years later from the same original, *Alemannisches Büchlein von guter Speise*. *Kochbuch des Meister Eberhard*, like these two from the first half of the fifteenth century, was the first by a professional author, the *Küchenmeister*, kitchen master or head chef of the duke of Bavaria-Landshut. Like its predecessors it offered dietary advice, including a large section copied from Hildegard von Bingen's *Physica*. A few years later, in 1460, Eberhard's colleague Meister Hans, he of the saffron rhyme discussed earlier, left a similar but even more extensive collection.

While the dining table represented a fundamental means of demonstrating status, the household manual became a way of committing to posterity a record of the privileges of wealth, as in the case of Ulrich

Schwarz, an Augsburg guild mayor and merchant who became wealthy through trading in wine and salt. He not only wrote a household book, but included in it a recipe collection.[6] Schwarz seems to have been an exceptionally ambitious politician, a reformer who aimed to increase representation among all classes and groups, but also eagerly furthered his own social aspirations. His clothes were ostentatious; his political decisions provocative. He appears to have written his household book during the 1460s. It is a combination of advice and information on the proper conduct of a household's daily routines, inside and out. After his death the work was passed down within the family, and entries were added by subsequent generations. Whereas Michael de Leone, the pronotary in Würzburg and author of *Daz Buoch*, had been interested in literature and poetry, Schwarz's interests were more practical. He noted down volume measures in use in different cities and rules governing the weather, and recorded political events and medical recommendations. His 137 recipes clearly show his social ambitions, culminating in the description of how to prepare 'good Westphalian pig's meat called ham' from a whole fattened pig.

Women are more prominent among cookery writers in Germany than they are in other countries. However they stuck to writing by hand even at a time when printing had become quite widespread, probably seeing their works as aides-mémoires intended for family use. The recipe collection of Philippine Welser from around 1545 was part of the dowry of the young bride from a wealthy Augsburg family (close competitors of the Fuggers) who secretly married the archduke of Tyrol in Innsbruck. The collection of Sabine Welser (probably from the same family) of 1553 reflects a similar (quite modern) combination of robustness, using local ingredients, but also taking imported luxurious ones for granted. Its specialities are *Pasteten* and *Torten*, pies and tarts, with a very liberal use of sugar, which many still regarded as a medicine rather than a sweetener. Here is her recipe for a strawberry tart:

> *Ain erbertorten zu machen:*
> *Mach das bedellin vnnd lass erstarcken jn der tortenpfanen. Darnach nim die erber vnnd legs darauf vmber aufs allernechst zusamen, darnach zuckeres woll aufs allerbast, lass darnach ain klein weil bachen, geuss ain maluasier darauf vmber vnnd lass ain weil bachen, so jst er gemacht.*

To make a strawberry tart
Make the base and let it go cold in the pan. Then take the
strawberries and put them on it tightly, then sugar it very
well, let it bake a little while, pour some malvasia over it and
let it bake a little while, then it's done.

Her recipe for puréed figs has some interesting aspects:

Ain feigenmusss zu machen:
Thu ein wein jn ain heffellin, vnnd wan er sieden wirt, so thu
geriben lezelten vnnd geriben semel daran. Saffera, mandel, wein-
ber, feigen thu darein vnnd ain wenig ain schmaltz.[7]

To make a fig purée:
Put some wine in a pan, and when it starts to boil, add some
grated gingerbread and some grated roll. Add saffron, almonds,
raisins, figs and a little lard.

Lard, in the south of Germany, would have been drawn (clarified)
butter, but even more telling and worth a short glance is the gingerbread Sabine Welser used and whose production was (and is) centred in
Nuremberg. Early recipes for it listed only honey, flour and spices as
ingredients along with a raising agent such as potash or *Hirschhornsalz*
(ammonium carbonate). The *Zeidler*, beekeepers, provided honey
from bees in the surrounding forest, later supplemented by the products of Germany's first sugar refinery, founded in 1573 in Augsburg. The
Lebküchnermeister, gingerbread bakers, formed their own guild in 1643,
while wealthy patrician families had long begun to demand richer versions that included almonds, nuts and eggs. The culmination of this trend
was a particularly rich version, *Elisen-Lebkuchen,* supposedly named after
a guild master's pretty daughter (to legally qualify for the title today, the
mix must contain at least 25 per cent almonds or other nuts and no more
than 10 per cent flour). The name *Lebkuchen* itself does not, as might be
supposed, derive from *Leben*, life, or *laben*, feasting, but most probably
has its roots in the Latin *libum*, a flatbread or sacrificial cake whose
origins can be traced back to ancient Mesopotamia. In its various shapes
it has always been something celebratory, a sweetened version of normal
everyday bread, but its preparation was never confined to specific feast
days or a particular season. Monasteries preserved such recipes from the

earliest times, since their pharmacies kept the necessary spices in stock, a convenience which also gave rise to several versions spread on wafers to prevent drying out. Besides Nuremberg, Germany's gingerbread tradition is based in Pulsnitz, northeast of Dresden/Saxony. In 1558 Pulsnitz bakeries received permission to bake *Pfefferkuchen*, literally peppercakes, leading to the evolution of an independent craft practised by small family companies to this day. The region was never rich, so the classic Pulsnitz *Pfefferkuchen* are still far more austere than the gingerbreads of Nuremberg, where the rival product is somewhat disparagingly known as *braune Ware*, brown stuff. Whereas Nuremberg's far richer *Lebkuchen* today are strictly associated with Christmas (although industrial manufacturers inundate the shelves with their wares as soon as summer is fading), *Pulsnitzer Pfefferkuchen* are produced all year round and are traditionally also given as presents on special occasions such as birthdays, graduations and so forth. Pulsnitz peppercakes are made by heating honey and/or syrup and kneading it into a mix of wheat and rye flour till it forms a thick dough. This is then matured in wooden barrels in a cool place for several weeks – or even months, depending on the recipe. It is then 'broken' in a special machine and mixed with spices and a raising agent – ammonium carbonate or potash – after which almonds, nuts and candied citrus-peel may be added for special kinds of *Pfefferkuchen* before baking. The Pulsnitz mix never includes eggs or fat of any kind, and presumably it is this type of *Lezelten* that recipes like Sabine Welser's call for.

Her home town Augsburg was, as we have seen, a city of rich Catholic gourmets with close links to Italy. The first German translation of Bartolomeo Sacchi's (commonly called Platina) *De honesta voluptate* was published here in 1554 under the title *Von der Eerlichen ziemlichen auch erlaubten wollust des Leibes*. Platina's work, the first cookbook to appear in print, around 1474, introduced the new, more restrained cooking style of the Renaissance, with minimal use of spices and less processing of basic foodstuffs. In contrast Germany's first printed cookbook, the *Kuchemaistrey*, was a rather modest compendium and still in the medieval tradition. It appeared in Nuremberg in 1485 and was hugely successful, with many new editions until 1674. The recipes do not differ much from earlier handwritten manuscripts, and the connection between humoral medicine, health, cooking and diet is still strong. Anna Weckerin's *Ein Köstlich New Kochbuch* (Amberg, 1597), the first printed cookbook by a woman, featured dishes for the poor and sick, possibly because of the fact that Weckerin was the widow of a Basel physician.

Title page of Rumpolt's cookbook from 1581. Note the cook's sturdiness; he is hardworking, but also well fed.

The first professional German cook to share his knowledge in a printed and thus more widely distributed book was Marx Rumpolt. His *Ein New Kochbuch* (A New Cookbook) was first published in 1581 by Sigmundt Feyerabendt. It has numerous vignettes and woodcuts by artists highly regarded in their time, such as Weiditz, Jost Amman and Solis, in the sixteenth-century equivalent of modern full-colour, glossy printing. In spite of the high price that the book presumably commanded, it was reprinted at least four times, in 1582, 1586, 1587 and 1604. Rumpolt's nearly 500-page work is the first true cookbook published in Germany, as opposed to a mere collection of recipes; a guide for professionals written by a professional. It covered instructions on staging banquets for members of different social classes, detailed the correct seating order, advised on servants and provided extensive tips on shopping.

It also included many menus for the emperor, kings, electors, archdukes, counts, noblemen, burgher and peasants, each with an alternative for meatless days. The higher the rank, the more dishes were served, with meals ranging from six to twenty or 30 dishes per setting. Here is a midday meal on a fast day for a peasants' banquet. In contrast, the imperial menu for the same occasion had 42 dishes for one course, not to mention the difference in ingredients and effort.

> The first course . . . a pea soup, boiled eggs. The other course . . . blue boiled carp with vinegar. The third course . . . a sauerkraut cooked with lean salmon and baked fish and roast fish on the cabbage, all served in one bowl. The fourth course . . . Yellow pike boiled the Hungarian way. The fifth course . . . a white jelly made from sour carp. The sixth course . . . all kinds of baked, cake and wafers . . . apple, pears, nuts and cheese, all served in one bowl.[8]

Approximately 2,000 systematically arranged recipes were followed by detailed instructions on winemaking. Rumpolt's work is still very much in the spirit of the Middle Ages, but the simple act of writing down and printing professional recipes made him a daring reformer: Rumpolt was the first cook in Germany to break the unwritten rule of the chefs' guild to protect their knowledge by passing it on only through word of mouth in professional kitchens. Despite Rumpolt's historical importance, frustratingly little is known about his life besides the date of publication of *Ein New Kochbuch*. However, careful reading provides a good idea about the man behind the book. At the time of writing he was the personal chef of the elector and archbishop of Mainz, who resided in Aschaffenburg (which belonged to the diocese of Mainz). He was Hungarian by birth, but his forefathers were driven out of the '*kleine Walachei*' (today part of western Romania) by 'the cruel and brutish arch-enemy of Christianity, the Turk'. Obliged to travel far and wide, 'from youth onwards to subsist among strangers, concerned as to how I would be able today or tomorrow to maintain a livelihood', he was unable to learn any foreign language, but devoted himself to cookery, 'with great effort and work . . . for many years now', suggesting that by 1581 he was no longer a young man. He seems to have been personal chef to the court of Saxony and possibly also to the Holy Roman Emperor, a Habsburg. He reports to have been 'at many lords' courts and have seen and heard a bit of Italy, the

Netherlands, Russia, Prussia, Poland, Hungary, Bohemia, Austria and Germany'; in short, a cosmopolitan self-made man in a period when this was exceptional. His insistence that he had tested everything he wrote down is worth taking note of, as it indirectly accused colleagues of merely copying from earlier works:

> Because as far as I am concerned I can testify with a good conscience that I have managed to excellently present to others and to communicate in the most beneficial way what I have understood and learned. And have not borrowed from other books and falsified what I have described here, but have made and arranged it all with my own hand at the masters' courts where I served.

Sigmundt Feyerabendt, the publisher of *Ein New Kochbuch*, was astute at publishing 'bestsellers'. Although Rumpolt sought to protect his work from unauthorized reprinting for a decade by a Holy Roman Privilege, by 1581 Feyerabendt himself had published a virtual copy of Rumpolt's work under the (widely used) title *Koch- und Kellermeystery*, attributing authorship to a certain Meister N. Sebastian. Publishers of the time certainly weren't afraid to take liberties. When the Latin version of Platina was printed in Cologne in 1529 and proved to be very successful, a publisher decided to combine two bestsellers by putting Platina's name on a reprint of the (anonymous) *Kuchemaisterey*. It is hard to avoid the conclusion that this abridged version of Rumpolt's work (the chapter on winemaking was reprinted almost word for word) was published with his knowledge and approval; a cheaper edition was made available for the less well-off after the expensive 'coffee-table' one had been popularized.

Posterity has barely acknowledged Rumpolt's achievement: in contrast to Sigmundt Feyerabendt, there is no entry under his name in the relevant reference works, nor is his *New Kochbuch* listed as one of Feyerabendt's publications. However, crediting Rumpolt with the first German potato recipe, as has generally been the case (also by this author), seems to be a mistake resulting from the recipe's title, *Erdtepffel*, literally earth-apples, the common southern German designation for potatoes (*Kartoffeln* in High German).

> Peel and cut them up, let them swell in water and squeeze them well in a cloth, chop them up and roast them in finely cut

bacon. Put a little milk with it and let them cook in it, so it will be good and tasty.[9]

It is highly improbable that Rumpolt would have known potatoes. They had reached Spain as part of the Columbian Exchange in the mid-1560s at the very earliest, were very slow to spread and as a foodstuff were regarded with suspicion. If he did, he would have referred to them differently, as the word *Erdtepffel* at the time designated a chervil-like plant today called *Kerbelrüben* (*Bunium* or *Chaerophyllum bulbocastanum*), which had cumin-like seeds and tuberous roots whose taste was often compared to chestnuts (more about potatoes will follow in the next chapter).[10]

In 1594, shortly after the publication of Rumpolt's work, Frantz de Rontzier's *Kunstbuch von mancherley Essen* (The Artbook of Various Dishes), was published in Wolfenbüttel/Lower Saxony. The author, personal chef to the duke of Brunswick-Lüneburg, recorded his recipes by dictating in the Lower German vernacular to a scribe who translated his words into High German. The result is somewhat less structured and convincing than Rumpolt's and was certainly less commercially successful, an indirect indication of Feyerabendt's skills. As an established publisher, Feyerabendt would have had a good distribution network, whereas the press in Wolfenbüttel was new and unproven. However, Rontzier's title indicates a change in attitudes: at least in some circles, cooking had passed from a craft to an art. The terms *Spisekunst*, the art of eating, and *Kochkunst*, the art of cooking, had become established and were clear signs of a sea change in German ideas about food.

It is hard to underestimate the importance of the fact that Germans now had a common language which in contrast to Latin was accessible to everybody in its effect on the burgeoning German culinary identity. Some culinary authors now presented their endeavours as specifically *teutsch*, German. Besides Hieronymus Bock and his *Teutsche Speisskammer* (German Larder), of 1550, Walter Ryff was one of the first authors to consciously reflect on national identity in German cooking-pots. The very long title of his work, published (possibly posthumously) in 1549, stressed food and beverages 'in daily use by us Germans': *Kurtze aber vast eigentliche nutzliche vnd in pflegung der gesundheyt notwendige beschreibung der natur, eigenschafft, Krafft, Tugent, Wirckung, rechten Bereyttung vnd gebrauch, inn speyss vnd drancks von noeten, vnd bey vns Teutschen inn teglichem Gebrauch sind*. As a prolific writer, Ryff has repeatedly been accused of plagiarizing various colleagues, but this makes the *Kurtze* a real treasure trove of insights into the food habits of his time. Studying those, it is important to bear in mind that the author was born in Alsace, but lived in Frankfurt am Main, Mainz, Nuremberg, Kulmbach and Würzburg, while his wife came from Rostock on the Baltic coast.

The *Kurtze* consists of 82 alphabetically arranged entries covering everything from *Acetum/Essig* (vinegar) to *Zythus/Byer* (beer). It is difficult to resist quoting them all, as they are immensely fascinating. Ryff tells us that garlic smells horrible, but that Germans could live without it. Almonds were now grown in Germany and therefore used far more frequently. Goose was more digestible when eaten young and goose lard was good for cakes. Spring asparagus (no mention, unfortunately, of the colour), though not cheap, was highly regarded and customarily boiled in a good meat broth and dressed with vinegar, salt and olive oil (like other authors of the time, Ryff used the term *Baumöl*, literally, tree oil). Parsley was the vegetable in most general use, both leaf and root, whereas gruel was 'a coarse dish for coarse people – tough, coarse and unfriendly'. He described basil as noble and fragrant but rarely used and noted that cabbage heads and greens were the most important stand-by in ordinary kitchens to fill empty stomachs, but that when they were served three or four times a day in the Bavarian style as sauerkraut, they made for an unhealthy, even evil diet. Butter was declared so essential to German cooking that not even a water-based soup could be prepared without it, and foreigners were right to call Germans *Grass-Alemant*, German fatties. Cheese was pronounced heavy and indigestible, especially when matured and made with rennet. No household, either rich or poor, could prepare a dish well without onions. The *Kurtze* also delved into a few regional food differences, explaining for example that in Alsace, Ryff's homeland, chickpeas were widely used in wealthy kitchens, though not at all in the rest of Germany. As for spices, Ryff thought that of all the spices used in German cooking, cinnamon was sweetest and best, whereas the green leaves of coriander were declared obnoxious and stinking (it is telling that coriander's Greek name at the time was translated into German as *Wanzenkraut*, bug-herb), but the seeds were considered useful in the kitchen and the pharmacy. Pepper is confirmed as the most common spice, and even peasants were using it to make their food more palatable, whereas saffron was delicious in meat broth and, although still expensive, was at last being grown in Germany. On poultry, Ryff reported that chickens were not cheap, but widely consumed, easy to digest and healthy, especially when young and a little fat. Pheasants made a noble dish but were always surpassed by a fattened capon. Partridges Ryff pronounced to be a little more common, but still very good when allowed to hang for a day or two, though not longer, as was the custom in Germany, 'where we are used to serve game when half-rotted and stinking'. Mustard might smell sour but couldn't be done without as it made a dish more digestible. The same effect was found in *agrest*, verjus, which also awakened the appetite. Finally beer in Germany was a cooling summer drink which dampened the drunkenness caused by drinking wine, which was why, according to Ryff, wine-sodden monks cooled themselves down at night by drinking beer.

German cookbooks at this stage were still a young genre as far as the writing itself and the level of detail were concerned. The Italian Scappi in his *Opera* of 1570 minutely described the many elaborate techniques that were needed for his dishes and gave precise measurements, assuming less knowledge and thus making his work accessible for a larger readership. The translation of Italian and French publications could present a problem if the translator in charge was not up to the job, leading to confusions that persist to the present day. For instance, historians have suggested that the alleged appearance of distinctive German national culinary habits at that time could be ascribed to the renaming of dishes.[11] Although their argument is similar to saying that the whole Mediterranean shares one cuisine because everybody uses olive oil, their studies are full of fascinating insights (they also show that it is not enough to classify recipes by names alone). *Sauce cameline*, the condiment mentioned earlier that was widely used in England, Italy, Catalonia and France, but supposedly not in Germany, is a case in point. Its composition varied considerably according to region, except for one defining ingredient: cinnamon. In Germany it just took a different name, as is shown by a late fifteenth-century Middle Low German recipe collection in which it appeared under the name *herensalsin*, lords' sauce. It shared all the characteristics of *sauce cameline*, namely the inclusion of a large proportion of cinnamon, bread-thickening and dilution with vinegar:

> One should take cloves and nutmeg, cardamom, pepper, ginger, all of equal weight; and as much cinnamon as there is of all the others, and add as much toasted white bread as there is of the others, and grind it together, and blend it with strong vinegar. And place it in a cask. It is called the lords' sauce, and it is good for half a year.[12]

It is often said that the combination of spices, sweetness, fruit and acidity still found in contemporary German dishes such as *Sauerbraten* is a German pecularity, a medieval remnant proving the cuisine's backwardness. Indeed, the combination of sweet and savoury seems to have been a German favourite in the fourteenth and fifteenth centuries, although the use of some kind of acidity was also popular in France at the time. At the end of the sixteenth century and from the south of Germany we get some comments on the combination of fruit and meat (besides much else of interest) from a highly sophisticated traveller, the philosopher and politician Michel de Montaigne. Embarking on a trip from his native Bordeaux to Italy in 1580, his journey took him through Germany and Switzerland. Possessed of an open and inquisitive mind, he enlisted his scribe and servant to keep a travel diary, recording daily life and culinary habits. The following observations are of the habits of the citizens of Lindau on Lake Constance:

> They [the Germans] make such an effort with their food and with [the help of] soups, sauces and salads bring such a diversity to the dishes, and everything in good inns is prepared with such good taste that the French aristocratic cuisine is barely comparable, seeing also that in our châteaux one would rarely find such ornate halls. Unknown to us were quince soup, soup with baked apples in it, and cabbage salad, as well as thick soups without bread, for example made with rice, which everybody shares, as separate plates are unknown. Noticeable is the richness in good fish, served with other meat in one dish; trout is not considered desirable and they eat only its spawn; game, snipe and young hare, which are very different to ours but prepared at least as well, are in abundance. We never saw meat dishes that tender as are served daily here. With the meat, cooked plums, pear and apple slices are served [a custom surviving in the form of poached pears and cranberries served with roast game to this day]; sometimes the roast is served first and the soup last, sometimes the other way round. As for fruit, there are only pears, apples which are very good, and nuts, then cheese. With the meat, silver or pewter cutlery is laid out with four containers with various pounded spices, amongst them caraway seeds or something similar that tastes savoury and hot and is sprinkled on the bread; the bread is more often than not baked with fennel seeds. After

the meal, full glasses [of wine] are served again together with two or three different things that further the digestion.

The scribe also noted:

> The Sire de Montaigne regretted three things on his trip. The first of these was that on departure he had omitted to provide himself with a cook who would have been able to study the local dishes and try them at home; second, that he didn't employ a German servant or seek the company of a local nobleman since, by relying on the good will of a miserable guide, he experienced great inconvenience; and third, that he didn't have a Münster[13] or something similar in his luggage. Although he had adapted himself so far as to drink wine without water, when there was competitive drinking and he was invited as a gesture of politeness, he never accepted.[14] Farmers here provide their labourers with flatbreads baked in the embers, sprinkled with fennelseeds, with bacon and some garlic.

Montaigne had chosen the right moment for his travels. By the 1590s a recession had set in, since the overland trade routes were declining in importance due to world trade shifting from the Mediterranean and Baltic to the Atlantic. When food and especially grain prices gradually inflated, the landed gentry was in a better position than urban manufacturers and tradesmen. In the territories to the east the nobles were able to buy the landholdings of the peasantry, sometimes taking over whole villages, and thus became lords over very large estates. In the west and southwest, after having played such an important political and economic role in the late Middle Ages, many townships lost their power to territorial rulers and became more provincial. Then, from 1618 to 1648, conflicting political and religious interests led to the Thirty Years War. International arguments meshed with German uprisings and escalated into extended clashes between foreign forces on German territory.

Even when times were peaceful the average peasant's housing could be called modest at best, but when the guards on top of the church tower shouted their warning that troops were approaching, the peasantry abandoned their dwellings and moved lock, stock and barrel – children, moveable goods and livestock – into caves and other hiding places that had often been deliberately fortified ahead of time, for example by planting thornbushes. In this prehistoric form of accomodation life was reduced to a matter of survival. Agricultural production was disrupted when farm buildings were destroyed, fishponds were emptied and livestock slaughtered or taken away by foraging troops, who often left nothing behind but literally scorched earth. The impact on the German economy and society at large varied considerably depending on time and place. In some cases producers of meat and grain, essential supplies for soldiers, could gain significant wealth and power by supplying the large armies, but as a result resources collapsed for the rest of the population. Historians are divided on the sharpness of the resulting drop in population, but agree that the worst-affected areas experienced losses of over two-thirds of the total, whereas some areas seem to have been virtually unaffected. The greatest killers were epidemics such as typhoid, plague and syphilis, all spread by armies on the move. Influenza was often fatal due to malnutrition and lowered resistance. Almost everybody born after 1600 who wasn't killed in battle was affected by hardship and the disruption of their livelihoods. Overall the damage to the economy was immense, and living standards in many areas of Germany took around a century to return to pre-war levels.

SEVEN

Coffee, Sugar and Potatoes, 1648 to 1815

As a result of the Thirty Years War, resilience and pragmatism gained an even stronger footing in German culinary culture. Whole regions were completely devastated: people struggled to get back on their feet and rebuild not only houses, but foodchains. A study of bakers and bread-baking in Weida in Thuringia illuminates the effects of the war on the food economy in a small town that had been almost completely destroyed. As was usual at the time, bakers were organized in a guild, and each master baker had to buy a place in the communal 'bread-bank', the bench, where an employee, usually an elderly person who couldn't do any other job, was in charge of sales. Before the war all twelve of the town's bakers had been allowed to offer their wares for sale. Afterwards, once more normal life resumed, a system known as *Wechselbacken,* alternating bake-days, was introduced because demand was much lower. This arrangement, first documented in 1680, allowed only one baker to bake each day, except on market days, when everybody could do as they liked. On Sundays and holidays no bread was baked unless there was a real necessity: in these cases a single baker was permitted to bake, provided that the bread wasn't delivered to the selling-bench before the end of the priest's sermon. Restrictions on permitted bake-days meant that in order to make a living the town's master bakers had to maintain their own cereal-producing farms and take up beer-brewing as an alternative source of income. The system, however, allowed them time enough to take care of these other businesses, while on bake-days sales were guaranteed. From the customers' point of view the advantages were less obvious, since reduced competition seems to have been detrimental to quality. These regulations remained in force until the second half of the eighteenth century, when the economy seems finally to have recovered. In 1789

Tuesday and Saturday were deregulated and became general baking days and in 1793 the restrictive regulations were reduced to the bread sold at the bread-bank, and each master-baker additionally had the right to sell their wares at their own bakery's window. From the nineteenth century onwards the system of alternating bake-days applied only to Sundays and holidays.[1]

The patronizing nature of the guild system was also reflected in the *Hausväterliteratur* (literally housefather literature), household companions directed at a growing bourgeois middle class. One of the earliest examples is the *Oeconomia* by Johannes Coler, a Protestant parish priest, published between 1593 and 1601. The subject-matter was very Lutheran, very comprehensive and very successful. Whereas books by professional cooks were clearly aimed at instructing colleagues searching for specialist knowledge, these works were more about guiding good (Protestant) Christians on the right path to a productive, moderate, quiet life, with recipes appearing almost as an afterthought. Just as Luther's wife Katharina took care of all aspects of household management, detailed instructions were provided for everything from agriculture and viticulture to the correct answers to religious questions. In later centuries this would evolve into a new and vital category of cookbook directed at young wives, based in some respects on the late fourteenth-century *Ménagier de Paris*, but eventually leading to an independent genre in the style of Madame de Saint-Ange.

Just as Luther's German didn't make for the disappearance of local dialects, the regional diversity on a culinary level possibly became even more pronounced (as within the European Union today). As a larger trend, however, it could be argued that with a common language and a confession of their own under their belt, Germans now felt bold enough to look for new inspirations for food. However, they didn't lose their love for everything Italian. By now those German kitchens that could afford these kinds of foodstuffs were familiar with lemons, cauliflower and Savoy cabbage (all originally from Italy). Rumpolt not only had a whole chapter of salad suggestions (likewise an Italian method), but also recipes for *Nudel* – pasta – dishes, including one for noodle soup and a kind of tagliatelle from flour and eggs which he served with grated bread, Parmesan and hot butter, a method he thought originated in Tyrol. After liberating themselves from the Roman church, Germans (or at least those at the upper end of the social spectrum), like the majority of Europeans in the late seventeenth and early eighteenth century, chose France as a cultural leitmotif (an orientation which would find its disillusioning end with Napoleon).

Manners, fashion and culinary habits took on a French veneer, and French phrases were incorporated into ordinary conversation. Everything turned fashionably *à la mode (des Français)*. Many German princes followed the example of the Prussian king Frederick II and developed a court culture on the French model. Princely palaces were built with ornately designed gardens in imitation of those of Versailles. Intimate dinners with guests seated at round tables encouraged intelligent conversation. The dining-as-spectacle banquets in which all, including beggars, had their place, became much rarer, further removing the common folk from contact with their rulers. In contrast to the all-powerful Sun King in Paris, Germany had a multitude of smaller political units governed by absolute rulers. The nobility, formerly independent, became court-attending aristocrats; self-confident burghers turned themselves into state-dependent bureaucrats, who were obedient and servile rather than acting as self-determined citizens. A fable by the Württemberg politician and writer Friederich Karl von Moser published in 1786 illustrates this:

> On the occasion of the birthday of a young eagle, King Eagle gave a banquet for his family and invited the entire sky's army to join the celebration. In deference to his power, thousands of birds waited on his table, admired the richness of the dishes and even more the heroic digestive powers of their king. 'We', the sated eagle finally announced to the watching crowd, 'have eaten.' 'But we haven't,' chirped a sparrowhawk plagued by hunger. 'You,' replied the sublime ruler, 'are my state. I am eating for all of you.'[2]

In previous centuries regional culinary differences had been most evident among the rural population – generally due to variations in the availability of raw materials – whereas upper-class cuisine was more uniform and international. In the kitchens of the educated bourgeoisie, these two styles merged, with cooks imitating and refining familiar regional dishes according to the dictates of French court cuisine. The result of the merger of sophisticated haute cuisine with peasant culinary traditions was a new culinary style, *Bürgerliche Küche* (this was a general European development, as witnessed, for instance, by Menon's *La Cuisinière bourgeoise*, published in 1746). Whereas the cookbooks of the previous century were based on the culinary culture of the Mediterranean and to a much lesser degree Eastern Europe (Poland, Hungary and Bohemia), hefty tomes like the authoritative *Die wohl unterwisene Köchin* (The Well-instructed Woman Cook) by Maria Sophia Schellhammer of 1697 now firmly looked towards France. The French added sweet desserts and meat dishes such as *fricassée*, *ragoût* and *côtelettes* to the German repertoire, complete with linguistic terms. Exotic spices were replaced by fresh herbs, cooking times were reduced and restraint and naturalness replaced the dietetics of old as a guiding principle. Somewhat to modern gourmets' surprise, England also played an important culinary role at the time, an influence undoubtedly furthered by the general trade connections. Marperger's kitchen dictionary of 1716 praised the cooks and dishes of England, among them the then fashionable boiled puddings.

The dominant economic phenomenon of the time was mercantilism, aiming for prosperity through trade. Rulers' coffers were filled most easily through perfecting the tax system. On the one hand this led to extensive land surveying and, in turn, to the first mapping and classification of vineyards. On the other, innumerable toll gates represented an obstacle: merchant barges on the Rhine, for instance, had to stop and pay tolls every 6 miles on average. Mercantilism thrived in a growing populace that mass-produced for export and fitted well into the ideas of the Enlightenment, whose efforts to educate and generally improve the plight of the lower classes were directed at 'good Christians, obedient subjects and efficient farmers'.

As a result, guild systems were increasingly identified as a hindrance to more efficient production methods, just as large, all-inclusive households gradually made way to the modern idea of a private, blood-related inner family. Civil servants and members of the educated middle classes were the first to implement the change, as the father of the family began to leave the house for work or retreated to his private office. Servants were banished to their own quarters, and children were increasingly excluded from the adult world. Fewer people worked in craft-based guilds and, with the rise of modern industry, manufacturers began to pay wages, a situation which led to more workers living independently as lodgers. At the same time, as an increasing amount of prepared food was bought in from cookshops, less space was needed in kitchens, whereas the salon became important for receiving guests.

Although the lengthy economic recovery after the Thirty Years War somewhat slowed them down in comparison with others, Germans took up the refined eating-habits of their French neighbours together with new ways in the kitchen. When cutlery became de rigueur for the nobility, the urban middle classes and affluent peasantry gradually followed suit. The use of fingers was now deemed uncouth and separate plates replaced communal bowls. From the end of the seventeenth century individual cutlery, including forks, was in general use. Tableware served increasingly to demonstrate social status. Preferences varied from region to region. In the north pewter was kept for daily use while costly silver dishes, set out when the occasion warranted, were otherwise stored in a special cabinet with a locked compartment. In the south luxury generally took the form of exclusive glassware.

In 1712 the inventory of a canvas merchant from Münster in Westphalia mentioned a tea pot, a special tea-table and silver cutlery, including knives, forks and spoons, as well as a porcelain dining service. The latter might well have been faience, since the Dutch had been striving to copy Chinese porcelain for half a century. These accoutrements, signs of an aspirational lifestyle, along with mirrors, paintings and other decorative elements, were becoming more and more common in private households. New rituals evolved, with the new and fashionable hot drinks served to visitors seated on elegant new furniture such as upholstered chairs and settees.

The way in which courtly cuisine and lifestyle trickled down through society can clearly be seen through the life and work of the writer, philosopher and scientist Johann Wolfgang von Goethe. Neither over-indulgent nor notably ascetic, Goethe's life appears to have revolved around his study and dining table, making him one of the first and most influential German gourmets. His mother's cooking at the family home in Frankfurt am Main was as renowned as the meals he served during his long and extremely active adult life in the yellow-painted dining room of his house in Weimar.

> I have eaten; but ne'er have thus relish'd my food!
> For when glad are the senses, and joyous the blood,
>   at table all else is effaced.
> As for youth, it but swallows, then whistles an air;
> As for me, to a jovial resort I'd repair,
>   where to eat, and enjoy what I taste.
> I have drunk; but have never thus relish'd the bowl!
> For wine makes us lords, and enlivens the soul,
>   and loosens the trembling slave's tongue.

Georg Melchior Kraus, *Evening Gathering at Duchess Anna Amalia*, 1795, watercolour. The poet Goethe enjoyed these informal gatherings where everybody indulged in their own interests.

> Let's not seek to spare then the heart-stirring drink,
> for though in the barrel the old wine may sink,
> in its place will fast mellow the young.[3]

Goethe's writings provide ample proof that he made no rigid division between disciplines, be it gastronomy, poetry or science. Food and wine influenced his poetry just as powerfully as did his scientific research. For him the traditional conflict between high intellectual ambition and a supposedly lowly preoccupation with the pleasures of the table did not exist. It could indeed be argued that it was Goethe's example that encouraged Karl Friedrich von Rumohr to publish his *Geist der Kochkunst* (The Essence of the Art of Cooking) in 1822. Goethe's early years were affluent. Born in Frankfurt, his father was a wealthy man who had studied law; his mother the daughter of a hotelier and wine merchant who inherited a wine cellar. Since Goethe's grandfather was among the highest ranking members of Frankfurt society, the young man was often a guest at important celebrations, such as the historic coronation of the Holy Roman Emperor, Joseph II, in 1764, when a whole oxen was roasted on a spit. Since 1356 the Frankfurt cathedral had served first as the election chamber of all German emperors, then as their place of coronation. The city's municipal grandeur was balanced, however, by modesty in the everyday life of its citizens. Goethe's aunt, for instance, was not too grand to run a delicatessen.

Expenditure by Goethe's own household in Weimar on food and wine was quite extravagant, and invitations to lunch were generously extended. White asparagus, very fashionable in elite circles, was among Goethe's favoured dishes. His father had planted asparagus between rows of vines in his small vineyard just outside Frankfurt's city wall and Goethe regularly sent asparagus (as well as strawberries) from his garden over to Charlotte von Stein, his muse, who lived just around the corner. As was usual then, every household grew as much of its own food as possible, both on rented *Krautland*, vegetable patches, and in their own gardens. Goethe brought home venison after hunting trips with the duke, but most of the rarer food items were supplied through a network of suppliers built up over the years. A friend of Goethe's regularly sent him fresh Dutch herrings, eel, salmon, lobster and oysters, as well as smoked tongue, pineapple, ginger and lemons. Most famous among those much valued supplies were *Teltower Rübchen*, an aromatic type of small white turnip from the town of the same name near Berlin, provided by his friend Zelter. The *Rübchens*' story is worthy of the great writer's merits.

The small white turnips are one of the oldest examples of a cultivar linked to a particular terroir. The district of Teltow, immediately south of Berlin is marked by sandy soils of low agricultural value. A search through the relevant literature reveals a wealth of recipes and references up to the present day. Possibly the oldest recipe is found in the *Brandenburgisches Kochbuch* of 1723 by Maria Sophia Schellhammer (based on the earlier *Die wohl unterwisene Köchin*). However, the renown of the little turnips extended well beyond mere recipes. Besides Goethe praising them highly, the gastronomic philosopher Karl Friedrich von Rumohr in his *Geist der Kochkunst* mentioned them as a characteristic speciality of Brandenburg. Theodor Fontane extolled the riches of the region in a poem dated 1898: 'Masses of asparagus around Halensee, dill, morels and Teltow Turnips, crayfish from the River Oder hither and thither . . .'. The Viennese *Appetitlexikon* (published 1894 by Habs and Rosner) described them in detail and the French *Grande Encyclopédie* of the 1880s included them, under the heading *navets*, amongst others, *de Berlin petit de Teltau*.

They were nothing new in Paris, having also been included in a *Traité des Jardins* published in Paris in 1789, where they were described as 'le Navet de Berlin . . . very small, white, a bit elongated, very tender and tasty'.[4] The success of the Teltow turnips seems to have been an almost worldwide phenomenon. Johann Christoph Bekmann wrote in his *Historische Beschreibung der Chur und Mark Brandenburg* (published 1751) about the trade on land and sea, linking Brandenburg with Spain and Portugal, St Petersburg, Constantinople, Batavia and Havana, as well as 'all parts of the world'. Among the exports were 'all manner of field and kitchen fruits, particularly the little turnips of Teltow, which amongst foreigners are considered as delicacies'. Other claims, however, particularly those made in regional publications from the early twentieth century, seem impossible to prove. They ranged from Teltow turnips being widely cultivated in Brandenburg during the Middle Ages and monks of Lehnin regularly sending them to the pope, to Liselotte von der Pfalz introducing them at the Versailles court of Louis xiv. In a similar vein legend had them served at the wedding breakfast of Napoleon and his second wife, Marie Louise von Habsburg, in 1810.

In contrast there can be no doubt about the work of generations of Teltow farmers who sowed the turnips at the end of August, around St Bartholomew's day, between the stubble left after the rye harvest. After eight or nine weeks – that is, at the end of October or the beginning of November – they were harvested. According to a report in the *Teltower Kreiskalender* of 1905, the turnips were in such high demand that they did not need to be offered at public markets. Instead the farmers had regular customers and exported large amounts to South Tyrol, Austria, Italy and Switzerland.

After the Second World War, for Germans living in the western part of the divided country, all this fame, history and excitement were difficult to understand. The turnips occasionally sold under this name had no special character. Grown on much richer soils near Hamburg, they tasted fresh, mildly acidic and rather watery, as turnips in general quickly adapt to local conditions. In East Germany Teltow seeds only survived in two private gardens. But since the early 1990s they have been once again become available commercially, cultivated by Axel Szilleweit, a Teltow market gardener. His *Rübchen* taste exactly as they are described in all the old books: aromatic, delightfully piquant and spicy-earthy, their sweetness and horseradish-like hotness wonderfully balanced.

Goethe was an experienced wine taster. On one occasion the duke had a red wine served blind after dinner and all present agreed that it was Burgundy, but couldn't come up with more precise details (showing us that blind tastings and guessing are not a modern invention). Goethe took longer than anybody else and finally declared that, never having tasted this wine before, he didn't believe it to be a Burgundy. He then correctly identified it as a wine from nearby Jena, stored for some time in a Madeira barrel. Goethe was equally interested in the scientific background of food and wine. He took great pains to describe the soil in Johannisberg in Rheingau (for him one of the best German vineyards) and correlate wine quality with location (terroir) and harvesting time, all of which remain vital to German wine production to this day. Goethe found beer too heavy and coffee made him '*trist*', melancholic, but he grew very fond of hot chocolate in his old age. He always had his own wine bottle at the table in Weimar (a sign of how bottled wine had become normal, at least in cultivated circles, which it wasn't a century earlier). His mother regularly sent him bottlings of his grandfather's old wines from her wine cellar in Frankfurt, which she tagged '*die alten Herren*', the old gentlemen. Goethe's favourite vintage was 1811, *der Eilfer*, the year of the great comet. Just hours before he died in 1832 in Weimar, he sipped wine, albeit diluted with water.

When François Le Goullon, former head chef to the duke's mother Anna Amalia, opened his own Hôtel de Saxe in Weimar, Goethe was a regular customer and frequently had dishes sent over to his own table, including *pâté de foie gras*. In 1829 Le Goullon published *Der neue Apicius*, a cookbook that included instructions on the composition of a proper meal as served in bourgeois circles. The first wine, he stipulated, should be a *Tischwein* or table wine, so called because it was set on the table, one bottle between every two guests. *Würzburger, Rheinwein, Mosel* and *Forster Wein* (from the Pfalz) were recommended whites, and Bordeaux, Tavel or Roussillon the preferred reds. These wines were to accompany the first course, a collection of somewhat simpler dishes. With the second, more elaborate course finer wines were served, such as Burgundy, *edle* (noble) *Rheinwein, Leisten* and *Steinwein* (two of Würzburg's best vineyard sites), plus red and white sparkling Champagne. This was to be followed by fruit and dessert accompanied by old Johannisberger, Xeres, Alicante, Cap de Constance and *ächter* (real) Hungarian Tokay (a selection that highlights how far trade had extended). According to Le Goullon (who by the way considered Teltow turnips fine vegetables to be pot-roasted with sugar and butter), dinner was to be completed with coffee, sugar water and liqueurs.

Coffee, together with potatoes and sugar, was one of the three culinary newcomers that had by then found their way on to the wider food scene.

53.4.

Johann Simon Kerner, 'Teltow Turnips', in *Abbildung aller ökonomischen Pflanzen* (Stuttgart, 1793). The tasty organic turnips grown by Axel Szilleweit today resemble this drawing.

Although they all fundamentally changed existing habits and continue to shape foodways up to the present day, the ways in which they conquered Germans' cups, plates and fancies were very different. The first report in German on *Chaube*, as coffee was called then, came from the Augsburg physician and botanist Leonard Rauwolf in 1582. Venice had its first coffeehouse around 1645 and London in 1652, although often existing inns just changed their names to adapt to the new fashion. When the drink was introduced to the French court in 1669, it became a social must-have in Germany as well. English and Dutch merchants opened a coffeehouse in Hamburg in 1677 (other sources mention 1679 or 1687). Leipzig followed suit in 1694 and Berlin finally joined the canon in 1721. In England tea quickly followed in coffee's footsteps, appearing at the same addresses from 1658. Since it was a particularly lucrative commodity it was heavily promoted and quickly surpassed coffee, whereas in Germany only the north really took to the dried leaves. East Frisians developed a tea culture that rivalled the English one, favouring a strong dark Assam type, the so-called *Ostfriesenmischung*, served with rock candy and liquid cream.

The rest of Germany embraced coffee. Coffeehouses became social meeting places, with not only the latest newspapers but a reputation for intense political discussion associated with intellectual progress and modernity (and in some cases social unrest). While men could socialize in public, women were relegated to *Kaffeekränzchen*, private coffee visits, which usually took place at home in the morning or afternoon. This ritual became so influential across all cultural sectors that the Jewish population developed a kosher adaptation for occasions where coffee was to be served after a meal which had included meat, replacing milk or cream with beaten egg white.

The coffee habit quickly spread to poorer households, popularized as a break from the monotony of the day's labour among those who worked at home. By 1780 coffee had replaced the morning bowl of soup or gruel, a development that was helped by the availability of more affordable coffee surrogates such as *Zichorienkaffee*, a coffee taste-alike made with roasted chicory root. During the 1770s chicory, a plant indigenous to Germany, created a whole new industry, with centres in Brunswick and Magdeburg. Ersatz coffee, known as Prussian coffee,

Mrs Everthirsty, born Coffeelove, and Hans Everthirsty, c. 1835, coloured etching.

experienced a real boom when Napoleon blockaded the seaports, with one factory alone employing 350 workers. Various other kinds of roasted cereals were also used to eke out the supply of expensive beans, producing a concoction known as *Bauernkaffee*, peasants' coffee, and along the Rhine as *Muckefuck* (a term often presented as a spoonerism of the French *mocca faux*, although this is questionable). References to coffee appeared in popular publications and were included in songs. A cartoon from around 1770 shows a distinctly well-nourished pair of townsfolk labelled Frau Kaffeeschwester, Madam Coffee-sister, and Herrn Bierwanst, Mr Beer-belly, while a folk song set to music by a Saxon music teacher remains popular to this day:

> *C-a-f-f-e-e, trink nicht soviel Kaffee,*
> *nichts für Kinder ist der Türkentrank,*
> *schwächt die Nerven, macht dich blass und krank.*
> *Sei doch kein Muselmann, der ihn nicht lassen kann!*

> C-a-f-f-e-e, don't drink so much coffee,
> the Turkish drink is not good for children,
> weakens the nerves, makes you pale and sick.
> Don't be a Muslim who can't leave it alone!

In 1734 the famous Leipzig composer and choirmaster Johann Sebastian Bach even composed a humorous *Kaffeekantate*, coffee cantata. In the aftermath of the Seven Years War (1756–63), which brought many French soldiers to the northwest and Saxony, coffee was so popular in these areas that the coffeehouses couldn't maintain their established monopoly. Even today Saxons are known as *Kaffeesachsen*.

As the coffee-drinking habit was adopted by all social classes, coffee consumption developed into something of a political issue. The ensuing discussions revealed the upheavals that society in general was experiencing at the time. Traditional social boundaries were called into question by Enlightenment ideas and increasing social mobility through prosperity and education, something the establishment, both liberal and conservative, found worrying, even threatening. How would the social order be maintained if everyone could drink coffee and wear the latest French fashions? Many were convinced that rulers had the right, even the duty, to interfere with people's private lives to protect them from any such harm. As in other countries, the 'coffee plague' was presented as an unhealthy and extravagant habit, especially as the drink was sweetened with equally expensive imported sugar. The anti-coffee crusaders also argued that coffee wasted fuel, corrupted the willingness to work and tempted the peasantry (who were expected to produce as much as possible for the urban population's tables) to consume an unseemly amount of their sweetest milk themselves. The clergy were convinced that the new black beverage was the devil's own brew and kept people from attending church. Coffee, it was said, weakened the German national character, while coffeehouses often had a bad reputation due to the prostitutes – known as *Caffe-Menscher*, coffee sluts – who frequented them. On a political level it was argued that much money was lost by importing an unnecessary luxury, thus running against the mercantilist ideal that the state maintain a positive trade balance. Coffee substitutes, in addition, were claimed to be a waste of good grain and, in the case of chicory, grown in fields that could be better used for other crops. Coffee was also accused of damaging the sale of beer and wine, both domestic products regarded as German national beverages. Beer consumption indeed fell during the eighteenth century, especially in the north, a situation which worried the landed gentry who collected taxes on brewing rights and public inns, a considerable source of income.

The first decree against excessive coffee consumption was issued in 1764 in Brunswick-Wolfenbüttel. It was probably never implemented, though, as there was no agreement on where the line should be drawn between rightful coffee drinkers and those who were abusing the habit. Other decrees followed, together with restrictions and inspections of all kinds, as well as taxes to limit the sale of both the raw material and the beverage. These measures resulted in a lively black market and large-scale smuggling. Most famous of the official measures was Frederick II of Prussia's introduction of *Kaffeeriecher* or coffee sniffers, some 400 invalided soldiers who patrolled the streets of Berlin searching out the scent of roasted coffee beans. The state held a monopoly on coffee roasting, and only the nobility, clergy and senior civil servants were permitted to purchase the less expensive unroasted beans. By the 1790s the wave of prohibitions on coffee consumption finally waned and it was no longer a subject of political interest (although it would reappear in the nineteenth century as a reaction to pauperization). Coffee did not fully achieve the transformation from expensive luxury to everyday pleasure until the 1960s, and even today coffee prices can be a sensitive political issue in Germany.

Sugar developed into an indispensable partner of the new hot drinks. While cane sugar certainly became more affordable during the sixteenth

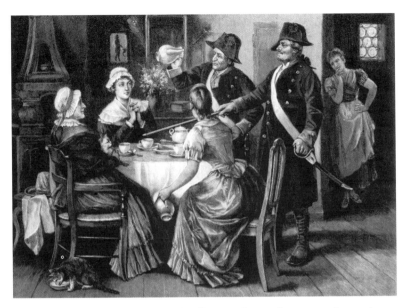

Louis Katzenstein, *Prussian Coffee Smellers*, c. 1785, wood engraving after a painting by Louis Katzenstein of 1892.

century, it wasn't until Brazil and the West Indies joined Sicily and Madeira as leading producers that sugar started to replace honey as a sweetener and rich desserts began to appear more regularly in recipe books. Sugar had long been an exclusive status symbol for the upper classes. Marx Rumpolt was the first to include in his cookbook of 1581 a chapter devoted to *Zucker-Confect*, sugar confections, explaining that his supplies came partly from the pharmacy. He never mentioned honey in the book, though he made clear that marzipan and *Zucker-Confect* were banqueting stuffs for the nobility, whereas the middle classes and peasantry had to content themselves with pastries, fruit and cheese. Affluent members of the middle classes, such as the patricians of Augsburg and Nuremberg, were early users of sugar, while the peasantry could afford it only on the most festive occasions and then tended to use it ostentatiously: highly visible 'red' sugar – possibly unrefined – was sprinkled over millet gruel, the festive dish mentioned earlier that was served at weddings and christenings until well into the eighteenth century (when it was replaced by rice, which was also trickling down the social food pyramid).

Following the example set by the French court, the new bitter-tasting hot drinks were not only sweetened with sugar but came with sweet pastries as a dessert at the conclusion of a meal or as a refreshment for morning or afternoon visitors. Additional models for sugar consumption provided by the French court were liqueur, lemonade, ices and chocolate pralinées. The last were supposedly invented by the cook of the Maréchal du Plessis-Praslin and introduced to Germany in 1676 by the French ambassador on the occasion of the Reichstag in Regensburg.

The new profession of *Conditor* (confectioner) included the production of *Confect*, a category which covered all kinds of sugar-coated fruit and spices previously regarded as medicine. *Conditoren*, in German also called *Zuckerbäcker*, literally sugar-bakers, also provided the nobility's banqueting tables with elaborate sugar decorations, though these were never actually eaten. Their recipes were shrouded in secrecy, ensuring that sugar confections remained the ultimate status symbol until social change shifted the use of sugar in late eighteenth century.

Once again, however, Germans were lagging behind: in 1800 the tea-drinking English wouldn't have lasted very long on the amount of sugar Germans consumed on average, just 1 kg per year, estimated to have doubled from a century earlier.[5] Hamburg was the leading centre in Germany for sugar refining and the sugar trade because of the large number of Dutch refugees in the city, who had long been familiar with sugar through their Caribbean plantations. The first Prussian sugar factories were founded in the mid-seventeenth century, but locally refined cane sugar was of inferior quality and expensive, in spite of protective tariffs. The future of sugar production altered dramatically in 1747 when Andreas Sigismund Marggraf and Franz Carl Achard successfully produced sugar from a strain of mangel wurzel (*Beta vulgaris*) known today as sugar beet. Achard founded the first beet sugar factory in 1801 in Cunern in Silesia. Because of a lack of funds and mismanagement, the

Max Liebermann, *Workers in Turnip Field*, 1876, oil on canvas.

venture proved a failure. The king refused to grant royal privilege, as he thought it important to include the existing sugar refiners in any future developments. In 1792 a Berlin cane sugar refinery took the form of a joint stock company with 71 shareholders, all of them Berlin merchants, pointing the way towards new and more liberal trading regulations. By 1799, however, as a result of the Napoleonic Wars and the Continental Blockade, sugar beet was considered necessary to satisfy demand in Prussia, and officials published instructions on cultivation of sugar beet and information on how to use the product in the manufacture of syrup, sugar in crystal form and spirits. They also offered financial rewards for anybody able to reach a certain annual production, although this only came to fruition when sugar taxation was simplified in 1810.

Between 1799 and 1815, 36 sugar beet refining manufactures were founded in Prussia, although many of them were short-lived and the rest only flourished due to the trade embargo imposed by Napoleon on England from 1806 to 1814. After the embargo the price of sugar and with it beet sugar production (which was still much less profitable than refining imported cane sugar, due to the exploitation of slave labour in the latter's production) dropped significantly in Germany. In France and French-occupied German territories, however, Napoleon strongly promoted the manufacture of beet sugar, going so far as to prohibit the use of imported cane sugar in 1813. At the time 33 kg of harvested beets yielded only 1 kg of unrefined sugar (and 2 kg of syrup), as compared to the 1 kg of refined sugar that can be made today from just 7 kg of sugar beet. This is as much a result of higher technical efficiency as it is of the development of modern beet varieties with a higher sugar content. Beet sugar production in France continued after Napoleon's demise, whereas Germany returned to refining cane sugar until the 1840s.[6]

In contrast to the craze for coffee and sugar, potatoes were accepted much more reluctantly, especially among the middle classes. Introduced first to the rich as a decorative exotic plant from South America, potatoes were not seen as food fit for humans and were often used as animal feed. Because of this potato cultivation in Germany spread unevenly, both in time and in space. The early history of the potato is difficult to trace because of the linguistic confusion, as we saw earlier in Rumpolt's recipe, between *Erd-Aepffel* or earth apple on the one hand, and the Latin term *Taratouphli* on the other. Whereas the latter stood exclusively for potatoes, *Erd-Aepffel* was a term for tubers in general and, in particular, for a chervil-like plant, *Kerbelrüben* (*Bunium* or *Chaerophyllum bulbocastanum*), whose tuberous roots were often compared to chestnuts in taste. Wolf Helmhard von Hohberg's *Curiosa,* a work published in 1682, had a recipe for *Erd-Aepffel warm und kalt zuzurichten* (earth apples prepared warm and cold), which has been claimed as the first potato salad recipe. However, the *Frauenzimmer-Lexicon,* published some 30 years later, had several recipes for *Erd-Aepffel* and declared them to be *Cyclamen*, which were said to taste like peas and were regarded as very common. An entry on *Tartuffeln* in the same volume makes clear that *Erd-Aepffel* were not potatoes: *Tartuffeln* are the 'roots brought from the American Peru to Germany, looking and tasting almost like *Erd-Aepffel* and now found quite frequently in German gardens'.[7] Until around 1700 the potato as food for people rather than animals was only found in German universities and the grander courts of the nobility. It is only after potatoes made it into the ground more widely that the term *Erd-Aepffel* would be used for these tubers.

In 1591 the ruler of Hessen-Cassel sent a present of *Taratouphli* to the elector of Saxony, mentioning their beautiful flowers. He recommended blanching the numerous tuberous roots first in water, then finishing them in butter, though this seemed to be based more on medical curiosity than serious culinary interest. Meanwhile, in the southern Netherlands, Ireland, England and Scotland, potatoes were already widely planted and accepted as a staple food. The picture is the same in Germany: in regions with soils good enough for reliable grain production, the potato took a long time to find its way into the fields, whereas in more mountainous and economically deprived areas, the population was encouraged to plant the new foodstuff by their priests, physicians, school teachers, civil servants and members of the judiciary, all anxious for the lower classes to be fed better and more reliably. The existing agrarian systems were gradually amended so that fields that had previously been left fallow in summer could be planted with potatoes, allowing production to move in from marginal lands. As it turned out, the potato was by far the most efficient crop on fallow land, although it was certainly not the best for restoring soil quality. It may well have been German mercenaries who promoted the potato's 'second coming', ensuring its popularity among the German lower classes. Eventually the adoption of potatoes into Germans' daily diet was furthered by the need to feed an increasing number of people who worked at home within a growing population. The earliest centres of cultivation were the Palatinate and the Vogtland. In 1731 a chronicle from this Saxon region mentioned potatoes as a staple food (now referring to them as *Erdäpffel*), declaring them as

> introduced fifty and more years ago as a new food. For poor people, they are meat and roast, although at first rather undigestible. They are also made into dumplings and a white starch is produced by squeezing their juice.[8]

The chronicler stressed that potatoes did better on poor soil and conveniently made up for a lack of grain. In neighbouring Saxony-Weimar, where soils were generally more productive, a ducal order of 1739 was needed in order to allow the planting of *Erdtufeln* (an interesting linguistic meddling), though only for the feeding of wild boar, since the duke was a passionate hunter.

The potato's advancement as a popular foodstuff was clearly furthered by heavy price increases in grain as well as bread shortages following war or famine. Because of the bread crisis of 1754 and '55 and in preparation for the Seven Years War, which started the following year, Frederick II of Prussia was keenly aware of how important it was to feed both the army and the rest of the population as the supporting cast in the advancement of his political ambitions. He strongly encouraged his peasants to plant potatoes, for example by distributing seed potatoes. The astute observer of human behaviour had potato fields guarded by his own men, thus arousing curiosity among farmers, and didn't hesitate to recur to a little benevolent force, as his initiative seems to have been not quite such a rapid success as is often thought. It was however made famous (in the patriotic late nineteenth century) through a painting that depicts the king himself inspecting potato fields in the marshlands of the River Oder. In Bavaria potatoes gained ground with the help of the innovative American Benjamin Thompson (later Count Rumford), who promoted his famous *Armensuppe*, a potato-based paupers' soup. Not much later, in 1819 (and thus a witness to varying regional acceptance), a monograph on the potato was published in Weimar/Thuringia.[9] By now the term *Kartoffel* had been forged and the work described 33 varieties in great detail, offering advice on their cultivation and use both for animal feed and human consumption. It gave instructions on cooking and preserving potatoes, as well as on making potato bread, butter, cheese and even wine. One of Germany's best-loved dishes, *Thüringer Klösse* or Thuringian potato dumplings, can be traced back as far as 1757. Dumplings had been

Potatoes prepared in various forms. Rice and noodles definitely play a secondary role. From the popular GDR cookbook *Kochen* (Leipzig, 1983).

prepared well before the introduction of the potato, but that year the weekly newspaper *Weimarisches Wochenblatt* recommended mixing two parts of boiled grated potatoes with one part flour and one part grated bread, adding a few eggs, milk, butter and salt to make dumplings for boiling and baking. When potatoes largely replaced the more expensive flour and bread in the diet of the poor, more sophisticated dishes such as dumplings allowed for social differentiation, despite the tubers' wide availability.[10]

The increase of the population through the second half of the eighteenth century that was sustained in particular by potatoes has been estimated at about 50 per cent.[11] This greatly pleased mercantilist and militarist rulers, but had its drawbacks. Land became scarce, since more or less all viable areas were already under cultivation. This resulted in steep rises in food prices. The public as a whole took a great interest in agricultural matters, leading to the hatching of a great many plans by economists. While these schemes were not always practical or successful, they pointed in the right direction, promoting new ideas such as bringing fallow land into summer cultivation, growing clover as animal feed, stabling cattle, improving seed banks and introducing new methods in animal breeding and husbandry. The model for these innovations was the agricultural system of England. At the time, economically as well as in land use, England was a century ahead of Germany. Many English agricultural publications were translated into German, and civil servants as well as the more affluent of Germany's farmers travelled to England to study modern agricultural practices and technology. However, all these initiatives were limited by the inflexibility of Germany's feudal society as well as related agrarian structures such as the commons. In spite of the emergence of new forms of industry and production methods (and in contrast to England), the majority of Germans still lived in villages or small rural towns where agriculture was part of most people's existence. Peasants were reluctant to experiment, since even one bad crop presented them with severe economic problems or hunger. Total yields varied widely from year to year, and productivity was almost impossible to increase due to the lack of manure. In a vicious circle of problems untended or poorly cultivated common land could feed only a limited number of animals, and even these were undernourished. Although in theory it may have seemed preferable to keep cattle permanently stabled, the labour involved in producing sufficient grain-feed and bedding straw was unsustainable. In addition the capital investment and other resources required to build large sheds were unfeasible for an impoverished peasantry.

The political situation of the peasantry improved slowly from around 1800 onwards. This was partly a result of the French Revolution and partly a response to economic necessity and the need to increase productivity while lowering costs. Some rulers turned against the feudal class system, since it was in competition with the state. Gradually serfdom was abolished, although the peasantry were often unable to meet compensation payments with the result that their freedom remained somewhat theoretical. Likewise the nobility in general was reluctant to abandon a lifestyle based on status and privilege. But gradually a new class system replaced the old one of feudal loyalty and the new mobility in the labour market was an important precondition for further economic development.

Arguably the most important German agronomist of the time was Albrecht Thaer, who published his *Grundsätze der rationellen Landwirtschaft* (Principles of Rational Agriculture) from 1809 to 1812. The work was a plea for efficiency in agriculture as a way of maximizing profitability, calling for the liberalization of market forces to allow production to regulate itself. With time land enclosure, an essential step towards more efficient cultivation, was put into practice, again following the English example. With the same aim, owners of smallholdings were moved out of their villages and resettled next to the fields they cultivated in regions such as the Allgäu. In others, like the drained marshlands of the Oder, whole new villages were designed with the sole purpose of increasing productivity. Important innovations included the introduction of new animal feed cultivars such red clover, alfalfa, onobrychis, turnips and ryegrass (a mix dubbed *Kunstgras*, artificial grass) into the cycle of crop rotation. Similarly pushing agrarian reform in Germany was purpose-built agricultural machinery such as clod crushers, seed drills and iron ploughs.

English livestock farmers also led the way with their selective breeding techniques that produced larger, faster-growing cattle and sheep that converted feed to meat and milk more efficiently. Among German economists, Friesians were renowned for their milk-producing qualities in the north, as were Simmenthal in the south, but it was clear that both breeds needed plenty of feeding if they were to successfully replace adapted local breeds which, if equally well fed, could be just as efficient. Average milk yields were around 700 litres per cow per year, with fresh milk rather than butter or cheese the most economically advantageous commodity (assuming the proximity of a suitable market). Sheep were mostly kept for their wool on large estates by landowners who could afford to crossbreed local varieties with expensive Merinos imported from Spain. Pig raising was of little economic value as they continued to be fattened in the beech and oak forests, remaining genetically close to wild boar and therefore not very vigorous.[12] However, with new lifestyles and rising demand from a growing population, the pressure on food production built up. The meat market provides good examples of the advantages and disadvantages guilds represented. Home slaughtering, a practice once common even among urban middle class households, was on the decline from 1750 onwards. With this came the move from salted to fresh meat, encouraged not least by health warnings against excessive salt consumption. While guild regulations restricted free trade, they made for equal opportunities for all buyers at meat shops and markets. Guild inspectors guaranteed that different kinds of meat were available at all times at set prices, and presented in an organized way, with the fattest meat regarded as the most desirable and lesser cuts priced accordingly. Battles between guilds and town officials sometimes ended with trial slaughters to determine the value of such meat as was available.

Bernhard Winter, *Slaughter*, 1924, oil on canvas.

Nevertheless the guild system increasingly proved a hindrance to the economically ambitious merchant. As production methods improved and became more efficient, economic pressure from overseas imports (nineteenth-century 'globalization') stimulated the market for mass-produced items. There had been manufacturing activities in the less fertile rural regions, particularly the lower slopes of mountainous areas, since the end of the Middle Ages. Over time these developed into dense production areas, in particular for textiles, made under the *Verlagswesen* or outworker system. Those who worked at home depended on their middle-men, the merchants, both to provide raw materials and to market the finished products. Unsurprisingly home workers were poor and their meals monotonous. Essentially based on potatoes and coffee, they lacked both the vegetables and meat eaten in the north, and the flour, fat, milk and eggs which provided a balanced meal in the south. A traveller's report from rural Silesia in 1783 described the only food available in a small village on the border of Bohemia as oat bread, butter, cheese and milk. Meat, said the traveller, was consumed only once a year at the fair in a neighbouring village.[13]

Ambitious rulers and their civil servants began to centralize production in urban areas, establishing *Manufakturen*, small factories. The Prussian kings were especially motivated by the need to increase production, since their population had grown by over 60 per cent in half a century, with about one-third of people then living in towns; an exceptionally high number in the German context. While trading centres such as Nuremberg and Cologne slowed or stagnated, cities like Berlin, Stuttgart and Munich blossomed, assisted by state subsidies and protectionism. Urban fields, stables and barns still provided additional food for town dwellers but were by no means able to satisfy the new demand. The modern food industry that developed from around the turn of the nineteenth century became the underpinning of the Industrial Revolution, each fostering and stimulating the other. When the Industrial Revolution really took off during the second half of the nineteenth century, the new factory jobs pushed up the wages for agricultural workers: even more rationalization in food production, as well as increasing imports, were the results.

This interdependent development was by no means smooth. Food production took some time to catch up to the economic growth that had begun in the luxury sector, where trade was less rigidly controlled than the market for everyday supplies, which was still under the guild system. But gradually the requirements of the urban population as well as growing official interest in the factories became more important than those of agrarian producers, who tried to limit the price of raw materials in order to keep food costs down. Eventually urban craftsmen were favoured over their rural colleagues. Specialist producers such as the *Pfefferküchler,*

Otto Günther, *Day Workers from Thuringia*, 1875, oil on canvas. The meat seems to be reserved for the oldest male at the table.

gingerbread bakers, and distillers needed an urban environment to run a successful business. Statistics from 1776 indicate that urban areas, particularly Berlin, had fewer bakers, butchers and millers per inhabitant than rural areas, but each had more employees, a trend that points towards concentration and increasing labour division. In smaller towns processing of expensive wheat flour was delegated to bakers, whereas everyday rye bread was mostly baked at home. Berlin was an exception to this rule, a foretaste of things to come. Here all bread was baked by professionals: 98.4 per cent of all wheat bread and 93.2 per cent of all rye bread was bought from the baker, compared to 81.3 per cent and 15.2 per cent respectively in small towns. In 1752 in Brandenburg (the city of Berlin and the province surrounding it) more than half of the value of all imports could be ascribed to foodstuffs, mainly sugar, wine, cattle, butter and cheese, as well as smaller amounts of herring, spices, citrus and tropical fruits, tobacco, fish and other seafood, along with coffee, tea and cocoa. By 1781 imports of coffee and sugar has almost doubled, as had those of grain, cattle and distilled spirits. Wine, beer and vinegar imports decreased during the same period. In the case of vinegar this was certainly due to the promotion of local industry. In 1777 Berlin businessmen founded a wine vinegar factory in Zossen, protected by higher taxes on imported vinegar, and in 1787 by a general import ban and a drastic reduction in taxation of local wine for vinegar production. In 1798 Berlin had eleven vinegar factories with a total of 25 employees – which could be interpreted to mean that at the time the wine produced around Berlin might have been better suited to vinegar production than to being drunk as such.

When Prussia began establishing factories it introduced even more protectionist measures to reduce expensive imports, favouring internal trade between her own provinces over trade with other German states. Unsurprisingly smuggling was widespread, mainly of coffee and spirits, since consumption proved difficult to limit. In 1800 the food industry, mostly involved in the manufacture of oil, sugar and chicory as a coffee substitute, was in the third most economically important industry behind the textile and metalworking industries.

During the same period agricultural production in Brandenburg increased, especially of potatoes and legumes, crops whose byproducts were used as animal feed. Dairy farming was thoroughly encouraged with *Holländereien*, state-supported dairies modelled on the Dutch system of state-sponsored dairy herds. A model dairy for teaching purposes was installed in 1780 at Königshorst northwest of Berlin by a family from East Frisia, and by 1800 Brandenburg had more than 100 dairy farms.[14]

Spreewaldgurken, the pickled cucumbers from the Spreewald region favoured by the Prussian king Frederick II, illustrate how food production was influenced by politics. The Spreewald region, now an hour by car from Berlin in the direction of the town of Cottbus and the Polish border, is a primeval landscape of forests and swamps. The flat land begins where the River Spree flows through the Baruth Urstrom Valley and continues into the Sorb enclave that reaches from this point through the Lower and Upper Lausitz to the German-Czech border. The roots of the Serbja or Serby, as the 60,000 Sorbian Slavs living in this region call themselves, go back to the migration period during the fall of the Roman Empire when many Slavic tribes left their original home regions in Eastern Europe. As a result of the expansionism to the east by German rulers, their realm shrunk until the Sorbs finally took refuge in the swamps along the Spree. Until well into the twelfth century the Sorbs shared this region with German immigrants, cutting tiny fields and meadows out of the moorland. They primarily cultivated millet, buckwheat and linseed. Experts are divided as to when cucumbers made their first appearance in the Spreewald. Some believe that seeds excavated from the early Slavic settlement at Tornow close to Calau prove that cucumbers were brought with the Huns and Tartars. However, the majority opinion is that the cucumber was introduced in the area by Dutch immigrants at the end of the 1600s. Etymology reveals that the German *Gurke* derives from the Old Polish *ogurek* (in contemporary Polish *ogórek*, which also goes back to the Middle Greek *águros*), though the Lower Sorbian *górka* sounds even closer.

When the German gastro-philosopher Karl Friedrich von Rumohr in 1822 wrote of sour or pickled cucumbers from the Lausitz, he unquestionably meant Spreewald cucumbers:

> However, it is the true destiny of cucumbers to be preserved in various ways, for their glassy-spongy cell structure makes them extremely receptive for every flavour which they can develop themselves or acquire from outside.

Here is his recipe for curing cucumbers:

> Lay larger but still unripe cucumbers together with fennel dill, vine, and cherry leaves in brine, allow a slight fermentation to

begin so that they keep the balance between salty and vinegar-sour, like a really tasty sauerkraut. Sour cucumbers are preserved in great quantities and excellent quality in Bohemia, the Lausitz and in a large part of the Slavic North.[15]

If we assume that the Spreewald Sorbs did cultivate cucumbers from the beginning, there is still no proof that they pickled them, although they did have all the ingredients necessary for this: good water, salt, onions, horseradish, dill, mustard, garlic, vine and sour cherry leaves. However, the Dutch weavers whom Joachim II von der Schulenburg brought in 1580 to Lübbenau, which then belonged to Saxony, certainly prepared them in this way. When they found that their weaving brought them little success they began growing cucumbers, which they knew from their homeland, and quickly found that the damp, warm, peaty-sandy moorland soil was ideally suited for the wind-sensitive and thirsty plants. Soon they were making more money from cucumbers than from weaving. At the beginning of the eighteenth century they were regularly transporting punt-loads of cucumbers to Berlin, where they proved a resounding success. However, the tight-fisted Prussian king Frederick William I was frustrated that the profits from this trade flowed out of his state into neighbouring Saxony, and persuaded 30 Lübbenau families to settle in the Prussian Lower Spreewald. His idea was that they should not only grow cucumbers but assist in the process of internal colonization. This led to the *Gurken Krise* or cucumber crisis, an exchange of diplomatic blows between Prussia and the Saxon court of August the Strong. But in no way did it affect the Berliners' enthusiasm for Spreewald cucumbers and they were a regular feature on Frederick II's menu during the second half of the eighteenth century. In the late 1860s the Berlin writer Theodor Fontane called Lübbenau 'the fatherland of sour cucumbers'.

Spreewald cucumbers saw more ups and downs in the twentieth century and their revival following German reunification is in part linked to tourism. Sorbs were heavily persecuted under the Nazis, but tolerated during GDR times, just as minorities in the Soviet Union were encouraged to assume a certain cultural autonomy. So on the one hand double-language signs and schools went up, while on the other the area around the beautiful Spreewald swamps was brutally affected by shallow brown-coal mining. The punts moored in Lübbenau, once the only means of transport, as well as the Sorbian women's traditional costume with their characteristic bonnets, are on the borderline between folklore and living cultural history. The Sorbian culinary influence has long become assimilated: jacket potatoes with quark and linseed oil, cucumber salad, potato pancakes and sausage with buckwheat groats are mostly identified in contemporary Germany as Eastern European rather than specifically Sorbian.

The difficulty of modernizing crafts and trades which had been established under the feudal system can clearly be seen in the way the *Mühlenbann*, grain milling ban (or prohibitions), hindered technical and social progress. Typically only one designated mill could be used by a community for grinding grain, guaranteeing the miller's livelihood and ensuring that his services were available. For a state interested in taxes, millers were a secure source of income, but the ban also meant that millers could not augment their income by taking in more customers and therefore had no incentive to improve service or invest in modern technology. The milling ban in Prussia was lifted in 1808 and replaced by a purchase tax. With free trade introduced as a general rule in 1810 and the labour market liberated from the constraints of the guilds, wages became the normal form of payment and competition increased. This almost immediately affected the grain growing industry: the number of mills increased, especially the more advanced and efficient Dutch windmills, with breweries installing their own in-house mills that used horsepower. In the 1820s more and more merchants investigated and invested in modern milling technology from England and the United States. Most importantly, steam-powered mills arrived in Berlin in 1824. With these the genuinely industrial revolution of the food industry became irreversible.[16]

As we have seen, this was closely linked to urbanization. In 1800 big cities were rare in Germany. Berlin was by far the largest, with almost 200,000 inhabitants, while Hamburg had just over 100,000 residents, Munich 60,000, Cologne 40,000, Nuremberg and Augsburg 25,000–30,000. In comparison London counted close to a million people. The food habits of the middle classes, who flourished in urban surroundings, gradually came to dominate the general picture.

Hamburg was particularly renowned for the good life, and paid special attention to food and drink. However, then as earlier, even wealthy households were often content with a simple meal: generally a soup followed by a substantial meat course, preferably boiled beef, veal or mutton (the least favoured). On special occasions non-seasonal luxury foods were introduced, such as cherries grown under glass in winter or lamb in December. Many affluent Hamburg *Bürger* had an ox slaughtered in autumn, and *Rauchfleisch*, smoked beef, was a famous Hamburg speciality praised by the romantic poet Heinrich Heine in his *Memoiren des Herren von Schnabelewopski* of 1832. Fish in general had become rare, possibly because of overfishing, and was correspondingly expensive, though herring made occasional and unpredictable appearances as large shoals. Bread came in all forms, from white wheaten loaves for the rich to the dark pumpernickel-like rye that was an important part of the diet of the poor. However, nothing was as popular as potatoes, which were eaten daily by everybody: by choice in affluent circles, out of necessity by the poor. Legumes, sauerkraut, celeriac and turnips were brought in by water from Magdeburg and Berlin, although fresh vegetables were too expensive for less wealthy families. Strawberries were cultivated on the drained marshes south of the city, and abundant for four weeks every summer, to be enjoyed daily with wine or milk. According to the same report from 1801, Hamburg had English and French restaurants, pastry bakers and even an *Italienerkeller*, supposedly an Italian restaurant or wine bar, frequented by young people and tourists. Ice cream was increasingly popular at feasts and offered in summer by almost every *Konditor* or pastryshop. So popular was the delicacy that after a mild winter a Hamburg company was able to ship ice in from Greenland and still make a good profit.

In a report from Stuttgart in 1815 the most important differentiation between the social groups was the gap between the poor (by far the largest group) and everybody else. The poor ate three meals a day, just like the rest of the population, but they lived mostly on potatoes (instead of meat and the traditionally favoured flour-based dishes), washed down with cider or perry rather than the wine enjoyed by the rich. Chocolate, tea and punch were likewise reserved for the more affluent, who served coffee with milk and rolls, usually at breakfast and often also after lunch, together with a pipe. It is striking that the report mentioned that they preferred their coffee without sugar, possibly a way of distancing themselves from the poor, who would drink sweetened but very thin real or ersatz coffee twice or three times a day in order to quell their hunger.

As for Munich, the Berlin academic and publisher Friedrich Nicolai, writing in 1785, was particularly struck by the level of beer consumption in that city, which far exceeded that of Berlin. In Munich, he noted, beer was drunk by all social classes, whereas in Berlin the common man drank more distilled spirits and women drank coffee:

The middle and lower classes in Munich eat copiously and rather coarsely, with flour-based dishes mostly very ordinary but regarded as special by locals . . . However in good houses and inns, the food can be very good and varied and better suited to a northern palate than in Austria, as it is less soft.[17]

Up to the present day, *Biergärten*, beer gardens, are a distinctive feature of Munich and Bavarian social life. They resulted from the loosening of guild restrictions in the early nineteenth century, when breweries started to sell their beer to thirsty souls directly from the cellar. Innkeepers obviously weren't too happy about this new competition, which proved particularly strong because breweries tended to be located near rivers, in cool, shady locations. This in turn went back to a decree from 1539 that banned beer brewing during the summer months because of the risk of fire. In reaction to this a new brew was developed that was stronger and contained more malt, so that it could be produced in March and kept over the summer if stored at low temperatures. Therefore breweries dug deep cellars, filled them with ice in winter and happily sold their *Märzen* (literally March beer). Their wooden benches typically stood under large horse chestnut trees, originally planted to cool the underlying cellars. To appease the angry innkeepers, the king limited the brewers' hospitality to beer – with the exception of bread, food had to be brought along. Today beer gardens are allowed to sell *Brezen* (pretzels), *Weisswurst* (white sausages), *Radi* (radishes), *Obazda* (a highly seasoned kind of cream cheese) and much else, but bringing along one's own hamper is still popular.

The culmination of Munich beer lust is obviously the Oktoberfest. This goes back to the same Bavarian king, the so-called König Max, Maximilian 1 Joseph, said to have been a gourmet and seen more frequently on the Schranne (a precursor of today's Viktualienmarkt) than with his troops. The crown prince's wedding in October 1810 was celebrated with a horse race on the Theresienwiese (named after the bride), then situated on the outskirts of Munich, but today more central. The popular king invited his people to celebrate with bread, mutton, sausages, beer and Austrian white wine while the newlyweds sat under an Osman tent, a spoil of the Ottoman war. Bavaria had recently added Franconia to its realm and the royal event was a useful way of stressing a unifying national identity. The following year the festival was expanded to include an agricultural show, and later also a shooting match. In 1819 most of

A. Adam, *Oktoberfest in Munich*, 1824.

the agricultural exhibits were replaced by stalls selling beer, wine and all kinds of food. Twelve brewers, one wine merchant, two coffee sellers, three liqueur merchants and one fruiterer, four pastrycooks, six cooks and three bakers offered their wares. The Oktoberfest had found its present form. With time the event acquired huge economic and logistic dimensions with over six million visitors today (as opposed to 100,000 in 1860). Many modern visitors sport the Bavarian *Tracht*, 'traditional' attire, which was actually invented in the late nineteenth century, including *dirndl* dresses for women and *Lederhosen*, leather knee breeches, for men – outfits much of the world takes to be traditional German national dress, just as Oktoberfest fare is thought of as typically German food. The almost 40 hectares of the *Wiesn*, as the locals call it, attracts many foreign visitors, especially from northern Italy and the u.s., and is as much a family destination as it is an occasion for companies to treat their customers to a night out. Everything from breakfast, to coffee and cake, to all kinds of Bavarian *Schmankerl* is on offer. *Brathendl* (grilled chicken) alone are consumed at rates of about half a million each season. Grilled *Haxn* (pork shanks) and grilled sausages are also popular. As in Munich's beer gardens, people can bring along their own food as well. The main action takes place in over 30 tents, some of them gigantic halls seating up to 10,000 people. They are run by the larger breweries or independent restaurateurs. All have live music, mostly *Blasmusik* by traditional brass bands. A special *Wiesnbier* is brewed for the occasion, which is somewhat stronger in alcohol. It is served in a *Mass* (a beer mug containing 1 litre). The original mugs were made of glazed earthenware, but due to repeated complaints about filling irregularities, they are now all glass. Then as now, the visitors' thirst remains vigorous: these years, more than 60 million *Mass* are emptied each year, an average of ten per visitor.

Bourgeois living room and kitchen, *c.* 1840.

EIGHT

Potatoes without Salt and Soup Kitchens: Pauperism, 1815 to 1871

Potatoes boiled in their jackets without salt, soup with black bread, a little lard, oat porridge supplemented by the occasional helping of 'black' dumplings (made from raw potatoes) – without potatoes, industrialization in Germany might not have happened, or at least not so quickly or so fully. Potatoes filled the bellies of the workforce and sustained their rapidly rising numbers. They could be grown in marginal soils and were ready to eat as soon as they were dug. Soon the poor almost abandoned bread. The change was remarkably rapid. While in 1800 legumes and bread were the staple foodstuffs in northern German poorhouses, 40 years later potatoes were set on the table twice or three times a day. The meal plan of the Brunswick poorhouse in 1842 recommended 1 kg of potatoes and 130 g of legumes per person per meal. White beans and potatoes were served on Sundays, pearl barley and potatoes on Mondays, carrots and potatoes on Tuesdays, lentils and potatoes on Wednesdays and Saturdays, peas and potatoes on Thursdays and swede and potatoes on Fridays. Additionally potatoes were served on three nights a week in the form of soup combined with oats, or just boiled in their skins.[1]

The circle was a vicious one in two aspects. On the one hand, reliance on a single foodstuff involved great risks in the form of plant diseases and resulting crop failures. On the other hand, with labour in abundance, employers didn't hesitate to exploit it, something that was still regarded as morally acceptable. At this early stage of industrialization, technology was less advanced than in competing countries and progress often depended on human muscle-power. Many industrial tasks were still very simple and could be done by unskilled labour, in particular in the mining industry, which provided the essential raw material for railways and trains, machinery and tools. There the lot of children was particularly bleak. Starting work at a very young age, they were forced to attend school after long shifts at work, and survived on a diet of black coffee-substitute, black bread, potatoes and salt. Often they lived so far from the workplace that their parents lodged them with the families of fellow workers. Child labour would be only legally regulated when draft officers on recruitment drives in industrial regions failed to raise the expected numbers because of the poor health of the candidates. In 1835 a newborn child from a noble family's chance of attaining his or her fifteenth birthday was 91 per cent, falling to just 58 per cent if they were poor and urban. The difference in attitude between British employers and those in Germany was underlined in a debate in the British parliament of 1846, when recommendations to limit the workday to ten hours were put forward but opposed; the naysayers gave as a reason the far longer hours worked in Germany.[2]

The nineteenth century was a period of great change in Germany. Personal freedom, universal laws and legal equality came to replace estates, privileges and feudalism. Motion and speed were the obsessions of the age. But there was a price to be paid. As the British economist Thomas Malthus observed in 1798, food production tended to lag behind population growth. Until around 1850, in spite of potatoes, the balance between the food supply and demand was at best fragile in Germany, although agricultural production rose by 40–50 per cent during this period. This wasn't yet due to technological efficiency, but was mostly the result of extended working hours, often by women. Climatic factors contributed to social and economic changes in this precarious situation. Mass poverty, a condition labelled pauperism by contemporary commentators, was a phenomenon of the age.

The eruption of Indonesia's Tambora volcano in 1815 led to the coldest summer on record the following year, which became known as the year without a summer. It ended in the disastrously severe winter of 1816/17. Famine followed, not least because food distribution was still disorganized. Prices varied widely from district to district and speculation was rampant. People in some rural areas walked many miles to reach towns where bread was marginally less expensive, while the destitute and desperate resorted to whatever they could find: moss, lichen, tree bark, grass roots, nettles, frozen potatoes, unripe grain, straw, sawdust and wood shavings. The same situation returned in the winter of 1846, when grain crops lost to frost had to be ploughed under and replaced by potatoes that then rotted with blight. From an agricultural point of view the situation was not disastrous, but when it was combined with an economic crisis that affected trade and the ability of banks to lend, and the fact that malnutrition and related diseases were rampant, mortality rates soared.[3]

For many hunger was a constant, whether they were in work or not. One often quoted report from 1844 by Friedrich List, a south German liberal revolutionary, mentions that in poor people's houses a herring would be tied to the ceiling with string so it could be passed around the table for rubbing onto potatoes as seasoning. Work that was done in the home, such as spinning and weaving, was increasingly poorly paid as a result of cheaper industrially produced imports from Britain. In Silesia the weavers' chronic situation was so well known that throughout the first two decades of the nineteenth century officials simply dismissed their misery as the normal way of life of the region. When the situation deteriorated in the 1830s bread was distributed to the poor and private organizations tried to help, but even their combined efforts weren't sufficient. In their misery those who worked at home repeatedly revolted, and in 1844 factories were destroyed by the workers. The general public, kept informed through newspaper accounts, was outraged, siding with the employers. The weavers were soon left to return to their own misery, and in 1847 famine and typhoid were rampant in parts of the region. According to reports from the early 1850s many of these people hadn't eaten bread, let alone meat, for years, some surviving on green potato leaves, old beans and cabbage, with a little tallow to bind the thin soup. Even salt was a luxury because it was subject to high taxes.

The lot of agricultural labourers wasn't much better. The population increase led to depressed wages, while in bad years they found themselves without employment. In Württemberg, Baden and the Palatinate the situation was particularly desperate, with local councils often imposing severe restrictions on marriages and new settlements in a vain effort to keep the situation in check. The expression *Kohldampf schieben*, feeling famished, is not, as might be supposed, a reference to a diet overly dependent on *Kohl*, cabbage, but apparently owes its origin to the hard times of the 1830s. It is a combination of two words for hunger in the Yeniche language, which was spoken by an impoverished nomadic people who travelled the roads of Central Europe at the time.

Revolution was in the air, and even the more prosperous middle classes felt increasingly threatened by pauperism. They were also still struggling to find their own food identity. *Bürgerliche Küche* in its

Biedermeier form was unobtrusive, good, solid fare. It was just as much about emancipation from the nobility, the middle classes' former role models, as it was about keeping an anxious distance from the lower classes. Porridge, gruel and related dishes by now symbolized rural backwardness and were deemed only suitable for old people and children. The higher incomes of the middle class translated into more variety in their diet, and they were much less vulnerable to rising food prices. Engel's Law, formulated by a German statistician in the 1850s, pointed out that the lower a household's income the higher the percentage spent on food; 70 per cent was by no means unusual. The prices for eggs, milk, butter and meat, though much more stable than those for grain and potatoes, were nevertheless always beyond the reach of the lower classes.

In retrospect it is easy to analyse this situation and come up with political explanations, but it still seems amazing that the hungry didn't resort to violent protests against the cake-eating upper classes, as they had done in 1789 in France. It could be argued that this was due on one hand to the belly-filling potatoes, but on the other to the essential drugs of the German industrialization, sugar-sweetened coffee and schnapps, as the tubers had also introduced the wider populace to harder stuff. Until around 1800 spirits had been very expensive to produce and were made mostly from grain. They were an exceptional treat mostly consumed in public inns. Distilling from potatoes was not only cheaper, but also capitalized on the fact that the tubers needed to be used in a shorter timespan, since they did not store as well as grain. Once potatoes began to be distilled, schnapps entered the daily diet of the poor.

Both coffee and schnapps were readily available, even to working women who were too time-pressed to cook; they kept workers awake and helped to overcome the feelings of powerlessness and anger as well as the pangs of hunger, be it on the fields, down the mines or, later on, in factories. It thus seems ironic that schnapps in particular was much lamented by the establishment. Miners would get drunk on payday rather than handing over their wages to their wives, the outraged middle classes claimed, while seated in their comfortable armchairs with no need whatsoever to seek an escape from reality. Even more ironically, strong spirits were rendered affordable by the state itself. Potato schnapps was mostly produced on the large estates east of the Elbe. Faced with difficulties in exporting their grain surplus, they converted significant areas to the potato, a cultivar that didn't require major capital investment and, if unsold, could be made into storable spirit, with the mash used as pig

The German borders in 1850.

feed. The state had succumbed to their strong lobby with extremely low taxation that more or less guaranteed a good market for the spirit. In another ironic twist Silesian home weavers, although extremely poor, had access to expensive real coffee, since the cloth they produced was sold by merchants to Central America in exchange for coffee beans. These were passed on to the weavers instead of money – a telling link between one form of slavery and another.[4]

In spite of these poor people's drugs, food riots did occur. In Bavaria, where potato consumption was relatively low, rising grain prices often led to riots. Landless and desperate unemployed day labourers and field workers resorted to blocking and plundering grain transports and attacking merchants, millers and bakers. Trouble in the grain market obviously affected the price of beer, which in Bavaria had long been considered a staple foodstuff, not least because viticulture had virtually disappeared there in the eighteenth century for climatic reasons. As breweries flourished their owners accumulated wealth and status. The long tables in beer gardens attracted an unusually wide span of social groups: labourers sat next to soldiers, and students mixed with middle-class families. When beer prices rose by more than 20 per cent in 1844, thirsty customers protested violently. In Munich in particular bar-room brawls spilled out onto the streets, especially when the heavier and more expensive summer beer was being tapped and the new season's price was announced. These beer riots, however, were poorly organized and achieved even less than the grain riots of rural Bavaria, since beer could not be stored at home. More innovative and considerably more effective were the beer boycotts staged by Munich factory workers at around the same time, the forerunner of a modern form of consumer protest that would be revisited in the 1890s by industrial workers in Berlin.[5]

In many cases the socially concerned members of the establishment set up local charities, trying to help as best they could. Private relief organizations joined town councils' efforts, in many cases distributing firewood and bread. Soup kitchens, the so-called *Rumfordsche Suppenanstalten*, opened all over Germany; they were based on the principles of Benjamin Thompson, Count Rumford. When he developed his famous recipe for a nourishing soup to feed the poor in the 1790s, Count Rumford was in charge of the Munich poorhouses. The ingredients of his inexpensive

L. Gradmann, *Soup Distribution*, c. 1817, aquatint. A soup kitchen modelled on the Rumford idea. The recipients look quite decently clad and pay for the soup.

but filling water-based soup that could be produced in large quantities were potatoes, pearl barley, stale white bread, salt and vinegar or sour beer, with the addition of a nominal amount of meat cut to the size of barley grains. In 1805 a magazine in Görlitz in the Oder region published a proposal to set up Rumford soup kitchens in medium-sized towns, complete with financial and organizational plans, since 'the growing distress of the poor, with the constant rise of prices in all areas, calls for serious thinking about the best way to reduce hardship and save a large part of a town's working inhabitants from total ruin'. The anonymous writer declared that the money distributed by relief funds was insufficient and therefore came up with a strategy in four points: to encourage industriousness, support agriculture, lower prices of the most essential foodstuffs with officials' help, and finally procure healthy and affordable meals for the poor. He further stressed his view that the soup should not be given away for free, as it wouldn't be valued appropriately.[6]

For various reasons emigration throughout the period was deemed by many as the solution to overpopulation and misery. Charity often took the form of collecting money to fund those who could not afford the passage to America. Cologne reported to Berlin in 1816 that 'frequently nowadays persons not provided with passports float down the Rhine on rafts towards Holland. Almost every day people arrive here both by land and by water with similar intentions.' The Dutch ports were crowded with German emigrants, especially from Baden and Württemberg, whose governments actively encouraged people to leave in their efforts to cope with pauperism. From 1830 onwards the economic situation deteriorated, with the imposition of monetary taxation in place of the system of tithes and ground rents paid in kind by the peasantry. To meet these demands peasants had to sell land, further reducing their ability to pay. Since industry was not yet developed enough to provide alternative work, the poor saw no other solution but to leave the country. Emigration remained high until the 1880s, the point at which German industry began to absorb the rural overpopulation. Thereafter and until the First World War, emigration decreased steadily, until it ceased completely during the war.

Labour-hungry Prussia and Russia were among the popular destinations at first, but throughout this period the United States took the vast majority of Germany's emigrants, with Brazil and Australia the next most popular destinations. Of the total number of immigrants to the u.s. from 1820 to 1924, Germans were the second largest ethnic group (only surpassed in numbers by UK citizens, which included the Irish until Eire achieved independence in 1920), representing about 15 per cent of the total populace. Most of them joined relatives and compatriots who had sent for them and often provided funds for their journey. The establishment back home distanced themselves from the lower-class emigrants by pointing at their supposedly unsophisticated food. This reaction was also seen in England, where it was known as 'trollopizing' after Frances Trollope's book *Domestic Manners of the Americans*, published in 1832 and three years later translated into German.[7]

Germans were by no means newcomers to the Americas. The first German-speaking immigrants had landed on American soil as early as 1607. By 1683 thirteen families from around Krefeld had founded Germantown in Pennsylvania. In the years that followed a steady stream of emigrants left Germany for America, particularly peasants from the Palatinate region around Mannheim, who were prepared to risk the expensive and hazardous crossing in order to escape from the poverty caused by interminable wars with France as well as religious and political persecution. These immigrants settled in New Paltz on the Hudson River at first but soon heeded William Penn's call for new settlers to take up the challenge of the South. It was among German immigrants of the East Coast that the style of cooking known as Pennsylvania Dutch was born. In spite of the implied connection with the Netherlands, the name is actually a linguistic corruption of *deutsch*, German; German roots are clearly visible in dishes such as *Schnitz un Gnepp* (apple slices and dumplings), *Schmierkaes* (quark), *Gfillder Seimaage* (stuffed pig's stomach) and *Ebbelkuche* (apple pie).

Most German immigrants quickly found their place in the new surroundings and many of their foodways became 'as American as apple pie'. In the 1840s German immigrants in New York were concentrated in the five- or six-storey brick tenements on the Lower East Side. The area became known as *Kleindeutschland*, Dutchtown, and soon stretched from 14th Street to Division Street in the south and from the Bowery to the river on the east. Low wages and high rents made for overcrowded, dark, stuffy rooms, conditions more suited to immigrants from urban areas, while rural immigrants tended to travel on to the farming regions of Missouri, Wisconsin and Illinois.

In New York many Germans made a living as tailors, printers and carpenters, but a large number worked as dairymen, grocers and butchers. By the late 1850s German family businesses dominated the baking trade.

A culinary place in time: Rogacki, a Berlin deli

Today Rogacki in Berlin's Charlottenburg district conveys some of the atmosphere New York delicatessens are renowned for. Unlike the rubbernecking tourists at luxurious department store Kadewe's famous sixth floor, people at Rogacki (www.rogacki.de) come to buy. In spite of offering more or less everything except fresh fruit and vegetables, its name above all stands for fish. In 1928 Lucia and Paul Rogacki started selling smoked fish in the working-class district of Wedding. Lucia looked after the shop while Paul went with his sister Marie and a handcart to the Alexanderplatz market. Business was good, and in 1932 they moved to the present address, where they started to smoke their own fish. The enterprise now employs 116 people and the present owner, Paul's grandson Dietmar, still uses the old so-called Altona ovens to hot-smoke herring, haddock, salmon and much more at the back of the store. Salads are homemade, as are all manner of pickled and salted herring and cucumbers, and the catering service, or *Stadtküche*, has no hesitation in offering decorated platters which include old-fashioned cheese hedgehogs and pigs formed out of minced pork. Food available to eat in store includes all the traditional German favourites: fried fish, *Schnitzel* and *Leberkäse* (meatloaf), blood and liver sausage, *Eisbein* (boiled ham hock), fried potatoes and potato and cucumber salad, with semolina pudding for dessert. All Berlin stands cheek-by-jowl at the narrow tables, overalls rubbing elbows with fur coats. Ignoring all trends, Rogacki remains unselfconsciously old-fashioned, providing a link to the pre-war food world in a mix of German and Eastern European elements typical of Berlin in the early years of the twentieth century.

Unsurprisingly their bread tended to be on the dark and sour side, and yeast-raised cakes were offered under the German term *kuchen*, cake. German grocers (whose range later on would often overlap and merge with Eastern European Jewish immigrants and the delicatessens of today) offered brine-preserved herring, while German brewers, similarly small-scale family enterprises, introduced Americans to German bottom-fermented beer: lager tasted more refreshing than the previously dominant English ale and proved very popular.

Besides beer, sauerkraut became synonymous with being German in America. Until the end of the Civil War itinerant *krauthobblers*, cabbage-shredders, went from door to door slicing cabbage for home-made sauerkraut, an activity which took place between late October and early December. Henry John Heinz of ketchup fame started his company in 1869 in Pittsburgh with grated horseradish. True to his family roots (he was born in Kallstadt/Palatinate), in the 1890s he built a sauerkraut factory on Long Island. In the bars, saloons and meeting halls of the city itinerant peddlers provided hungry patrons with potato salad as well as sauerkraut and frankfurters, which were kept hot in a metal container slung round their necks. Surprisingly sauerkraut was

Traditional sauerkraut making in our times at the Kimmich factory near Stuttgart.

explicitly kept to a minimum on ships of the Lloyd Line which brought emigrants to the New World. In 1878 official regulations indicated that between-deck passengers were entitled to morning, afternoon and evening tea or coffee with milk and sugar, and white and rye bread with butter; the midday meal was to consist of soup with fresh or dried vegetables, along with 1.7 kg meat per person per week. The meat was to be fresh on two occasions (a hint at the general order of preference), while the third could be salt-cured and take the form of sauerkraut with bacon and potatoes. This requirement, however, might not have corresponded to reality, much like the optimistic assumption in a German historian's dissertation of 1939 that 'good cooking on the emigrant ships was guaranteed by a law which decreed that an experienced cook had to be on board.'[8]

German speakers were renowned for dining as a family and enjoying their food, often congregating in large groups. Shooting clubs and singing societies hosted parades, picnics and *Volksfeste*, open-air festivals. Some of those were impressive affairs, with herring salad, sauerkraut, potato pancakes, Frankfurter sausages, beer and honeycake on offer. Cavernous beer halls lined the Bowery with hearty simple fare including wurst and pretzels. More sophisticated luncheon rooms, known as *Raths-keller* or *Postkeller*, attracted an additional client base of non-German fellow Americans. In 1882 August Lüchow, a waiter from Hanover, took over a simple beer hall at 110 East 14th Street and transformed it into a huge multi-roomed palace lavishly endowed with German *Gemütlichkeit*, coziness. Lüchow's was possibly the most successful and longest running of all German restaurants in the u.s. The restaurant served traditional German and Austrian fare using local ingredients, and offered imported beer from Würzburg and Pilsen as well as the best American beers and the finest Rhine wines. Customers were serenaded by live music from opera to brass band, and in December the restaurant installed a Christmas tree of legendary height. Lüchow's closed in 1986 after having moved to the Theater District two years earlier.[9]

Lüchow's was paradise on earth compared to paupers' situation back home in the 1830s and '40s, where even minor offenders in their desperation often insisted on serving prison sentences in order that they would be fed (needless to say, with price rises, offences involving food increased exponentially). Compared to Silesia's hard-pressed home workers, inmates of institutions such as workhouses did indeed live a life of luxury: meals might well have been meagre, but at least they were guaranteed. The meal plan in a Munich prison at the time consisted of bread and soups made with flour, beans, peas or potatoes, to which meat was added twice weekly.[10] Prison food had always been controversial. Those involved in nutritional science, a growing area of study, made it clear that water and bread did not represent an adequate diet. The public view was that inmates only deserved the barest minimum. As new scientific findings redefined what this should be, fears were expressed that too much food would lead to an increase in the prisoners' sex drive. A more genuine problem was developing a meal plan that could cater to a diversity of age groups, be affordable and keep prisoners reasonably healthy.

Hospitals, prisons, poorhouses and workhouses established in the eighteenth century typically began as independent economic entities that produced most of their own food. With the help of inmates, they grew vegetables and fruit, kept dairy cattle and pigs and processed their own grain and meat. By the early nineteenth century, however, these institutions were becoming ever more crowded. The rapid growth of cities converted rural areas into urban ones, with a subsequent loss of productive farmland and animal husbandry. At the same time the institutions themselves were obliged to tighten their belts and take a long, hard look at food costs. Outsourcing was often cheaper than home production. In prisons as well as hospitals, the goal was a quick and cost-efficient reintegration of inmates into the workforce while providing re-education in good citizenship. Until around 1850 medical care in hospitals took second place to general care, since most patients, predominantly unskilled labourers, servants, craftsmen and travellers suffering from minor complaints, were accepted because they couldn't cater for themselves.

Until that point sickness had commonly been countered by fasting as a direct method of purging the body of 'poisonous' substances. The medical standard of the time (before the advent of modern science) was set by Christoph Wilhelm Hufeland, a friend of Goethe and personal physician to the Prussian queen Louise. In 1797 Hufeland published his very successful *Kunst, das menschliche Leben zu verlängern* (The Art of Prolonging Human Life, renamed *Makrobiotik* in later editions) which was focused not on illness but on the human being as a whole. Hufeland recommended balance and harmony in all things. This was in fact a return to classical medical ideas and a sign of how former influences had not been forgotten, in spite of the obsession with all things French and the court in Versailles: the Grand Tour to Italy was popular and when Goethe went to Rome, he returned with a love of virgin olive oil, artichokes, stufato and Parmesan cheese. A return to holistic medicine meant that

An inmate of the municipal workhouse of Rummelsburg in Berlin receives his meal: a bowl of soup and a slice of bread, c. 1900.

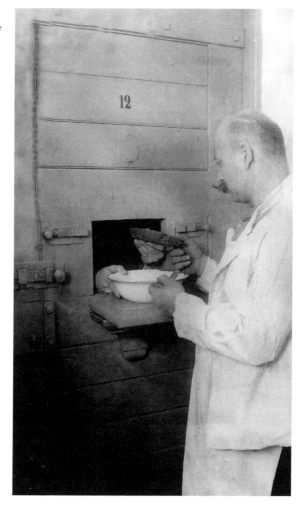

the connection between health and food was renewed – as long as you ate right, you'd be all right. This conviction would be reinforced – albeit underpinned by a new system – in the course of the nineteenth century by the nascent field of food science. It has stuck in the German culinary psyche up to the present day.

Hufeland spawned a whole generation of cookbooks based on his classification of foodstuffs and preparation methods, and stated that the cook's duty was to follow dietetic principles. His recommendations were to become the foundation of vegetarianism and the *Lebensreform* or life reform movement. In 1791 one of Hufeland's colleagues, Johann Christian Reil, had published a rant against *apicische Lekkermäuler*, gluttony in the style of Apicius (anticipating the like-minded gastro-philosopher

Karl Friedrich von Rumohr), while the Wolfenbüttel physician Johann Bücking in his *Diätetischer Hausarzt* (The Dietetic Family Doctor) gave very exact recipes on the same theme. In the 1820s and '30s numerous works followed based on homeopathic principles. These were first conceived in 1796 by the German physician Samuel Hahnemann and were based on the belief that like cures like. They followed the principle that remedies were only needed in extreme dilutions. Under this school of thought, the use of spices in the kitchen was to be extremely reduced and all foods that might interfere with the efficacy of remedies were prohibited, among them cheese, sausage and fish as well as beer and coffee.

Physicians and medical men in general increasingly regarded institutions as a rich source of material for research. The consequences of this were given a public airing by the writer Georg Büchner, who studied medicine. His stage play *Woyzeck* (written in 1836 but published posthumously in 1879) dealt with the establishment's reaction to pauperism. Out of desperation the impoverished protagonist sells himself to a ruthless physician for food-based experiments, referring to the first feeding experiments (on dogs) which took place in the 1820s, during the early days of nutritional science. Medical men became the ultimate authority on hospital food. By 1880 standardized meal plans had been introduced into all institutions. Compared with standard practice in 1800, these plans offered considerably less bread and much more meat, some fish and above all fresh milk, which was regarded as digestible, nourishing and healthy. Potatoes, however, didn't make an appearance until the early years of the nineteenth century, and even then were only recommended in comparatively small quantities. Alcohol was progressively banned, while coffee was only introduced at the end of the nineteenth century, when it was prescribed as a stimulant for medical reasons. Nevertheless, records from the Berlin Charité in 1819 indicate that nurses were enthusiastic consumers of coffee, especially on night shifts. Finances, meanwhile, became more secure as hospital costs were increasingly covered by insurance schemes. Kitchens were better equipped and staff better trained. Public opinion, however, required that meals should not exceed what the average workman could afford, although views differed on what a workman actually ate. After all, institutions were run by middle-class administrators concerned with maintaining appropriate social differences, as symbolized by food. Such limited statistics as are available for workers' households reveal that institutions in general spent more on meat and milk and less on bread, potatoes and vegetables than workers, while hospitals served a richer diet than the average working family could afford. However, records from Berlin in 1879 also show that physicians and staff consumed most of the meat, sausage, fish, butter, cheese, eggs, bread, potatoes, vegetables, fruit, sugar and beer that appear in hospitals' consumption statistics. Patients were only allowed their fair share of milk, rolls and legumes. It is similarly difficult to know how much of the prison food that was officially bought in was actually consumed by inmates, as it might have been sent back as unwanted, or been subject to underhanded deals by the staff.[11]

In the 1840s the liberal ideals that almost paved the way to national unity and a constitution had long been around in the kitchens in the form of *Hausmannskost*. 'Houseman cooking' is the literal translation of a term whose origin can be traced back as far as the final years of the Middle Ages. It fitted the spirit of the nineteenth century well, since it stood for simple, down-to-earth, everyday fare, the very opposite of the nobility's upper-class excess. One of the strongest advocates of the idea that simplicity in food was preferable to indulgence was the German art critic and historian Karl Friedrich von Rumohr. He published his *Geist der Kochkunst* (The Essence of the Art of Cooking) in 1822 in Weimar under the pseudonym of his chef, Josef König. Rumohr was a highly rational, reality-obsessed empiricist whose culinary masterwork preceded Brillat-Savarin's *Physiologie du goût* (1826) and represented the intellectualization of cookery begun by Grimod de la Reynière in his *Almanach des Gourmands* (1803–12). Rumohr's guiding principle was to 'develop out of edible things that which best suits their natural characteristics'. To prove his point, he ridiculed the classical cuisine of the Romans, 'which through mixing and working completely destroys the original character of the dish', and wrote admiringly of the philosophical principles of Horace and Rousseau. Declaring himself in favour of simple meals, it was, he explained, much more important to eat well every day (though not more than was appropriate) than to indulge in occasional extravagant feasts. Even dishes commonly associated with the lower classes and therefore deemed untouchable by the good bourgeois, like soup, were in his opinion viable, and he cited *Olla podrida* as a case in point, presenting this popular stew from the Middle Ages as a culinary relict. Originating in Spain, this rather wild mix of edibles could take awesome dimensions. In 1581 Marx Rumpolt's recipe ran to several pages, bringing together capon and game with offal and garlic, but was pronounced fit even for the king. The patrician upper middle class of the time developed special serving dishes for the *Holiprotiden*, with liquid and solids served separately. In late seventeenth century the term was also used for a ragout made from crayfish, morels and sweetbread, reminding modern German cooks of *Leipziger Allerlei*. At the French court, from the late seventeenth century, all the lowly ingredients in the *pot d'oille* were gradually eliminated: cabbage and leeks were replaced by delicate primeurs, and pork by smoked ham. The result was served in expensive silver dishes, making soup, once a lowly dish, respectable, and in the eighteenth century the base for restorative consommés. Rumohr himself claimed to have rediscovered and modernized the *Olla* on the occasion of a stay in Rome and his health problems with its (in his perception) heavy cuisine. The courtly version of the dish disappeared with the Habsburg monarchy, whose palace in Vienna had a separate Spanish soup kitchen with its own cook. At that time the *oglio* (or *olio*) was a clear soup served at midnight in small cups on the occasion of large court balls. A pared-down version of the Spanish original, certainly much more to Rumohr's taste, survived in Alfred Walterspiel's classic *Meine Kunst in Küche und Restaurant* (My Art in the Kitchen and Restaurant), first published in 1952. It used carrots, Savoy cabbage, leeks, onions, potatoes and some herbs as well as bacon, a shoulder of mutton, a chicken and, if possible, two fried partridges or a pheasant and some ham, with some small sausages, chickpeas and finely shredded lettuce added to the resulting clear broth.

Among Rumohr's contemporaries who also disapproved of excessive consumption at mealtimes were Eugen von Vaerst, whose *Gastrosophie* was published in 1851, and Gustav Blumröder, who published *Vorlesungen über Esskunst* (Lectures on the Art of Eating) in 1838. The same ideas were taken up by novelists such as Adalbert Stifter, who vigorously deplored 'general wretched depravity' in his fellow citizens. Heinrich Heine, a fervent admirer of French cuisine, likewise denounced the gluttony of the moneyed classes of the Biedermeier period in Germany, filling his pages with food-related incidents as examples of culinary vice or virtue.

The middle classes found themselves caught in the same dilemma with music. As with food, they had to feel their own way between upper-class excess and the perceived vulgarity of the streets. In households that consulted and followed works like Sophia Wilhelmine Scheibler's *Küchen-Zettel-Buch* (1832), a collection of menu suggestions, music was an established aspect of the ritual of dinner. For dinner on a Tuesday night in January, Scheibler proposed potato soup, pike made blue (cooked with vinegar) with horseradish and butter, stuffed milk rolls, roasted partridges and a pie. Additional side dishes included anchovies, potatoes, cherries and cabbage dressed as salad, while dessert consisted of either apples, meringues, macaroons, a cake or butter and cheese. Music was played during meals and at in-house concerts both before and after dinner. Bursting into song at table, as is described in the novels of Theodor Fontane, was considered perfectly normal. Johann Sebastian Bach had thought nothing of playing in church one day and in a coffeehouse the next. Nevertheless table music was increasingly regarded as an inferior genre, rejected not only by Rumohr but by serious musicians, and dismissed out of hand by Richard Wagner. The tradition nevertheless continued in the form of light entertainment in spa towns and as an attraction in city cafes. At the opening of Café Kranzler in Berlin in 1825 a band from Italy was announced as a 'divertissement'. Light music was also an important feature of the drinking gardens of Dresden, Leipzig, Berlin and other major cities, where customers were offered artificial mineral water, created in 1820 by physician Friedrich Adolf Struve and based on the medicinal spring waters of Karlsbad.[12]

In a further effort to distance themselves from the lifestyle of the nobility, their indulgence in luxury and the pursuit of leisure, bourgeois circles reprimanded those women who only issued orders to their servants. Many expected them instead to take an active part in the management of the household and join the servants in the kitchen. During the nineteenth century cookbooks changed accordingly: for instance, they took into consideration the fact that urban households increasingly depended on buying their food instead of producing it themselves. Shopping and storage needed special knowledge and diligence. Scheibler in the *Küchen-Zettel-Buch* strongly advised against keeping anything prepared in any way longer than a day, especially in summer. Technological improvements rarely extended to cooling, mostly consisting of new cooking stoves, which permitted a more efficient use of fuel. From the 1860s onwards the most widely accepted of these was the *Sparherd* or economic stove originally developed by Count Rumford. It was a closed iron range equipped with regulated air supply and up to five hot plates with a separate oven and hot-water cistern; factory-produced, it was easy to transport and install, making traditional stove fitters redundant.

Pauperism and the ensuing migrations disrupted the traditional transfer of cooking skills from one generation to another, adding to the rising demand for cooking advice. Girls of working age from large rural families were obliged to learn new ways when entering service in urban households. When they returned home to marry, these young women in turn brought their household and kitchen experiences with them, imitating their employers' lifestyle in so far as economic conditions allowed, an enterprise ably assisted by practical cookbooks such as that of Henriette Davidis.

Davidis was a pastor's daughter from the Sauerland region of Westphalia. Her mother, a Dutchwoman from an urban background, originally found herself without any of the skills necessary to maintain a rural household. She often found this lack very embarrassing and it led her to take steps to ensure that her thirteen children would be better prepared. Living in a region that had seen early industrialization, young Henriette was familiar with the lifestyle of the lower classes. Religiously and socially motivated to better herself and her fellows, she found work as a teacher and governess. The future cookbook author sympathized with the young women she observed trying to run a household on a tight budget without servants. Her *Praktisches Kochbuch* (Practical Cookbook), published in 1845, was intended as a helpful companion to these young housewives, not least since much of the work previously undertaken in rural households had gradually disappeared, making cooking the focus of attention. Written in a thoroughly accessible style, the book was immensely successful, reaching its 21st edition within the author's lifetime and going into its 61st edition a century after its first publication. German immigrants took the book to the u.s, and in 1879 a German bookstore owner published its first American edition in Milwaukee. This was followed by the first English translation in 1897.[13] Interest in the work was not confined to the kitchen. In 1891, German novelist Wilhelm Raabe pointed out in *Stopfkuchen*, a work of fiction which examined the lot of outsiders in a small town in northern Germany in the middle of the nineteenth century, that Davidis's cookbook would always repay study, if only as an opportunity to dream of other worlds. Contemporary proof that Henriette Davidis's masterwork is still regarded as a culinary bible can be found in Nobel Prize-winner Günter Grass's novel *Der Butt* (The Flounder) of 1977, in which Davidis is used as symbol for the bourgeoisie.

A proliferation of female authors followed in Davidis's footsteps. Among those who were successful and went into numerous new editions were Sophie Wilhelmine Scheibler, Marie Susanne Kübler, Mary Hahn and Katharina Prato. The authors often used regional titles for their books, though the content was designed to appeal to certain social groupings rather than focusing on regionality. Not infrequently the same content was sold under several titles, while dishes described as regional were usually stereotypical rather than distinctive or authentic.

In many cases the word *wohlfeil* (affordable) was included in titles, appealing to the conscience of both middle-class author and audience. Among these, first published in 1815 in Berlin, was Sophie Scheibler's *Allgemeines deutsches Kochbuch für bürgerliche Haushaltungen oder gründliche Anweisung wie man ohne Vorkenntnisse alle Arten Speisen und Backwerk auf die wohlfeilste und schmackhafteste Art zubereiten kann* (General German Cookbook for Bourgeois Households; or, Thorough Advice on How to Make All Kinds of Dishes and Bakery Goods Without Any Prior Knowledge in the Most Affordable and Delicious Way). While the title promised thrift, the book included recipes for luxuries such as chocolate, asparagus and all kinds of meat, including pigeons, capon and game, along with elaborate cakes and frozen desserts.

A similar contradiction surrounded horsemeat. Long tainted by Christian taboo for its association with pagan rituals, during the nineteenth century it returned to the menu. On the one hand it came to be associated with the poor, while on the other *Hippophagen-Vereine*, horsemeat-eating associations, promoted it as nutritious. In 1848 Henriette Davidis published *Praktische Anweisung zur Bereitung des Rossfleisches*, offering practical advice on the preparation of horsemeat. However, horse slaughter, butchering and selling of the meat was restricted to separate establishments by law (a requirement in place till 1991). In 1860 an economist mentioned the opening of horse butcheries for the less affluent in several large cities in northern Germany. Berlin counted seven of these in 1868, with around 1,300 animals slaughtered in 1863–4. According to official records, in 1895 in Saxony, the state reputed to have the greatest horsemeat consumption, between 1 and 2 per cent of all meat consumed was horsemeat. Today consumption is about 50 g per head per year, with *Rheinischer Sauerbraten* frequently cited as being originally made from horse.[14]

Another new category of cookbooks were those for children, by now regarded as a distinct social group. The dolls' cookbooks of Christine Charlotte Riedl and Julie Bimbach, both published in 1854, were followed by Henriette Davidis's *Puppenköchin Anna* (Anna the Doll Cook) in 1858. Adult concern for children's well-being did not preclude strictness. In addition to professionally written recipes, in Davidis's work the voice

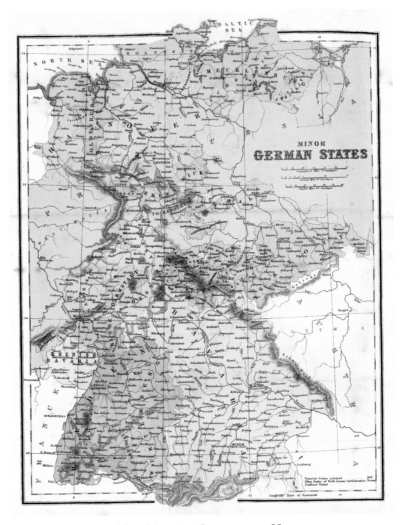

Map of the minor German states, 1864.

of the schoolmistress can be heard stressing the importance of politeness, thankfulness, thrift and cleanliness. *Struwwelpeter*, literally shaggy Peter, was another enormously successful book directed at children and even more open in its educational purpose. Consisting of ten short stories, it was originally written in 1844 by a physician in charge of the Frankfurt lunatic asylum as a Christmas present for his three-year-old son. From a food historian's viewpoint the most interesting of those stories is *Suppenkaspar*, about a small boy, Kaspar, who refuses to eat his soup and is dead within five days. While this may well be the first case of anorexia nervosa described in literature, in the context of pauperism it

Henriette Davidis,
Anna the Doll Cook
(1858).

Dr Oetker, childrens'
cookbook from 1961.

becomes particularly intriguing, since the title, *Suppenkaspar*, is used to this day to admonish difficult children at table.

In the second half of the nineteenth century food crises still occurred, but they were less severe and more local. Pauperism didn't disappear overnight, but in the wake of the famine of 1846/7 the economy improved and by 1850 the remains of the feudal system were abolished all over Germany. Hardship was not seen as god-given any more, and insurance companies and banks attempted to share burdens among a larger proportion of the population. In some regions redemption payments by the peasantry to former landlords were state-funded. In the long term, with increasing industrialization, employment in urban factories offered an alternative to the paupers' misery, and the poor gradually became the urban proletariat.

The actual timing of the switch from agrarian to industrial society depends on one's point of view, as in the 1840s the agricultural sector made for less than half of the net inland product but still employed more than half of all working people until the 1870s (the percentage declined, but absolute numbers were stable or rose as agricultural production intensified). At the same time the industrialization of the agricultural sector only started in the 1870s, with yields rising significantly from the 1890s, mostly due to the introduction of modern technology.

Although in 1840 Germany's economy still lagged more than 50 years behind that of Britain, by the end of the century Germany would be one of the leading industrialized nations. Two factors above all others were responsible for this dramatic change. The first was the abolition of internal trade tariffs, a process initiated by Prussia and leading to the foundation of the *Deutscher Zollverein*, the German tariff union, with eighteen states and a population of 23 million under Prussian leadership forming a single market. The other factor was the development of faster and cheaper transport, above all by ship and railway, allowing raw materials and labour to meet at new urban production centres. The iron industry moved to the coal mines in the Ruhr area, the Saar region and upper Silesia and began to use steam power. As with the first modern agricultural equipment, early locomotives had to be imported from England. But by 1858, 1,000 engines had been domestically produced.

The percentage of the population working in factories rose from 4 per cent in 1850 to 10 per cent in 1873. In response to this the feminist writer Lina Morgenstern started large *Volksküchen*, or people's kitchens, in Berlin. These offered affordable, healthy takeaway food. The first opened in 1866, and within three years a total of ten were operating in the city, providing up to 10,000 meals daily at cost price. Only one dish was cooked each day, and the list of these provides what is effectively a roll-call of Berliners' favourite dishes: green peas with smoked bacon and potatoes, rice pudding with braised meat, sour potatoes with pork and beef, kohlrabi, potatoes and beef, potato dumplings with dried fruit and bacon, potatoes with apples, pork and beef, braised cucumbers with bacon and potatoes, spinach with potatoes, pork and beef or meatloaf. Berlin's rival gastronomic outlets rose in protest against what they saw as unfair competition, but Morgenstern persisted, publishing her *Volksküchen* recipes in the form of a cookbook in 1868. Even more importantly, the plight of injured troops and prisoners during the Franco–Prussian war in 1870/71 led her to form a committee to hand out meals in the barracks at Berlin's railway stations, thus establishing a precedent for more humane treatment of the victims of war.

NINE

Stock Cubes and Baking Powder: The Industrialization of Food, 1871 to 1914

Soup made from stock cubes, margarine on white bread, cake made with baking powder, canned fruit for dessert and packed biscuits as a snack on the train – during the new age shaped by modern technology, urbanization and rapid transport, Germans shook off their old food habits and embraced modernity. Following the declaration of one unified German state under the leadership of Prussian king William I as German emperor in 1871, knowledge, skills and energies were on the one hand concentrated under the roof of one nation, and therefore more efficient, and on the other could flow freely. As soon as they could afford it, urban factory workers traded potatoes for white bread and salted herring for meat. The middle classes reacted by doubling their efforts to distance themselves from the working classes, keeping up a facade of pompous affluence no matter how much some housewives struggled to make ends meet, dishing up all the complex fare then deemed indispensable. The food industry, increasingly well equipped with modern technology and knowledge, was more than happy to oblige. German engineers rose to the occasion, standardizing, developing and rationalizing foodstuffs with the same efficiency they had shown in building up the railway system. Then as now the aim was to optimize the use of resources, labour and capital to produce a reliable result, modelled on the pioneering work of the American industrialist Frederick Taylor, who sought to streamline the production process by reorganizing workers, machinery and products. In spite of protectionist warnings, the international food trade flourished and in the perception of the time food seemed almost to fly around the globe, anticipating the current state of affairs. But just as there is today, there was a limit to how much of the new people were comfortable with. *Lebensreform* or life reform was the green movement of the time.

As we have seen, in Germany modern food technology had started in the 1820s with the introduction of steam engines in flour mills. The limitation of machinery, unlike human beings, is a lack of adaptability, which leads to the need to standardize the raw material. Industrial flour mills and commercial bakeries set up laboratories to analyse gluten and starch content, an expense that only became justifiable once large-scale production could be provided by 'endless' tunnel ovens. While the origins of modern food science lie in the early nineteenth century, its findings started to make a real impact on the food industry in the 1870s. There was at the time a strong belief in strict determinism, which in principle could be applied to all natural processes. Reinforced by modern chemical analysis and physiological experimention, this allowed scientists to understand the composition of foodstuffs with more accuracy. Justus von Liebig, Carl von Voit and Max Rubner were particularly prominent in this field. Using earlier findings by colleagues in other countries, they analysed nutrients, conducted feeding experiments and assessed the human body's ability to absorb foods by examining excrement. The result of this detailed study of organic chemistry was the identification of proteins, carbohydrates and fatty acids. The chemist Justus von Liebig integrated these findings into a coherent system, while the physiologist Carl von Voit, working with Max Pettenkofer on the human metabolism, further refined our understanding of human nutrition.[1]

The roots of the food industry at least partly go back to the need to find new ways to feed the army. Military requirements could play havoc with vulnerable food prices, either pushing up the cost of food as a result of additional demand or creating shortages due to uncontrolled foraging by troops. In Prussia, from the mid-eighteenth century onwards, experiments were conducted on the preparation of dried powdered meat, which could be stocked and transported more easily. Another method was devised by French physicist Denis Papin, inventor of the steam digester, a pressure cooker first presented in 1681 in London. Papin used it to boil bones. The resulting gelatin was praised as cheap and nutritious and later became the basis for many soup kitchen recipes as well as so-called portable soup, a bouillon in tablet form. In 1756 the Prussian army was offered a 'powder against hunger', a forerunner of the famous *Erbswurst*, ground dried peas pressed into the shape of a sausage.

Rationalized production in a biscuit factory, *c.* 1938.

It is said to have been invented by a Berlin chef as part of soldiers' iron rations in the Franco–Prussian war of 1870–71 and is still available today.

However, from 1864, the real star of all these efforts was Liebig's meat extract, Germany's first mass-produced, branded and mass-market food product. It appeared only a few years after Gail Borden had launched his similarly successful condensed milk in the u.s. under the Eagle brand. Like Borden, Liebig didn't invent the process but he was responsible for assembling all the previous research on the subject. Liebig's Extract Company Ltd was the brainchild of a German engineer combined with Belgian (and later English) capital and quality control assured by Liebig. The project linked the immense cattle herds of the South American prairies with European customers. While previous imports had been confined to hides, horns, bones and suet, it exploited the high regard in which meat essence was held. Production in Fray Bentos, Uruguay, rose very quickly. At peak production, 1,000 cattle a day were slaughtered daily at the large processing plant: 30 kg of meat had to be boiled down to produce 1 kg of completely fat-free extract. In 1870 alone 478 tons of extract were produced, as well as corned beef and salted meat. By the 1880s the company had extended its range to include liquid stock and the first commercial stock cubes under the Oxo brand. At first they were sold to army catering establishments and hospitals, moving into more general markets as affluent private households increasingly gave up boiling meat for soup and stock and bought Liebig's instead. The main selling point was that the product could be used as a tonic for convalescents and a fortifier for the family's provider. Cookbook authors embraced the product enthusiastically, and in 1870 Henriette Davidis published a booklet recommending Liebig's. However, meat extract's nutritional value became a controversial subject much discussed among Liebig's colleagues. In the end his opponents convinced experts and the general public that the extract had little value as a food source, but encouraged appetite and aided digestion. Competition followed rapidly. In the 1880s Julius Maggi of Kemptthal in Switzerland (a Swiss-German company, but very much part of the Germanic food world) and Carl Heinrich Knorr of Heilbronn in Württemberg marketed products that were primarily based on ground legumes, dried vegetables, pearled sago and tapioca, an alternative to Liebig's extract that was similarly directed at busy housewives and time-pressed cooks but was much more affordable. At an industrial exhibition in 1897, Knorr displayed a cubic-metre-sized soup cube prepared from dried vegetables which represented 70,000 soup portions. Real commercial success came when in the early 1900s refrigerated transport by ship did away with Liebig's erstwhile advantageous preservation method of fresh meat at its point of slaughter. At the end of the First World War Liebig's had lost its dominance in the German market.[2]

Margarine, though not actually developed in Germany, became popular in the 1880s when Dutch manufacturers transferred production to Germany as a way of avoiding protectionist import tariffs. In the early 1900s, with the introduction of new technology capable of solidifying any fat-containing liquids, large oil mills were constructed near northern German ports and along the Rhine to process copra, linseed, sesame seed, palm kernels, soy beans, groundnuts and cotton seed. At the time, in addition to 470,000 tons of real butter, Germans consumed 200,000 tons of the new *Kunstbutter*, artificial butter, per year. This was more than one-third of the total world production, and one can't help being reminded of Walter Ryff's mid-fifteenth-century remark about *Grass-Alemant*, German fatties. From 1897 the law required that margarine had to be 10 per cent sesame seed oil to differentiate it from butter in laboratory tests. Nevertheless producers unashamedly used the butter association in their advertising. *Aha! Sanella! Das gibt ein feines Butterbrot!* – 'Ah! Sanella [a big margarine brand]! That will make fine bread and butter!' shouted an advertisement in 1905, adding *Pflanzenbutter-Margarine* in small print in a corner. In 1932 a new law prohibited any allusion to animal fat or products in relation to margarine and artificial fat, although Rahma (a brand whose name could be translated as Creama, since *Rahm* in German means cream) simply omitted one letter in its brand name and continued to market itself under the name Rama.[3]

Until around 1900 in Germany (unlike in the U.S., where the Californian gold rush in particular had pushed demand), industrially produced food in cans was mostly consumed by the army and the navy and as ship's supplies. With the exception of a few luxury products, canned food rarely featured in private households, not least as a result of the high prices of the cans themselves (the tin plate to make them had to be imported from England). Canned peaches brought the delights of midsummer to a select few in the middle of winter. The first small canning factories were established in the 1840s in Brunswick and Lübeck and centred on the equally luxurious asparagus. This led to agricultural specialization, but also the development of a parallel industry to supply raw material for packaging. It appears that the market for canned food at the very end of the century evolved largely due to department stores, which ran their own quality controls and demonstrated the content of cans in glass jars in their windows to convince customers.

In domestic households special glass jars instead of cans came to be used for preserving. Developed and patented in 1892 by the chemist Rudolf Rempel, these jars had a glass lid sealed with a rubber band. They were boiled in water in a special sterilizing pan, weighed down by a weight or stone, which was soon replaced by a metal clip. After the businessman Johann Weck bought the patent he quickly came to dominate the trade, and because his name featured prominently on each jar, the Duden dictionary of 1907 listed the verb *einwecken*, to preserve, which is still used to the present day. Apples, pears, cherries and plums were mostly preserved by drying. *Pflaumenmus*, a thick plum concentrate, was a legacy from the time when sugar was still a luxury, since it was boiled down without sugar. Its ubiquity led to complaints among servants. The first commercial jam factories started in Dresden in 1843 and Brunswick in 1861 but they were small, artisanal affairs. Jam remained a luxury product and until the turn of the century was mostly imported from Britain (where its production relied on fruit imports from Germany to a considerable extent).[4] The German jam industry only expanded when domestic beet sugar reached the necessary quality level in the years immediately before the First World War. Since the railway system increasingly facilitated

Weck advertisement for preserving jars, probably early 1930s.

the wider distribution of perishable foodstuffs such as fruit, the area of orchards in Prussia more than doubled during the last quarter of the nineteenth century. Westphalian peasants sent cherries to the cities on the Rhine and sales of quinces and plums from the banks of the Main helped to finance the local vineyards.

Until 1900 canned meat such as corned beef was imported from America. At that point the inspection rules that had originally been introduced in 1879 (based on earlier regional laws) to control trichinosis in pigs were extended to include all meat, acting like a protectionist tariff. Imports almost stopped, opening a window for domestic producers that provided the army with their rations, but also supplied canned luxurious ragouts, fricassés and venison dishes to the customers of up-market delicatessens. The industry's greatest success was canned *Würstchen*, literally small sausages (frankfurters), developed in 1896 by a butcher in Halberstadt, a small town between Brunswick and Magdeburg. Canning meant that the salt level could be low, making for a finer taste, and the method was soon copied in Frankfurt, hence the name.

Sausage factory,
c. 1915.

For the urban housewife, storage problems made it difficult or impossible to stock up on provisions in the traditional way, since many flats didn't have suitable cellars or larders. In affordable accommodation the latter, if present at all, were often situated next to the toilet. Refrigerators only began to appear in domestic kitchens after the Second World War and even the icebox, an insulated wooden box that had to be filled with bought-in iceblocks, could only be afforded by more affluent households. A popular alternative method of preservation at the time was salicylic acid, originally obtained from willow bark or the herb meadowsweet, which was used to prevent mould or rot and also mixed with butter and milk.[5] Refrigeration, developed in the 1870s by Carl von Linde among others, was first used in breweries and helped to commercialize bottom-fermenting beers. But the industry soon became aware of the vast advantages this new technology offered, and perishable foodstuffs acquired a new status on the market. Germany's first refrigerated meat stores were installed in 1882 in Bremen and 1883 in Wiesbaden, while the

fish industry used a combination of refrigerated transport and canning
to extend its markets inland.

Cattle breeding had been intensified and feeding regimes optimized
to achieve higher yields of both meat and milk. As the agronomist and
writer Josef von Schreibers predicted in 1847, modern dairy farming
could only move in one direction: 'The animal has to be turned into a
machine, destined to transform the given feed in the shortest time and
in the least amount of space into the maximum amount of milk.' Milk
was now generally recognized as a valuable food, and deemed particularly
important for invalids and children. From 1850 on specialized milkmen
(and women) sold milk in the cities from *Abmelkwirtschaften*, urban stables
with cows that had just calved. These relatively un-commercialized stable
arrangements developed into large-scale dairies and cooperatives that
could afford the modern equipment required to guarantee hygiene
standards. The success of promoting milk as a healthy alternative to coffee
and alcohol was limited – the lower classes considered it to be not much
more exciting than Count Rumford's *Armensuppe* and perceived it as too
expensive. Until the end of the nineteenth century milk consumption
remained significantly higher in more affluent households, while the
lower classes preferred to consume dairy products in the form of cheese
(the fattier the better, its production facilitated by industrially prepared rennet) and butter, both of which were gradually becoming more

Hortitzsch, 'Central Post of the Wille Milchcuranstalt in Dresden', from
Gartenlaube magazine, 1883.

affordable due to the introduction of modern centrifuges. Condensed milk, first produced commercially in Germany in 1886 by the Pfunds dairy in Dresden, was advertised as a natural product especially good for children.[6]

Belief in progress through science was the orthodoxy of the age. God-given famines were simply no longer accepted. In 1855 Hermann Klencke published *Nahrungsmittelfrage in Deutschland vom Standpunkt der praktischen Naturwissenschaft* (The Food Question from the Point of View of Practical Science). His aim was to provide a scientific answer to the problems of the first half of the century: food crises, high prices and scarcity. How could foodstuffs, he enquired, be re-evaluated? Characteristically this prolific writer on medical science addressed his book of 'answers to vital questions' to a male audience. But he followed it up in 1867 with *Chemisches Koch- und Wirthschaftsbuch oder die Naturwissenschaft im weiblichen Berufe* (The Book of Chemical Cookery and Housekeeping; or, Sciences in the Female Vocation). This somewhat cumbersome title was addressed to 'thinking women' and came with a motto: 'The difference between the educated and the uneducated lies in the fact that the former is always aware of the reasons for his actions. Chemistry has been entering men's factories and workshops to great advantage – why shouldn't it, keeping up with the times, bring enlightenment to the woman's workshop, the kitchen?' Furthermore, he contined, cooking had so far been a purely mechanical activity that would benefit from the introduction of reflective thinking. Fielding accusations that he promoted industrial surrogate foodstuffs, Klencke promised greater efficiency in terms of both cost and time.

Meanwhile, von Liebig, von Voit and their colleagues were busy in their laboratories. Voit's ideas translated into the new field of *Ernährungslehre*, nutritional science, and were enthusiastically adopted by those concerned with the ever-present social problems. In 1883 the medical scholar Max Rubner introduced a new idea, the concept of calories, which would form the basis of the Atwater system. Over time institutional meal plans became more differentiated according to the age, occupation and state of health of the individual.[7] Tables were devised that recommended ideal menus for different work requirements and age groups. Most important was the provision of sufficient protein and fat, while the understanding grew that a good diet had to be varied and balanced, since no single foodstuff could provide complete nourishment on its own. Excessive consumption of potatoes or rice was thought to lead to undernourishment and lethargy, whereas meat and a proportion of fat delivered dynamic, healthy workers. Legumes were identified as an affordable substitute for meat.

The availability of statistics obtained through national surveys contributed to greater understanding of what the German population actually consumed. Meat consumption was clearly linked to social conditions. Consumption of pork in particular had greatly increased, as distilleries and the commercialized dairy industry provided feed in the form of mash and whey. Sausage of all kinds was particularly appreciated by the labouring population since no preparation was required and it could be bought as needed. At the same time wheat consumption rose significantly, and in 1910 overtook rye as the cereal of choice. From 1900 onwards consumption of potatoes slowly declined, whereas milk, butter and cheese increased rapidly, rising from 6 kg of dairy foods consumed per head per year in 1860 to 11.6 kg in 1910.[8]

Studies indicate that from the mid-1880s the general state of public health in Germany improved in spite of more frequent and longer stays in hospitals (between 1877 and 1910 the number of hospital beds more than tripled, not least due to the national health insurance introduced for workers in 1883). These were partly due to the institutions' improved medical reputation, and partly to the introduction of workers' state insurance. Infant mortality began to improve from 1900, although as before, the higher a newborn's social class the greater the chance of its survival. From the mid-1880s life expectancy between the ages of fifteen and 30 in the larger cities was on the rise, while general improvements in hygiene, rather than medical progress, made for a decline in infectious diseases. In sum, by 1900 the lower classes were significantly better off and even among them the percentage of real income spent on food was gradually decreasing.[9] This turn for the better for more led to widespread worries about social hygiene which, it was feared, was leading to the gradual degeneration of the Germanic race. Regional rural diets were increasingly idealized, as indeed were folk traditions in general, and admired as naturally balanced by instinct. Even seen within the perspective of the time, this romantic view was often mistaken, since agricultural trade meant that the peasantry didn't always eat what they were growing. In fact sufficient meat and fat were only within reach of better-paid workers, families with few or no children or those who could grow a fair proportion of their own food and raise a pig.[10]

The new food science had become accepted, indeed fashionable, among the educated classes. Combined with further new findings (particularly in the 1920s on vitamins), it fundamentally altered ideas on the connection between medicine and diet. In the 1890s the imperial health office issued its own interpretation of the new thinking: the *Gesundheitsbüchlein*, an educational health booklet that included nutritional advice (and saw numerous new editions until the 1940s). As in England at the time, warnings on the dangers of food adulteration bordered on hysteria. Every cookbook advised its readers to check almost everything for illegal additions, colourings and the like: cocoa might have ash added, chocolate might include rice flour, coffee beans and tea leaves could be artificially coloured. Even flour and salt were suspect and fish could be inflated so it would look larger and stuffed so it would weigh more.[11] Milk adulteration was indeed widespread; it was diluted with water or skimmed milk or had flour or sugar added, as well as all kinds of chemicals intended to delay deterioration. At the same time milk was often unclean due to sloppiness in the milking parlour and during transport. In 1875, in response to the problem, special pasteurized, high-quality, full-cream milk from better-fed cows that were subject to veterinary supervision came on the market, albeit at three or four times the usual price.

It soon became obvious that consumers, in spite of all the advice offered, weren't able to check food quality themselves. The first German food law was introduced in May 1879 under the auspices of the imperial health office, itself created three years earlier. The official health policy of the time appears modern even today, making the connection between general health and social standing, environment, nutrition and so forth.

Laboratories were set up to undertake regular controls. However, the law's implementation rested with regional governments and the text lacked exact definitions of categories to differentiate between the original, adulterated products and outright imitations. The law allowed the police to enter businesses, take samples and check on hygiene, but the resulting jurisdiction tended to diverge significantly from region to region. In Saxony egg noodles had to have a minimum egg content, but not so in Frankfurt; honey made with glucose syrup that had been made from potatoes was deemed adulterated in Dresden but not in Magdeburg. For new products such as margarine and jam, standards had to be defined from scratch. For glucose syrup this represented a problem. Produced from potatoes since the 1870s on a large scale on the agrarian estates east of the Elbe, it was a much-used ingredient of the developing confectionery industry. In jam, however, adding glucose syrup was considered as diluting the fruit, leading in 1910 to the introduction of a legal minimum fruit content. Public discussion was most concerned with health issues regarding preservatives, since industrial interests lobbied for certain additives, deemed essential for modern production, to be classified as legal.

Then as now, food scandals flared up in spite of all official efforts. Beer scandals in Bavaria in 1884–5 resulted in the discovery of all kinds of illegal additives, though these proved not to pose actual health hazards. In 1910 *Maratti-Fett*, cardamom oil bought in England and imported from Ceylon, had been used in the production of certain margarine brands in Hamburg, causing widespread serious illness. The new field of food chemistry, led by Joseph König, could hardly keep pace analysing the new substances that were constantly developed, such as the flavourings cumarin and vanillin. Salicylic acid was declared illegal in 1902 and after long debates boric acid followed. In some cases, such as in the shrimp industry, preservatives appeared to be used as a remedy for deplorable hygiene. In other cases, such as the Brunswick asparagus canners and the German chocolate industry, producers instigated their own health regulations that exceeded legal requirements. In general legislation evolved towards allowing only thoroughly tested additives and colourings, setting maximum content levels and having them declared on the packaging, enabling consumers to take their own decisions. In 1912 the canning industry introduced standard sizes and labelling, including net content. Saccharine in contrast, developed as an artificial sweetener in 1878, alarmed the beet sugar industry but was soon embraced by the public, since rising affluence led to modern health problems such as obesity and diabetes.[12]

As Germany's population grew by over 50 per cent from 41 million in 1871 to 67.7 million in 1914, the number of Germans who lived in towns with more than 2,000 inhabitants almost doubled to over 60 per cent. The new urban areas were mostly in the Rhineland and Westphalia, but no city grew faster than Berlin, illustrating the profound changes that Germany as a whole was undergoing at the time. Previously a rather provincial Prussian royal seat, its population tripled, with many new residents streaming in from Germany's eastern territories, hoping for better opportunities and making it the only European city to grow at a comparable speed to the industrial cities of North America, such as Chicago. Like the uncertainties faced by those who emigrated to America, the move to Berlin from a poor village in Silesia must have been a daring and risky undertaking. Many families counted themselves lucky to rent a place at all, no matter how cramped and primitive. The working classes' living quarters were called *Mietskasernen*, tenement barracks. In 1890,

40 per cent of the city's inhabitants lived on the third floor or higher and averaged, in 1875, 72 occupants per building.[13] Unsurprisingly modernization in the form of a sewage system, electricity and gas as well as easy access to the public transport system came to more privileged areas, far away from the factories' noise and filth, before they arrived in workers' quarters. Few could afford more than two rooms, of which one served as kitchen, central living area and workroom as well as bedroom, with communal toilets and no central heating. Among the poorest privacy was almost non-existent, and public space had to be used as much as possible; the complete opposite of the bourgeois ideal. *Eckkneipen*, corner pubs, proliferated, said to number 'five on four corners' in Berlin. The poorer the family, the more important it was for women to maintain good relationships with neighbours and small shopkeepers so that help might be sought in the form of borrowing or credit. This support was however criticized by middle-class do-gooders as at best a waste of time and at worst evidence of an inclination to idleness. Few understood that these women had to meet all their family's needs from weekly wages which for the most part barely covered necessities.

Berlin was obliged to bring in staple foodstuffs early in her history, but with the metropolis exploding from 1850 onwards, the food situation changed dramatically. State-built roads and the railway, first opened from Berlin to Potsdam in 1838, joined the waterways as a convenient way to provision the city. Freight trains increased by a factor of twenty within just twenty years, whereas passengers only tripled. Food production took new forms to satisfy the exploding demand. Berlin's first *Backfabrik*, baking factory, opened in 1856 as a joint stock company. The factory could process up to 250 tons of rye flour per day, producing one-third of all the rye bread needed by the city. Local bakers worried that they might lose custom, but even with this substantial output demand rose faster than production, although mechanization allowed the *Backfabrik* to offer traditional products such as *Schrippen*, white rolls, at lower prices than bakers.

At the time meat was bought from small butchers and a few privately owned slaughterhouses. Yet by then it had became clear, as the Berlin physician Rudolf Virchow argued at council meetings in the 1860s, that the city needed meat that was not only affordable but healthy, and that the council needed to invest in the city's infrastructure to that end. It took until 1881 for the central cattle market and slaughterhouse to open in the east of Berlin. Covering an area of over 38 hectares, with its own railway connection, it also made it much easier to implement meat inspection rules.

The city council then instigated a building programme to replace the open-air markets. As market days had been extended, with more stalls to satisfy the ever-growing demand, hygiene was an increasing problem. In 1850 the city had fourteen markets (the largest being the one on the Gendarmenmarkt) with 6,000 stalls, whereas by 1880 there were twenty markets with more than 9,000 stalls. In 1886 a covered central market on Alexanderplatz opened, combining wholesale and retail. Like the central slaughterhouse, the Alexanderplatz *Markthalle* had direct railway access, significantly reducing the number of horse-drawn carts on the streets and enabling deliveries of up to 15,000 kg per hour which could be stored in an ice cellar under the central building. Six years later, fourteen covered retail markets were spread all over Berlin and the old outdoor markets were closed down.[14]

The milk trade also underwent significant changes: in Berlin consumption of milk quadrupled between 1893 and 1913. In addition to the *Abmelkwirtschaften* mentioned earlier, milk was brought in by rail from increasing distances. In 1879 the builder and businessman Carl Bolle decided to tap into Berliners' thirst by opening a milk garden on Lützowufer, south of the Tiergarten. Within two years he had expanded his business into bottling and delivering milk supplied by rail from producers in the surrounding countryside, installing Berlin's first steam-powered centrifuges to allow the surplus to be turned into butter and cheese. The fresh milk was transported in hygienic tin plate churns (made in the company's own workshop) and quality-checked in the company's own laboratory. Bolle's business rapidly grew into Europe's largest milk distribution company. By 1907 Bolle was running 300 horse-drawn white milk carts that sold around one-seventh of all milk consumed in the city. They had fixed itineraries and rang a bell to attract potential customers' attention. One contemporary expert asserted that Bolle's high standards had done more for milk quality in Berlin than any food legislation or police intervention.[15]

Overall, food retailing saw significant reorganization, with new specialist stores selling coffee, delicatessen goods and tobacco. Over time some of these expanded into chains such as Kaiser's Kaffee and Bolle's dairy business (later diversifying into general grocery stores). In addition small corner food stores increased rapidly in number. They were mostly run by women and offered all kinds of daily necessities, with prices as flexible as their opening hours and readily available credit. The first *Warenhaus*, a department store initially aimed at those on a tight budget, developed out of *Konsumvereine*, buying co-operatives formed by housewives' associations. Understandably these were not popular with retailers deprived of their profit, as prices for luxury products such as tropical fruit and canned food, but also toilet paper, could be as low as half those of regular shops. Over time some department stores ironically became temples of luxury housed in grand purpose-built premises, such as Wertheim on Leipziger Platz, opened in 1897, and the Kaufhaus des Westens, or department store of the west, Kadewe for short, opened in 1907 on Wittenbergplatz. Fresh food could only be handled by the larger of these stores as it posed particular storage problems and in any event offered smaller profit margins. This was the domain of specialized luxury delicatessens, which often came with a sophisticated restaurant. One of the most famous of these deli-cum-restaurants was Borchardt, near the Gendarmenmarkt. Opened in 1853 by a Pomeranian, August Friedrich Wilhelm Borchardt, it quickly developed into a favourite of the aristocracy and upper classes, moving into newly built and imposing premises in 1895.

Ordering food from Borchardt or his most prominent competitor, Julius Fehér, was a clear sign of social distinction. Some time during

The Fehér delicatessen store in Berlin, *c.* 1910.

A culinary place in time: Borchardt in Berlin

The restaurant exists to this day, housed in the building on Französische Strasse that was previously the delicatessen. The building was still more or less intact in 1946 and its colourful history continued under the GDR regime. Ironically legend has it that the Socialist United Party (SED) originated here, although the official ceremony took place at the nearby Admiralspalast. Before its new incarnation as a Gastmahl des Meeres (a GDR chain of seafood restaurants), Borchardt in November 1948 was one of three so-called free Handelsorganisation (HO) restaurants in Berlin, under the name of Lukullus. Later on it was turned into a dance hall for the young and in the 1980s a canteen for construction workers when the Friedrichstrasse was rebuilt. Reopened in 1992, once again it has become a meeting point for the political establishment, its imposing high ceiling and large columns reminiscent of Paris fin-de-siècle brasseries (www.borchardt- restaurant.de).

the first decade of the new millenium, Fehér published a collection of recipes using the exotic fruit and vegetables his stores in Hamburg and Berlin offered under the title *Die internationale Küche* (International Cuisine). In it he wrote:

> The limits imposed in earlier times by poor transport technology are disappearing. Today nothing keeps the gourmet from delighting in game, fruit and vegetables from foreign continents.

Indeed, the menus his catering business proposed sound remarkably modern: grapefruit the Californian way; chicken and okra soup; veal chop and nasturtium salad; grilled kangaroo tail with root-artichoke purée (actually the tuberous roots of Helianthi strumosu, a sunflower closely related to the Jerusalem artichoke); *crêpes Parisienne* and cheese to follow.[16] At least the wealthy (as opposed to those belonging to the right social group, as during feudal times) could choose their meals from what the world had to offer, seasons and distance shrinking to bare logistical details. Over time this would develop into one of the basic principles of modern supermarkets: everything, any time, anywhere.

At the time national trade policy was the subject of intense public debate. On one side were the advocates of unhindered economic growth through industrialization; on the other, those who pleaded for a minimum level of agricultural self-reliance. The latter deemed the pace of industrialization too rapid and feared it could lead to a fatal dependancy on imports. Rye had been imported since 1852, barley and oats since 1867 and wheat since 1876. The agricultural sector was part of an international market strongly affected by cheap grain imports, mainly from Russia and the U.S. where, following the end of the American Civil War and with immigrants increasingly settling in the Midwest, wheat cultivation had doubled within fifteen years. This had combined with the extension of the railway system and the lowering of transport costs by ship to Europe, and ordering had been made easier via the telegraph. This did not only apply to Germany. By 1900 Britain was importing four-fifths of its grain, three-quarters of its dairy products and almost half its meat.[17] However, in Germany the old landowning *Junker* class, the agrarian elite east of the Elbe whose interests were directly opposed to those of the various industrial parties, still dominated politics in spite of their gradually declining economic power. In 1902 new tariff laws were introduced in favour of them, virtually locking out cheap Russian imports and leading to significantly higher bread prices.

In the search for nourishing, affordable home-grown food alternatives soybeans came under consideration. They were first grown on an experimental scale in Vienna in 1875, and two years later in Germany from seeds imported from China. Soy was found to be nourishing, tasty and equally suited to humans and animals. The crop was more robust than maize, ripened early in the year and seemed well adapted to the Central European climate. Nevertheless the new cultivar failed to acquire general acceptance, remaining locked into the research programmes of agricultural institutes until the aftermath of the Russo–Japanese war of 1904–5, when imported soy beans began to arrive as raw material for the manufacture of cooking oil and margarine, with animal feed as a by-product. Since other nations were able to source their oilseeds from their respective colonies, Germany became the chief European importer of soy beans from 1910 onwards, as land formerly devoted to home-grown oil-bearing crops such as linseed and rape had been converted to more profitable cultivars such as sugar beet. In 1913 a company offered the first soy products in the form of milk and flour, while soy was also introduced as an ingredient in the popular instant sauce powder produced by Maggi. German consumers, however, never fully embraced soy and its derivatives.[18]

As the nation's disposable income increased and urban households had more money to spend on convenience products, choices were no longer only dictated by economic constraints and the distance between producer and consumer widened. Advertising replaced the market cries of old. The pioneers of this new method of selling included new luxury foodstuffs and products which needed explanation, such as cocoa, coffee substitutes and margarine. The responsibility for marketing food products moved from the seller to the producer. Branded products in sealed packages couldn't be tasted before purchase and were sold in a fixed size for a fixed amount, thereby significantly reducing the storekeeper's role or replacing it altogether, as in vending machines like those for Stollwerck chocolate. Package design became very important and products were valued for their 'shop window quality'. Major producers not only ran massive advertising campaigns but provided shopkeepers with ready-made promotional material and advice.

Shop windows illuminated by gas light started to appear in Berlin in the 1860s and by 1884 the main boulevard, Unter den Linden, was equipped with electrical street lighting. Evening strolls became a new leisure activity, and arcades augmented shops with restaurants and cafes. In 1914 restrictions that ordered the covering of shop window displays on Sundays were lifted. Larger cities were soon converted into a backdrop for billboards, with illuminated signs (made from single light bulbs, not yet neon) on walls and roofs, the most eye-catching of these animated. A contemporary commentator raved:

> Electrical light sparks from a fantasy sparkling wine bottle pouring automatically into a pointed glass a never-ceasing stream of sparkling Champagne. An ad for a sparkling wine characterizes Berlin as thirsty for Champagne, a city where sparkling wine and whiskey are flowing.[19]

By the 1890s the use of advertising as a form of mass-communication had been well established among food manufacturers and department stores. Thanks to a standardized postal system, mail-order companies became profitable, offering coffee, butter, honey and even poultry. Affluent households were inundated with catalogues and special offers. The first *Litfasssäule* or advertising pillar was erected in Berlin in 1855. Advertising campaigns took the form of flyers and simple posters much like those for exhibitions and events, and in some cases came to be elevated to an art form. In the 1880s Julius Maggi himself designed the characteristic bright yellow and red label which adorned his liquid seasoning, and employed the young writer Franz Wedekind to produce the advertising copy. Modern technology provided new design possibilities: specially shaped bottles for beer and lemonade and printed tins for biscuits, tea, coffee and the like, as well as luxury printing methods for all kinds of packaging, became an important part of branding. In 1891 Liebig's success was followed by *Leibniz-Cakes*, small flat biscuits designed by the Hanover merchant Hermann Bahlsen to sustain hungry travellers. Bahlsen imported modern chain ovens from Glasgow, while the packaging was as distinctively designed as the advertising. In 1911 the biscuits, named after the German philosopher Gottfried Wilhelm Leibniz, a native of Hanover, were Germanized to *Keks*. In 1891 August Oetker, a pharmacist in Bielefeld, hit upon the idea of selling baking powder and custard powder in small, standardized envelopes, imitating American custom. He branded them with a logo under the Dr Oetker name and ran an advertising campaign assuring consumers of their quality. His marketing strategy included the publication of a *Schulkochbuch*, a cookbook for school kitchens, and he was later to pioneer the advertising of food products on TV.

Besides Liebig's, Bahlsen and Dr Oetker, other innovative companies included Kathreiners Malzkaffee, Henkell and Stollwerck, all of which used American and English expertise and ideas for their marketing. Their campaigns included demonstrations and lectures, recipe competitions, customized magazines, calendars, cookbooks and short films that were shown in cinemas. Recipes and serving suggestions printed on packaging replaced the sensory impressions delivered by unpackaged wares that could be touched, smelled and tasted. Serialized picture cards were often added; these could be collected in customized albums. In the 1890s Stollwerck packaged their chocolates in cardboard Easter eggs, and advertising postcards were distributed at exhibitions such as the *Gewerbeausstellung* of 1896 in Berlin, confirming the overwhelming importance now attached to visual information and the truth of the German saying *Das Auge isst mit*, the eye also eats.

Postcard from 1915, part of a series issued by the Bahlsen company to promote their product and proudly display the Germanized *Keks*.

The introduction and expansion of the railway system was a key factor in the movement of people as well as foodstuffs throughout the period. Within a few decades people embraced the new mobility and the distribution of perishable foodstuffs increased markedly. Instead of *Postwartestuben*, waiting rooms along the old postal lines, *Bahnhofs-restaurants* now catered to travellers in the larger train stations. Soon first-class passengers could order a warm meal at the station to be served at their seat on the train, and in 1880 the first dining car on the European continent was introduced on the line linking Berlin to Frankfurt am Main. When *Baedeker*, the German equivalent of Murray's red books for English travellers (and a follow-up of the Münster Montaigne missed on his trip in the 1580s), was first published in 1835, it was advertised as a handbook for fast travellers. Cultural tourism was on the rise. In 1816 the first steamship on the Rhine was English, but eleven years later it was joined by a German equivalent. The idea of travelling out of curiosity or for relaxation or entertainment was immediately attractive to Germans. A slim cookbook, *Junggesellen- und Touristen-Kochbuch*, published in 1896 and aimed at bachelors, included travellers in the title. Just over half a century after the first railway line opened to passengers, overnight express trains were taken for granted. In towns and cities the number of travellers prepared to pay for accommodation saw taverns and inns replaced by hotels and *Höfe*, courts. Many of these were endowed with seemingly aristocratic names and initially were reserved for men. Towards the end of the century establishments which offered nothing more than a set menu were considered outmoded and replaced by large hotels with restaurants, many of them financed by shareholders. These luxurious establishments offered travellers more modern amenities than they could afford at home and were greeted with great enthusiasm.

Before 1871 most places – like Gebrüder Habel, opened in 1779 on Unter den Linden in Berlin – had been more solidly bourgeois than openly extravagant. After that, however, the restaurant scene fundamentally changed. William I had French chefs but was comparatively modest at table, whereas his chancellor Bismarck was a gourmet who loved large amounts of good food. In 1878, on the occasion of the Berlin congress, the British delegation noted somewhat disparagingly: 'Prince Bismarck, with one hand full of cherries, and the other of shrimps, eaten alternately, complains he cannot sleep and must go to Kissingen [to take the waters].'[20]

From the economic boom of the so-called founding years (mainly based on the substantial French reparation payments after the Franco–Prussian war of 1870/71) and the pompous lifestyle favoured by William II all kinds of new hotels and restaurants emerged, anticipating the excesses of the 1920s. In Berlin in late 1877, the imposing Vienna-style Café Bauer opened opposite Café Kranzler. It was lavishly decorated by well-known artists. Seven years later it was the city's first restaurant with electric lighting. It offered 600 newspapers and magazines as well as a separate room for unaccompanied ladies. Besides coffee and tea in many variations, its menu included eggs for breakfast, various cold cuts, beer (with porter and pale ale the most expensive), spirits, wines (German, Austrian and French) and champagne.[21] At the same time taverns such as Lutter & Wegner were converted to restaurants serving wine, a move designed to compete with the beer palaces with their extravagant Tivoli-style entertainments. This development was by no means restricted to Berlin. Germany's largest such wine restaurant was the Nymphenburg Volksgarten in Munich. Opened in 1890 and modelled on the Copenhagen Tivoli and the Vienna Prater, its many rooms had a total of 6,000 seats and a variety of entertainments including an *Almhütte*, an alpine dairy, since guests had clearly come to expect more than just good food and drink.[22]

One name to feature prominently in Berlin's gastronomic life was that of Kempinski. The Kempinskis' story is typical of Berlin. Like many other Jews at the time, in the early 1860s Berthold Kempinski had moved from Posen, the least economically developed of Prussia's eastern provinces, to Breslau in Silesia, trading in Hungarian wines. Ten years later he moved to Berlin and started a wine company on the Friedrich-strasse. His wife prepared and served simple dishes to customers in the small tasting room, and over the years this developed into one of Berlin's largest and most successful gastronomic businesses. In 1907 Kempinski opened new premises on the Leipziger Strasse, decorated in the art nouveau and early art deco styles characteristic of the time. Here numerous restaurants could seat 2,500 guests catered for by several kitchens, a bakery, a patisserie and a butcher. In addition there were workshops to maintain the vast amount of silver and copper items, glass and china painting, a steam-powered laundry, an incinerator and refrigerated storage rooms. Oysters, a Kempinski speciality from the start of the business, were sold in impressive quantities. A delicatessen and a catering service completed the complex in 1912. Wine remained the core of the Kempinski business and it owned vineyards in many of the country's growing regions. Its wine stock was stored in vast cellars on Friedrichstrasse and thousands of bottles were sold every day. But what marked Kempinski out from competitors like Dressel, Hiller or Borchardt was the fact that it catered for many different social groups. At Kempinski's wines were priced to attract all comers, from the upper classes down to the lower bourgeoisie. You could splurge on melon with crayfish, poached salmon, loin of venison and strawberries with thick cream, or you could sit in exactly the same impressive surroundings and be served by the same elegant waiters, but order less expensive dishes, or smaller portions at half price.

In contrast the Dressel and the Hiller restaurants on the central boulevard Unter den Linden were both famous, expensive and intimidatingly exclusive. The Hiller had been owned by Lorenz Adlon before he opened his monumental hotel opposite the Brandenburg Gate in 1907. Lorenz Adlon had come from Mainz and originally trained as a carpenter. Early in his career, however, he discovered a talent for restaurant organization and worked his way up the professional ladder in Mainz, Düsseldorf

Diners at Kempinski, *c.* 1910.

and Amsterdam before settling in Berlin, where he bought the renowned
Hiller. In 1890, together with his colleague Dressel, he bought the Hotel
Continental next to the Central Station on Friedrichstrasse, and from
1899 on the two ran the highly successful and lucrative *Zooterrassen*, a
café and restaurant in the zoological garden. At the same time, Adlon
established himself as a wine merchant. All of this seems to have been
with one ambition in mind: building the Hotel Adlon. When the Adlon
opened, it was full of marble, expensive tropical hardwoods and the
latest technology in the form of elevators, heating, telephones and
modern conveniences.

Many legends surround Hotel Adlon and it is often very difficult to
uncover the solid facts. Lorenz Adlon's extremely expensive and therefore very risky undertaking must in some way have had the backing of
William II. The enterprise fitted the emperor's vision of a new, modern
and luxurious Berlin, and he therefore allowed the demolition of a historic Schinkel building, the Palais Redern, to make way for the new hotel.
The emperor is often quoted as saying, '*Kinder, wenn ihr baden wollt* [a
different version goes: '*wenn ihrs gemütlich wollt], geht ins Adlon!*' (children,
if you want to have a bath/comfort, then go to the Adlon). Rumours
had it that he paid a yearly retainer for the entertainment of his guests,

topping the sum up if needed, and used the Adlon as an unofficial extension of his own, considerably less luxurious palace. But that could be a clever modern manipulation of reality, just as some people insist that the famous French chef Auguste Escoffier presided over the Adlon kitchen for a while, for which there is no evidence at all.

Back then Escoffier's recipes were as important for the German gastronomic scene as for that of France and French was the culinary language of the time. However, the rampant nationalism of the time also found its way onto menus. Chief promoter of the idea was the *Allgemeiner deutscher Sprachverein*, the general German language association founded in 1885 in Brunswick, 'with the aim of maintaining the true spirit and the real essence of the German language . . . thus strengthening the national identity among the German people'.[23] The three stated goals of the language association were defined as cleaning the language, protecting the specific Germanic character and, finally, re-establishing German national traditions. The very first *Verdeutschungsheft* or Germanification manual, published by the association in 1888, was *Die deutsche Speisekarte* (The German Menu). The thin volume contained examples of German menus (now called *Tischkarten* instead of *Menü*), two drawings to illustrate the correct terms for cuts of beef and veal and a dictionary of the most common dishes, with German phrases substituted for foreign terms. The work also suggested German spellings for those foreign terms that had 'become' German, and accepted some 'irreplaceable' ones like *Kakao*, cocoa, and *Schokolade*, chocolat. In the fourth edition, published in 1900, the author made a special case of the 'controversial' word 'sauce'. Translations given in the first edition – *Tunke*, *Beiguss* and *Guss* or *Brühe* – had not caught on, he wrote, and he therefore declared *Sosse* as acceptable. 'Those who can't warm to this substitution,' he went on, 'should do as the German Kaiser and make no special mentioning of the *Sossen*.' In 1888 William ii had decreed that, as far as possible, all imperial menus were to be written in German. Following his decree, the first of these Germanized menus, for a meal for officers ordered to attend the imperial table on September 10, was published in the newspapers:

Windsor-Suppe. Zander in Rheinwein gedämpft. Burgunder Schinken mit Gemüsen. Pasteten von Rebhühnern mit Trüffeln. Hummer nach Ostender Art. Pulardenbraten, Salat. Mehlspeise von Äpfeln. Butter und Käse. Gefrorenes. Nachtisch.

Windsor soup. Pike perch steamed in Rhine wine. Burgundy ham with vegetables. Partridge pies with truffles. Lobster the Ostend way. Roast chicken, salad. A flour dish from apples. Butter and cheese. Ice cream. Dessert.

French linguistic (and culinary influence) in Germany went back a long way. In some places, such as Berlin, this influence acted at the top level of society – from the mid-seventeenth until the mid-nineteenth century the Prussian court, in common with many others, spoke French – as well as at lower social levels, where French was heard first from the Huguenot immigrants welcomed by the Great Elector of Brandenburg after the abolition of the Edict of Nantes by Louis XIV in 1685. In Berlin in 1698 the French colony made up one-quarter of the city's population. It appears that on a lower social level many Huguenots quickly assimilated and thus the languages mixed (an influence still perceptible to this day), while the elite of the *réfugiés* hung on to the more prestigious French longer. French occupation followed in 1806–08 and again in 1812/13. It was only from the second half of the nineteenth century, when the British Empire was at its zenith, that English started to compete with French. In the *Speisekarte*, the 'wondrous mix of French and German which nowadays are joined by some English words' was put in the dock, and words like *souper, service, restaurant* and *menu* were quoted as examples:

> Even for the simplest dishes of the bourgeois cuisine, which have not come to us from France, French expressions are used . . . *gekochtes Rindfleisch* [boiled beef] is too common, so it appears as *boeuf bouilli* . . . and the disgusting *à la* . . . could as well be *nach*.

Prior to the Franco–Prussian war efforts to attain linguistic purity had been mostly moderate and seen as a means to a more general and better comprehension of the German language, encouraging public discourse. But with growing German nationalism throughout the reign of William II, linguistic purity became an end in itself and took the form of *Fremdwörterjagd*, a paranoid hunting of foreign words as a method of unifying the nation against the enemy. Around the turn of the century, Ernst Lössnitzer, a Dresden-born chef and teacher, was one of the driving forces behind the Germanizing movement in the restaurant scene. In the introduction to his *Verdeutschungswörterbuch für Speisekarte und Küche* (Germanification Dictionary for Menus and Cookery), first published in 1888, Lössnitzer denounced the predominance of the French language, which had become fashionable in the wake of the Thirty Years War, resulting in the downgrading of German to a servants' language. Prior to this, he claimed, Germany had a distinctive national cuisine, while nowadays there were French menus for German people on German soil. This disgraceful situation had to end, he wrote, since Germany had won back full independence as a state, psychologically and economically, meaning that there was no further need for the bastardized '*französeln*', the German version of Franglais. Lössnitzer's book was the most extensive foreign to German dictionary on the subject, and undoubtedly also a sign of German professional chefs' renewed self-esteem. They had formed an association in 1896, with international exhibitions and annual culinary 'Olympics' taking place in Frankfurt am Main since 1900. Even before that, the *New York Times* reported in May 1884:

> The movement some time ago started in Berlin to secure reforms in German cooking, by introducing French methods and making cooking a profession, is meeting with much success. The reformers have arranged to hold a great public exhibition of the German arts devoted to cooking, baking, and confectionary, in Berlin, from Aug. 17 to Aug. 24 next. The enterprise will be extensively advertised, and many prizes will be offered to competitors.[24]

In the book's second edition of 1903, Lössnitzer mentioned a letter of thanks from William II and other German royalty. What Lössnitzer failed to mention is that from the start the linguistic associations had strong opponents. In 1889 a group of 41 writers, journalists, philosophers and academics, among them Rudolf Virchow and Theodor Fontane, signed a public declaration against the *Sprachverein*. They accepted that a 'cleaning' of the German language was necessary, but strongly opposed official coercion in the form of strictly defined rules, and opposed the introduction of a state-run institution modelled on the Académie Française. The Germanizing movement grew stronger during the First World War, but lost its appeal afterwards.

At the time German wine was a source of great national pride. German winemakers flourished throughout the nineteenth century, their international reputation established with the vintage of 1811, the *Kometenjahrgang*, the famous comet vintage referred to by Goethe as the *Eilfer*, eleven. Excellence was a matter of timing. In 1811, for the first time, almost all Rheingau vineyards were picked late (a custom established at Schloss Johannisberg in 1776 as a reaction to the positive result of the accidental delay in the previous year), yielding exceptionally rich and long-lived wines. In 1845 the young Queen Victoria and her German husband, Prince Albert, had visited Hochheim on the River Main to explore the origins of Hock. Demand for Rhine wines increased in the new urban centres, not least as a result of better and more affordable transport, and this, along with patriotic fervour, combined to make the best German wines more expensive than those of the renowned châteaux of Bordeaux. In 1901, as a result of anxiety about food adulteration in general, the legal term *Naturwein*, natural wine, was introduced as a description of wines with an entirely natural alcoholic content, produced

Poster advertising the cookery exhibition of 1894, which featured 'Cooking, pastry, baking, troops' catering, the people's nutrition and all related trades'.

from a single vineyard in a single vintage. In 1913, following repeated complaints about cloudy wines from overseas customers, the wine commission agent Theodor Seitz patented a method for sterile filtration using asbestos (deemed harmless at the time).

Wine consumption was restricted to the middle and upper classes and provided a highly ritualized marker of social status. Sparkling wine, considered both prestigious and modern, enjoyed considerable success, not least through promotion by the nascent advertising industry. In contrast to beer or strong spirits, its target group included women and young men. Lutter & Wegner in Berlin had built its reputation and success on the much-repeated story of the invention of the word Sekt. The writer E.T.A. Hoffmann and his actor friend Ludwig Devrient were regular champagne drinkers who one night in 1825 quoted Falstaff's line from Shakespeare's Henry IV, *Bring er mir Sect* (Bring me a cup of sack), from which casual reference came the new term for Germany's sparkling wine. In 1902 the *Sektsteuer*, a tax on sparkling wine, was introduced on the initiative of Admiral von Tirpitz, minister of naval affairs, as national pride called for an extension of the imperial fleet for the ostensible purpose of protecting Germany's sea trade. Germany was a largely unsuccessful latecomer to the colonial game, copying the brutal exploitation of indigenous peoples practised by the longer-standing European colonial powers. Concentrating on the Pacific and sub-Saharan Africa, copra, coffee and cocoa were mostly produced on the agricultural side. In the 1900s the expenses of the navy construction programme escalated and led to repeated financial crises. From 1909 the *Sektsteuer* was graded according to price, resulting in the increased consumption of less expensive wine. The tax is still levied today at €1 per 750-ml bottle, and graded according to bottle size.

Legislation affecting champagne was much less strict than it is today, and region and name frequently diverged substantially. Thomas Mann in *Die Bekenntnisse des Hochstaplers Felix Krull* (Confessions of Felix Krull), first published unfinished in 1922 and set in the decades following 1871, portrayed a notorious fraud's father as a corrupt sparkling wine producer who lived in a villa on the Rhine. Bottles of his Lorley Extra Cuvée were described as looking much better than they tasted, and, faced with bankruptcy, the pleasure-seeking father shot himself. Mann frequently used food to define his characters; in *Buddenbrooks, Verfall einer Familie* (The Decline of a Family) of 1901, grand and overly sumptuous meals make the young hero sick as the family is gradually ruined.

In the restaurant scene as in the private sphere, appearances became increasingly important. It is reported that William II was a thoughtful, quiet man in private, but the face he showed to the world was that of an all-powerful imperial ruler. Friedrich Schiller, intentionally or not, had supplied the leitmotif for this in his poem of 1799, *Die Glocke* (Song of the Bell), much quoted at the time: 'the man must to go out into hostile life . . . whereas inside rules the modest housewife, the children's mother'. German households came to be modelled on his example. According to the law, it was a wife's duty to keep house while the husband took care of all important economical and financial decisions. Married women acquired their social standing and creditworthiness from their husbands (it was not until 1977 that husband and wife would be considered fully equal under the law). Women were expected to take responsibility for home and family, including cooking, in accordance with their 'natural' inclination, most people at the time agreed. Official statistics never listed 'housewife' as a distinct occupation, but grouped them with other un-waged situations such as children, the homeless, the mentally ill and inmates of prisons.[25]

As in Britain and many other Western countries at the time, every-day meals had to be kept as simple and affordable as possible, but still had to be tasty and varied and include the husband's favourite meat-laden dishes, even if his wife didn't share his preferences. Women would often content themselves with smaller portions or have no meat at all, just as sisters didn't question the fact that they had to look after their brothers. The scholar Victor Klemperer, born in 1881, remembered his father being served schnitzel when the rest of the family had to make do with sandwiches. The master of the household alone ate stewed apples and apple cake every day. It was seen as the duty of the entire household to keep the family provider in the best possible health, and wives must not disturb their husbands with their worries during meals. Even educated, independent women took it for granted that they were the ones at the stove, as the cookbook *Für Zwei in einem Topf* (For Two in One Pan) by the highly regarded actress Luise Dumont-Lindemann showed. Published in 1912 in Düsseldorf, its recipes for two were directed at 'housewives who can't spend more than 1.5 to two hours in the kitchen each day'. Dumont-Lindemann made good use of leftovers and suggested replacements for ingredients which might prove difficult to procure. Thrift was admired as much as before, but for middle-class women the notion now included the task of presenting an impressive front to the world, even on a tight budget. To this end housewives were expected to create impressive dishes out of inexpensive ingredients. Resources had to be juggled so that sumptous meals could be served on special family reunions or when there were guests. China, cutlery, glasses and a male servant were often hired on these occasions to give the 'right' impression in an effort to imitate aristocratic ways. Such meals were expected to include at least two main courses which featured rare and correspondingly expensive ingredients, often imported. A menu from a middle-class household in 1900 lists

> Oysters, Batavia soup prepared with birds' nests sourced from India, chicken vol-au-vent, loin of venison with truffled artichoke-hearts, lobster salad with mayonnaise, a salmis of duck, cheese, pineapple ice cream, fruit and coffee.

To make budgets go as far as possible, housewives were advised to keep a ledger to record all expenses. The moral pressure to be thrifty

Adolph Menzel, *The Ball Supper*, 1878, oil on canvas. In some respects this is the pendant to the workers' grimy world: eating hastily and in a crowd.

was further intensified by cookbook titles such as *50 Pfennig-Küche oder die Kunst billig und gut zu kochen* (50-pence-Recipes; or, The Art of Cooking Cheaply and Well, 1894). It was directed at all classes rather than simply the least affluent. Meatloaf, potatoes, herring and legumes featured heavily. Housewives were constantly being urged to make good use of leftovers and a filling soup was recommended as a first course in order to save on the main course. The culinary shortcuts the new food industry offered proved a double-edged sword: unlike in Britain or France, any time women saved in the kitchen was expected to be reinvested in home and family instead of providing a short respite from wifely or motherly duties.[26]

The idea that a wife's work might be considered hard – let alone openly declared to be so – was unthinkable. Households went to great lengths to hide the reality of a housewife's situation, cultivating instead the illusion of relaxed idleness. Social aspirations among the lower middle classes often led to the employment of a servant girl to establish the wife's all-important non-working status, in spite of the fact that this stretched the funds. Ironically, at the same time housewives were also legally obliged to earn an additional income should their husbands not be able to fully provide for the family. In more affluent households outside help was hired for the harder jobs such as washing or the preparation of special meals when entertaining. In the larger apartments of the time the kitchen was sited right at the rear and was generally accessed by a separate servants' entrance. The very opposite of the grand salon at the front of the house, the kitchen, including the laundry, was often dark, stuffy and small, directly reflecting women's status and the work assigned to them. In detached houses or villas it was always in the basement. Servant girls were paid part of their wages in the form of board and lodging. Food was a frequent reason for complaint by servants although, in theory at least, the *Gesindeordnung* or servants' law guaranteed food of acceptable quality in sufficient quantity. Nevertheless employees were unlikely to complain of employers who could all too easily find replacements.[27] In 1902 the left-wing economist Oscar Stillich published a bleak survey of female servants in Berlin. Most of the young women, he reported, didn't have enough time to eat and were given reheated leftovers, sometimes even buying additional staple foodstuffs from their meagre earnings in order not to go hungry. More specific complaints were that meat which had been boiled and reboiled in the preparation of fashionable bouillons for the master was reused to prepare meatloaf for the servants, and that the aptly named *Dienstbotenkaffee*, servants' coffee, was undrinkable. Other sources maintain, however, that food allocated to household servants was usually good, since a healthy workforce served the employer's interests; there was also a fear that gossip among young female household servants which revealed penny-pinching by the master of a household would damage his social credibility.

Discussions about women's rights intensified as more affluent middle-class women clamoured for a choice between marriage and salaried work, demanding that housekeeping be recognized as a job that needed proper training. In 1873 the first urban housewives' associations were founded, followed in 1898 by the precursor of Deutscher Landfrauenverband, the German Countrywoman's Association. They tried to reconcile many different goals, among them integrating housewives into the feminist movement, which at the time consisted of unmarried women who had different ideals in life. The reality, however, was that such associations supported the old patriarchal structure by making it easier for housewives to perform their tasks within the existing system. By the turn of the twentieth century the discussion had already moved on. The most progressive suggestions included cooperative kitchens to lighten the load on housewives who worked outside the home, since salaried jobs were considered essential for the achievement of true emancipation. August Bebel, leader of Germany's socialist movement, pronounced these *Einküchenhäuser*, one-kitchen co-operative ventures, a solution to the main problem and a way of providing everyone with a nourishing meal of meat and vegetables using modern ingredients enhanced through the use of new technologies. Originally this idea had been promoted by the social democrat feminist Lili Braun as part of a far-reaching life reform as early as 1900, but had been strongly opposed as counter-revolutionary by Clara Zetkin. Another proposal was that husbands should pay for their wives' work with half their salaries, making women economically independent – an idea well ahead of its time – while countering the pejorative term *Nurhausfrau*, only a housewife. However, during the First World War the notion that a woman's natural place was in the home was readily abandoned when the conservative, male establishment saw the need. Then it was suddenly considered equally natural that women leave their kitchens and children to replace their men in the factories.[28]

Usually the cards were stacked against women who worked either from choice or necessity. While upper-class working women were seen as un-feminine, if they came from the lower classes, such women were deemed a real social threat. To prevent socialist agitation, feared above all by the establishment in an ordered society where everyone theoretically knew their place, by the mid-1880s owners of large factories had started to open housekeeping schools. They published books with titles such as *Das häusliche Glück* (Domestic Happiness), which contained advice on how to make a home comfortable and cosy for men. Although this particular work saw many reprints and numerous regional and international editions, its target audience were those most inclined to reject both the books and the schools as exploitative at best, and at worst an unacceptable infringement on their private lives.

It was, the middle classes maintained, a woman's natural duty to provide a hot meal at midday, while a lack of housekeeping and cooking skills was put forward as the main reason for poor health in children and the tendency of workers to spend their leisure time in pubs, wasting money on alcohol and causing trouble. Working-class meals were published in learned journals and found wanting when analysed according to the latest nutritional theories. The mostly male authors came up with solutions to the problem of feeding a family, none of which sounded particularly enticing. One example from 1891 proposed black bread, skimmed milk, lard, coffee (half real beans and half barley) and salt for breakfast, followed by lentil soup with bacon and herring with potatoes for lunch.[29] Legumes, quark and cheap fish were regularly recommended as replacements for expensive meat. Potatoes were seen as overly filling, leading to a monotonous diet lacking in nutritional value. Even on the tightest budgets, women were expected to produce special meals on Saturday nights and at midday on Sunday to give their menfolk a reason to bring the pay-packet straight home rather than spending it elsewhere.

Middle-class women often extended their motherly role to alleviate the lower classes' lot for the sake of the nation, as we have seen in the case of Lina Morgenstern and her *Volksküchen*, a commitment triggered by the Austrian–Prussian war in 1866 when the Prussian State called craftsmen, peasants and workers to take up arms without providing for their families. Together with many fellow well-off middle-class women, Morgenstern's aim was to keep the poor from starving, thereby preventing urban uprisings. Her Berlin-based *Volksküchen* charged a modest sum for meals in order to preserve people's self-esteem and distance the initiative from the soup kitchens run by the city council for the poor. She also saw rapid industrialization as a cause of accelerating hardship in the cities, leading her to replace the original takeaway outlets with simple dining halls. These proved popular among craftsmen, lower-grade civil servants, soldiers and servants, as well as teachers and families struggling to make ends meet. Hedwig Heyl was another notable figure in this field. She not only took over the post of acting factory director upon the death of her husband in 1889, but committed herself wholeheartedly to the women's movement in Berlin, earning herself the sobriquet 'Berlin's best housewife'. Like Morgenstern she was convinced that women's role was to counteract the hardships that came with industrialization. In her eyes good housekeeping depended on information and organization – home economics – rather than relying on female instincts. Her cooking lessons were based upon the latest scientific findings and first took shape in 1885 with women from upper-class families, later expanding to young working women of all classes.

To the bourgeoisie pubs and taverns were synonymous with socialist meetings. Morgenstern was concerned with moral education and allowed neither alcohol nor tobacco on the premises. One of the main reasons for excessive alcohol consumption was seen in the popularity of pubs and taverns where landlords imposed a *Trinkzwang*, or drinking rule. No food could be consumed without ordering alcohol, most often beer, the main source of profit, since the pubs were usually owned by breweries. The tighter the budget, the fewer the alternatives were for socializing and refreshment. But crowded housing conditions left workers no other place to gather and eating places such as *Hammelkopf*, mutton head, were popular. This simple pub near the new central slaughterhouse of Berlin had originally catered to butchers and meat buyers, offering *Bouletten* (meatballs, obviously a Huguenot contribution), pork shanks, cold pork chops and potato salad. The food was said to taste better than at home, its popularity assisted by beer, schnapps, card games and friendly service.

In a similar vein, though quickly growing into a chain, the Aschinger restaurants became immensely successful. Though limited to Berlin, these fast food outlets could be seen as the precursors of modern international fast food chains. The Aschinger system relied on food that was centrally produced according to high and exacting standards. Between 1892 and 1900 the two Aschinger brothers from Württemberg, one a cook, the other a waiter, opened more than twenty *Bierquellen* or beer pubs in all parts of Berlin. Usually a new Aschinger location meant that the brothers bought the whole building and turned the upper floors into staff accomodation, thus attracting (mostly women) workers from outside Berlin. The offer of staff meals at half price tied them even more

Housekeeping course, *c.* 1900.

effectively to the company. The pubs' blue and white decor signalled the serving of Bavarian-style bottom-fermented lager, which was seen as more sophisticated and modern than the traditional acidic, top-fermented lactic-tasting Berlin *Weisse* or wheat beer (*Weisse mit Schuss*, with the addition of sweet fruit syrups, most commonly green woodruff or red raspberry, to counteract acidity, goes back to that time). However, the food on offer at Aschinger's was actually Berlin-style and affordable without exuding even a whiff of poverty. At first it was confined to *belegte Schrippen* or sandwiches presented in glass showcases, just like the goods in the new department stores. Most popular was *Hackepeter*, raw pork mince with onions. The menu was soon extended to include *Löffelerbsen*, yellow split pea soup, and *Bierwurst*, sausage with salad, as well as more expensive dishes like roast goose with apple sauce. Fresh rolls from the Aschingers' own central bakery were served free in unlimited quantity with any order. The Aschinger establishments were the opposite of the typical Berlin *Eckkneipe*, corner pubs, since the food was reliably good and affordable and the premises looked modern and clean – even elegant – and thus were acceptable to a very wide range of social groups. In the early 1900s the group extended to include numerous *Konditoreien* and most spectacularly the *Weinhaus Rheingold*, a wine restaurant, as well as several hotels. Like Kempinski, Aschinger's became a Berlin institution mentioned by many writers of the time, such as Yvan Goll, Elias Canetti and Alfred Döblin.[30]

On Sundays many Berliners tried to get out of the city, heading for the parks or the beer or coffee gardens. Some of the latter were run as private gardens, open to travellers in need of refreshment. Unlike urban coffeehouses and restaurants, they were deemed acceptable for women and families. Around 1830 Zenner in the suburb of Treptow put out the first sign declaring *Hier können Familien Kaffee kochen*, here families can make their own coffee. This was the result of a royal decree directed against the numerous unregulated gastronomic ventures beyond the city's border, prohibiting the sale of refreshments there. The ingenuity of the Berliners found a way around the problem, and private hostelries from then on sold hot water instead of ready-made coffee, although families on a limited budget had long since brought their own coffee and cake. For many of them this would have been generous slabs of *Streuselkuchen*, yeasty white dough often covered with a layer of fruit – usually cherries or apples – and spread with buttery crumble made with sugar and as much butter as they could afford. Back in the eastern provinces, where many of them had come from, the large sheets would have been sent to be baked in the baker's oven after the bread. Now they either made smaller versions themselves or bought them from bakers. Ground poppyseeds as a cake topping, in a rich mixture with almonds, raisins and a little milk and sugar, were particularly typical of Silesians. For Christmas they would

Aschinger (on Alexanderplatz) interior, *c.* 1935.

Hans Baluschek, *Families Can Make their Own Coffee Here*, 1895, mixed technique on paperboard.

prepare *Mohnpielen*, an uncooked bread dish made from sliced *Schrippen*, white rolls soaked in milk with raisins and ground blue poppyseeds, made into a mush and shaped into dumplings on the plate: it was traditionally eaten on Christmas Eve after the late evening church service, although some families served it on New Year's Eve. In contrast the fancy fare of the middle classes included more luxurious confections. The moment and place of birth of *Schwarzwälder Kirschtorte*, Black Forest cherry gateau, a chocolate, cherry and cream-stuffed creation, are notoriously difficult to pin down, but the cake embodies the pompous spirit of the time.

Everyday life for the urban working classes was as stressful as it was for the mining communities that assured the ever-growing demand for coal, and obviously this wasn't restricted to Berlin. In 1890 the theologian Paul Göhre took three months off after graduating to disguise himself as a jobless, penniless scribe. He went to work in a metal factory in Chemnitz, Saxony, in order to experience how the working classes lived at first hand. Shortly afterwards he published his findings in a booklet full of illuminating insights. The majority of Göhre's co-workers were Saxon locals, most of whom had taken in one or more lodgers in spite of the overcrowded accomodation in order to make ends meet, so privacy was virtually non-existent and even a bed of one's own was regarded as a

Schwarzwälder Kirschtorte, or Black Forest gateau.

luxury. Göhre reported that salaries were largely sufficient to meet basic needs but didn't provide for emergencies, luxuries or longer absence on military service. The factory in which he took employment was situated in an industrial suburb where old houses mingled with newly built, spartan two- or three-storey tenements. Most families only had one or two rooms, lacked a kitchen and confined their cooking to an oven standing in a corner. Göhre described the work at the factory as physically exhausting. The workday started at six and lasted almost eleven hours, with a twenty-minute break at eight o'clock for breakfast and one hour allowed for lunch. Only the young apprentices were allowed another half hour in the afternoon at four o'clock; the rest snatched a bite to eat as necessary in order to finish work earlier. Most brought their prepared breakfast from home, either sitting out in the courtyard if the weather permitted or taking it in the simple dining hall. There wasn't much washing of hands, since everybody was eager to get to their sandwiches. These

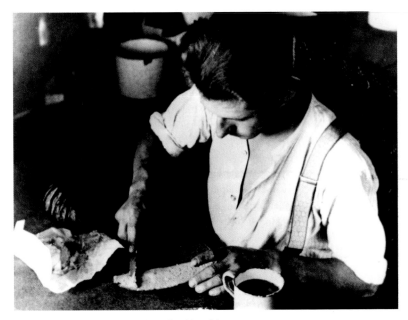

A workers' breakfast, *c.* 1920.

packed meals usually consisted of bread and butter with sausage, meat or cheese, and occasionally also hard boiled eggs or pickled cucumbers. Supplies could also be bought in the factory's canteen. Coffee was brought from home in metal containers in winter, with buttermilk the alternative in summer. According to Göhre, dark beer was increasingly consumed instead of schnapps, since beer was now available in bottles thanks to the recently introduced swing stopper.

Although some workers returned to the dining hall at midday if they lived too far from the factory, everybody else went home for lunch as soon as the whistles blew at noon. Göhre's notes make clear how important he deemed this meal, whose quality depended more on the housewife's diligence and ingenuity than her budget. It was the focal point of the family routine and could not even be replaced in its complete significance by a similar meal served at night. Workers without families, such as himself, went to simple restaurants nearby, where he described the food as plentiful and decent enough: alternating roasted and boiled meat was accompanied by vegetables, potatoes and bread as well as a glass of brown beer. The municipal soup kitchen provided simple but decent meals for even more modest budgets.[31]

Long working hours profoundly affected eating habits. Wherever possible workers returned home for lunch, walking or, if they could afford it, using public transport. But with time they came to favour shorter lunch breaks to be able to go home earlier. They came to work armed with packed sandwiches and a coffeepot and soup or stew in a *Henkelmann*, stacked metal containers resembling India's tiffin boxes that could be reheated in a hot water bath often provided by factories. Alternatively wives or daughters brought something along at lunchtime. In between a quick sip from the *Flachmann*, the hipflask, often served as a substitute for food. Numerous abstinence organizations laboured to educate against this, often joining force with other initiatives such as the women's movement. For women alcoholism was mainly an indirect problem since they consumed much less of it, having restricted access to pubs and restaurants. Instead housewives had to deal with its effect on the household budget as well as absent or drunken husbands. Feminist activists such as Ottilie Hoffmann opened numerous alcohol-free eating houses in northern Germany that also offered evening entertainment and came to be one of the origins of the *Volkshochschulen*, adult education centres, founded in 1918.[32]

From around 1900 factories started to offer hot meals in canteens. A forerunner of the arrangement was the organized midday delivery to the

Adolph Menzel, *Iron Rolling Mill*, 1872–5, oil on canvas. Note the hastily gulping workers in the bottom right-hand corner.

Constructions such as this one were provided by the factories for workers to reheat the lunch they brought along from home.

Hans Baluschek, *Lunchtime*, 1894, oil on canvas.

From 1891 to 1927 the WMF company operated the so-called *Knöpflespost*
to collect workers' lunches from their home.

factory. WMF, a large metalworks in Württemberg, collected the *Henkelmann*
containers prepared by housewives by horse-drawn carriage from workers'
homes. This service, dubbed *Knöpflespost* after a popular kind of homemade noodles, operated from 1891 to 1927. Canteens in large-scale factories
were originally called *Speiseanstalt*, *Werksküche* or *Menage* and were
above all intended to provide for unmarried workers. However, with
growing distances between the workplace and home, fewer and fewer
workers were able to go home at midday. In 1750 it took twenty minutes
to cross Hamburg on foot, which rose to 30 minutes in 1850, but by 1900
this had grown to a full hour, a situation made worse by the trend for
shorter lunch breaks. Although employers still promoted the ideal of
family meals, they also wanted to curb alcohol consumption and keep
their workforce well fed for the sake of efficiency. Initially distrusted as
a patronizing self-interested measure, reinforced by the fact that the
higher ranks tended to take the meals in their own more comfortable
premises where better fare was provided, it was only after the Second
World War that workers' canteens were unreservedly embraced and
such segregation disappeared.[33]

The moral insistence on family midday meals was also rooted in the fear that children might become lifelong dependents on soup kitchens, since their school days very rarely extended into the afternoon. In contrast to what happened in England and France, food was often given directly to families so that mothers could cook at home, preserving traditional family structures. An organization initiated in 1883 by Agnes Blumenfeld risked distributing breakfast for hungry children in Berlin schools after strictly checking their needs and taking care that the children themselves went to the school director's office to collect their breakfast. The composition of these free meals differed widely, ranging from a piece of bread and a cup of cocoa in the working-class district of Neukölln to a litre of milk and a roll with butter in upper-class Wilmersdorf. The same organization also gave food to families and helped with firewood, blankets and other necessities.

Many workers' budgets didn't allow for much leeway and an increase in food prices could quickly lead to mass protests, a fact of which officials were well aware. The flashpoint was now the price of meat. The price of both bread and milk also rose in the years before the First World War, but public reaction to these increases was much less violent; a sure sign of where preferences lay. When meat prices rose in 1912 because of protectionist import restrictions, the Berlin authorities organized the sale of Polish meat at reduced prices. The meat was to be offered without any profit margin by regular butchers in the covered markets. However, butchers in Wedding, a working-class district, wanted to sell their regular wares at normal prices and refused to offer the 'Russian' meat they declared to be of inferior quality, pretending that their colleagues in the affluent suburbs were offering better cuts. As a result, as described in contemporary newspaper accounts, the women who had flocked to the markets hoping for cheap meat started punching and bombarding the butchers with fruit and vegetables. The police closed the markets, whereupon the furious housewives' riot spread to nearby butchers' shops. On the following day events escalated when the women were joined by local agitators, and the police used force to protect shopkeepers and other customers. However, the women were ultimately successful: on the second day almost all covered markets were obliged to offer cheap meat.[34]

This kind of valve for letting off steam against perceived unfairness or excessive infringement on one's personal life was not available to the middle classes. Many of them increasingly suffered under their self-imposed stuffiness, with its endless ritualized menus, and the rapid changes around the safe havens of their homes. Theodor Fontane (a self-confessed gourmand who clearly enjoyed his food and often described it in loving detail in his work) highlighted the moral dilemma experienced by the bourgeoisie in in reconciling themselves with progress in an unfinished poem, 'Retrorsum' (Backwards), commenting on *Automatenrestaurants*, vending machine restaurants. The first super-modern fully self-serviced Automat restaurant opened in 1897 on Berlin's Leipziger Strasse. Its interior, modelled on public vending machines that delivered cigars, perfume, chocolate and other sweets, was functional and clean in accordance with the new ideal of speed, social freedom and unhindered access under the slogan: 'No tip, serve yourself, casual, fast and good.' By 1914 *Automatenrestaurants* had appeared in all major German cities.[35]

Some of the bourgeoisie reacted to the changes by adopting aristocratic manners, joining the reserve officer corps and taking up their drinking and duelling habits. Others threw off the constraints of the

Postcard from 1904, showing the Brandenburg Gate on the back and promoting the Automat restaurants on Friedrichstrasse and Leipzigerstrasse in Berlin, also advertising cigarettes and cognac.

established order by embracing the ideas of the *Wandervögel*, a hikers' youth movement emerging in the 1890s in Berlin. The *Wandervögel* and others campaigned against materialism and the presumptuous idea of unbounded human mastery of nature. Their plea for a return to a healthy, pre-industrial lifestyle soon spread to all areas of life and could be summarized under the slogan 'back to the purity of nature'. In time the *Lebensreform* or life-reform campaign became almost a kind of secular religion, the cult of unspoiled nature as a modern paradise regained. This moral countertrend to conservatism and industrialization in many ways resembled the modern green movement. However, its health-conscious, youth-orientated and temperate followers also declared all alcohol as well as tobacco and coffee to be harmful drugs. New alcohol-free, sweet, fizzy beverages were enthusiastically promoted, among them *Sinalco*, literally 'without alcohol', a citrus lemonade still available today from a factory founded in 1908. In addition the first alcohol-free wines and beers were produced.[36] Nudism was as ardently practised as *Kleiderreform*, a new, reformed style of clothing which advocated domestic linen and wool instead of imported cotton. Expanding waistlines among the bourgeoisie came to be regarded as evidence of lack of willpower and personal neglect, while a slender, muscular body could be taken as evidence of youthful energy, self-discipline and high expectations. Then as now, advice on how to deal with problems of obesity varied widely, with fasting, abstaining from meat and eating raw food the most popular. The first recorded cases of anorexia appeared in the 1920s when women abandoned the lace-up corset and adopted the new less structured fashions with shorter hemlines and fewer layers.[37] Anti-vaccination clubs formed and *Vollkornbrot*, wholemeal bread, was seen as a superfood as opposed to the white rolls workers loved and could increasingly afford. The Catholic priest Sebastian Kneipp developed *Kneippkaffee*, a coffee surrogate made from malted barley. He also offered a hydropathic treatment that included walking barefoot in damp meadows and advocated the use of indigenous herbs instead of imported spices. A cookbook based on his teachings and published in 1897 included recipes for powdered soup made from sage, stinging nettles, woodruff, oak leaves, strawberry leaves and other similar ingredients.[38]

Just as it is today, for many vegetarianism seemed like the perfect answer to civilization's perceived unnaturalness. The ancient Greek vegetarian ideals found in Orpheus and Pythagoras had emerged among the educated classes with the onset of the Enlightenment, recommending vegetables, fruit and herbs for therapeutic as well as moral reasons, with French philosopher Jean-Jacques Rousseau as its major influence. In his writings, especially the book *Emile* (1762), Rousseau worshipped nature as a de facto religion, presenting the unspoiled child in contrast to grown-up man degenerated by civilization, the carnivore as brutal and unnatural in contrast to the peace-loving herbivore. In Germany Gustav Struve was one of the most important pioneers of vegetarianism. Converted in 1832 after reading Rousseau, the following year Struve published the first vegetarian-themed novel in German, *Mandaras Wanderungen* (Mandara's Travels). The narrative details a young Indian's letters home as he travels through Europe about a Christianity demoralized through meat-eating while defending the vegetarian lifestyle of his homeland (for the German audience the grass was obviously greener in far-away India). In 1869 Struve continued the theme with *Pflanzenkost – die Grundlage einer neuen Weltanschauung* (Plant-diet as Basis for a New Philosophy of Life), providing the movement with the necessary theoretical foundation. In contrast to the new scientific approach to health, medicine and nutrition that promoted meat as the perfect superfood, he proposed vegetarianism as the holistic approach to human health and an all-encompassing life reform as the solution to the social problems of the age. The theologian, philosopher and anthropologist Eduard Baltzer was another ardent and influential German vegetarian, converted in 1866. The following year he founded the *Deutscher Verein für natürliche Lebensweise* (Association for a Natural Lifestyle), continental Europe's first vegetarian society, later renamed *Deutscher Verein für naturgemässe Lebensweise* (Lifestyle True to Nature). Three years later, a national umbrella organization, *Deutscher Vegetarierbund* (German Vegetarian League), followed. Thereafter numerous vegetarian cookbooks of all kinds were published, often combined with comprehensive advice on health and life in general.

Obviously vegetarianism was part of the romanticization of agrarian life in general which carried the life reform movement. Whereas earlier forms of agromania had aristocratic ladies posing as milkmaids, the new trend involved a much larger part of the populace. Urban working families were encouraged in various ways to return to nature and appreciate the countryside. One of these was *Gartenstädte*, based on an English idea. The cooperative structure of these garden cities was seen as ideal though rarely realized, Hellerau near Dresden being one of the notable exceptions. Garden suburbs began to appear at the edge of large cities, as did *Schrebergärten*, allotments named after the Leipzig physician Daniel

Moritz Schreber. Schreber's publications discussed children's health and the social consequences of over-urbanization, advocating physical exercise in the countryside. Allotments came to be used for food production as much as recreational purposes. The largest garden project still in existence is Eden, a settlement dedicated to fruit growing founded in 1893 in Oranienburg near Berlin. For the first seven years the project was strictly vegetarian, but thereafter relaxed its rules. It produced a whole range of *Reformwaren* or reform products including fruit and vegetable juices, vegetarian margarine and *Kraftnahrung*, powerfood, a vegetarian meat and sausage lookalike, precursor of today's tofu sausages. Designed as the food for a new reformed natural lifestyle, these products and many similar ones were sold in special shops known as *Reformhaus* (the first of which opened in 1887), precursors of the organic stores that joined them from the early 1980s onwards. Sporting events such as races to prove the strength of vegetarian athletes were immensely popular.

The principles of wholesome food as a source of health and a way of life were later articulated by anthroposophist Rudolf Steiner when he outlined the principles of biodynamic agriculture in a lecture, *Landwirtschaftlicher Kurs*, delivered in 1924 to landowners in the Silesian town of Kobernitz near Breslau. Based on anthroposophy's holistic approach, Steiner placed agriculture in a larger, cosmic context, emphasizing independent self-sufficiency as the ideal structure for farming communities. As an alternative to the new industrial fertilizers and chemicals, he recommended natural preparations made from mineral, herbal and animal components, as well as the use of cow dung to increase soil fertility while discouraging pests and disease.

Steiner was convinced that spiritual powers enabled all life on earth and that the cosmos and humanity all work together to influence plant growth. He regarded human taste as an essential element for detecting the intrinsic quality of foodstuffs and for understanding the connection between production methods, geographical location, and the characteristics of different types of foods.

Maximilian Bircher-Benner, a Swiss-German physician, was among the strongest opponents of Justus von Liebig and the new food scientists and became one of the guiding culinary voices of the reform movement. After studying the much-hyped hydrotherapy and visiting reformer colleague Heinrich Lahmann's renowned sanatorium in Dresden, he opened his own sanatorium in Zurich. Named *Lebendige Kraft* (Living Power), it targeted the wealthy who suffered from the long-term effects of the

A culinary place in time: Hof Marienhöhe

One of the very first biodynamic estates in Germany was established at Hof Marienhöhe near Bad Saarow, one hour's drive southeast of Berlin. When Steiner's disciple Erhard Bartsch arrived at the estate in 1928, the soil was dry and sandy, covered with heath and a few robinia trees. It was deemed completely useless for agriculture. But Bartsch's intention was to test Steiner's methods under extreme conditions. The first plantings were 4 km of hedgerows, and Marienhöhe has been under cultivation ever since. Today the estate consists of 120 hectares of small fields surrounded by a ring of lush forest. Cereals, potatoes, root vegetables and salad greens flourish, alternating in a seven- to nine-year cycle with legumes and fodder for the farm's pigs and cattle whose milk is hand-processed into cheese. It is largely to the work of organic and biodynamic farms that Germany's new cheese culture can be ascribed. In 1992 about 60 dairy farmers and cheesemakers founded the *Verband für handwerkliche Milchverarbeitung*, an association for artisanal milk processing (www.milchhandwerk.info), which today has over 600 members.

overeating encouraged by the economic boom. The idea proved extremely successful and attracted businesspeople, writers and artists from all over the world. Among those who spent time at the sanatorium was Thomas Mann, who wrote in a letter in 1909: 'Best wishes from a grass-eating Nebuchadnezzar who crawls on all fours in his airbath.' The sanatorium, he said, was a prison of hygiene where one had to get up at six in the morning and lights were off at nine in the evening. Treatments included long walks in the adjoining woods, abundant sleep, gymnastics and modest vegetarian meals that favoured raw food, and patients were to avoid stress and stimulants as much as possible – very much like an expensive modern-day spa. Bircher-Benner's colleagues were dismayed by his methods, rejecting his teachings as heretical. But he remained firm in his belief – based on new scientific findings in thermodynamics – that processing diminished food's nutritional value. He was convinced of the fundamental importance of the fact that plants transform solar energy into carbohydrates. Green leaves and fruit, he maintained, were 'sun-food'. Like many other pioneers, Bircher-Benner took his ideas to the extreme, and for him cooking was a compromise to be avoided as far as possible. Whereas the pro-meat faction of the time saw meat as equivalent to cultural and social superiority and therefore especially important for men, Bircher-Benner declared the consumption of flesh to be a dirty and an inefficient energy source. His sister, placed in charge of the sanatorium's kitchen, didn't ban it completely from the menu, possibly in an attempt to accomodate as many wealthy customers as possible. Red cabbage, stuffed veal breast, macaroni with grated cheese, lettuce, Turkish rice pudding with raspberry sauce and fruit on a Sunday in January were followed the next day by salsify with tomato sauce, green beans, potato pancakes, lamb's lettuce, cheesecake and fruit. However, the famous Bircher-Benner müesli (a Swiss diminutive of *Mus*, mush) was invariably served for breakfast. It consisted mainly of fresh fruit, above all grated apple (including the skin and core), soaked oats, a small amount of ground hazelnuts or almonds, lemon juice and sweetened condensed milk, the latter favoured by the doctor over fresh milk for reasons of hygiene, in spite of the processing involved.

TEN

Hope and Hunger, *Vollkornbrot* and Swedes, 1914 to 1949

In retrospect the tussle between free traders and autarchist protectionists appears to be a harbinger of things to come. To be torn between the relaxed and confident embrace of all the new and exotic tastes and aromas which the world at large had to offer on the one hand, and the much more cautious locavore who promised reliable familiarity on the other, was a conflict that would repeatedly and profoundly mark the German diet during the twentieth century. It recurred in different forms. The life reform movement was one of them: as soon as pauperism had been halfway overcome and society at large started to believe in a future of meat and white bread for everybody, sceptical voices called for reforms, a return to a supposedly better past of wholemeal bread and vegetables. But the real shock was still to come. Instead of a glorious repetition of 1871, as most of them expected or had been led to expect, with the outbreak of war in 1914 Germans were drawn into a relentless strudel of rationing and shortages. Eventually they were reduced to eating swedes – also known as cattle fodder – and even they were in short supply. Women's lot reflected the general dilemma; they were supposed to be feminine, but now had to hold their own and run the show on the home front. Faced with empty shelves and cupboards, it was primarily they who had to find an answer to the moral conflict about civil obedience. But who would have hesitated very long between decrees, propaganda and hunger on the one hand and autonomous action to procure at least a minimal daily ration on the other, disregarding the law if necessary? The confusing rollercoaster of food-centred feelings, questions and issues would haunt Germans again and again and left its traces in their culinary DNA.

Ironically the fleet everybody had been so obsessed with in the pre-war years was never fully deployed during the First World War, but it was the naval construction programme that put Germany on a collision course with Britain. The British reaction to the appearance of a rival naval power was a radical one: they cut Germany off from its external food sources. This blockade, a historical switch from military to economic priorities in maritime warfare, was widely regarded as being contrary to international law, as it expanded the list of contraband and put pressure on neutral countries. At the onset of war, Winston Churchill, then first lord of the British admiralty, openly declared his intention to 'starve the whole population – men, women, and children, old and young, wounded and sound – into submission'.[1] The outcome of war no longer depended on military plans and materiel, but on how long civilians could endure hunger and hardship. Food had become one of the decisive battle grounds.

According to official estimates, German food imports, whether direct or (equally important) indirect in the form of animal feed, represented roughly one-third of pre-war consumption. This was by no means exceptional at the time, as by 1913 foodstuffs made up 27 per cent of the world's export trade.[2] Supplies for the army, numbering about one-sixth of the population, as well as the rural population, accounting for about one-third, couldn't be cut far below pre-war levels. The result was that without any imports only one-sixth of the usual supplies were available for the remaining half of the population. Centralized distribution might have offered a slim chance of making this work, at least for a while, but rural producers were not interested in supplying the urban and industrial areas through a middleman. So far as food was concerned, Germany had lost the war by early 1917.

Prior to the war agricultural output had risen steadily due to the use of fertilizers, mostly imported, and there was initial optimism about reserves and future yields. Germany had forged a place in the international food community by refining raw materials, such as converting feed grain via cattle into meat, fat and milk. In time of war this made for a fatal dependency on imports, which became difficult or impossible to obtain even from neutral countries. Many factors combined to reduce food production at a time when it was most needed: agricultural labour became scarce because of the call to arms, machinery was difficult to find as German factories were increasingly used for armament production, horsepower represented a problem since horses were needed at the front, and fertilizers such as Chilean nitrate could no longer be imported. The latter problem had already been addressed by Fritz Haber, who had developed a chemical method to produce fertilizer by synthesizing ammonia, a process subsequently made commercially viable by Carl Bosch and the BASF company of Ludwigshafen. The method, however, was still expensive and mainly used to produce explosives (with Haber also playing an unfortunate essential role in the push for gas warfare).

As a result of these factors, crop yields declined and attempts to increase the area under cultivation failed. Even seemingly ample crops such as potatoes and sugar quickly became scarce, as people compensated for the lack of fat and meat by consuming more starch and sweets. German officials were much criticized for their lack of preparation and mishandling of the food supply. However, the task was not only immense but without precedent, and it seems to have been impossible to deliver a satisfactory result. At the start of the war official strategies for dealing with scarcity were virtually non-existent. Stores and warehouses were filled to the brim and after the initial panic buying no hardships were noticeable. The government didn't build up any stocks, since the necessary laws for this were difficult to steer through parliament, and war preparations were deemed inappropriate from a psychological point of view. Soon, however, export embargos and import tariff exemptions for important foodstuffs were followed by state attempts to buy food in neutral countries. The conservative agrarian lobby refused to join the war effort on a political level, hindering efficient centralized food distribution, while small producers were unwilling to give up their precious wares for the official maximum prices, which were kept deliberately low. At the same time transport for perishable foodstuffs, particularly potatoes, was problematic since trains and roads were needed for the army. As it became obvious that the war would not be over any time soon, the authorities saw no other solution but to step in and become actively involved in food production and distribution. From January 1915 grain production was nationalized and its distribution centralized. New ministries and offices, complete with the necessary administrational apparatus, came to manage supplies of everything from potatoes, meat and eggs to legumes, salt herrings and sauerkraut through fixed maximum prices, allocations and rationing.

Bread was largely replaced by potatoes, but its supply was considered essential to maintaining civic order. Official efforts concentrated on making grain supplies last as long as possible and sought to disguise potatoes as bread, at least to some degree. As early as October 1914 it was decreed compulsory to include 5 per cent potato products (mostly in the form of dried flakes) in all rye bread. With an even higher potato content (up to 20 per cent) this was sold as *K-Brot*, leaving it up to consumers to decide if they were eating *Kriegsbrot* (war bread) or *Kartoffelbrot* (potato bread). As Germany's main grain-producing territories in the east weren't suited to wheat growing, from January 1915 regulations obliged millers to include a proportion of rye when milling wheat and higher minimum grinding levels were set. Night baking was declared illegal in an attempt to reduce the consumption of wheatflour rolls, a popular breakfast indulgence. Since the home-grown grain available to the bakeries had a higher water content than the previously used imported varieties, all bread was somewhat heavier than in pre-war times, and the potatoes in *K-Brot* added to the load. By June 1915 bread was rationed. As the situation deteriorated during the course of the war and potatoes became scarce as well, *K-Brot* was made with the addition, depending on availability, of maize, peas, beans, soy beans, manioc, tapioca, acorns, swedes and even animal blood. The educated classes nevertheless endorsed the new national loaf with patriotic fervour, leading the British prime minister Lloyd George to comment that the German 'potato-bread spirit' was more dangerous than German militarism.[3] Beer supplies were considered a similarly delicate matter. Before the outbreak of war, Germany had been the second largest beer producer worldwide (behind the u.s.). In spite of grain shortages many breweries carried on, though national production was reduced to one-third of its previous total, beer became lighter and thinner and many small breweries eventually had to close down.

The introduction of rationing cards was without precedent and a complex apparatus was required to make the scheme work at all. In spite of this new kind of state socialism the system favoured self-governance. Regional authorities, responsible for implementing state decisions, were faced with immense practical and administrative tasks. In many cases they not only produced their own food to complement official allocations, but had to solve storing and control problems – all this while confronting the complaints of the angry and desperate. Early in the process, working-class women in particular didn't hesitate to vent their anger when faced with price increases, leading to riots and looting.

Certain official decisions seemed particularly short-sighted and driven by panic, such as the so-called *Schweinemord* or pig slaughter. In December 1914, shocked by fast-diminishing stocks of potatoes and grain, officials sought to reduce the use of animal feed by declaring pigs competitors with humans for valuable food. As a result, in the following spring a government order was issued calling for higher slaughter numbers. Sources widely differ in their assessment of numbers, but the market was certainly inundated with meat and fat, as many communal authorities were unable to cope with preserving the meat, which often came from animals slaughtered too young. Prices collapsed for a time only to reach even greater heights later in the year. Left as the main source of meat (as well as milk, fat and fertilizer), cattle in their turn became scarcer and the breeding stock gradually deteriorated. Whatever action was taken in one part of the market led to a serious lack in another without solving the underlying problem. The introduction of a maximum price for pigs in November 1915 drove the market almost completely underground, by then a familar response to all attempts at regulation. Maximum prices for cattle followed in March 1916, and by May, when few foodstuffs were left without regulation, the KEA, *Kriegsernährungsamt* (Office for Food in Wartime) was created as a coordinating body. The authorities, it seemed, had no choice but to stumble from one measure to another in their attempt to establish a centralized structure in spite of regional and group interests. Attempts to solve shortages were only put in place when these became too severe to ignore. The reality was that supplies were insufficient, whatever official policymakers might do or say.

The rationing system defined Germans neither by their social nor financial status, but according to their relevance and importance to the wartime economy. The army and armament industry had absolute priority. The latter used fat and sugar to replace blocked imports of glycerine (glycerine required for nitroglycerine can be manufactured from sugar by fermentation in the presence of sodium sulphite[4]), while exporting sugar, potatoes and coal to neutral countries in exchange for raw materials for their factories. Army provisioning still relied on a law dating back to 1873, but the authorities realized that with urbanization and industrialization the situation had profoundly changed. Instead of calling for regional supplies as in the past, army provisions were bought on the free market by a central office. In spring 1917 it was estimated that 70 per cent of all food available was consumed by the army. However, the provision for soldiers listed in an imperial decree of 1909 was undoubt-edly soon reduced to mere theory: 750 g bread, 10 g roasted coffee beans, 180 g raw meat plus 40 g suet (or any other kind of animal fat), 250 g legumes (which could be replaced by 125 g rice or 1.5 kg potatoes) and 25 g salt as well as 'other necessary foodstuffs' were to be provided daily.[5]

To complement the comparatively meagre civilian rations, the populace was strongly encouraged to collect and consume anything that held the promise of a few calories as well as to forage for food in the wild. Schoolchildren in particular were roped in to collect anything and everything they could find, from bones, fruit stones and potato skins to all kinds of wild plants, including beechnuts. They were also taught to attack pests such as caterpillars on cabbages. In some regions the woods had to be closed for certain periods to allow nature to recover from ravenous collectors. By late 1916 it became obvious that in spite of the activities of numerous charities, more had to be done to prevent famine. Following experimental efforts to relieve the worst effects of shortages in Berlin with what were known as *Goulaschkanonen*, goulash cannons, the KEA pushed for more and larger *Massenspeiseanstalten*, literally 'dining institutions for the masses': communal soup kitchens that would make more efficient use of foodstuffs. Official propaganda presented these soup kitchens as a civilian equivalent of the soldiers' field kitchens. Initially developed to provide for soldiers' families and the unemployed, they were soon established in most towns and increasingly became open to everybody. In Berlin the initiative was put under the command of the dynamic home economist Hedwig Heyl, the local women's movement pioneer. *Massenspeiseanstalten* usually offered a simple stew at lunchtime which could also be taken away. At some point the authorities even discussed compulsory attendance in cities; a utopian de-privatization of cooking and eating that was never realized. On the contrary, attending them was often perceived as shameful. Only at the beginning, when meals were provided without the need to produce a ration card, did they enjoy some popularity. Women in particular not only criticized the prices for the quality and quantity offered, but resented the perceived intrusion into their private sphere. Many regional authorities came to realize that soup kitchens were not actually more efficient in their use of scarce foodstuffs. Nevertheless, towards the end of the war, the system pushed meagre official supplies in that direction, and for many the soup kitchens were the last resort.

By the last months of 1916, the official daily regular civilian ration stipulated 271 g bread, 357 g potatoes, 11.4 g margarine and butter, 36 g meat, less than a tenth of an egg, 26 g sugar and 9.8 g pearl barley or other starch, a total daily allowance of 1,344 kcal.[6] Given that supplies were so meagre it seems somewhat absurd to consider recipes in cookbooks, even assuming that additional supplies might be self-grown or

Potato peeling in a Berlin central soup kitchen, catering for 9,000 jobless each day.

obtained from illicit sources. As it happens, leaflets dealt rather better with the constantly changing situation than any cookbook. Daily newspapers also provided regular instruction on how to deal with ration cards, unusual ingredients and substitutes, and how to cook 'without' the various ingredients in short supply – particularly fat, milk and eggs. The market for surrogates of all kinds flourished, in April 1916 reaching at least one-eighth of all expenditure on food. Some of these substitutes were familiar modern industrial products such as margarine, stock cubes and custard powder; others were of very questionable quality and origin, or ersatz-ersatz, such as coffee surrogates made of swedes, acorns or heather. Some products made by profiteers had no merit whatsoever – ersatz salad oil made from yellow coloured vegetable substances, coloured maize or potato flour posing as powdered egg and pepper made from ash. A brand called Topol, sold as *Nährhefekraftmehl* (nutritious yeast flour), promised to replace fat, meat and milk in one go. Under great logistical difficulties, the market in ersatz foodstuffs was officially regulated, and by July 1919 there were 837 officially sanctioned sausage substitutes, more than 1,000 stock cube surrogates and a choice of 511 branded stand-ins for coffee.[7]

Books such as the *Kriegskochbuch*, a wartime cookbook written by Luise Holle (editor of the Davidis cookbook from 1892), were undeniably published with the best of intentions, advising a return to soup mornings and evenings. Holle provided recipes for meat dishes made with non-rationed offal, low-fat dishes, cheap desserts and austerity baking. Nevertheless, the ingredients still included such unobtainables as fifteen Pfennig-worth of candied lemon peel, 200 g ground almonds, four eggs and 250 g chocolate.

Housekeeping had become almost schizophrenic. On the one hand private initiative and the old subsistence skills were needed and implicitly encouraged. The worse the quality of the raw material, the more work and creativity were needed to turn it into something palatable. Housewives associations joined official propaganda efforts by organizing talks and cookery demonstrations to promote thriftiness and ingenuity. Every available patch of ground was to be cultivated, be it balcony, windowsill, public park or allotment. Potatoes, vegetables and fruit were planted; goats, rabbits and poultry were kept for milk, meat and eggs. *Balkonschweine*, balcony pigs, are often mentioned in this context, supposedly showing the desperate desire of urban families to keep pigs, though the term usually referred to rabbits. On the other hand, the consumption of all officially traded foodstuffs was highly regulated and deprivatized. Private households were checked to prevent hoarding and overconsumption, and precious reserves were subject to confiscation. Forward planning was impossible, as foodstocks were completely unpredictable and depended on what was available after seemingly endless queueing, sometimes all night long, a system christened *Lebensmittel-Polonäsen*. On top of all this, even when successfully making do with official rations, women were repeatedly accused of selfishly 'over-caring' for their families by making food taste good. Cooking was to be a patriotic requirement; the goal was to avoid pleasure and overindulgence.

Besides the shortages, unequal distribution of scarce supplies caused many complaints, leading to demonstrations, riots and strikes. The discrepancy between urban and rural populations grew and was in turn augmented by the gap between city folks with rural connections and those without, as well as between rich and poor. For a wealthy minority, food was still available – a reality made painfully obvious in delicatessens, restaurants and hotels. Officially these outlets had the same status as the soup kitchens, and were restricted in their offerings by the obligation to serve rationed food only with the necessary coupons. However, money procured a comparatively sumptuous meal at most places, especially as non-rationed game and poultry often found their way into restaurant kitchens. On official meat-free days (introduced in 1916), menus offered dishes containing meat as 'bread with topping'.

The food situation reached its crisis point in the winter of 1916–17, known as the *Kohlrübenwinter*, turnip (or more precisely swede) winter, when the potato crop failed and the winter months were particularly cold. Until summer 1917 swedes had to stand in for potatoes as a staple food while also appearing in the form of jam, bread and sausage. Previously swedes had been regarded as cattle fodder, and relying on them for survival represented a severe blow to German morale, much worse than having to fall back on paupers' potatoes. Metaphorically people felt they had been reduced to the status of cattle, reflecting the state of those being sent to the slaughterhouse at the front. Even so there was too little to go around, even for money. Average rations in this period fell below 1,150 calories per person per day, well below subsistence level. The resulting famine was widespread and has been compared to the situation in Ireland in the 1840s.

This might have been decisive in ending the war forthwith had it not been for the German decision to resume and expand submarine warfare against Allied merchant vessels. Hunger isn't only a bad cook, as a German saying goes, but also a bad advisor, as it gave the u.s. the final excuse to enter the war on the Allied side and further tighten the blockade. Food-related propaganda in Germany was relentless in persuading consumers to accept restrictions and sacrifices in the name of patriotic duty, preaching the return to the supposedly healthy, natural diet of old (picking up on *Lebensreform* slogans) and appealing to people's sense of responsibility in posters, leaflets and lectures. But the longer the war continued, the less the population identified with official views on food policy. Towards the end of the war official contributions from the agrarian regions to the centralized food distribution had been reduced to minimal amounts, and official rations shrank to a fraction of pre-war consumption. With the exception of the winter of 1916–17, potatoes were the only food supplied at anything close to pre-war levels, whereas meat rations in the second half of 1918 were down to 11.8 per cent, eggs to 13.3 per cent and butter to 28.1 per cent of pre-war consumption. In cities this represented half the protein required by an 'average' adult, one-quarter of the fat, three-fifths of the carbohydrates and a little over half the calories.[8]

As the situation deteriorated, anarchy crept in and almost everybody cheated on everybody else at all levels: regional governments exaggerated population numbers to receive higher allocations, farmers exploited their position to get higher prices from urban customers and factories cheated on the system by providing workers with food acquired through 'self-help', that is, illegal bartering. City folks hoarded food bought directly at the farm gate, an illegal activity facilitated in many districts by special trains conveniently scheduled in addition to the official timetable. Illicit trading increased in importance as state-sanctioned supplies of food diminished (along with clothing, shoes and lighting material). Official estimates suggest that only about half of all rationed food was legally distributed. The government seemed to tolerate the status quo for the simple reason that illicit trading was probably the only way the nation could survive (it was only in March 1918 that illicit trading as a professional activity was declared a criminal offence punishable with a prison sentence). Women were fully aware of the fact that official rations were totally insufficient and that soldiers at the front were often in better physical shape than their families back home. They didn't hesitate to turn to 'self-help' and commit criminal offences in trying to keep their families alive. The *Heimatfront* (home front) turned into a battle between people and authorities. The less the state was able to guarantee food supplies, the more the *Schleichhandel*, illicit trading, flourished (the term *Schwarzmarkt*, black market, was only introduced into German during the Second World War).[9]

In cities and industrial regions people began to suffer from famine-related illnesses such as oedema, tuberculosis and rickets, the same fate that had earlier afflicted those reduced to strict official rations in institutions. Schoolchildren, young people, the elderly and the chronically ill suffered the most, but scarcity and the lack of any stimulants such as chocolate, spices, coffee, tea and tobacco led to general depression and apathy. Mortality rose among all age groups and was particularly severe in the large cities when the influenza epidemic in 1918 took its toll. While war casualties among the military were calculated between 1.9 and 2.4 million, between 700,000 and 800,000 civilians died of starvation or related illnesses. Officially this situation did not exist. Propaganda seemed to have learnt a lot from the new art of advertising. At late as spring 1918 a poster in doctors' waiting rooms declared:

> We must persevere. We can persevere. Our nutrition is sufficient and secure. It is expected that the situation will soon become better. The general state of health is satisfying. We have been spared from epidemics. Rheumatism and gout have completely disappeared.[10]

Everybody who saw this knew it was a lie and whether in the trenches or at home, people were increasingly unwilling to fight for the so-called authorities behind them (it is notable that the situation in Britain was quite similar).[11] Having appealed to the u.s. for an armistice, Germany was expected to surrender her merchant fleet as well as rolling stock in the form of locomotives and freight wagons in good working order 'to ensure the supply of foodstuffs to Germany'. However, those few of the wagons that were still in working order were needed to distribute such little food as there was. German officials hesitated to sign a document which sentenced their country to continuing hunger and starvation, risking anarchy through famine. At the least they expected to be able to buy food for the starving population in return for the merchant fleet. But France had borrowed heavily during the war to meet her own food shortages and kept insisting that German gold reserves be used for reparations instead of buying food supplies. Consequently the blockade was further extended into the Baltic Sea, suspending German rights in those fishing grounds. German industry ground to an almost complete halt from lack of raw materials and the inability to feed its workers. Depression and hopelessness were even more acute than in wartime, threatening moral collapse. A British commissioner reported in 1919, after an inspection trip in Germany, on the appalling quality of the potatoes: 'It was with difficulty that one could believe the potatoes I referred to could be eaten by any human creature; only the pangs of direct hunger would make their consumption possible.'[12]

It is rarely mentioned how negatively these hardships affected the way the Treaty of Versailles was perceived in Germany. Also, there can be no doubt that the deep food trauma of the First World War shaped Nazi strategies. Some historians even claim that the experience turned a whole generation, the schoolchildren of that time, into enthusiastic Nazi followers, adding conviction to their theory that Germany's economy needed to expand east to achieve *Lebensraum*, or living space, a concept that had been coined by Friedrich Ratzel in the late 1890s.[13] Finally, in March 1919, the German delegation agreed to part with the merchant fleet. During the following weeks food arrived in German ports, most of it organized by the American Relief Commission, although restrictions remained until the blockade was lifted with the official signing of the peace treaty in late June 1919.

In 1919, depending upon region, 20 to 40 per cent of the population were unemployed, with their allowance from the state constantly eroded

A group of poor unemployed people during lunch on a bench, 1920–29.

by rising inflation. From 1920 onwards American and British Quakers organized the provision of additional food to as many starving German children as possible, reaching 25 per cent of all those born between 1907 and 1919. The Quakers were seen as apolitical and impartial as a result of the help they gave to civilians and German POWs in France and Belgium during the war. They were careful not to interfere with German ideas about family structure and cautious in the way they offered assistance: these provisions, they explained, were

> meant to be a supplemental meal. We do not want to raise the burden of support from the shoulders of the parent any more than necessary. The meal is given at ten o'clock in the morning, or at two or three o'clock in the afternoon so as not to coincide with the meal at home.

Perhaps due to these sensiblities, the state authorities were reluctant to take up the role of providing extra food from the Quakers when they stopped sending food and money in 1925, although the need for school meals was obviously acute. In 1922 more than 60 per cent of all school-children in the larger cities were malnourished. In 1924 an American visitor noticed:

You can't tell from their faces how old they are; so you don't know how undersized they are. It is just the expression and color as well as the odd lines and wrinkles that one cannot imagine on a child's face.

Once again it was left to private initiatives and charities to care for hungry children in the large cities while the authorities reverted to admonishing housewives to prepare sensible meals with little money, continuing to offer advice rather than assistance throughout the depression of the early 1930s.[14]

In 1922 meat consumption remained at wartime levels: 22 kg per head per year, less than half the 52 kg available in 1913.[15] Obliged to spend up to half their income on food, the urban middle classes felt reduced to a social and economic level unacceptably close to that of the lower classes. It has sometimes been said that the First World War made for a growing social homogenization, a 'socialization' through shortages. However, in retrospect a general loss of confidence as well as the rise of egocentric principles based on the idea of the survival of the fittest seem more characteristic of the First World War and the post-war period. The anarchic spirit of self-help that had developed during wartime led to food riots. Disillusioned and frustrated that peace hadn't brought a return to their pre-war lifestyle, the less fortunate were by no means ready to accept private profiteering and extortionate prices. In contrast to those in work, they were unable to express their feelings through striking. The police had to be called, often in vain, to protect shopkeepers from looting. In Berlin the situation reached a new climax on 5 November 1923 when the city authorities were unable to distribute unemployment allowances due to paper money shortages. Sparked by mounting anti-Semitism, thousands stormed the Jewish Scheunenviertel quarter in the centre of Berlin, looting Jewish shops and robbing, beating up and stripping naked any Jewish-looking person unfortunate enough to cross their path. Most of the people in this mob had known only hunger, misery and frustration and saw group action as their only chance of wielding any kind of power. A wider spectrum of society involved itself in much less violent incidents of lawlessness, and those who stole food from shop displays were almost apologetic to shopkeepers. Meanwhile farmers and wholesalers were holding back their goods in anticipation of currency reform, which eased the tension on 15 November 1923.[16]

Finally, after almost a decade, life in Germany was becoming less bleak, not least due to the easing of reparation payments under America's Dawes Plan and increased acceptance of Germany as a political and economic player. During the so-called *Goldenen Zwanziger*, Golden Twenties, at least some of the urban middle classes adopted a more relaxed lifestyle, warmly embracing modernity. An underlying need for escapism made people search out amusement, sometimes almost desperately, albeit with a certain flourish. On Berlin's Kurfürstendamm the density of cafes, bars and restaurants was even higher than on the Linden boulevard. All tastes were catered for at all hours. Sitting out on the pavement to watch passers-by was part of the attraction year-round. In winter some places even put out tall coke-fired ovens very similar to the outdoor gas-heaters of today, adding further to 'the Paris feeling'.[17] American-style amusement parks modelled on Coney Island, *Luna-Parks*, replaced the pre-war coffee gardens. Restaurants serving wine and beer became ever larger, louder and more colourful gastronomic experiences. Among the best-known of these establishments was Café Piccadilly on Potsdamer Platz, which had 2,000 seats on two floors.[18] Opened in 1912, it had been renamed Kaffee Vaterland, fatherland cafe, in 1914. In 1928 the Kempinski family reopened it as Haus Vaterland; it offered entertainment as well as food and drink and could seat 3,500. Music and entertainment of every kind started at midday, while a wide range of themed restaurants and bars offered the equivalent of a world tour. The best known of these places of entertainment as well as refreshment was the *Rheinterrasse*, a simulated Rhine landscape complete with vineyards and looming castles where revellers experienced a 'genuine' thunderstorm over the Rhine at regular intervals. Vienna was represented by a Grinzing *Heurigen* wine bar where guests were serenaded by schmaltzy violins while gazing across a panoramic vista of the Austrian capital. In a Moorish palace, where the Golden Horn and Constantinople complete with mosques and minarets were visible on the horizon, Turkish hookahs were set on Turkish tables and Turkish coffee was served from copper pots along with proper Turkish raki. Rice wine was on offer at the Japan-Bar, a Texas band played in the Wild West, sherry could be had in a Spanish bodega, Tokaji wine was served in the Csardas-Stube – and, of course, there was ample provision of beer and wurst at the Bavarian Löwenbräu beerhouse, while an *Altberliner Bierstube* was aptly named Teltower Rübchen, Teltow turnip. Music and artists were to be heard and seen everywhere, but the heart of the whole endeavour was a vast dancehall. On the tenth anniversary of the opening of the complex, Haus Vaterland claimed to have welcomed ten million visitors who had consumed 3.5 million bottles of wine from the Kempinski cellars and eaten food provided by more than 100 cooks working in the main kitchen on the fifth floor. Berliners themselves, it was said, visited Haus Vaterland once out of curiosity, then left the place to tourists and newcomers, since natives of the city much preferred the catering at the original Kempinski establishments.

For Hotel Adlon the Golden Twenties were golden indeed. With its cellars well-stocked with wine, the hotel was financially stable in spite of inflation, welcoming increasing numbers of international visitors who appreciated the ambience even more than Berliners did. In 1928 the dinner menu had become a relaxed international mix: *scotsch* (sic) *woodcock* and *poule au pot* were mentioned next to *holländische Tunke*, *sweet potato* and *omelette au confiture*. At the dinner gala evenings announced for every Thursday, the chef heeded the call of the exotic even more enthusiastically, offering a wild mix of Florida, Londonderry, Rhodesia, Souvaroff and Stroganoff.

Cafés on the Westberlin Kurfürstendamm in the 1920s provided coke-fuelled heaters to prolong the season, 'following the Paris model'. Today gas heaters are used even in the midst of winter.

249

In contrast in private households women were increasingly obliged to contribute to finances to make ends meet. Fewer and fewer families could afford servants, by now a scarce and expensive commodity. Taking their inspiration from the u.s., home economics associations endeavoured to highlight the virtues of modern technology. Of the many American publications which dealt with the subject, the most influential, Christiane Frederick's *The New Housekeeping: Efficiency Studies in Home Management*, was translated into German in 1920. Households were regarded as workplaces in need of rational organization based on modern scientific findings. Nevertheless traditional ideas lay behind the supposedly modernist vision: it was never questioned that housework and childrearing were women's tasks. In addition the war had shown the importance of housework as an economic force, and its rationalization in Germany was not intended to promote consumerism, leisure activities or any of the other selfish white urban female indulgences enjoyed in the u.s. Housework was intended to assist economic recovery and help the nation meet reparation payments; for the same reason, buying imported goods was considered unpatriotic. In that respect nothing had changed in the aftermath of war. Performing the duties of a wife and mother was still widely regarded as a woman's main task in life. Taking part in any other activities – including spending more time than necessary on household chores – was to cheat the husband and children of the time they deserved with their wife or mother.

Bauhaus architects, industrialists, Social Democrats and feminists were all united in promoting the need to rationalize women's daily chores. In 1926 these uncomfortable bedfellows came together in the creation of the Home Economics Group of the Reichskuratorium für Wirtschaftlichkeit (RKW, National Board of Trustees for Productivity), forerunner of the Rationalisierungs- und Innovationszentrum der Deutschen Wirtschaft (German Economic Centre for Rationalization and Innovation). For some this seemed to offer a convenient means of controlling the spending habits of the lower classes, thus limiting wage demands; for others it could be considered an opportunity to criticize the proletarian lifestyle for scientific reasons – an excuse to deplore knick-knacks in the kitchen, chattering with neighbours and frequent unplanned shopping trips as wasteful and causing a nuisance for the rest of the population. Cooking, cleaning and washing, it was felt, should conform to the same processes that governed industrial labour by delivering maximum output for minimum input through the elimination of waste. A large show on the subject, *Die Ernährung* (Nutrition), was held in Berlin in 1928. It was designed to demonstrate that hunger would never return thanks to the new, modern, rational kitchens on show, assuring visitors that home-making and housewifery were central to the whole economy. The Berlin trade fairgrounds had been started for the first automobile exhibition in 1921 and were situated next to the Avus motor racing track. The new *Funkturm* radio tower was finished when in 1926 the first *Grüne Woche* ('Green Week') agricultural fair took place there. It soon also featured a restaurant at a lofty 52 metres off the ground.

The nation's home economists were tireless in developing new materials such as Cromargan, a type of stainless steel, and Durax or Jena, fireproof glass, as well as more affordable and easy to clean utensils made from aluminium and enamel. Every tool and kitchen activity was monitored and reviewed in the search for more efficient implements and methods, leading to calls for the standardization of furniture, appliances and kitchenware. The board even examined household tasks such as peeling potatoes, though an exhaustive search for the ideal instrument and method for the task proved inconclusive. Advice then focused on saving energy and avoiding exhaustion caused by incorrect posture and poor working conditions. Industrialists, charities and the government promoted the board's ideas in schools and pamphleted the populace at large. At the forefront of the campaign were electrically operated food processors with numerous applications – bringing the technical revolution into the home environment and ensuring the industrialization of private kitchens. However the majority of the households targeted by the campaign used coal or firewood to cook, as most couldn't afford electricity until after the Second World War. Like war propagandists, the rationalizers were always ready to turn events to their own advantage: 'The vacuum cleaner will be superfluous in the home which does not allow dust the possibility of collecting', wrote Erna Meyer, one of their leading advocates, in 1927. Germans were by no means alone in holding up rationalization as the answer to domestic drudgery, but the notion seems to have had an unusually strong appeal there, at least in the abstract. With hindsight, this seems to anticipate the irrational acceptance of the absurd idea of resettling the conquered territories in the late 1930s and early '40s: as long as we stick to the right principles, we'll manage anything.[19]

In the wake of the economic recovery of 1924 new housing projects enabled the introduction of modernist ideas into the home. However, it is important to keep in mind that at the time the functional layouts that enabled the rationalization of work in kitchens equipped with water and heat sources derived from gas or electricity were too expensive for most working-class families. In these new spaces the kitchen was placed at the centre of the household but was largely reduced to cooking and related activities. Living and eating in the same room had come to be regarded as unhygienic, and as requiring a room deemed too large for rationalized labour. Only in very small flats was it declared acceptable to combine cooking and eating activities in a single space. The ideal new kitchen was sited next to the living or dining room. It was small, well-ventilated and had plenty of light. The best known of several new kitchen models was the *Frankfurter Küche* designed in 1926 by the Viennese architect Margarete Schütte-Lihotzky. Commissioned by Frankfurt am Main's city council, it was modelled on the kitchens installed on steamships and in dining cars on trains. The prototype was

Margarete Schütte-Lihotzky's Frankfurt kitchen.

A culinary place in time: Musterhaus am Horn

Germany's very first fitted kitchen was installed in the
Bauhaus model house Musterhaus am Horn in Weimar in
1923 on the occasion of the first Bauhaus festival. Bauhaus
represented a lifestyle in which art and technology were
seen as one. The kitchen here is all in white, with milky
glass tiles, and its use is restricted to food preparation and
the cleaning of dishes. Visually and functionally it is the
very opposite of the traditional lower classes' Wohnküche
or kitchen-cum-living-room. Unlike the Frankfurt
Kitchen, ceramic containers (which are still in industrial
production today) are used for flour, sugar and similar
provisions. The Musterhaus was conceived as a model for
a new kind of building but remained a one-off. Just as the
ideal of a classless society was unable to overcome inflation,
massive unemployment and political instability, all of which
worked against women's emancipation, any notion of
democratization through the standardization of living
space as proposed by the Bauhaus was strongly opposed by
conservatives who wanted to hang on to the traditions
which gave them a favourite position in society. The Haus am
Horn was lived in until 1938. It was restored and declared
a world heritage site in 1996 and is open to the public
(www.hausamhorn.de).

---

furnished according to the Taylor system and complied with efficiency
studies in home management. Three different types were proposed, giving
away the project's middle-class target groups: for households with two
servants, for those with one, and for those with no servants at all. They
all included an ironing board that opened out from the wall, moveable
lamps and *Schütten*, small aluminium drawers for flour, sugar and other
necessities. The smallest model was 6.5 m square and narrow in shape
with a single window at the short end. It had wooden cabinets painted
blue, a colour with a supposedly hygienic 'anti-fly' function. It could be
argued that Schütte-Lihotzky valued simplicity for aesthetic reasons, for
even at the time her design was criticized for isolating the housewife. In
response she developed an additional model with a glass wall facing

the living or dining room, aestheticizing the housewives' isolation rather then ending it.

The Nazi regime appropriated and exploited many of the life reform movement's ideas. Not only was the lawn of Berlin's Olympiastadion maintained according to biodynamic principles, but the concentration camp in Dachau also ran a 150-hectare farm growing a wide selection of herbs following Rudolf Steiner's ideas, which were sold in a shop on the premises.[20] *Körperkultur* – body culture – became an Aryan, neo-pagan cult closely linked to the vegetarian ideal of a 'pure' and thus healthy body. At the same time the Nazis were deeply suspicious of the vegetarian movement itself, which they considered both pacifist and sectarian. In 1935, the same year that Johannes Haussleiter provided a history of vegetarianism in antiquity, *Der Vegetarismus in der Antike,* Germany's vegetarians' association, the Vegetarierbund, disbanded to avoid being forcibly absorbed into the Deutsche Gesellschaft für Lebensreform – German Life Reform Society – founded by the Nazis.

In Nazi ideology farmers were idealized as the backbone of the Aryan race, providers of the life source and embodying the link between *Blut und Boden,* blood and soil. As early as 1933 the agricultural sector was brought under the direct control of the *Reichsnährstand* (national food estate). The regime mounted a far-reaching campaign for self-sufficiency in food production to reach independence from food imports. Obviously this was one of the lessons which they had learnt from the First World War; self-sufficiency was considered essential in preparing the country for war. Programmes initiated during the late nineteenth century, designed to create more usable land from swamps and coastal areas, were restarted as *Landeskulturmassnahmen,* and grassland was brought under the plough.[21] However, agricultural productivity lagged behind the industrial sector. Chemical fertilizer, by now industrially produced, was expensive and would soon become scarce as its production had rival requirements with the armaments industry. Farms were often small and fields widely dispersed, a result of Napoleonic inheritance laws which led to fragmented landholdings in some regions. The Nazis tried to consolidate farms to make them more efficient, an essential prerequisite for the replacement of horses and oxen with tractors. The model for these new farms was to be the *Erbhöfe,* so-called ancestral estates, whose owners (who had to be of pure Aryan descent) had safeguarded their farms from splitting up and thus becoming inefficient. However, like most regulations at the time, this had the ultimate goal of tighter

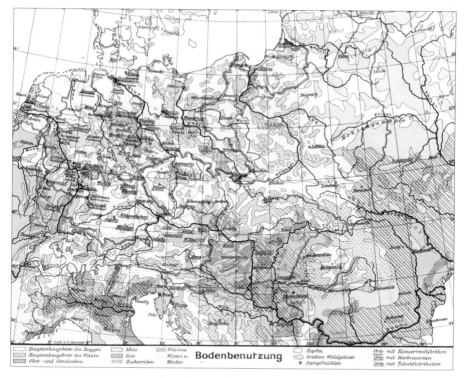

Agriculture in Germany in 1930.

state control (and substantial *Flurbereinigung*, the re-parcelling of land, only took place after the Second World War). *Lebensraum* in the east was considered essential to provide the land and resources the German race deserved. Once the east was conquered and its former inhabitants forcibly removed or murdered, German agronomists in their mega-lomaniac fantasies intended to build an agricultural empire modelled on the American Midwest as well as earlier European colonial efforts in the tropics.

From the beginning, Germany's 'battle for food' ran into severe problems due to below-average crops and bureaucratic deficiencies. In addition migration away from rural areas made for deep-rooted labour problems during the harvest. When a bread crisis threatened in the winter of 1935–6, drastic steps such as rationing were only narrowly avoided, leading to renewed efforts and even stricter agricultural regu-lations in the years that followed. Sport and dance halls were confiscated to house national grain reserves in preparation for war, and the build-ing of silos and store rooms was subsidized by the state. The need for migrant workers in armaments production led to the official promotion of machinery on farms. A the same time inexperienced members of the Nazi Youth were sent to provide cheap labour in stables and fields.[22]

The Nazis promoted *Vollkornbrot*, wholemeal bread. However, they didn't invent it; indeed the concept and term were by no means as timeless as some would have liked them to be. The history of *Vollkornbrot*, bread made of the whole grain except for the husk (or chaff), went back to the 1890s, when bread reformers lobbied against the commercial white bread made with flour from modern mills where bran and germ could be easily separated. The first documented use of the term is from 1910: then as now (up to a point) it not only stood for the use of wholegrain flour, but the idea of a complete, indeed full – *voll* – reconnection with nature. There had, of course, been earlier versions of non-white breads, above all in the north of Germany, where more rye was consumed than in the centre and south. The darkest and heaviest of these virtue-bestowing breads was Westphalia's *Pumpernickel*. Originally known as *Swattbraut* or black bread, there are many stories attached to its seventeenth-century beginnings, though historians remain divided as to the roots of the name. To this day pumpernickel is made from coarsely ground wholegrain flour kneaded with water and salt and formed into large, long, rectangular loaves that steam rather than bake for 24 hours in a sealed oven, producing a sweetish, almost syrupy flavour. Since the 1890s reform bakers had come up with various new wholemeal breads. At the start these were called *Ganzmehlbrot* (literally wholemeal bread), among them Steinmetz, Simons and Schlüter breads made from rye and Graham bread made from wheat, all named after their 'inventors' and encouraged by new scientific findings which promoted the idea that food should be unadulterated, 'natural' and complete. The term *Vollmilch*, full-fat milk, was also coined then and was legally defined in 1899 as linked to fat content.

Official Nazi policy declared that the quality and colour of the daily bread was directly linked to the general health of the German race, an almost mythical notion perceived at the time as threatened with degeneracy. However, since the hardships of the First World War, dark bread made with bran had a negative connotation in not so mythical daily life, and many people were convinced that it made more sense to eat more digestible white bread and feed the bran to animals for meat and milk. In 1923, with hyperinflation under control, a general shift from rye to wheat bread mirrored that of the comparatively prosperous late nineteenth and early twentieth centuries. Political discussion once again was divided between those who advocated free trade and wheat imports on the one hand, and supporters of a conservative campaign favouring rye bread and designated wheat-free days along with the imposition of import restrictions on American wheat on the other. As the depression took hold in Germany in 1929 home-grown rye gained ground once more, and wholemeal bread was seen as a more sustainable and thrifty way to use precious home-grown nutrients, as well as a source of the newly discovered and already popular vitamins.

In their quest for German supremacy the Nazi party appropriated and exploited this trend, initiating an impressive systematic campaign in favour of *Vollkornbrot* on the basis of domestic economy and health, in particular the fight against tooth decay. The master race, it was assumed, would thrive and flourish on a diet of domestically produced, 'natural', wholesome food. In a survey of bread consumption in 1936, black and wholemeal bread made up 6 per cent and rye bread 50 per cent, while bread made from a mix of rye and wheat – to this day one of the most popular types of bread – was at 20 per cent and wheat bread at 24 per cent. In the same year autarchy in food and military self-sufficiency were officially declared the main political goals, along with the mobilization of the entire German economy for war as a prelude to the expansion of Germany to the east. *Vollkornbrot* was one of the most important elements of these preparations for war. Having learnt their lessons from the First World War, officials didn't attempt to standardize bread production in general. Instead they called for the regional family-run bakeries that were widespread in Germany (in contrast to Britain where the bread industry was already dominated by large-scale industrial producers) to come up with their own wholemeal breads based on the *Vollkornbrot* principle. An advertising campaign using posters, leaflets and educational materials for kindergartens, schools and dental practices sought to inform and convince instead of 'force-feeding' the population; it was later augmented by short films shown in cinemas detailing the 'battle for bread'.

In 1939 the Reichsvollkornausschuss or National Wholemeal Committee was founded with the aim of increasing consumption of wholemeal loaves to between 30 and 50 per cent of the total. Bakers were required to submit samples of their respective breads for quality control. Upon approval and for a fee, they received advertising materials and an official sticker featuring the general health committee's logo with the old runic sign symbolizing life (which came to be used on over 150 different foodstuffs officially approved as healthy) and the words

Vollkornbrot ist besser und gesunder, wholemeal bread is better and more healthy. At the same time the committee trained bakers to optimize quality and advocated the production of wholemeal rolls and pastries. Official prices for those wholemeal goods were slightly higher than those for ordinary ones in the hope that the higher margin would serve as an incentive to increase production, one of the major problems of the whole operation.

Vollkornbrot became a national symbol. It entered the school curriculum and was made compulsory in soup kitchens, canteens, restaurants and hospitals. Instant food products for infants using wholemeal flour were introduced. On the somewhat delicate subject of digestibility, officials assured people who complained about flatulence that their degenerate digestive systems only needed time and training to gradually return to full capacity. Statistically the campaign was a success. Between 1937 and 1939 consumption of black and wholemeal bread rose steadily almost everywhere in the country. In spite of all the propaganda, however, *Vollkornbrot* never fully shed its association with wartime and hardship, and many equated it with the fortification of margarine with vitamin A; a necessity associated with shortages and a lack of personal choice.

As soon as German troops marched into Poland in early September 1939, a totalitarian food regime took full effect through rationing. Once again lessons had been learnt and in contrast to 1914 everything seemed well prepared. It was only logical that only racially pure Germans were entitled to *Vollkornbrot*. From 1942 onwards *Vollkornbrot* couldn't be produced in adequate quality and quantity, and porridge and gruel were increasingly recommended instead. This was partly due to failed crops, in spite of the often ruthlessly inhumane exploitation of the conquered countries. Ironically this failure led to a return to what actually were Germany's original foodways. In the post-war years, as soon as white bread became available once more, national preferences reasserted themselves, although in the 1970s environmental concerns saw a return of *Vollkornbrot*, fortunately this time without a grim ideology.[23]

On a more psychological level, *Eintopf* was another element in the Nazis' attempt to mobilize and involve the whole populace in the war effort. The term *Eintopf*, one pot, means quite literally that only one cooking vessel should be used for the whole meal. As with *Vollkornbrot*, this was by no means a new invention, since stews and hotpots are the kind of dishes whose origin is universal and cannot be ascribed to any particular time or place. The word *Eintopf* itself was a Nazi attempt to

exploit the romanticizing of the outdoors that motivated young hikers and boy scouts. A simple foldable tripod to hang a pot over a fire was as much a part of their equipment as a guitar to encourage group singing. In some circles even individual plates came to be seen as degenerate, evidence of a lack of community feeling. The Nazis positioned themselves as honest and down to earth, officials deliberately posing as men of simple tastes. During the Second World War *Eintopf* was commented on by the writer Bertolt Brecht:

> *Die Oberen sagen, im Heer*
> *Herrscht Volksgemeinschaft.*
> *Ob es wahr ist, erfahrt ihr*
> *In der Küche. In den Herzen soll*
> *Der gleiche Mut sein. Aber*
> *In den Schüsseln ist*
> *Zweierlei Essen.*

The ones up there are saying, in the army we're all one people. The same courage should prevail in our hearts. But in the bowls are two kinds of food.[24]

From October 1933 *Eintopf-Sonntage*, stew Sundays, were introduced to reinforce the feeling of community. All Germans were asked to serve and eat a simple stew instead of the usual roast lunch on the first Sunday of every month from October until March, donating the pecuniary difference to the newly founded *Winterhilfswerk*, Winter Relief Organization, to support and show solidarity with the unemployed. The money was collected by party members, and though officially declared optional, social and political pressure made support for the campaign far from it; a characteristic Nazi strategy. Specialized cookbooks offered recipes suitable for these Sundays which were marked in calendars in the same way as public holidays; recipes were printed in newspapers along with pictures of the Führer himself eating *Eintopf*. In January 1935 the menu at Hotel Adlon listed *Suppentopf Hausfrauen Art oder Möhren mit Pöckelkamm bürgerlich* – housewife-style stew or carrots with salted pork à la bourgeoise offered at 2.20 marks, the price being composed of 0.80 basic costs, 1.20 *Winterhilfe* donation and 0.20 service charge.

With gold and foreign currency reserves not only low but urgently needed for importing raw materials for the armaments industry, the Nazi regime was under severe financial constraints. At the same time purchasing power rose following economic recovery, threatening inflation. Officials deemed it essential to steer food consumption in the right direction. Initially health was used as the prevailing argument. A poster from the 1930s delivered the message loud and clear: 'Eat fish and you'll stay slim and healthy.' As a result, fish consumption rose from 8.9 kg per head in 1932 to 12.5 kg in 1938.[25] It was not long before economic and political necessities dictated more direct interference, although the authorities were always careful to mask their real motives. From 1934 the building of new fishing boats was state-subsidized, neatly connecting job creation with rearmament efforts, since the owners of the boats were legally bound to convert their vessels to become part of the war fleet when required. In the same year, 1934, an effort was made to steer private demand even more directly by establishing the first modern market research society, Gesellschaft für Konsumforschung (GfK), as a privately funded body. In 1937 the GfK issued a *Reichsspeisekarte* or national menu listing foodstuffs appropriate to every month while generally recommending higher consumption of potatoes, quark (widely popular since ancient times), low-fat cheese, fruit and fish, all perceived as produced domestically and in abundance. Butter, lard, bacon, margarine and oil were to be used sparingly, and jam was promoted as a substitute on bread. As a result of state subsidies, jam production tripled between 1933 and 1937. Many companies supported these efforts by including the GfK's meal recommendations in housekeeping courses they offered their female employees.[26]

Bakers were now legally obliged to sell *Vollkornbrot*, wholemeal bread. State funding went into various research projects designed to promote self-sufficiency and develop protein and oil-rich plants such as rape (advertisements promoted *Erstes deutsches Rapsfett*, the first German rapeseed fat). The cultivation and use of soy beans were once more heavily promoted (though for various reasons the campaign proved unsuccessful everywhere but in the occupied Ukraine). The whaling industry was revived, fish farms were set up and farmers were encouraged to plant root crops to replace grain as animal feed. Dairy products became a sensitive subject. A decree of October 1938 prohibited the production and distribution of liquid cream and all related products between 15 September and 14 May of each year, leading to all kinds of ersatz recipes, often using egg white and resembling a kind of syllabub. From the start of war only low-fat milk was distributed. In the attempt to get hold of every single gram of milk fat a decree of 1940 even aimed at the confiscation of farmers' butter-making equipment, although it is difficult to know how far this was implemented. In spite of the regime's motto *Kanonen statt Butter*, 'canons instead of butter' – corresponding roughly to Churchill's famous 'blood, toil, tears and sweat' – the importance of butter as a contributor to the national feeling of well-being cannot be overstated. Butter had been rationed since 1937, but quantities remained constant until spring 1942, when regular allocations were cut from 150 to 125 g per week. In 1943, 60 per cent of all butter consumed in Germany came from domestic production, an increase of 30 per cent on 1939, although the quality of this wartime butter was far inferior and led to the coining of the term *gute Butter*, good butter – that is, the real thing – which still rings familiarly in the ears of those like myself who grew up in the 1960s.

After German troops had marched into Austria in 1938, German tourists apparently descended in hords on Austrian coffeehouses, hungry for badly missed delicacies such as *Torte* and *Schlagobers*, whipped cream, causing the official ss newspaper to comment: 'One would think Greater

Germany was only created so that this raving Philistine rabble can wolf down whipped cream.' The ss commentator, naturally enough, did not mention that while the cream-eaters were gorging themselves, Austria's Nazis were beating up Jews in the streets.[27]

Official propaganda declared the purchase of imported tropical fruits unpatriotic, promoting German apples and presenting rhubarb as a patriotic replacement for lemons. This (and similar attempts to control advertising) only worked up to a point. Leaders of the Women's Bureau, Frauenwerk, the Nazi successor to the housewives' associations, tried their best but frequently admitted how difficult it was to effect permanent changes in consumption patterns in spite of all their efforts through cookery courses, leaflets, radio programmes and recipes in newspapers. The Frauenwerk's list of recommended foodstuffs for October 1937 featured 'fish, cabbage, jam, quark, skimmed milk, grapes and porridge oats'.[28] It should come as no surprise that many women clung stubbornly to regional and personal preferences in the attempt to preserve their self-esteem and self-identity. The suggestion to replace the cold evening meal of buttered bread with cold cuts with a warm cooked dish met with particularly strong resistance, even if this was promoted as more flexible and therefore better suited to accomodate fat and meat shortages. Thrift, the old bourgeois ideal, was lifted to new heights of pettiness: restaurants were subject to official guidelines on leftovers and housewives were advised not to use wooden spoons as these might soak up precious fat, while butter and jam were to be spread directly onto bread to avoid waste on the plate. In a similar vein women were discouraged from shopping in department stores as this could lead to impulse purchases.[29]

Some of this advice on food and cooking sounds perfectly familiar and sensible. It is only the political background – the imposition of social pressure and constraint through lack of alternatives, all with the goal of brutal imperialism – that makes these efforts more than questionable in the historical context. *Pellkartoffeln*, potatoes boiled in their skins, can be delicious as anyone might wish, particularly when served with quark – the official alternative to butter – when both are chosen freely and without the indigestible background of racist ideology and dictatorship. The point is well illustrated in a passage from a report of the *NS Frauenschaft* from 1936 which sounds as familiar to contemporary ears as the Nazi campaign against food waste: 'City women had actually come to ignore the growth and cycle of the natural environment that surrounded them. Fresh strawberries in winter were now simply seen as a delicacy.'[30]

Overall consumption of fruit declined, although in 1938 Germans still ate 7 kg per head of unpatriotic imported tropical fruit, down from 10 kg in 1930. In spite of the fact that alcohol and tobacco were presented as unhealthy, particularly for women, cigarette consumption almost doubled between 1932 and 1940, not least as result of the young, elegant women depicted in advertisements who were undoubtedly representative of consumers' desires. Brandy consumption among adults rose by 40 per cent between 1930 and 1937, while coffee became a highly controversial subject, since demand notoriously exceeded supplies. The black market in coffee flourished from the start. In 1939 the propaganda minister fulminated about unnecessary needs:

> We don't want to go so far as to apply the drastic antithesis of 'First guns, then coffee', but it seems necessary in face of the difficult state of affairs of the world to judge stringent German rearmament as more important than supplying our *Kaffeetanten* (coffee-aunts) with sufficient coffee.[31]

The Nazi philosophy was full of contradictions. In spite of all the nostalgic agrarian romanticism, the regime also promoted modern technology in households and advanced new methods of food production. Consumption of electricity in private households and small businesses rose by 38 per cent between 1933 and 1940. In the effort to avoid waste – driven home with yet another campaign, *Kampf dem Verderb* – and build up stocks for war, convenience foods became a priority for state-subsidized research. New kinds of food packaging were developed. The output of cans as a means of preserving fruit and vegetables almost doubled between 1933 and 1937, and mass production of frozen food started in 1938. However, while the state promoted the virtues of frozen food, foraging for wild food and vegetable gardening were also strongly encouraged. Later on potato and vegetable peelings were collected for local pig farmers in return for some *adelige Milch*, literally noble or blue-blooded milk, the skimmed milk naturally tinged with blue which was given to pig farmers by the dairies to feed their animals. Temporary restrictions on sought-after luxuries were made more palatable by the promise of a better future: Hitler's vision was of a modern consumer society modelled on that of America, with refrigerators, radios, washing machines, holidays and a car affordable by every family. However, the Volkswagen Beetle project was as unrealistic as similar schemes promising affordable household goods –

the first car was delivered to a private customer in 1946. Nevertheless for a while such promises made people feel good. Many working-class families remembered the years between 1935 and 1939 as 'good years', times when they were feeling more affluent than in 1932 and better off than before the depression, though this had more to do with expectations than actual living standards. In the late 1930s Germans had to spend about 45 per cent of their income on food but consumed only one-eighth more meat than during the depression, 48.6 kg per head and year. The *Frankfurter Zeitung* commented in January 1937 on the 'intensive impression of popular enjoyment making itself felt in restaurants, beer-gardens and open-air cafés . . . [although] customers often could not afford to purchase more than a cup of coffee or a glass of beer.'[32]

After the rise of the Nazis to power, the Germanizing Sprachverein perceived itself as contributing to the official party line, calling itself 'our Mother Tongue's SA' (the SA or Sturmabteilung was the Nazis' paramilitary troop).[33] But the association's members had misunderstood the Nazi agenda. The Fascist ruling party often deliberately used certain foreign words as euphemisms, preferring *Sterilisation* to the much more widely comprehensible German term *Unfruchtbarmachung* proposed by the association. In November 1940 Hitler, who was very much aware of the fascination little-understood foreign words possessed for the masses, decreed:

> The *Führer* does not wish any kind of forcible Germanizing and does not approve of the artificial replacing of foreign words that have long since been integrated into German by words that are not in the spirit of the German language and mostly insufficiently render the sense of the foreign words.[34]

Nevertheless some very German terms are used on a menu from the Adlon Grill from June 1939, among them *Tunke*, *Edelpilze* and *Marseiller Fischsuppe* instead of *Sauce*, *Champignons* and *Bouillabaisse*, but in general the menu still sounds quite cosmopolitan, offering *ragout fin*, *Scotch woodcock* and *Welsh rarebits*. Guests are also encoraged to drink wine: the saying 'A meal without wine is like a day without sunshine' is printed in both German and English. The official activities of the Sprachverein ceased as the Nazis increasingly instrumentalized language for propaganda purposes while severely regulating it in the public domain. With the exception of the infamous *Eintopfsonntage* discussed earlier, food is rarely mentioned in the linguistic studies of the period. References are generally oblique rather than direct. A German journalist of the time gives an account of a woman in Berlin in 1941

> who was less than complimentary about the quality of the *Magermilch* (low-fat milk) which people were being served, and as a consequence had to go to the police station every day for three months and recite 'There isn't any skimmed milk. There's only skimmed fresh milk' (*entrahmte Frischmilch*).

It is impossible not to be reminded of George Orwell's *1984* and the language of Newspeak:

> The whole aim of newspeak is to narrow the range of thought. In the end we shall make thought-crime literally impossible because there will be no words in which to express it . . . The Revolution will be complete when the language is perfect.[35]

Cover of an Adlon menu from 1939.

Aryanization, another characteristic euphemism of the Nazi regime that masked the forced sale and later dispossession of Jewish businesses, in many cases helped to consolidate buyers' fledgling enterprises and led to immense and often shameless personal gains by 'good' Germans. One prominent example is the sale of the Kempinski group to Aschinger in 1937. The depression had put an end to the sybaritic escapism of the late 1920s and everybody in the hospitality industry was struggling. The Kempinskis had not only managed to stay afloat but had even made profits. Aschinger, however, in spite of a legendary reputation that lingers to the present day, had been too lofty in its ambitions, and in the 1930s the gastronomic empire ran into serious financial trouble. The group abandoned the provision of free rolls and turned to the authorities for help. The enterprise became the Nazis' main caterer at all major events, including the Berlin Olympic Games in 1936.

During the aggressive anti-Jewish campaign introduced as soon as the Nazis came to power in 1933, shops under Jewish ownership were boycotted, with customers' entry actively hindered by paramilitary SA pickets. Like other Jewish-owned stores and hotels, those under Kempinski ownership had to mount signs declaring themselves as such. While the industry in general recovered from the economic crisis, the Kempinskis' business suffered considerably and from 1933 no further profits were made. In the years that followed the management tried to scale down the company by selling some of their holdings. Whereas Kempinski had been cultivating their own vineyards in several regions of Germany and exporting wine worldwide, they now ceased to bottle their own vintages and were obliged, like other Jewish companies, to accept a designated Aryan manager. In addition, faced with constant social defamation and the deterioration of their reputation, they were forced to retire from all official committees. After the Olympics anti-Jewish attacks became ever more open, and the Kempinskis' financial position weakened further. In common with many other Jewish companies, at a certain point they were forced to sell as they were simply squeezed out of the market and rendered insolvent. Aschinger and Kempinski were business partners who cooperated on many levels in the close-knit industry. After lengthy negotiations in 1937 Aschinger took over Kempinski 'under very favourable conditions', though regarded as legally correct under the prevailing system, thereby solving Aschinger's financial problems. The Aschinger production facilities had in any event been oversized and had suffered from a lack of outlets. Under the new arrangement the two companies

Haus Vaterland's menu from October 1943 promises second helpings of potatoes, but signals that free rolls (*Gratisbrötchen*) can only be had against wheat coupons, promoting the official propaganda slogan: *Esst Vollkornbrot, es ist gesünder!*

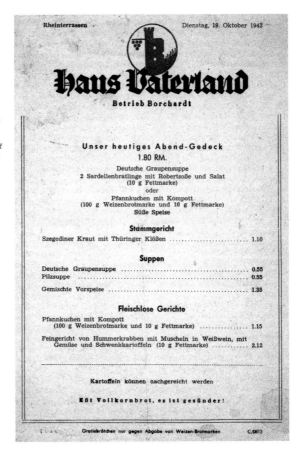

could be streamlined into one and resources could be rationalized. Advertisements made it known that the Kempinski restaurants were now socially acceptable and the takeover proved to be thoroughly profitable for Aschinger. When in 1941 Jewish company names were declared illegal, Aschinger managed to buy the highly respected restaurant and delicatessen store Borchardt and use the name for the whole operation. As a result Aschinger's turnover doubled between 1936 and 1943. In those years, as people sought at least temporary escape from the daily problems caused by war, restaurants and bars were busy. During the war Aschinger was able to offer potato and vegetable dishes without requiring ration cards, and in 1942 the company employed German Jewish women as well as forced labour from 26 nations. Conditions were close to slavery: workers were payed a pittance with the foreign workers housed in barracks.

Since the start of the war in September 1939 blackout regulations had made for complete darkness after sundown, with air raid wardens patrolling the streets. Urban bars greatly profited, offering refuge from the dark outside. Haus Vaterland continued to provide entertainment and meals until November 1943, when it was partially bombed out. A menu from October of that year offered German pearl barley soup, fish cakes, salad and pancakes with stewed fruit as well as Szegedin sauerkraut with potato dumplings and a *Feingericht*, a fine dish, of prawns and mussels in white wine with vegetables and sautéed potatoes. Second helpings of potatoes were on offer, and the bottom line reminded everybody to eat wholemeal bread: *Esst mehr Vollkornbrot, es ist gesünder.* Officials were aware that food was crucial to maintaining military and civilian morale. They knew that supplies would not last long in spite of all strategic preparations, so the intention was that the war should be short. Campaigns like the one for *Vollkornbrot* tried hard to suppress excessive demand and match consumption with domestic production, but also aimed for a healthier population able to withstand wartime restrictions. White bread made of wheat was denounced as leading to anaemic blood, the very opposite of 'racial fitness'. Whereas before women had been told to do the 'right' thing for the welfare of their families, the discharge of their duties was once more portrayed as for the benefit of the whole nation.

After a blitzkrieg of just three weeks (during which Aschinger's trucks helped to carry men and arms to the front) Poland was divided and Slavic families were chased from their homes to make room for ethnic Germans from outside Germany. Young women serving their *Pflichtjahr*, the mandatory year of service introduced in 1938, were sent to help the immigrants adopt a 'proper' German lifestyle. This included orderliness, cleanliness and observation of the Christmas rituals that had become hugely popular during the late nineteenth century and now formed a firm part of German national identity. Supply problems back home were countered by the systematic and unscrupulous exploitation of the conquered territories, including the drafting of foreign labour, first voluntarily, than forced. In summer 1943, 6.5 million foreign workers were living in Germany, representing a slave labour market in many respects. Those from eastern countries received particularly small rations of frequently bad quality food, mostly turnip soup, some bread and occasional weekly allocations of tiny quantities of margarine and meat. Prisoners of war didn't fare much better. After a twelve-hour day of hard physical labour a British soldier interned in Upper Silesia was issued

about a pint of watery vegetable soup, usually mangold or
sauerkraut .. three potatoes boiled in their jackets, and a loaf
of black bread between twelve men, and sometimes a minute
piece of ersatz margarine.

The bread and margarine were intended for breakfast with a cup of
ersatz coffee. Survival in these camps often depended on Red Cross food
parcels. In non-military prisons food rations were set at an even lower level;
they were to all intents and purposes a death sentence in themselves.[36]

With the rationing of fuel, clothing and food introduced in late
August 1939, even before the invasion of Poland, food allocations went
down to below pre-war standards, although the need for calories was
increased by additional physical activity, including collecting water or
walking to work and shops. Fat supplies barely balanced carbohydrates
in the form of staples such as *Vollkornbrot* and potatoes. Potato dishes
were everyday fare, with *Kartoffelgemüse* particularly popular. This, a
dish of sliced potatoes in a flour-based sauce, could be varied in many
ways, with the addition of vinegar, a little sausage, pickles, herring brine
or fresh herbs. If no fat at all was available, people 'roasted' the potatoes
with cold ersatz coffee and made 'meatballs' and 'meat-spread' out of
potato skins. Unlike in Britain, the rationing system in Germany echoed
that of the First World War in being unequal in entitlement and extremely
complex. Army rations were set at 4,200 calories per head per day,
compared to 3,600 for those engaged in heavy labour and allocations
for *Normalverbraucher*, regular consumers, at 2,400 calories. Children,
pregnant women and nursing mothers, assuring the future of the
master race, were entitled to additional milk, butter and sugar rations.
Ration cards were colour coded and issued by the municipal authorities
for four weeks at a time, allowing for constant adjustment.[37]

In the 1940s academic nutritional studies examined the precise
amounts of calories different occupations needed and at what time of
the day warm meals were most efficient for productivity. The domestic
economy section of the *Reichsnährstand* redoubled its educational
efforts, publishing in 1940 a new edition of the *Einschlachtheft*, guidelines for pig-slaughter and sausage-making, with an appendix on
Kriegs-Sparmassnahmen beim Schlachten, wartime saving-methods as
applied to butchering. Other titles in the same series advised on eggs, wild
fruit and quark. Women developed their own methods of preparing
starch from potatoes and syrup from sugar beet. Culinary ingenuity

came up with mock meat chops prepared from boiled cabbage and a marzipan lookalike made with grated potatoes or semolina mixed with sugar and artificial bitter almond flavouring (other available artificial flavourings were lemon, vanilla and rum).

As during the First World War, theoretical entitlements in the form of rations per head per day were not the whole story, and what people could actually obtain often differed significantly. As a result of the constant barrage of food-related propaganda of previous years, many households seem initially to have been well prepared, stocking up on basic supplies while continuing with the housewifely habit of preserving fruit and vegetables against winter and other hard times. However, after 1941 shortages extended to many everyday items such as shoelaces, candles and toilet paper. Queuing was obligatory and most supplies were ersatz – copies of the real thing. Pigs were in competition with humans for foodstuffs such as grain, potatoes and turnips – another reminder of the First World War – and in 1944 meat supplies were half those of 1933, as

Poster, *Hamster Woman, Be Ashamed of Yourself*, December 1939. This propaganda warns against the hoarding of food (shown are macaroni, linseed and olive oil, palm fat and a sausage) as well as shoes or wool.

general food shortages led to fewer and leaner pigs. In 1943 and 1944 regular consumers were eating 40 per cent less fat, 60 per cent less meat and 20 per cent less bread than in 1939, though this was still considerably more than during the First World War or in the invaded countries at the same time, and did not lead to actual starvation.

The Nazis' plans greatly counted on Ukraine for grain. This meant cutting off supplies to Russian cities, where the official Nazi *Hungerplan* scheme led to the greatest death rate since the Thirty Years War, just as Stalin was ready to let the Leningrad population starve instead of evacuating the majority and abandoning the city when it became clear that the German army was prepared to lay siege to it. In general the German army was expected to live off the land, ruthlessly requisitioning whatever was needed. German troops pillaged, plundered and destroyed even the very means Ukrainians needed to produce grain. The harvest of 1941 was much lower than expected, while transport problems meant that the army's food supplies were frequently simply in the wrong place. In addition the police systematically searched Ukrainian houses to confiscate hidden supplies of food. Even so brutality never extracted enough from the eastern territories to feed the entire German army, as had been the original plan.

But even on the eastern front soldiers were able to siphon off goods from the black market. In 1940 the introduction of the *Schleppererlass*, literally hauling decree, allowed German soldiers to loot as much as they could carry. In France in particular, the troops lived off the fat of the land, dining in Parisian restaurants and sending back and taking home butter, coffee, wine, champagne, cognac and other luxuries, even whole pigs and sheep. These riches were both looted – 'organized' – and paid for in the local currency, as German soldiers were well paid in comparison with those of other nations and were expected to spend money in situ to reduce inflation back home. Many of the occupying forces were also sent additional money by their families to spend on delicacies and luxuries. In May 1942 each individual soldier was allowed to send home an extra 20-kg parcel in addition to the usual forces' parcels, and customs officers were officially instructed not to check their contents. A father returning to his family from Paris is recorded as bringing

> fabric for clothes, stockings, dried beans, writing paper, liver sausage, carrots in meat sauce, gloves, fabric for underwear, belts, shoes, soap, washing powder, pears, almonds, cinnamon

and pepper. The table was full [of these goods] and [the practice] has now become a habit in Germany. Wherever the men are, whether in Holland, Belgium, France, Greece, the Balkans, Norway, they're buying.

This meant that for those back home who had the right contacts, life could be quite comfortable. The architect Julius Posener was shocked to see young women in white clothes on the ruined streets of Cologne when he returned from Italy in April 1945, where people had died from starvation in the streets: 'The people didn't correspond to the destruction. They looked well, rosy, lively, looked after and reasonably well-clad.'[38]

In the course of the war agricultural productivity in Germany went down as a result of shortages of agricultural machinery, labour and draught animals. Many farms were run by women with the help of forced labourers and POWs, some of whom were treated like slaves and others like family, the latter case being the exception and against official regulations. Plans for a mass-migration of German farmers to the European California in the new eastern territories – with the Slavic 'subhumans' taking the role of the Native Americans – were never realized. Those few who followed the call were full of expectations but in the main were unable to cope with the new climate and soil conditions, and were often ambushed by partisans, many of whom were the former owners of the farms.

The Nazi mantra was that others must suffer before German rations would be cut and that all of occupied Europe could be regarded as a perfectly legitimate source of food for Germany. Thus hunger was ruthlessly exported to all the occupied countries, leading to severe famines and malnutrition as the grain imports on which some of these countries depended, particularly Greece and Italy, were also cut off. Estimates say that about 45 per cent of the grain used for bread in Germany during the war and 42 per cent of all fat and meat came from outside Germany, mostly produced through forced labour.[39] French agriculture struggled as a result of labour shortages, while farmers increasingly retreated to self-sufficiency and the black market as means to make a living. The urban population there could only survive with the right connections and appropriate financial means. Italy and Norway were equally squeezed dry. In fact, western Europe contributed more food to wartime Germany than the occupied Soviet Union, with vast amounts of meat and grain imported from France, Holland and Denmark. The latter represented a special case, as the Danes were regarded as fellow Aryans and were initially left more or less alone in their internal affairs. Denmark's pricing policy encouraged agricultural production, a black market barely existed and Denmark provided Germany with about a month's worth of butter, pork and beef a year (200,000 tons of butter in 1940–43, compared to 49,000 from France). Unlike Germany, but similar to Holland, Danish agriculture was very efficient and based on the latest scientific knowledge.[40]

As on earlier such occasions, the food situation in wartime Germany differed significantly between urban and rural areas. Particularly on the large estates in the east, food could still be plentiful, whereas great efforts were needed to produce meals from the monotonous urban supplies of mostly bread, potatoes and legumes in the industrial areas in the west, where cooking once again became the art of making something out of nothing. As during the First World War many city dwellers depended on 'hamster tours' to the hinterland to complement their rations with milk, butter, eggs, vegetables or fruit. Rural connections replaced the social hierarchy of old. By 1942 open spaces in cities had once more been converted to vegetable patches, with trees cut for firewood. Rabbits and chickens were kept in suburban gardens and on balconies. When the Berlin zoo was hit by Allied bombs in autumn 1943, people feasted on crocodiles' tails, deer, buffalo and antelope, followed by bear ham and sausage. During the latter stages of the war, reports from all over Germany repeatedly mentioned the spontaneous and savage butchering of dead horses in the streets. The black market became ever more important, increasingly operating through barter or with tobacco (or tobacco coupons) as a substitute currency, often leading to complicated networks of exchange. Once again it was mostly women who had to bear the additional load. In spite of all the Nazi propaganda illegal trading has been estimated at at least 10 per cent of average household consumption, but was probably much more important in large cities.[41]

Many small farmers were disappointed with Nazi politics. They disapproved of the centralized collection and distribution at fixed prices and withdrew into self-sufficiency and profiteering, making good contacts even more important for town folks seeking to top up official rations. Special courts were set up to deal with those involved in illegal trading and they occasionally handed out very severe punishments (just as looting following air raids was often punished with death), but it seems that many, including officials, took the risk anyhow without any sense that what they were doing was wrong. In 1943 August Nöthling, a Berlin

delicatessen trader, was found to have provided large amounts of luxury
and/or rationed goods such as ham, venison, butter, fat, poultry, tea,
cocoa, sugar, oil, sweets, honey and fruit without coupons to an impressive group of the Nazi elite, including the chief of the Berlin police. He
committed suicide in his prison cell.[42] Until most restaurants (as well as
theatres, dance clubs and the like) had to close following the declaration
of total war after the defeat at Stalingrad in early 1943, real feasts could
still be had at places such as Horcher's in Berlin for the select few with
the necessary pecuniary means. Waiters clipped the relevant coupons,
while menus offered all kinds of non-rationed luxuries such as oysters,
lobster and champagne, fish, fowl and pasta. However, the further the
war progressed, the less the reality on the plate tended to correspond to
the printed words. Less prestigious places were accused of cheating their
customers of their ration allowances by asking for coupons without
using any of the ingredients they covered. While some members of the
Nazi regime made it a principle to strictly follow their own guidelines,
others openly indulged. As for Hitler's table, sources differ, making it
difficult to differentiate between propaganda and reality – tales of frugal
vegetarian meals on one hand and roasted pigeons followed by fancy
cakes on the other – reflecting the contradictions of the Nazi realm as
a whole.

Once again the British imposed a total blockade against Germany,
her allies and occupied countries, cutting most of continental Europe off
from the world's food suplies. German officials welcomed any excuse to
save calories that could be considered wasted on 'unnecessary eaters',
be they slave labourers, the populations of occupied territories or otherwise deemed unworthy. Those in institutions, among them the mentally
ill and disabled, were systematically starved to death on an official diet
of potatoes, turnips and boiled cabbage without the addition of protein.
Non-Aryan citizens' rations were set considerably lower and choice
was much more restricted, leading to gradual starvation. The systematic
exclusion of the Jewish population from public life also took the form
of restricted shopping times. From July 1940 in Berlin Jews were only
allowed to buy food between four and five o'clock in the afternoon, and
even then Aryan customers were to be served first. Shopkeepers were
not allowed to reserve or deliver anything to Jews, whose rationing
cards were marked with a capital J, and Jews were frequently prohibited from buying specific produce: rice, sugar, oranges, pastries, fresh
vegetables, frozen food, almonds, nuts, even salt herrings, eggs, cheese and

condensed milk. In October 1942 those Jews remaining in Berlin were only allowed to purchase fresh vegetables once a week, and then only white cabbage, swedes or beetroot. The same year it was decreed that even non-rationed food was to be sold only to Jews after everyone else's needs had been satisfied.

During the exceptionally cold and long winter of 1941–2, potatoes froze during transport, leading to food shortages. Coal supplies were equally scarce, adding to the misery, with schools, theatres, bars and factories not involved in the war effort closed for lack of heating. The general mood of the German public threatened to turn against the government. Hitler and some of the Nazi leaders had always wanted to eradicate Europe's Jews, and now they had a 'rational' reason to actually do so, eliminating even more 'useless eaters'. In the camps food rations in general were below all imagination, with barely any fat to go with the bread and watery soup, so that inmates' bodies consumed themselves after using up their fat reserves. Individual food situations differed according to the status of the camp, the inmates' nationality and their category. In general ss supervisors installed a hierarchical system using food privileges as a means of coercing inmates. Obviously any jobs involving food were sought after. Working in the kitchen of the concentration camp Bergen-Belsen in July 1944 meant cigarettes, raw vegetables, meat broth and hot sweetened coffee, according to one report. Those in the 'hospital' section at the death camp Auschwitz were allowed to eat the rations of their unconscious fellow inmates. In general constant hunger made people egotistical, undermining solidarity and making for few revolts. Hunger often led to an obsession with food, fantasies about meals, recipes and orgies, called stomach-masturbation in another report. In his account of Auschwitz, Italian writer and death camp survivor Primo Levi wrote:

> Lager [the camp] *is* hunger: we ourselves are hunger, living hunger . . . How weak our flesh is! I am perfectly aware how vain these fantasies of hunger are, but dancing before my eyes I see the spaghetti which we had just cooked . . . at the sorting camp when we suddenly heard the news that we would leave for here the following day; and we were eating it (it was so good, yellow, filling), and we stopped, fools, stupid as we were – if we had only known! . . . this way of eating on our feet, furiously, burning our mouths and throats, without time to breathe, really is '*fressen*,' the way of eating of animals, and certainly not '*essen*,' the human

way of eating, seated in front of a table, religiously. '*Fressen*' is exactly the word, and is used currently among us.[43]

In 1940 the British Royal Air Force had started 'morale bombing' to undermine Germany's will to fight by openly targeting civilians (in violation of international law). Once again Churchill was determined to starve, kill or cure the Huns, as he called the entire German population. Initially the German government offered generous compensation to those who had lost their homes and/or possessions in the form of money or ration coupons, occasionally distributing extra rations of white bread, meat, schnapps, wine and tobacco. As prices were fixed and purchases rationed, this often fuelled black-market activities. Equipment and comfort in shelters and the large public bunkers differed greatly from place to place. Where bombings were a regular feature, people went to bed in their clothes, leaving suitcases ready packed with valuables and food. Nevertheless life didn't come to a halt: children were born under the most primitive conditions and birthdays and holidays were celebrated in the shelters. Feeding newborn infants was a particular problem, as many women found difficulty in producing sufficient milk for breastfeeding due to nervous stress and malnourishment or the need to suckle their babies at irregular times. The effect of major air attacks was much like that of an earthquake, sometimes followed by firestorms, creating an inferno in which temperatures could rise to over 1,000°C. Thousands of people were literally cooked, burned to death and completely incinerated or suffocated. Allied aerial bombing began to seriously affect food production and distribution, especially in the cities. Rations were cut in order to be able to supply bombed-out, homeless people with hot meals. For many factory canteens were the last resort. The long-term effect of constant living in fear and nights without sleep combined with food shortages and lack of medicine left its mark on the general health of the populace. Morale on the home front plummeted; conditions deteriorated.

Officially the German food supply system did not collapse until the very last months of the war. Nazi propaganda not only made sure that both the origin and the moral price of foodstuffs were either unknown or ignored, but partly reduced any impression of deprivation through constant indoctrination. In collective memory Germany's civilian population did not go hungry until the war was over, and the regime's conduct was perceived by many as the very model of crisis management. Hitler was seen as a safeguard against starvation, hunger an Allied weapon no less than bombing. Historians have been trying to show how restricted the national wartime diet really was, and the extent to which women's everyday efforts ensured that people had enough to eat, frequently going hungry themselves in favour of husbands or children.[44] As recently as the 1960s public voices ascribed the supposedly successful management of food supplies during the Second World War – with the exception of the very last months – to the fact that while home production might not have reached the ideal of complete self-sufficiency, production had increased enough for rations to stay well above the required minimum, omitting to mention the export of hunger to the occupied territories and the mass murder of 'undesirable' eaters.[45] In fact from 1942 onwards the populations of Greece and Belgium suffered severe undernourishment, while France, Norway and Holland seriously struggled.

By the spring of 1945 it was obvious to all but the most fanatical Nazis that the war was lost. For most people, particularly those in what was left of the cities and the large numbers of refugees, survival was all that mattered. A report from March 1945 speaks of empty food shops, the few that had survived that long, and a saleswoman greeting a customer with the discouraging news: 'Whatever you might want to ask for, it's not available.'[46] Finally the myth that the Nazis had the food situation under control was exposed as yet another of their lies. Untold numbers of refugees streaming in from the east struggled to find food and shelter for the night in improvised camps. Some had been able to pack and prepare provisions; others had been forced to leave without anything. Milk for children became an ever scarcer resource and mothers resorted to every possible trick to save their children from starvation. In early May 1945 Germany surrendered unconditionally and the Allies assumed supreme power. What was to have been a 1,000-year empire vanished after no more than twelve. Food had become a weapon of mass destruction used by all sides and the result was brutal devastation, physical as well as psychological. Over 70 million people had died, more from hunger than from any other cause, a number so immense it would be impossible even to begin to grasp the misery it represents. The Nazis' policies had robbed German culture of almost all its Jewishness. Generations of young Germans would grow up without any knowledge of gefilte fish, challah, cholent or kugel.

As each occupying force came to terms with the territories under their command, differences between them very quickly became apparent. Most radical were the changes in the Soviet zone. In 1945 and 1946 a land

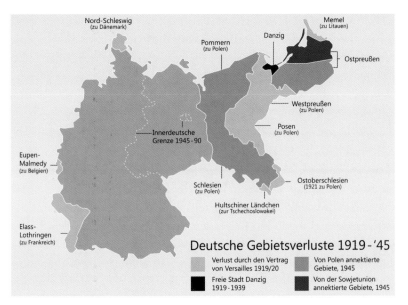

Restructuring of the German borders after the First and Second World Wars.

reform carved up all farms larger than 100 hectares and those belonging to former members of the Nazi party into small parcels. While some of these were redistributed to peasants, landless workers and refugees, others fell into the hands of the state. In the western zones the primary concern was purely material survival. Food production and distribution were close to collapse. To further confuse matters, many of the borders of the occupied zones stretched across former economic areas. Crop yields in 1946 and 1947 were significantly lower than average because of the destruction wrought on farmland and equipment throughout the years of fighting, leaving much agricultural land unusable. In addition the agriculturally rich former eastern territories were now under Polish and Soviet rule. As had been the case throughout the war, hardships in all areas of life differed greatly. Some households lacked the bare necessities while others were preoccupied with luxuries such as children's toys or the need to safeguard their precious wooden floors. Contrast between the bombed-out cities and rural areas were particularly extreme. While autumn 1945 saw the bottling of a top vintage at Schloss Johannisberg in the Rheingau region, the estate praised by German connoisseurs including Goethe, the writer's parents' house in nearby Frankfurt am Main was reduced to rubble, along with almost the entire city.

Distribution of food rations resumed almost immediately after the surrender. It was now organized by the occupying forces but basically used the same structures and systems. Allocations changed slightly and ration cards were linked to registration for employment. Survival strategies were basically the same as during the last years of the war, but under drastically worsened conditions. Improvised soup kitchens were set up in many cities. Queuing was essential for everything and information on stocks came by word of mouth. At the end of the war public and army storerooms had been opened and in most cases looted by whoever could get hold of something without being caught. Most survived on the twin essentials 'organizing' and 'hamstering', leaving the elderly without family, single women and war widows with small children often hit hardest. The differences between urban and country conditions became extreme. In many reports of the time farmers are depicted as tight-fisted profiteers, but sometimes their fields were plundered by hungry refugees.

By now most of the surviving civilian population were female, many of them unmarried or widowed. Most worked extremely hard to set the next meal on the table, trying to look after their children as best they could and working as nurses or leading refugees on the long trek home from the east. Women whose fathers or husbands had been party members were initially forced to work without pay as *Trümmerfrauen* – literally rubble women – clearing the ruins. For others, sorting out what could be reused from the rubble, while not enthusiastically embraced as an occupation, had the advantage of coming with a slightly larger food allocation. Though certainly not at brutal as in the Nazi camps, hunger now targeted the population at large. Women who were undernourished or exhausted simply collapsed and died while clearing the ruins. One woman reported from Hamburg in the summer of 1945:

Tired, tired! This summer is so much harder than the previous one. Everything is so scarce, and all thinking gradually concentrates on food! With the lack of fat, the cravings get worse all the time and fantasies become more excited; sausages, beef steaks, wonderful cakes, whipped cream, large bowls with fruit, sophisticated platters with vegetables full of young peas, beans, red tomatoes, delicate green cucumbers, pale cauliflower and lusty thick asparagus spears are dancing in a teasing and inviting way before one! These are the torments of Tantalus, being served at Michelsen [a delicatessen restaurant] a tiny sliver of meatloaf with dried vegetables – straw made somehow palatable! – no potatoes

In the rubble and debris, life goes on: fine food store reopened, says the sign.

Historical wine restaurant Lutter & Wegner in Berlin, 1946.

and preceeded by an undefinable broth! If only one could give
up eating altogether![47]

Food rations were distributed every ten days, and many ate everything
up at once and then had to survive on beets and foraged greens. Some
women reportedly looked at pictures in cookbooks while eating a watery
soup. Virtually everything was ersatz, a copy of something else: 'goose-
lard' was semolina flavoured with marjoram, softened with water and
very little fat; chocolate cake was coloured with 'coffee' grounds made
from roasted chicory root. Quality food did not exist. Potatoes were
often half-rotten and stinking; bread made from bran was virtually empty
under the crust. People who still had a home but no job often stayed in
bed all day to save energy. Some survived on what they grew themselves,
while many children went begging. Dogs and cats ended up in the cooking pot. Acorns were ground into flour as a substitute for wheat and
rye. In 1945 beechnuts were plentiful and avidly collected to include in
baking or in exchange for cooking oil. Memories of the immediate post-
war years are marked by constant hunger for bread, a longing described
by Heinrich Böll in his novel *Das Brot der frühen Jahre* (The Bread of Those
Early Years, 1955).[48] Many people lived in former air raid shelters or
in cellars which were little more than holes in the ground without light
or windows after having been bombed-out several times. Ever present
amid the rubble and ruins was the smell of rotting corpses, which were
being eaten away by rats. Heating materials were very scarce and distribution unreliable. In those areas where electricity and gas was available,
supplies were frequently interrupted, as they had been following heavy
bombing during the war. Cramped accommodation translated into the
sharing of inadequate sanitary and cooking facilities in those households
which still had coal-fired ranges. Households that lacked even the most
basic cooking facilities used a few bricks to build makeshift fireplaces
on balconies or doorsteps, fuelling them with little more than twigs.
Many counted themselves lucky to have salvaged some kind of cooking
pot; others had to fetch their meals from soup kitchens. All manner of
seemingly impossible containers were transformed into cookware to
replace items that had been lost, stolen or burned during the war. Many
of the first cooking vessels produced in the post-war years were made of
helmets and other military hardware.

In September 1945 Britain herself was on the verge of bankruptcy
due to the war, but managed to avert mass starvation in the zone under

The author's paternal grandmother's scrap-metal pan from the immediate post-war years.

her control by using the UK's gold and dollar reserves to buy food. While a number of British NGOs supported the humanitarian effort that had started in those European countries formerly occupied by Germany, the general public in the UK tended to resent such assistance, particularly when bread and flour rationing had to be introduced throughout Britain in July 1946. The result was that private food parcels to Germany were declared illegal, while Germans themselves were described as ungrateful and unaware of the sacrifices required from the British. In Germany itself the general population didn't seem to know what to expect and just carried on as before, surviving by keeping their heads down.

Not all were unforgiving. There had been voices in Britain opposing the total food blockade and 'obliteration bombing' of civilians, among them the Bombing Restriction Committee and the Food Relief Campaign, who pleaded with the British government to allow small quantities of special foods to pass through to children, mothers and invalids in the German-occupied territories. Victor Gollancz, a successful Jewish London publisher, was among those who campaigned relentlessly for a more humanitarian attitude to the former enemies. Gollancz visited the British zone for six weeks in the autumn of 1946, writing numerous letters on the dire conditions in Germany to all major newspapers on his return:

> The most horrible of my experiences has been a visit to the camp at Belsen, where I saw the tattoo marks on the arms of the Jewish survivors. I am never likely to forget the unspeakable wickedness of which the Nazis were guilty. But when I see . . . boys and girls in the schools, and find that they have come to their lessons without even a dry piece of bread for breakfast; when I go down into a one-roomed cellar where a mother is struggling,

and struggling very bravely, to do her best for a husband and
four or five children – then I think not of Germans, but of men
and women.

In early November of the same year, Gollancz described the situation
in Düsseldorf:

The normal consumer's ration is supposed to be one of 1,550
calories a day, about half ours in England. But this week four
of the items that account for most of this bogus figure – bread,
cereals, skim milk, and even vegetables – are either non-existent
or in horribly short supply; and the same has been the case, in
varying degree, ever since I've been here.

When describing the bread famine, a particularly dire situation which
left many empty-handed after hours of queuing, he added that those
who could not supplement their ration through the black market had to
make do with anything from 400 to 1,000 calories a day. In conclusion
he pointed out: 'The youth is being poisoned and re-nazified. We have
all but lost the peace – and I fear that this is an understatement.' Many
died from starvation or simply froze during the extremely hard winters
following the end of the war, in particular the elderly and the very
young, with refugee children in urban areas most severely affected and
infant mortality in some regions and at some points extreme. Hunger-
related diseases spread at great speed, among them tuberculosis, hunger
oedema, typhoid fever, emaciation and other effects of deficiency.
Undernourishment was normal: a weight deficiency of 30 per cent was
considered as by no means uncommon, with dizziness and stomach
cramps a common part of everyday life.[49]

Connections with the occupying forces could procure life-saving
food, particularly with the end of the non-fraternization rule in October
1945. Rape was a brutal fact of women's lives, and not only, as is often
assumed, in the Soviet zone. Prostitution and friendly relationships gradually became difficult to tell apart. American soldiers in particular were
well supplied with luxuries. German children begged them for leftovers,
sweets and chewing gum as well as Coca-Cola, official supplier of sodas
to the American army. The company had had bottling plants in Germany
since 1929 and had been intensely involved in promoting the Olympic
Games in Berlin. In 1940, to deal with wartime shortages, the company

German survivors: 'These six did everything in this room.' Victor Gollancz's caption ran 'wooden walls, leaking roof of wood and paper, 162 square feet. Old man 84, TB feared for one child.'

invented the brand Fanta, a drink originally based on whey and deriving its name from *Fantasia* or *fantastisch*, fantastic, to avoid the economic effects of anti-American tendencies. The Billy Wilder film comedy *One, Two, Three*, staged in Berlin in 1961, was to star James Cagney as Coca-Cola's head of operation.

From 1946 onwards food parcels began to arrive from the Cooperative for American Remittances to Europe (CARE), a privately funded aid organization that sought to relieve suffering and hunger in Europe following the Second World War. Further supplies were sent by more or less distant American relatives and friends. The CARE packages contained preserved meat and fat, tinned and dried fruit, honey, chocolate, sugar, powdered eggs, milk and coffee, along with much needed medical supplies. Displaced persons, many from the Baltic countries, received particularly generous numbers of CARE packages, the contents of which tended to fuel a flourishing black market. The equivalent in the Soviet zone was on one hand the *Soli-Paket* that could be sent via Switzerland and on the other the more ideological Soviet *Pajok*, distributed to artists, engineers and intellectuals. In Germany itself the black market flourished unchecked. As Victor Gollancz wrote in autumn 1946:

The general decline of public morality under the impact of the growing despair and financial chaos in which the grey and black sectors constantly encroach on the legitimate one, and the mark becomes more and more meaningless. Technically illegal transactions are, indeed, so open that the epithet 'black' is a misnomer.[50]

In Berlin in 1947 1 kg of sugar could be had on the black market for seven or eight American cigarettes; 1 kg fat for 23 to 25. Larger transactions were usually done by men, with some companies using their mass buying power to procure food for all their employees. Even the authorities participated in this moneyless alternative economy: in 1947 Ruhr miners worked extra shifts to supply Hamburg with its energy needs; in return Hamburg theatre companies went to perform in what was to become the Ruhr Festivals.[51] Few Germans realized how much greater

A young couple studies the content of an American CARE package, 1948–60.

A culinary place in time: Kempinski on Kurfürstendamm

The Kempinski Hotel reopened on Kurfürstendamm in West Berlin in 1952 is an example of reconstruction financed by the American Marshall plan. At the end of the war all Kempinski/Borchardt hotels and stores were bombed out, with the original house in the Leipziger Strasse totally destroyed. In the Soviet sector Aschinger's holdings were confiscated and formed the basis for the state-run Handels-organisation (HO) chain of retail stores and restaurants. Fritz Aschinger stayed in the west, reopening ten Aschinger pubs and restaurants in 1945 and 1946. He was accused of war crimes (after denying any involvement in Aryanized Jewish business transactions) and committed suicide in 1949. The last Aschinger Bierquelle near the West Berlin Zoo station closed in 1976. His main business partner presided over the opening of the Kempinski hotel on Kurfürstendamm in 1952. Most members of the Kempinski family had emigrated to Britain and the U.S. Only Walter Unger, a great-nephew of the founder, had stayed behind, hoping to save some of the family's fortune. He was forced to sell everything he owned, paying a substantial 'Jewish property tax' on sales and renouncing any claims in the event of his death. He then was deported and eventually murdered in Auschwitz in October 1944.[52]

had been the hardships the Nazis had inflicted on the occupied countries, believing themselves let down by the occupying powers. In February 1947, when food distribution was made extremely difficult by the exceedingly cold winter, hunger riots erupted in the Ruhr region, Rhineland and Westphalia, soon spreading to Hamburg and Bavaria. On the occasion of the royal wedding in London in 1947, the Young Düsseldorf Workers' Association sent the couple one day's ration as a wedding present: this consisted of 300 g bread, 12.5 g meat, 2 g cheese and 40 g starch (this could have been semolina, pasta or oatmeal).[53]

Meanwhile, because of inflation and price controls, there was no incentive for farmers or industry to produce food or goods. When from April 1948 onwards the Marshall Plan gave western Europe access to

foreign exchange, most was used for the purchase of imports from the
u.s. in the form of food, animal feed, fertilizer and building material,
though it also acted as propaganda for the American way of life.

The introduction of the Deutschmark in June 1948 was of great psychological importance, providing the seed corn from which grew the
Wirtschaftswunder, Germany's post-war economic miracle. Suddenly many
things were on regular offer again in shop windows and on shelves, though
many people had to watch every Pfennig they spent. Quickly a large gap
developed between the old rich and newly rich on the one hand (industrialists, politicians and many profiteers from black market activities and
hoarding of illegal goods waiting for the currency reform) and the large West
German majority, who were mostly somewhat better off than immediately
post-war, but could only gasp at luxury when it was suddenly displayed.
The black market didn't disappear immediately, but ration coupons quickly
became unnecessary. German farmers brought in a very good crop in
1949. In the western zones rationing officially ended in May 1950 and in
the Soviet zone in 1958. By this point many people didn't even bother

Farmer women
selling vegetables in
Nuremberg just after
the Second World War.

to collect the cards and shops didn't ask for coupons any more.[54] With hindsight it is amazing how quickly economic recovery set in.

Food supplies soon became a crucial weapon in the developing Cold War. In June 1948 the Soviets made an attempt to cut off the western Allies' ties to Berlin, Germany's erstwhile capital embedded in the Soviet zone, by closing all land and water access to the city. In response to this blockade the western Allies instigated the *Luftbrücke*, an airlift without precedent, flying in all essential supplies to a city which had long been a symbol of Prussian nationalism and Nazi militarism, thereby trans-forming it into a symbol of western freedom and democracy. For almost a year until May 1949, *Rosinenbomber*, literally the raisin-bombers, landed on the city's three airfields almost every three minutes on average. The same aircraft which had brought death and destruction a few years earlier now 'bombarded' the city with life-saving food. On the busiest days 896 planes flew in about 7,716 tons of goods; in total 274,718 flights brought in over 2.2 million tons of supplies, mostly food, coal and medicine. Besides tinned meat, most foodstuffs were provided in dried form – a saving in both space and weight – among them potatoes, vege-tables, fruit, milk, eggs and soy beans. For those feeding their families, new strategies in the kitchen were needed to deal with this situation. Strangely the *Operation Vittles Cook Book*, compiled by an association of American Women in Blockaded Berlin (1949), made no mention of short-ages, but depicted German cooks as backward, ignorant and clumsy, with a notorious inclination to serve dark, heavy bread. War and the blockade lived on in West Berliners' minds. In the 1970s many still had emergency food rations stored in a corner.

Even after the end of the blockade Berlin's situation remained pre-carious. A Berlin woman born in 1934 who had a job in West Berlin and lived there in the 1950s made ends meet by shopping for food in East Berlin during her daily lunch break, like most Berliners, since Western currency could be changed into Eastern at rates of one to four or even five. In retrospect she reflected:

> it was very sad really, as at times East Berliners had nothing to eat because we all went shopping there. Those in the east came home from work at night only to find that those from the west had already bought up everything . . . for us it was the only way to make a living, right through the 1950s, for others it was rather a sad story.[55]

Officially the East German regime agreed with this version, but internal papers admitted quite the opposite; food shortages in the East were compensated for by East Berliners shopping in the West.[56]

The developments of the the first half of the century changed Germans' eating habits in numerous ways. One of them was a wider acceptance of street food. Until the Second World War eating quickly and in the street had mostly been a necessity for those without hearth and home. For the bourgeoisie the habit was associated with the lower classes. Hardship, hunger and entire cities reduced to ruins made it easy to overcome old behaviour patterns and improvise. Drink kiosks, *Trinkhallen* or *Wasserhäuschen* (water houses), as they are called in Frankfurt am Main where they are regarded as a special local phenomenon, had sprung up in industrial areas during the second half of the nineteenth century.[57] They were the cities' attempt to contain the workers' thirst for beer and schnapps by selling recently invented beverages such as carbonated mineral water and other non-alcoholic drinks, later including tobacco and, in defiance of all good intentions, beer and schnapps. Only occasionally was food available in the form of cookies or biscuits. Over time these kiosks, which were not subject to compulsory closing hours, developed into public meeting points as well as small grocery stores, often selling newspapers and food and acting as lottery agencies. In the years immediately after the Second World War they were used, along with improvised shacks on bomb sites, as outlets for whatever food was available, providing a model

Currywurst, Berlin's trademark streetfood.

for a new kind of fast-food outlet. In Cologne, for instance, some offered fondant sweets, potato fritters or fried meat patties. Soon after currency reform, more varied foods were to be had, including goulash and hot sausages. The 'invention' of Berlin's trademark street food snack, *Currywurst*, curried sausage, is generally agreed to date from September 1949, when it was introduced by a certain Herta Heuwer at her stall on the Kantstrasse in West Berlin. Her creation consisted of a fine-textured ready-cooked pork sausage, grilled and served with a sauce made of tomato purée, curry powder and Worcestershire sauce. In 1959 Heuwer had the preparation registered as a *Spezial-Sosse* under the name of *Chillup*. A rival claim, however, dated the invention back two years earlier in Hamburg and ascribed the ketchup and curry powder to provisions a woman received from an American soldier.[58]

ELEVEN

Kasslerrollen and *Toast Hawaii*: Post-war Indulgence, East and West, 1949 to 1990

Af[A]ter a twelve-year-long exercise in locavorism (even if it was sustained by unscrupulous plunderings from helpless victims), hunting and gathering for whatever was available while continuously being told what to eat, even what to crave, followed by some real hunger, Germans were ready to indulge. As the rubble was cleared, houses, towns and entire cities were rebuilt, traffic and industry got once again on track, and the economy was at last on the up, waistlines quickly expanded. But it wasn't quite that simple. There was yet another layer waiting to add to the culinary complexities that had built up since the gruel of old, a giant experiment that would divide the Germans into two groups and subject them to contrasting political systems. How would they react? Would they develop equally contrasting cuisines? Would West Germans succumb to American-style consumerism and the lure of the brave new world, while their compatriots in the East filled their larders according to communist principles, adopting Russian recipes and drinking vodka?

The answer is that they did indeed move in opposite directions up to a point. But in many ways the differences that later emerged after re-unification in 1990 were due to regional preferences and pecularities that went back much further. Yet the different political systems the two parts of Germany were part of had another effect. While West Germans were free to discover the Western world on their plates (either at home or through travelling), East Germans, with a few exceptions, were much more restricted in their choices and stayed closer to home in their cooking (and travel). The GDR wasn't on a completely different food planet, but because of its economic problems got caught in a kind of time warp. West Germans would often comment upon the nostalgia they experienced during visits to the East, as food there seemed less industrialized and more homemade, the style of cooking more down to earth.

While the 1950s on both sides of the new internal German border were a period of rebuilding, rationing on the eastern side lasted significantly longer, until 1958. The Politburo was more than optimistic at that time, announcing that the GDR would surpass the FRG in food consumption levels by 1961. Officials were convinced that to expand local production and make the country independent from food imports, individual private farmers had to be completely eliminated and replaced by a centrally planned, state-run agriculture based on the Soviet model. In 1959 and 1960 *Landwirtschaftliche Produktionsgenossenschaften* (LPG), or agricultural collectives, were formed by force. Reactions among farmers ranged from resignation to emigration and suicide, making for a significant loss of specialist knowledge and motivation. In 1960 the combination of a failed crop with unsuccessful experiments in open stabling for cattle almost made for a crash in food production. As meat, bread and many other things became scarce, the populace reacted with panic buying and angrily threatened with riots and strikes.

This brought the communist experience to another level, with the regime ordering the complete closure of the border between East and West in August 1961. Following this, a certain economic and social stabilization set in. Cut off from the Western free market, an egalitarian ideal of stable prices and zero unemployment seemed tangible. By 1963 food supplies had gradually normalized. Choicer meat cuts and ham continued to be scarce, but basic foodstuffs were reliably available; nobody went hungry because of food shortages. Quite the opposite: generous portions became a way of life, with butter and pork in particular consumed in impressive quantities. A meal without meat was not taken seriously at all. Minced meat, *Jagdwurst* (a kind of scalded, smoked pork sausage) and *Kasslerrolle*, brined pork neck, were much-loved standards. *Kalter Hund* (cold dog), thin biscuits layered with a chocolate mixture rich in fat and sugar, was a cake favourite among children.

Unsurprisingly egalitarianism had its problems. Some citizens of the workers' and farmers' state were more equal than the rest and thus higher up in the food chain. The very small political elite group of the Politburo lived a very isolated and luxurious life. Their highly secluded and secured settlement a short drive north of Berlin, first in Pankow, then Wandlitz, had its own leisure facilities, hospital and bunkers and was amply provided for, with many goods imported from the West. As was

Kasslerrolle, deboned brined pork: always available, forever popular. From the GDR cookbook *Kochen* (Leipzig, 1983).

to be expected, the lonely group at the top quickly lost touch with the real world beyond their small secluded realm and increasingly dismissed expert knowledge when taking decisions. They insisted on increasing crop production with vegetables completely unsuited to the areas in question, just as they were puzzled to find on a rare outing that sugar cube production didn't cope with demand. Complaints about shortages were usually blamed on some local subordinate and often met with a simple reshuffling of distribution instead of basic reforms. But citizens' *Eingaben*, petitions, could also lead to political actions at the highest level if the regime deemed the issue politically sensitive. Thus in 1977 shortages of coffee (which had to be imported against hard currency) led first to the introduction of *Mischkaffee*, a mixture of ersatz ingredients such as chicory, rye and other grains with a minimal addition of real beans. After more complaints, this time about the unpalatability of the ersatz coffee, the regime engaged in secret weapon trading to get hold of coffee beans from Ethiopia, Angola and other 'new nations' such as Vietnam, Laos and the Philippines. Eventually in 1978 Western coffee brands such as Tchibo and Jacobs were introduced in exclusive Delikat shops, albeit at horrendously high prices.[1]

In fact since 1948 rationed goods had been offered, albeit at much higher prices than in regular shops, in state-owned Handelsorganisation (trade organization, HO) stores. This 'state-run black market' aimed to lure shoppers away from private shops as well as soaking up the monetary overhang – people had more money in their hands than available goods in the shops to spend it on. Officials praised the state-owned stores:

> In the food stores of the state organization you'll find all you need – from tropical fruit to smoked herrings. The simple people you'll meet here are shopping in their own shop, just like you. The state's own retailer offers you everything without anybody making a profit on it.[2]

When rationing was abolished in 1958 the HO group continued as a normal retailer and came to include restaurants, hotels and the large Centrum Warenhäuser department stores. In addition private restaurants were provided with the HO range of special foods and imported beverages. In the long term the HO group made a massive and continuing loss which weighed on the government budget. As costs for raw materials and energy rose over the years, state subsidies for food were huge due to the fixed prices officials didn't dare to adjust, as they deemed holding them at the same levels vital to safeguard the precarious political balance. Instead they continued to offer scarce, highly desirable goods in special stores at much higher prices, opening the first Exquisit shops with fashionable clothes and shoes in summer 1961, followed in 1966 by Delikat, a new chain of luxury food shops. By the 1980s both Exquisit and Delikat had developed into a standard source of supplies for a large part of the population. Anything a bit more refined than the most basic goods could be found there, from wine, spirits, fish, cheese and chocolate (regular GDR quality containing as little as 7 per cent cocoa), to meat, sausages, special bread, export beer and much else, in packaging that was up to Western standards. Some of these special Delikat wares were even found in a section of regular stores in rural areas. At a certain point the Delikat stores' success undermined general supplies. As demand exceeded supply, ordinary foodstuffs were elevated to Delikat ranks and normal shelves were stocked with lower quality produce. Meat in sausages was made to go further by the addition of potato starch, blood plasma, powdered skimmed milk or liquid egg, leading to complaints about their taste and extremely short shelf-life. The introduction of a supposedly superior Delikat butter in 1988 at almost triple the regular price caused much uproar. A pensioner wrote in:

> Also, butter is now sold at Delikat, the 250 gram piece for 6.80 marks. What is this supposed to be? What is the butter we are eating for 2.40 marks? I mean, what is going on? Did we, who are pensioners today, build up our republic that badly and what did our hundreds and more of voluntary hours of work for which we only received coupons and not 5 marks, count for at all? Are the values we have created nothing?[3]

Delikat and Exquisit had been preceded by Intershop stores. First started in 1955 at the Baltic port of Rostock and aimed at the hard currency of seamen and travellers, Intershop stores proved so successful they were quickly extended to ferries, airports and large hotels, offering the usual array of spirits, cigarettes, sweets and coffee. They acquired an even more important status after the Berlin Wall's construction in 1961, as they were installed along the transit routes between West Germany and West Berlin as well as at all checkpoints and in railway stations. From 1967 a select group of GDR citizens, such as diplomats and artists, were allowed to use them as well. From 1974 their selection was extended to food and they were officially opened to East Germans, as the government tried to get their hands on the population's hard currency, whether received from friends and family or illegally traded. By 1976 as much as 85 per cent of the Intershop revenue came from GDR citizens. At the related chain of Interhotels (which were run according to the same principles) 80 per cent of all customers were East Germans.[4]

Food parcels from 'the West' were part of life for many East Germans, mostly, but by no means exclusively, at Christmas. At some points these private imports of chocolate, coffee, clothes and shoes surpassed the GDR's own production.[5] The grateful recipients in turn typically sent back *Stollen*. Paradoxically the rich Christmas cake associated with Dresden was made from almonds, raisins, candied peel and other commodities that were scarce and had to be imported against hard currency. It is in this context that the GDR Institute of Nutrition proudly announced in 1981 a newly developed method to candy (domestic) green tomatoes, with the result declared almost identical to standard citrus peel.[6]

Access to Western currency or special connections created a separate consumer class, corrupting socialist collectivism. In the late 1970s GDR citizens could be categorized like this: first and lowest were workers, pensioners and others with low income and no access to hard currency (and who therefore couldn't buy coffee at Intershops); they were followed by citizens with an income high enough for Exquisit goods; who in turn were topped in this ranking by people who could get hold of West German currency and therefore were able to satisfy their needs at Intershops. Finally there were the very privileged, mostly high-up state functionaries who could buy at 'special shops' and drive expensive Western cars and who were not affected by any of the economic hiccups. Everybody in the GDR knew that this was how the system actually functioned. Nevertheless, in 1977 the ever-optimistic regime claimed that 'of course, these [Inter]shops weren't a permanent companion of socialism'.[7]

The GDR became nearly self-sufficient in basic foodstuffs, but above that consumer choice was often limited and quality patchy. Egalitarian ideals didn't always translate into flexibility or good service, just as nationally defined goals were tricky to coordinate with individual production plans. Food distribution suffered from bad planning and lack of coordination as well as disinterested carelessness. Good quantities of fish would be caught on the Baltic but never made it inland due to the lack of refrigerated transport. Tomatoes, cherries and even precious imported grapefruit and peaches rotted because workers didn't feel like doing overtime. Only red and white cabbage as well as apples were sturdy enough to be reliably available. HO stores and Konsum cooperatives had a bad reputation concerning cleanness, selection and presentation. Customer service was almost unheard of. Dissatisfaction was rife and in spite of contemporary nostalgia surrounding GDR food culture (which will be discussed in the next chapter), petitions in 1979, the East German state's thirtieth anniversary, included many questions and complaints. Was it true that rationing coupons would be introduced for meat after the elections? Why were many high quality products either exported or sold only in Exquisit shops where normal people couldn't afford them? What were the reasons for shortages in bed linen, cars and vegetables? Would the situation be even worse in the coming years with no elections and no state anniversary? In 1986 the GDR's own market research institute found that 40 per cent of all food was of lower quality than in 1980.[8] Propaganda slogans tried to transform the populace into politically and socially responsible consumers who would obediently buy what was on offer instead of clamouring for what wasn't. Nevertheless a petition from 1987 stated: 'Never has shopping caused so much worry and effort as lately.' Perceived as a socialist shop window to the capitalist West, the GDR capital had absolute priority in everything, including food supplies. In popular opinion Berlin housewives went shopping, whereas in the rest of the republic they went out searching for food. Some East Berliners felt like Westerners, supplying their compatriots in the neglected provinces with scarce goods. Frequently people queued without even knowing what they were queuing for and then bought more than they needed to compensate for the effort. Even in expensive Delikat stores shop assistants often kept the most wanted goods under the counter for preferred customers as *Bückwaren*, or bending ware. Home production was widespread in the form of immensely popular *Schrebergärten*, allotments, with preserving and later freezing fruit and vegetables being common practice. Some of the produce from these private ventures was also bought by the state, which paid higher rates than the fixed shop prices, then sold the produce at a loss in the HO stores, demonstrating the absurdity of the economic system. Statistically living standards rose in the 1970s and '80s. Increasingly households could afford TVs, refrigerators, washing machines and cars. However, waiting lists were long as the economic capacities of the GDR were overstretched due to the building up of heavy industry (a declared priority) and maintaining its own sizeable army.

Kindergarten in Oberschweissbach, GDR, January 1980, during lunch. Note that the young woman is not eating with the children, but seems to be just supervising them.

The state desparately needed women in the workforce due to the demographic imbalance resulting from the Second World War, which was followed by the loss of an important number of young males to the West before August 1961. Occupation among women of working age rose from 66.5 per cent in 1964 to 82.6 per cent in 1976.[9] Childcare was amply provided and a birthrate decline in the 1970s was countered with very generous maternity leave provisions. Collective feeding programmes in schools and factories were an essential part of East German socialism. This required a radical remaking of traditional German eating culture. Home cooking was reduced to simple evening meals (traditionally cold) and Sunday lunch. In 1978 almost every second GDR citizen ate his or her main weekday meal in a school or works canteen. The latter also provided workers with half-cooked meals, prepared vegetables and peeled potatoes to take home; factory shops were able to offer scarce goods such as condensed milk, pork fillet, strawberries and higher quality beer. With the state producing seven million dinners daily, this could have been the opportunity to positively change people's food habits, but once again official theory and the reality on plates massively diverged; on the one hand there were campaigns for healthier nutrition patterns, and on the other the lack of any initiative to instigate them in communal meals.[10]

Although in the 1970s (in contrast to West Germany) GDR women were proud of being able to do men's work, they soon noticed that in spite of all propaganda they still lived in an unequal, gender-divided society that expected them to carry a double burden. Role models of old regarding household chores, hierarchies in the workplace and women's representation in political and social committees didn't change significantly, since society's understanding of men's role remained unchanged. In 1970 a study found that of the weekly 47.1 hours on average spent on housework per household, women did 37.1 hours, men did 6.1 hours and 'others' (mostly grandmothers) did 3.9 hours. The state-run HO restaurant chain in 1960 advertised its catering services for *Jugendweihe* day (the youth initiation ceremony for fourteen-year-olds that had replaced Christian rituals and took place on a Sunday in late spring) by promising working mothers 'a day which many families will have discussed and saved for during the whole preceeding year', with 'the advantage that mother and grandmother can celebrate like everybody else'. Warm and cold dishes, even entire meals including plates and cutlery, could be ordered from the central HO kitchen. It is difficult to know how many families actually had a chef come and prepare mushroom soup, tongue in red wine with vegetables and potato balls and then lemon cream as dessert, bringing all the necessary pots and pans along and taking away the dirty plates with him after the meal.[11]

By no means all official planning was doomed. Goldbroiler, a chain of diners selling grilled chicken, was a huge success. The idea was born in 1964 when the Soviet Union threatened to reduce food deliveries. The East German regime, ever scared of political destabilization, sought to close the 'meat gap' with domestic production. To achieve this they were prepared to import Western technology. From 1965 a special committee was put in charge of building up modern industrial poultry production and thus set an example for the further development of GDR agriculture. Dutch, West German and British technology was imported via Yugoslavia, and from 1966 set up in state-owned *Kombinate für Industrielle Mast*, industrial feeding combines. Even with the exceptional empowerment granted directly by the party leaders, Goldbroiler was financially precarious. But the project persevered, mostly due to its perceived political importance, and eventually those in charge could admit to the politically delicate fact that their model had been the hugely succesful German diner chain Wienerwald (founded in 1955 and selling grilled chicken). When the first Goldbroiler restaurants opened in late 1967, the broiling equipment still needed to be imported from the 'capitalist enemy'. Partly because poultry at the time was regarded as a luxury, partly because these restaurants were true family places, they proved to be an immense success that put the chicken-producing *Kombinate* under enormous pressure to meet the demand.[12]

The name Goldbroiler seems ironic, as GDR language politics in many ways resembled those of 1870s Germany. But in officials' books, conveniently ignoring its American origin, *Broiler* had been adopted from the Bulgarian industry as a special meat-rich chicken breed. Most streetfood was linguistically nationalized to detract attention from its Western capitalist origins. Hot dogs, served in special buns with cucumber ketchup, were rechristened *Ketwurst*. *Krusta*, a square version of pizza with a darker, rye-bread-like dough was introduced in the early 1980s. It came with all kinds of toppings ranging from the exotic Black Sea to the homely Spreewald. Hamburgers were called *Grilletta* and consisted of a pork burger sandwiched in a crusty bun with the addition of sweet and sour chutney, although some remember it as gratinated with cheese and vegetables. All this upmarket fast food was initially and mostly directed at the crowds on Berlin Alexanderplatz, one more of the capital's many privileges.

A culinary place in time: the Konnopke sausage stall in Berlin-Prenzlauerberg

Max Konnopke was born a farmer's son in Cottbus in 1901 and moved to Berlin in the late 1920s. After working as a day labourer on construction sites, in 1930 he and his wife tried their luck as *Wurstmaxe*, venturing out each night (as daytime sales were heavily regulated) with their *Wurstkessel*, a metal pot containing different kinds of sausages in hot water, on a folding table protected by an umbrella. Nightlife in the Prenzlauer Berg district was good for business. When meat became scarce at the end of the 1930s, they sold *Kartoffel-puffer*, potato pancakes. In 1947 they moved into two wooden sheds, which were soon replaced by mobile carts. Later their son-in-law joined the company, expanding it to various weekly open-air markets and the Christmas market. When their son trained with a West Berlin butcher in 1960 he discovered Currywurst, as yet unknown in the East – at least that's how the Konnopke website tells the story. The Konnopkes, always quick at spotting an opportunity, created their own version of tomato ketchup and the new dish became extremely popular with factory workers, craftsmen, nightowls and other Konnopke aficionados, sometimes being referred to as an Indian dish. Max worked until 1976, passing the business on to his daughter Waltraud, who built a new kiosk in 1983. Today the kiosk, situated next to the Eberswalder Strasse subway station, is run by Waltraud's son Mario and his wife. With the fall of the Wall, the urban landscape gradually changed. Students and tourists replaced the workers and opening times are now ten to eight, with Sunday closed. Konnopke has become a cult, but the sausage is still skinless, and said to be an East Berlin speciality (www.konnopke-imbiss.de).

Almost simultaneously with Goldbroiler, another successful restaurant chain started. This one was based on fish and called Gastmahl des Meeres, banquet of the sea. At the time fish was rather plentiful due to the large GDR fishing fleet. The idea came from Rudolf Kroboth, responsible for sales at the VVB Hochseefischerei, the combineed deep-sea fishing cooperative in Rostock on the Baltic. The first Gastmahl des Meeres opened in Weimar in 1966 and was quickly followed by fifteen others all over the country. The menu and design (in blue and white) were the same in all outlets, said to have been based on American family restaurants. Like these the restaurants were advertised in magazines and in cinemas, but also through Kroboth's own TV cooking show, *Der Tip des Fischkochs* (The Fish Chef's Tip), every week from 1961 to 1972. The self-trained Kroboth regularly summoned his head chefs to Rostock for training sessions. The Gastmahl des Meeres menu offered up to 100 different dishes, mostly simple, solid fare such as potato salad with baked fish or fried herring with boiled potatoes. Although herring, pollock and cod featured most prominently, customers could also indulge in Russian keta caviar.

Food magazines or critical restaurant guides as such didn't exist in the GDR, but many newspapers and magazines ran a section with recipes and nutritional advice. One of those was *Liebe, Phantasie und Kochkunst* (Love, Fantasy and the Art of Cooking) by the agricultural writer and journalist Ursula Winnington, printed in the popular monthly *Das Magazin*. She combed literary sources for foreign dishes such as *asparagi alla milanese*, Chicken *gangbao* or *Imam bayildi*, Turkish stuffed aubergine, but was also allowed to travel internationally and collected recipes on those occasions.[13] In its 1983 edition the West German restaurant guide *vif Restaurantführer* included GDR restaurants. A West German food critic had been taken to 55 restaurants and hotels on two state-organized trips. Although he liked and recommended some places, above all the Müggelsee-Perle, a tourist destination in the south of Berlin, GDR authorities didn't appreciate his efforts and confiscated the specimen copies the Hamburg publisher sent to the featured chefs. An article about the guide in the West German magazine *Der Spiegel* from November 1982 made clear what the reasons for this might have been:

> Only British gastronomy has an even worse reputation than the German democratic one. Long waiting times, seating regulations, rude service, meagre offerings, 'hunting meals' at which plates are grabbed from eaters as soon as they put down the fork – all this is part of GDR everyday life.[14]

The restaurant guide pronounced regional food such as *Lausitzer Hochrippe* (Lausitz rib roast) and *Thüringer Klösse* (Thuringian potato dumplings) best, but admitted that it wasn't exactly lean cuisine. The GDR publication *Gastronomische Entdeckungen* (Gastronomic Discoveries, 1984), could be seen as a reply to this West German impudence. It presented restaurants and regional specialities from all over East Germany. Pork and sausages featured prominently. The author Manfred Otto, quoting a GDR survey on Thuringia, said that over a third of East Germans associated the region around Weimar and Erfurt with *Thüringer Klösse*, the famous dumplings made mostly from raw potatoes and stuffed with croutons, while the rest thought of *Thüringer Rostbratwurst*, bratwurst. He declared Thuringians to be real foodies, loving anything good and porky, but also the wild watercress that grew (and still grows) along streams and rivers between Erfurt and Eisenach.[15]

East Germany's 26,000 restaurants were categorized in five official price groups, with over 70 per cent belonging to the two lowest ones – which also meant they were the lowest in the supply chain. In many personal recollections East German gastronomy is described as limited and unpredictable, with only *Soljanka* and *Letscho* available with some reliability. *Soljanka* originated as a Russian or Ukrainian soup made with pickled mushrooms, cucumbers or vegetables, tomato, lemon and sour cream; Hungarian *Letscho* is a spicy dish of bell peppers, tomato and onions, somewhat in the style of an Italian *peperonata*. East German restaurant offerings mostly represented very liberal variations on those originals, based on supplies. *Würzfleisch*, a kind of ragout, was another stalwart at gastronomic outlets. Waiters are often remembered as surly at best, rude at worst. Seating regulations in restaurants (unheard of in West Germany at the time) forced people to queue in spite of empty tables, as the staff were generally slow in clearing tables and often refused to serve outdoors as it was too much bother. True to socialist ideals of equality, nobody expected any form of service from anybody else.

But there were exceptions, in particular among privately owned and run restaurants. Although many of the remaining private craftsmen and small companies had been forced to sell out to the state in 1972 (following a pattern somewhat reminiscent of Jewish dispossessions in the 1930s), private shopkeepers and restaurants later came to be quietly encouraged, as they proved more efficient than the state-run establishments. In 1989 they accounted for 43 per cent of all restaurants.[16] Ambitious chefs included Doris Burneleit at the Italian-themed restaurant Fiorello, which she opened 1987 in Berlin, and Rolf Anschütz (self-taught, like Burneleit), who from 1966 gradually transformed the Waffenschmied (Armourer) in Suhl/Thuringia into an extremely traditional Japanese restaurant complete with naked bathing rituals, kimonos, chopsticks and sake. Both Burneleit and Anschütz had to study their chosen foreign cuisine in whatever literature they could find and make do with what they could get their hands on in the kitchen. Frequently improvisation was needed – Burneleit marinated Edam cheese in white wine and dried it in a well-aired chimney to stand in for the unobtainable *parmeggiano*. Anschütz was lucky: Japanese guests were so impressed that they supplied him with original ingredients by post. In 2011 his story was made into a film, *Sushi in Suhl*. The Konnopke family with their sausage stall in East Berlin's students' and artists' district Prenzlauer Berg was more pragmatic: they temporarily switched to fish when meat was scarce in the early 1960s. At the ambitious Hotel Neptun in Warnemünde it helped that the director could offer holiday stays when bartering for food. The five ethnic restaurants opened in 1978 were said to be the most expensive venues in all East Germany. They featured Cuban, Hungarian, Russian and Scandinavian cuisine as well as local seafood. The Neptun, like other high-end hotels built by a Swedish company, opened in 1971 and was based on the highest international standards. Offering 757 beds, the hotel was fully booked until the fall of the Berlin Wall in 1989. It was unusual in that it eventually welcomed both East Germans (80 per cent) paying with their own currency, and international guests (20 per cent), who had to exchange their respective currency into 'hotel money' to level out black market rates.[17]

By 1965 holiday trips were high on many East Germans' wish lists, but most people necessarily stayed within their own country's borders. Against widespread perception, travelling was not all state-organized, but long waiting lists were the norm, particularly for trips to neighbouring socialist countries. Young people often risked hitchhiking and camping was very popular. Travelling seemed much more easy in cookbooks. *Kochen*, together with its sister publication *Wir kochen gut* the most important East German cookbook, in its sixth edition of 1983 dedicated a chapter to international dishes based on holiday trips. Bulgarian *Tarator* (a cold cucumber soup), Czech *Kuttelflecksuppe* (tripe soup), Hungarian *Palatschinken* (pancakes), Caucasian *Plow* (pilaf), Polish *Gurkensuppe* (cucumber soup) and Roumanian *Mititei* (grilled ground meat rolls) were all lovingly mentioned in the introductory text. The recipes that followed were mostly from Russia and Central and Eastern Europe, but also included some French classics such as *rillettes*, onion soup and *bouilla-baisse*, an Indian pumpkin stew and *minestra* (made with potatoes and

Italian cuisine's appeal didn't stop at the inner German border: pizza and spaghetti. From the popular GDR cook-book *Kochen* (Leipzig, 1983).

spaghetti). A special section with the title 'Foreign specialities for curious minds' started with *Süsssaures Schweinefleisch*, sweet and sour pork, and Szegedin goulash followed by *Burgunder Bohnen* (green beans with carrots, bacon and unspecified red wine), *Bami*, paella (with pork and fish), stuffed vine leaves, short ribs braised with white cabbage and apples, beef fillet in puff pastry, ravioli, *Pelmeni* and *Honigbroiler* (whole fried chicken glazed with honey, mustard and curry powder) as well as apple pie, Russian carp (served on sauerkraut) and *Fisch mit Gemüse*, fish with vegetables – a mix of international classics, imagined exotica and perfectly normal fare. As was the case in West German recipes of the time, exotic ingredients were replaced by what was locally produced and available, such as domestic *Erwa* or *Bino* food seasoning, which stood in for soy sauce. However, to include eight recipes involving bananas, which were exceptionally rare, seems to border on the sadistic.

Some of those dishes were also presented by East German TV chef Kurt Drummer in the fortnightly half-hour series *Der Fernsehkoch empfiehlt* (The TV Chef Recommends). Unlike his colleague Rudolf Kroboth, Drummer was a professional who commandeered the stoves at a number of large Interhotel kitchens. His tasks on TV seem to have included directing consumers towards available foodstuffs, and he adjusted his cooking presentations accordingly. However, without a hint of irony, the cookbooks that went with the series featured Italy and Austria next to Cuba and the Soviet Union.[18]

Particularly during the 1980s, culinary inspiration beyond sauerkraut and potato salad could have been gathered closer to home. Although the GDR was perceived as a monocultural state, refugees and students workers from fellow socialist countries provided foreign influences. From 1987 Vietnamese represented the single largest foreign ethnic group among them. The regime had declared its solidarity with the fellow socialists who urgently needed economic help after the Vietnam war and the following socio-economic crises. Investing in local pepper and coffee production, East German officials in return saw a chance to deal with their own lack of labour, mostly due to inefficiencies in their centralized planning. In theory foreign workers were extremely segregated in every aspect of life. Although the reality turned out to be both more lax and more severe, depending on the circumstances, their culinary influence nevertheless seems to have been minimal. Sources on GDR contract workers, for instance, never mention factory canteens offering special meals. The populace had not been told that each contract worker helped to reduce

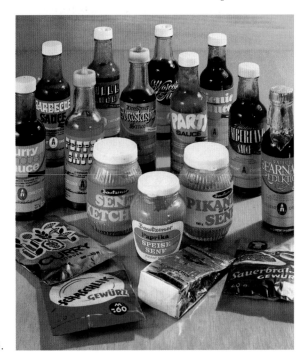

GDR versions of Worcestershire sauce and ketchup, from *Kochen* (Leipzig, 1983).

the state deficit; they only saw that authorities had not planned for the Vietnamese workers buying rice, pork, sugar and poultry and thus blamed them for even more patchy supplies on the shelves.[19]

On the evening of the GDR's fortieth anniversary on 7 October 1989, the Politburo members dined in style with international state guests, among them the Romanian Ceausescu, the Palestinian Arafat and the Soviet Gorbachev, at the Palast der Republik, the Republic's Palace. Built on the site of the demolished imperial Schloss and opened in 1976, this was the GDR's most ambitious and expensive building project. Behind bronze-coloured reflective glass, it housed not only the parliament, but also two large concert halls, a theatre, art galleries, a bowling alley and a discotheque. Needless to say, the thirteen restaurants also to be found under its flat white roof never experienced any supply problems. They specialized in theatrical performances such as flambéing and preparing steak tartare at the table. That evening the menu was conceived to impress: quail breasts were served with creamed corn as a starter; then came

Window of Café Central in Leipzig on the occasion of the SED party convention, 1987.

trout rolls with dill sauce and trout caviar, followed by turkey soup with pistachio dumplings and tomato royale, all accompanied by domestic Rotkäppchen sparkling wine. *Filet-Ensemble Trianon* followed as main course, composed of veal fillet with ham duxelles, beef fillet with a vegetable bouquet and chicken medaillons with half a peach. Dessert was an ice cream creation on a chocolate-marzipan sponge cake, appropriately named *Surprise*. By then a 3,000-strong crowd of mainly young protesters had marched over from nearby Alexanderplatz where a celebratory fair with dance music had been held, chanting *Freiheit* and *Wir sind das Volk* – freedom, we are the people. Just five weeks later the Berlin Wall fell and West Berliners would welcome their former and future compatriots with sparkling wine and bananas.

The 1950s in West Germany have often been labelled as *Fresswelle*, or wave of gluttony, but at closer inspection this turns out to be an oversimplification. Admittedly eating one's fill for many was a top priority immediately after post-war hunger. A woman remembered April 1949, after the Deutschmark had been introduced:

> Suddenly in the shops there were such mountains of butter, eggs aplenty, those milk shops, you could buy cream, liquid cream. And white flour, white flour, oh, that was so nice. And then the fat on top and a bit of coffee, real beans.[20]

Following the founding of the FRG in May 1949, West Germany quickly adopted a free-market economy and deregulated food prices, although they were indirectly influenced by the state regulation of the agrarian market (later on the EU level), protecting German farmers. Buyers valued the quickly growing freedom of choice, furthered by the introduction and rapid success of self-service stores and supermarkets. At first they were few and far between: just 39 in 1951 in all of West Germany. However the American food industry was keen to change this in order to conquer the German market (on a political level, the resulting higher living standards were also thought of as an essential way of fighting the communist threat). In 1953 an American exhibition on the subject toured through Germany, but the turning point came at the ANUGA food show in Cologne in 1957, where a special exhibit with almost 40 modern self-service shops was displayed. From then on, numbers as well as turnover quickly rose: from 326 stores in 1955 to 53,125 in 1965. Their share in turnover of the retail market for food went up from 4.4

per cent in 1956 to 34.8 per cent in 1960 and 62 per cent in 1964. As the investments necessary to remodel existing shops were substantial, independent shops tended to form chains, such as Spar, founded in 1953, and in the long term the number of independent bakers and butchers declined substantially.[21]

Until then everything had been weighed individually in front of the buyer, often into their personal receptacles such as bowls or bottles, which could easily take twenty to 30 minutes. Now food needed to be uniformly prepacked instead of being delivered in large sacks or bags, barrels or boxes. People commented that they missed the small talk of the old shops, but they also valued the time saving and being able to choose freely and at leisure. Generic food items were gradually replaced by brand names, with a rising number of options available. New foodstuffs such as margarine, chocolate, cocoa powder, condensed milk and baking powder were the pioneers. Brands provided printed guidance, replaced the verbal sales talk of old, and promised reliable quality. For these reasons packaging played an essential role, with new synthetic materials such as cellophane on the rise and gold the most successful colour. Industrial convenience food such as *Puddingpulver*, custard powder, Maggi soup seasoning, packet soup and tinned ravioli (the latter introduced in 1957) were or became increasingly popular.

The currency reform of 1948 marked the end of the standardized 'regular consumer' and the 1950s were more about diversification than just gluttony. Even working-class families with restricted budgets longed for something special and refined. Thrift was still considered essential, and housewives continued to be admonished to act responsibly and save. Invariably seen as naturally suited to the job, they were portrayed as responsible for their family's happiness, farmers' success, avoiding shortages or otherwise hampering a prospering economy (by shopping for domestic produce according to seasons), the integration of refugees and much else. Initially consumption for most was still limited, but not monotonous: for instance, Christmas and Easter were marked by special meals including meat and sweets, as were Sundays, with white rolls for breakfast and chocolate pudding for dessert. The often quoted waves (as the *Fresswelle* was supposedly followed by a general emphasis on house and home, then on travel and finally on health as top priority) might have their origin in individual experience, as people remembered being gradually able to afford more: first a Sunday roast, then wine in the evening, then a refrigerator, then a short holiday trip in summer. While slowly catching up with American consumers, the delicacies people had been dreaming of weren't taken for granted, since they remembered the first this and the first that very clearly as something special, such as the first roast goose for Christmas. Slowly expenditures on food went up, but with wages rising as well, they came to represent an ever smaller proportion of disposable income: an average of 46.4 per cent in 1950 decreased to 36.2 per cent in 1960. A worker needed to work for about four hours to buy 1 kg of butter in 1950 (as compared to about one hour for workers in the U.S.), down to about two hours in 1960 and one hour in 1970.[22]

For most West Germans in the 1950s meat was special and far from affordable every day. Between 1950 and 1960 annual consumption of pork per head rose by 50 per cent while that of poultry tripled, especially because prices for the latter went down from the mid-1950s on due to industrial production. Much less non-white bread was eaten, but rye bread remained dominant, at least in working-class households: a four-person household in 1950 consumed on average 23.2 kg of non-white bread per month and a little under 5 kg white bread. The last figure stayed more or less constant up to the early 1960s, whereas the former declined steadily to 14.9 kg.[23]

Until the mid-1950s, in rural areas, grain was still sent to the miller who in turn gave the flour to the baker who then made one's bread for a fee, and also baked large sheet cakes prepared at home. But the general tendency was to bake less at home and buy at the baker's instead: the amount of flour purchased went down by half whereas expenditure on baked goods doubled. This included *Teilchen*, small Danish pastries, during the week, marking the start of a less strict differentiation between Sunday and weekdays. However housewives still had to demonstrate their skills. *Obsttorte*, a baked base covered with fresh, tinned or steamed fruit and a glaze, became a favourite. It was easy and quick to make and was considered tasty and healthy. The Dr Oetker company, a leading producer of baking powder, compensated for losses in sales by launching a similarly packaged powdered jelly glaze in 1950. It was an instant hit.[24]

West Germany developed into an important import market for fresh fruit and vegetables. Allotment gardens lost some of their importance in daily food supplies as transport became ever better at dealing with delicate and perishable foodstuffs. Women still preserved fruit and vegetables, but younger generations were less likely to do so, and then mostly only to save money. Over 80 per cent of imported vegetables (with the Netherlands the dominant source) were of just five varieties: tomatoes (which shot up in popularity as they filled a seasonal gap and were deemed very decorative), cauliflowers, onions, cucumbers and lettuces. At the same time the consumption of potatoes went down, as did that of legumes. Especially in urban areas potatoes were increasingly consumed in the form of convenience food, such as dried potatoes used for dumplings or frozen chips. Rice was gradually accepted as an alternative, with parboiled boil-in-the-bag rice first offered in the late 1950s. From 1958 significantly more fresh fruit was eaten: mostly *Südfrüchte* (citrus and tropical fruit) besides the traditional apples and pears. When tinned fruit and vegetables became more widely affordable in the mid-1950s, they quickly became very popular. Tinned vegetables were considered handy, tasty and time-saving (with peas, peas and carrots and green beans top of the list), whereas tinned fruit was thought of as something special for dessert on Sundays or for guests, with pineapple a favourite through all social strata.

Margarine remained the dominant fat consumed in working-class households, but from the mid-1950s its consumption (as well as other vegetable fats, suet and in particular lard) went down in favour of butter. The consumption of full-fat cheese shot up, with *Schmelzkäse*, spreadable processed cheese, a favourite. Interestingly quark consumption also rose considerably, almost tripling. With the ban on cream officially lifted in 1952, consumption of fresh liquid cream went up but stayed at somewhat moderate levels, while condensed milk in tins became immensely popular.

For many real coffee remained a special treat, and only overtook ersatz products in volume in 1955. Total expenditures on so-called *Genussmittel*, luxury goods, including coffee, tea, wine, beer, spirits and tobacco, rose both in percentage and in absolute quantities, but tobacco and cigarettes moved down the ranks and were replaced by beer and spirits. Above all beer consumption shot up, most of it bottled and consumed at home. A similar urge to catch up resulted in chocolate consumption quadrupling, with the favourite flavours being (in decreasing order) milk chocolate, milk and nuts, coffee and cream.[25]

The *Frankfurter Küche*, the modern fitted kitchen, made a return in the 1950s and '60s in a modernized and more adaptable form that came from the u.s. and Sweden and was integrated in the many new housing projects. *Praktisch, sauber und pflegeleicht,* practical, clean and easy-care, was the slogan of the time, with modern materials such as Formica popular, as were wipeable plastic table covers somewhat later. With fitted kitchens came electrical appliances, trickling down from higher to lower income households. A *Küchenmaschine*, or food processor, became an essential wedding gift. The hand-held electric mixer was used much more frequently, however, as the time needed to assemble and clean the food processor was deemed too great for smaller tasks. Modern kitchen machinery not only saved muscle power but changed the status of certain preparations; lengthy beating and whipping now didn't take one's own energy or that of a servant, but could be done at the flip of a switch. Refrigerators were at the top of most people's wish lists (followed by vacuum cleaners and washing machines), but they were expensive. According to a survey, only 10 per cent of all households owned one in 1955, but almost every second household wanted one, and by the early 1960s they had one. This meant that women no longer needed to go shopping several times a day and could buy larger quantities at lower prices. Most insisted on a freezer compartment, often thinking that they would make their own ice cream. In fact they used it to store bought-in ice cream as well as frozen food. Frozen food started to appear in 1955, with an official presentation at the ANUGA food fair that year in Cologne. Once stores and private kitchens were equipped for it, consumption rose quickly, from 150 g per person and year in 1956 to 400 g in 1959 and 2.7 kg in 1963. *Fischstäbchen* or fish fingers, introduced in the early 1960s, proved to be a long-term success.

Housewives didn't necessarily gain personal leisure time through all this modern technology, as expectations also changed: laundry was easier and more quickly done now, so everybody wanted a clean set of clothes more frequently than before. Many of these tasks had been previously outsourced and now returned onto women's to-do lists. Whenever possible a warm midday meal was expected to appear on the table. On Sundays and special holidays these had to be extravagant, often including a soup and dessert. In 1949 Edeka (the oldest German food retailers' cooperative, founded in 1898) started to publish a widely distributed free customer magazine with the title *Die Kluge Hausfrau* (The Clever Housewife), first fortnightly, then weekly.[26] Initially the recipes included were still modest, with meat and fat making rare appearances and shortages frequently mentioned. In summer 1950 the lunch suggestions were the following:

MONDAY: cauliflower soup with star-shaped noodles, buckwheat porridge with fruit juice

With modern technology came new tasks for housewives which had been previously outsourced. The Piccolo of the 1950s shreds and mixes, but can also vacuum, polish or spray-paint.

TUESDAY: stuffed Savoy cabbage with boiled potatoes, cherry soup with semolina cooked in milk
WEDNESDAY: fried mushroom dumplings with Béchamel potatoes, lettuce
THURSDAY: broad beans and roots, diced bacon and mashed potatoes
FRIDAY: steamed mackerel in caper sauce, boiled potatoes, sugared berries
SATURDAY: sour aspic with mashed potatoes, *Rote Grütze* (a red berry dessert) with milk
SUNDAY: clear soup served in cups, kidney and heart ragout in a rice ring, an assortment of vegetables, apricot dessert.

Already for Christmas 1950 butter was taken for granted as an ingredient in Christmas baking, as were roast goose and veal. For New Year's Eve a cold buffet was suggested and its logistics (clearing your husband's desk and covering it with a large white cloth) explained in detail. It was a harbinger of things to come: all the dishes were to be elaborately garnished in bright colours using tomatoes, parsley and lettuce. Everything was to be easy and quick to prepare, so that the housewife had time to apply make-up and look fresh and just as decorative as the food.

An Italian salad for the New Year's Eve buffet of 1950 announced a new internationalism. The culinary horizon was widening, at least in recipes' titles. The phrase *Mailänder Art*, or *alla milanese*, was to be used frequently for pork fillet, veal, sausages and asparagus, mostly indicating the use of tomato puree and grated cheese (which from 1958 was *Parmesan*, parmeggiano, instead of the more general term *Reibekäse*). For Easter 1951 mock turtle soup made a comeback and *Weincreme*, wine cream, added a posh note by using the French spelling. On the same occasion *Huhn auf französische Art* (chicken the French way) was combined with *Risipisi*, the Frenchness of the chicken being guaranteed by the use of cognac. The small tin of green peas (still expensive and considered very modern) added to boiled rice for *Risipisi* further marked the special occasion. During the following years Frenchness signified various combinations of cognac, garlic or red wine (French cuisine as such was deemed ambitious and only became truly popular in the 1960s).

Clever housewives first heard of China in 1953 with an extremely freely adapted version of (Indonesian) *nasi goreng* and then again in 1961 with a number of sweet and sour recipes. In 1955 Toast Hawaii made its

Toast Hawaii and other dishes for parties from the early 1960s.

first appearance in the magazine, the same year the first West German TV chef, Clemens Wilmenrod, is said to have invented the gratinated concoction of boiled ham, tinned pineapple, cheese and a dollop of tomato puree, all on white bread. It was symptomatic of the pseudo-international cooking style that would soon reign. In 1958 *Die Kluge Hausfrau* invited her readers on a culinary world tour: Italy was represented with cod *alla milanese*, Portugal had a spinach roulade and France a Parisian omelette, while Dutch cooking was represented by a brain soup and Africa (as one entity) a banana salad. If nothing else, this last dish makes clear how arbitrary these recipes were, being much more concerned with preconceptions than authenticity. As the internationalization of recipes in *Die Kluge Hausfrau* progressed, regional German dishes came to be categorized as *Hausmacherart*, home cooking.

Working hours gradually decreased, and as more families could afford their own cars, holidays became immensely fashionable. In 1969, 25 million West Germans took a summer holiday trip, and over half of them went abroad.[27] This brought German tourists to Italian beaches, creating a lasting demand for *wurstel con kraut* along the Italian coastline and eventually leading to a renewed popularity of Italian food in Germany that is still pervasive. Since the end of the nineteenth century, Italian ice-cream makers, mainly from the region of the Dolomites, had been a feature of all major cities in the summer months, but during the 1950s and '60s many of them moved to Germany for good. To this day many ice cream parlours are in Italian hands and known as *Dolomiti*. The first German pizzeria, Sabbie di Capri, opened in 1952 in Würzburg. It was run by an Italian from the Abbruzze region who had worked for the U.S. Army in Nuremberg. He found that American soldiers loved the food he was familiar with as poor people's fare from his homeland, and soon his clientele expanded to include locals.

During the 1950s it was common to ask one's friends around for an evening of drinks and snacks accompanied by music, singing and dancing. Punch and bowle were very popular, and from the mid-1950s so were whisky and brandy. *Kaltes Büffet*, a cold buffet, could include herring in cream, sardines in oil, tuna in oil, anchovies and a platter with cured ham, boiled ham and finely sliced Italian salami. *Die Kluge Hausfrau* boldly suggested serving a whole slab of Gorgonzola on a wooden plate, with a bowl of butter shaped in balls and a large basket with sliced white bread, black bread, crisp bread and *Pumpernickel*. For dessert seasonal stewed fruit and fresh fruit were recommended, with cheese biscuits, cheese with quark or ham and banana rolls to be offered during card games.

The word *Party* became a very trendy Anglicism, and with the introduction of the *Partykeller* (party cellar), the basements of people's houses were finally converted from dark shelters to the brighter side of life. TV changed the way people spent their evenings as well as what they ate. The very first private TV sets in West Germany were introduced in 1952. Twelve years later more than half of all households had at least one (and almost 100 per cent in 1980). Cinema almost immediately started to decline in popularity as people drank and ate in front of the small screen. In particular men seemed to appreciate long evenings with plenty of good food in the form of *Fernsehhäppchen* (literally TV bites) and *Schnittchen* (small open sandwiches). *Knabbereien* such as saltsticks, crisps, roasted peanuts and the like became immensely popular, with the first crisps produced in Germany for the German market in 1959. The first TV food advertising in 1957 was for sparkling wine, chocolate, coffee and wine.[28] Clemens Wilmenrod, the first West German TV chef, was a trained actor. His bimonthly (later monthly) ten- to fifteen-minute shows were shown live from 1953 to 1964. In these he conjured up a full meal without any restraints on the use of convenience products, letting his fantasy run free in terms of names and connotations. Producers of food as well as appliances soon noticed how efficient it was to be mentioned by the talkative entertainer. Freely embracing brands, he became entangled in serious arguments with the TV stations on the subject of plugs and product placement.[29]

Towards the end of the 1950s, recipes in cookbooks and magazines became increasingly complicated, even overblown. Instead of straightforward buttered bread with cold cuts, suggestions for the cold evening meal recommended bananas with ham on a bread plinth or tomato aspic. *Schnittchen* were garnished ever more lavishly and recipes' titles frequently included the words *Schlemmer, Lukull, Delikatess* or *Gourmet* – now West Germans were seriously indulging. *Bunte Platten*, lavishly garnished arrangements, consisted of everything imaginable from red-capped 'mushrooms' made of hard-boiled eggs, half a tomato and dots of mayonnaise to a fleet of halved and hollowed pickled cucumber 'boats' filled with a meat salad and garnished with an onion 'sail' on a toothpick.

In the 1960s an opposing trend set in, with health-conscious recommendations and the appeal to stay slim or lose weight. Sugar, fat and overcooking were presented as the antithesis to natural health and slimness. As early as 1950 a magazine article had advised on how to stay slim:

Together with that whipped cream and those ham rolls, the chocolate and the smoked eel the worries about one's figure have reappeared. Worries – of course that's something quite different than these sighs caused by the good life, pangs of conscience about having overdone it out of joy about the re-appearance of good things. But still: the coat is too tight, the jacket won't close . . . and *Herr Müller* has to ask his small son if his shoes are dusty as his belly blocks the view. One thing is for sure: We've been eating too much lately, or rather been eating the wrong way . . . To get slim and stay slim, a sensible way of life with a sensibly mixed diet is needed. That means we prefer vegetarian to meat-eating, eating vegetables (prepared without flour and preferably eaten raw), salads (without oil and bacon, but with a lot of herbs), fruit and fruit juices. We avoid fatty meat and meat fried in fat, baked fish or fat fish such as eel, and for a while heroically say goodbye to sweet pastries, *Torten*, choco-late and other sweets. Quark and milk, boiled fish and boiled eggs enrich our menu. Instead of beer we rather drink a glass of Mosel wine and above all, as a general rule, we never drink during the meal, but only before or after and never too much.[30]

Officials had already taken action: in the early 1950s a West German government delegation went on a trip to the u.s. to study nutrition. In their subsequent publication they recommended higher consumption levels of fresh milk and fresh fruit, as well as fruit juice, and pleaded for nutritional education at all levels. Nutritional advisers needed to link up with science and the food analyses of old had to be reexamined. But the commission also pointed out that any reforms in Germany would have to come from private organizations, due to the fact that the popu-lace was tired of being told what to eat by officials. In 1953 the Deutsche Gesellschaft für Ernährung (German Nutrition Association), was there-fore founded.[31]

Meat producers took note and delivered meat with less fat from younger animals. Pigs in particular had to shed fat through revised breed-ing and feeding programmes. For beef, young bulls came to be preferred, with oxen and their marbled meat almost disappearing. At the same time meat became more affordable: in 1950 a worker needed to work for over three hours (198 minutes) on average to buy 1 kg of pork chops, whereas by 1984 this had reduced to less than one hour (58.7 minutes).

In 1958 Lufthansa introduced its 'Senator' first class service.
A chef steward looked after passengers' culinary needs.

The quality of the meat, however, often reduced with the fat, and West Germans continued to eat more than they needed as hard physical work tended to be replaced by sedentary office jobs. In 1981, 3,500 calories were consumed per person on average per day, and fat intake had tripled since the early 1950s.[32]

As in earlier decades, housewives were often presented as the culprits. A study of 'inappropriate nutritional behaviour in times of affluence' published in 1979 accused them of feeding their families too much and at inappropriate times, regularly neglecting breakfast and putting too much emphasis on midday meals. Meal plans were pronounced to be 'remarkably monotonous'. Soups were accused of furthering obesity and too little healthy fish, fresh and raw vegetables were eaten, although the latter had largely replaced legumes, deemed indigestible. Obesity was declared the most imminent threat, with every fifth child in West Germany suffering from it – again, mostly mothers' fault. It is striking that neither anorexia nervosa nor bulimia nervosa were even mentioned at this point.[33]

It is worth noting that the study openly recommended convenience food. Freezers and frozen food had arrived for good in German households, of which more than half in 1978 had a freezer or freezing compartment. Fish fingers were followed in 1970 by the first frozen pizza produced in Germany; it was a huge success. That year the average West German consumed 10 kg of frozen goods on top of ice cream, a number that was to quadruple during the following four decades. Modern convenience food had started with canned ravioli and the immensely popular Miracoli pack introduced by Kraft in 1961, a cardboard box that contained spaghetti, tomato sauce in a pouch, grated cheese and a herb-spice mix. Ready-made meals gained ground with the advent of microwave ovens, owned by one-third of West German households in 1989 (and virtually every single one could store frozen goods by then), a number that would double in the following three decades.[34]

Undeniably shopping and cooking were still women's tasks. In 1964 a study found that most West German married men didn't like their wives to work, although because of economic restraints, over one-third of all women with children under fourteen were doing just that. One-third of all husbands first of all expected their wives to be good at cooking and housekeeping. A study published in 1976 described the typical average housewife as 35 years old, having married at 21. She had two (school) children, both planned. Her husband was six years older than her and the sole earner, although she did some low-paid work before the children arrived. She had no higher education and enjoyed being a housewife, with a working day that stretched from 6.30 am to 10.30 pm. Without any hired help or servants, she cleaned the four-room flat, did the shopping, prepared three meals a day and supervised the children's homework. She usually found a few hours for herself which she spent with household-related activities, such as doing her hair, needlework, repapering the walls or preserving and freezing fruit and vegetables. Weekends were more relaxed than weekdays.[35]

However, change was on its way. Alternative lifestyles like *Wohngemeinschaften* (groups sharing an apartment), *Kommunen* (communes) and *Ehen ohne Trauschein* (cohabitation) superseded patriarchal family structures and meals followed suit: one-pot dishes and pasta became favourites. Kitchens changed once more from purely functional cubicles back to more multifunctional spaces, with large tables and much social interaction. At the time rapid economic growth started to show its drawbacks. Industrialization and materialism were seen more and more critically, and it seemed time for another call back to nature, a resumption of the *Lebensreform* ideas of roughly a century earlier. In fact, *Vollkornbrot*, wholemeal bread, saw a revival. Berlin's first (post-war) *Vollkornbäckerei*, wholemeal bakery, Weichardt opened in 1977. It strictly followed Rudolf Steiner's anthroposophical principles and milled organically certified grain on three stone-cut mills on the premises. Besides championing environmental causes and nuclear disarmament, the burgeoning green movement fought for women's emancipation. West German nutritionists were hard to convince, though. The midday family meal still stood for the integrity of the family, physical and spiritual health, economic stability and material well-being. To this day the pattern of limited preschool childcare followed by short school days with free afternoons makes life difficult for working parents.

In spite of the political protests against the establishment, the 1970s also saw the beginnings of a new generation of restaurants. When the first German Wimpy outlet (a British burger chain) opened in 1964 at Bochum central station, it was regarded with mere curiosity. West Germans were still into chicken: the Wienerwald grilled chicken chain of family restaurants had been eagerly embraced from its start in 1955 in Munich. Their slogan *Heute bleibt die Küche kalt, wir gehen in den Wienerwald* (today the kitchen stays cold, we're going to Wienerwald) became immensely popular. In 1971, the year McDonald's made its debut in Munich, the Austrian chef Eckart Witzigmann started at Munich's Tantris restaurant. In 1979 he became the first German-based chef to be awarded the coveted three Michelin stars with his own restaurant Aubergine, also in Munich.

When the Michelin inspectors started to test German restaurants in the mid-1960s, their general verdict wasn't exactly positive, but they put it diplomatically: 'German cuisine doesn't stand out through refined cooking techniques but rather the excellent and sumptuous composition of its dishes.' One of Germany's first Michelin stars had been awarded to the Keller family's self-confidently French-orientated restaurant Schwarzer Adler in the Kaiserstuhl region near Freiburg in 1969. Both the young Witzigmann and Franz Keller junior had trained with the French chef Paul Bocuse, who in turn was a disciple of Fernand Point. True to its Roman past, but undoubtedly also due to the proximity of French colleagues and shopping opportunities accross the border in France, Germany's southwest was a hotbed of restaurants that were up to French standards. But even here, somewhat oldfashioned sounding dishes featured on starred menus, such as 'chicken breast Pompadour', 'veal liver St Tropez' and 'duckling Three Musqueteers'.

Bocuse's bestseller *Cusine du Marché* was to change a lot of this. Published in 1976, it appeared the following year to great acclaim in a German translation, bringing the master himself to Frankfurt am Main for the occasion. The original title had been translated to *Die neue Küche,* new cuisine. While *Nouvelle Cuisine* in France went back to Michel Guérard and his fat-stripped, generally lean *Cuisine Minceur*, it all became one on German plates. *Nouvelle Cuisine* proved to be a great success in spite of some disparagingly calling it *Ikebana-Küche* because of the small and decoratively plated portions. Bocuse and his clever business advisers understood that French lifestyle, food and cuisine represented valuable export goods. France had started a large advertising campaign for French wine in Germany as early as 1959, and by 1975 Bocuse and his pâtissier colleague Gaston Lenôtre both had outlets at the Kadewe department store in Berlin. Even in Bocuse's pared-down version, which was by no means as demanding or as complicated as the *haute cuisine* of old, French cooking was regarded as inherently superior. Whereas Bocuse in his original book addressed housewives as his target readership, the German edition was directed at mostly male *Feinschmecker*, gourmets, and *Laien*, amateurs.

Neither of them expected to find the right ingredients and quality needed for these dishes in Germany. Regional products such as oysters from the Northern Sea island of Sylt were still in their infancy and only started to be commercially viable from the mid-1980s. As we have seen, West German agricultural policy aimed at efficiency rather than the individual quality that was still to be found in France's many deeply rural and less populated regions and its traditional centralized distribution system. Karl-Heinz Wolf, an ambitious restaurateur in Bonn, started to drive once a week to the wholesale market in Rungis near Paris to buy fish, poultry, crème fraîche and so on to supply his kitchen. He soon took orders for colleagues as well and in 1978 founded his hugely successful company Rungis-Express, importing fine French food on a commercial scale. Until the end of the 1980s, the menu at almost all ambitious German restaurants was determined by the twice-a-week delivery of the truck from Rungis-Express.

By then, some German chefs had gradually realized that their restaurants were not actually situated in France. It was a painful process of reorientation. When Gerhard Gartner started to use German products and look at his mother's recipes for inspiration at his two-star restaurant Gala in Aachen from late 1986, colleagues and restaurant testers accused him of excessive nationalism and culinary fascism. They agreed that serving domestic pike-perch instead of loup de mer and ceps in place of truffles could make for new impulses to German cuisine, but most feared losing their customers if they offered German cheeses and waited for local asparagus and strawberries. In hindsight Gartner turned out to be one of the most prominent prophets of new German cooking. Chefs increasingly started to look for and encourage local producers as well as integrating regional recipes into their cooking. The onset of the *Neue deutsche Küche* or new German cooking was marked by a TV series and a book that went with it called *Essen wie Gott in Deutschland* (Eating like God in Germany). The title played on the German saying *Leben wie Gott in Frankreich*, living like God in France, which describes a sumptuous meal or way of life. The profession of chef became more attractive, with the stereotype changing from unreliable drunkard to star artist. New technical equipment made kitchen work less physically demanding, and during the 1980s the almost exclusively male profession slowly opened up to women, although they are still in the minority.

In a trend that trickled down from exclusive restaurants' plates into cookbooks and food magazines, recipes and pictures of finished dishes became less decorated and 'cleaner'. At the same time dieting became popular and all the internationally acclaimed versions from Atkins to Hay and South Beach found their way to Germany. So-called 'light' products, diet foods with reduced fat, sugar or fat content, became a very successful new market for the food industry. The first brand, called *Du darfst* (you may), was introduced by Unilever in 1973 with a low-fat margarine, followed by cheese, jam and spreadable sausage two years later. It was mainly directed at women and promoted not as reducing weight but as helping one to avoid putting it on – arguably an even larger market than those who needed to shed the kilograms. Other brands followed suit. Soon almost any industrially produced food product, including ready meals, was available in a reduced fat version with artificial sweetener replacing sugar.

The new energy in the restaurant kitchens quickly translated into a new kind of food journalism. Arguably the most successful German food journalist is Wolfram Siebeck, who started as a columnist for the youth magazine *Twen*, founded by German art director Willy Fleckhaus in 1959. The first restaurant review Fleckhaus commissioned took Siebeck to Maxim's in Paris, following in the footsteps of his role model, the American writer Joseph Wechsberg. He later moved on to the food magazine *Der Feinschmecker*, published since 1975 by the Hamburg-based Jahreszeiten Verlag. His cookbooks have become bestsellers. Just like most of the chefs who brought restaurant cooking in Germany up to the French level, but did not create their own style (at least in the beginning), in Siebeck's world French culinary culture has been the sole guiding star, and he frequently shows his impatience, even despair, with uneducated German palates and minds. His colleague Gert von Paczensky started as foreign correspondent, but went on to write restaurant reviews for the magazine *Essen und Trinken* (Food & Drink), published since 1972 by the Hamburg publisher Gruner & Jahr. On West Germany's small screens, the actor Wilmenrod had been joined and followed by chef Hans Karl Adam (1915–2000), journalist Horst Scharfenberg (1919–2006), chef Max Inzinger (born 1945) and journalist Ulrich Klever (1922–1990). Up to the late 1980s food journalism and anything related to it was mostly focused on the harmless, pleasant aspects of food rather than critically analysing the larger picture of food production and environmental issues.

After the Second World War West German agricultural policy clearly aimed for higher productivity. Generous state subsidies went into far-reaching reparcelling of land for more efficient cultivation at larger farms, with some in narrow villages moving out to new buildings on greenfield sites. The number of tractors multiplied by six within a decade, combine harvesters went from rare experiments in 1950 to bringing in one-third of all grain in 1960, and milking machines became the norm.[36] Like the European community as a whole, West Germany soon produced more than the market could take. Better seed quality, significantly increased use of fertilizers, pesticides and premixed feeds, improvements in animal breeding and the veterinary system, a growing number of greenfeed silos and the increased use of cutting and turning machines all combined to make ever-rising production levels. The number of dairy cows rose only slightly, but the yield per cow went up significantly. Milk and butter prices were a constant point of contention – consumers found them too high and often opted for (imported) margarine, although domestic butter production by the early 1950s was exceeding domestic demand. On top of that, neighbouring countries were pushing onto the West German market with their agricultural products, and threatened to stop buying German industrial products if they were obstructed. The French were not the only ones to target the German market: from 1961 Dutch butter and cheese was marketed with the help of *Frau Antje*, a pseudo-Dutch Meisje complete with wooden clogs and white lace bonnet, created by a German marketing agency.

Meanwhile intense mechanization and other investments led to increasing debts among farmers. In the mid-1960s wages were about one-quarter lower than in comparable industrial jobs. The *Bauernverband* (farmers' organization) was always busy fighting for better economic conditions for its members. It tried to present them as a uniform group, although differences in their incomes were significant: in 1965 around 1.5 million agricultural businesses in total ranged from large farms to very small ones run as a side concern. Of these, 143,000 had more than 20 hectares, 300,000 were family-run with 10 to 20 hectares and around 1.1 million were even smaller than that. Children's work was amazingly common. It was normal that children over seven in rural areas had to help out during the summer. When they reached the ages of thirteen or fourteen their parents were reluctant to let them go to school any longer, feeling they would be more useful at home. Non-farming parents in tight circumstances also sent their children to work on farms. Although officials were anxious to preserve traditional social structures in rural areas, it shouldn't surprise us that the numbers of those working the land went down due to modernization: from almost one-quarter of the employed West German workforce in 1949 to 13.3 per cent in 1960 and 6.5 per cent in 1975.[37]

The landscape kept changing. Between 1980 and 1990 the number of farms decreased by another fifth, while total agricultural production, particularly of wheat, sugar beet, milk and eggs, rose by 14 per cent.[38] Rural districts tried to attract industrial enterprises, and commuting farmers who had a second occupation to make ends meet contributed even further to mixing of rural and urban lifestyles and living standards. In the 1970s rural towns and villages that were not situated in the catchment areas of the industrial cities had been considered doomed, but by the mid-1980s about half of the West German population lived in rural areas, although only 3 per cent of the total population were full-time farmers. Nevertheless village structures changed as supermarkets came to dominate the retail trade; with increasing motorization they were often situated on the edge of towns and cities.

Artists using food as their medium often were more politically minded and critical than the food journalists of the time. The best known among them is Joseph Beuys, who frequently combined animal fat with felt in his sculptures, but also used butter, chocolate, fruit or sauerkraut in his *Partitur der Sauerkrautfäden* (The Sauerkraut Strings' Score) (1969). The same year, he created a piece called *Beethovens Küche* (Beethoven's Kitchen) for the Argentine composer Mauricio Kagel's film *Ludvig van*. He refused to drink wine from the German state estates in the Rheingau

(*Ich trinke keinen Staatswein!*, 1974) and in 1977 planted potatoes in front of a Berlin gallery as a performance. His colleague Sigmar Polke, painter and photographer, had 'discovered' potatoes for his sculptures and ideas in the 1960s. The German-speaking Swiss artist Daniel Spoerri is best known for his *Fallenbilder*, in which he preserved the debris left on tables after long dinners. In 1968 he started a bar, restaurant and gallery in Düsseldorf where Beuys pinned baked herringbones to the wall, calling them 'Friday objects'. The Swiss-German Dieter Roth, another Eat-Art representative, used chocolate as his favourite medium for sculptures and portraits, documenting decay. The Viennese Peter Kubelka developed a unique combination of experimental filmmaking and cooking and taught both at the Frankfurt Städelschule from 1978 to 2000. He pronounced cooking to be the mother of all arts. German *enfant terrible* Martin Kippenberger taught at the Städelschule in the 1990s; his prolific work in the 1980s included frequent quotations from Joseph Beuys's *Wirtschaftswerte* of 1976, multiples of East German packed foodstuffs signed by the artist.

A signature dish of the time was *Dialog der Früchte* (Fruit Dialogue), created by Hans-Peter Wodarz at the Ente Vom Lehel restaurant in Wiesbaden at some point in the mid-1970s, as culinary legend has it, originally for Andy Warhol. The swirled pattern of three different fruit purées, highly decoratively served in a large soup plate, replaced the sorbet often served between starter and main course and in its fresh straightforwardness was symbolic of the new health consciousness. In 1970 the German sports association started the get-in-shape *Trimmdich* movement. A legal blood alcohol limit behind the wheel was introduced in 1973, originally set at 0.8 milligrams of ethanol per gram of blood, and reduced to 0.5 in 1998. In both parts of Germany alcohol consumption had risen with the post-war economic recovery in the 1960s. Alcoholism was viewed first as a sort of punishable criminal behaviour, then increasingly as an individual mental illness to be treated in closed institutions. The frequently abominable conditions encountered there were the subject of a undercover investigation and report by the journalist Günter Wallraff. The national stereotype however swerved away from the boozer to make way for the hardworking and reliable German who enjoyed the occasional recreational tipple, linked to German festivals like Oktoberfest. In fact the trend in alcohol consumption has been going down since 1980 and as of 2010 was below 10 litres of pure alcohol per head each year.[39]

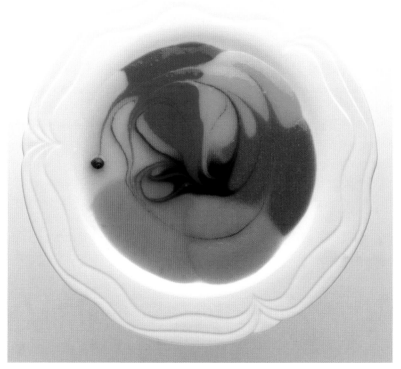

Dialog der Früchte or dialogue of fruit, a swirl of puréed fruit, replaced the traditional sorbet in the 1980s in trendy high-end restaurants. The signature dish was created by Hans-Peter Wodarz, one of the key players in Germany's Michelin-starred Nouvelle Cuisine scene. Like many other dishes at the time, it was documented by food photographer Johann Willsberger in his hugely influential magazine *Gourmet*.

Another subject Günter Walraff investigated undercover during the 1980s was the large 'underclass' of migrant workers. Disguised as a Turk, he worked in a McDonald's outlet and in the steel industry and took part in clinical studies, publishing his experiences in a series of reports and bestselling books.[40] As in the GDR, *Gastarbeiter*, guest workers, had been recruited through state agencies in reaction to acute labour shortages at the height of the economic boom. Mostly young males, they first came from Italy in 1955, but the programme was quickly extended to many more of the less industrialized Mediterranean states: Spain (1960), Greece (1960), Turkey (1961), Portugal (1964) and Yugoslavia (1968). As the industry requested more experienced labourers, many of them settled down and were soon joined by their families. They all left their culinary traces. When they lost their jobs in the factories due to the economic crises of the 1970s, these immigrant workers had to look for alternative business opportunities; one option was opening a food store, a food stall or a restaurant (in 1978 in Nuremberg one-fifth of all restaurants were Greek, Italian, Yugoslav or Turkish).[41] Yugoslav restaurants were widespread until the war in former Yugoslavia, introducing modern-day Germans to the gastronomic concept of the wood-fired grill. Some of them renamed or reinvented themselves as *Balkanküche* (Balkan cuisine) or later Croatian.

The strongest Turkish culinary impact came at the beginning of the 1970s when the first *Dönerbuden* (doner kebab stands) opened in Berlin. Doner quickly became *Currywurst*'s strongest competitor as Germans' most widely eaten fast food. Although it is just as popular in Turkey, and with few exceptions is prepared by Turkish immigrants, the German version of doner is different to the original. It does not have much in common either with the historical Persian dish, where mutton or lamb is roasted on a turning spit, nor with the main course served under that name in contemporary Turkey, where the spit-roasted meat is served over cut-up pide flatbread with melted butter added and the whole crisped quickly in a hot oven. In Germany meat is marinated with salt, spices, onions, milk, or yogurt and layered on a spit, the final product containing a minimum of 60 per cent ground meat. Originally mutton, it is now often mixed with beef, and modern variations include chicken or turkey. Most of the doner blocks (which legally are considered to be ground meat) are made by specialists, who produce up to 300 tons daily in Germany. The meat is served in one-quarter of a Turkish pide (pita) flatbread cut open to form a pocket or, more recently, as *Dürüm Döner*, wrapped in a very thin bread called *Yufka*. Usually green lettuce, tomatoes, onions and red cabbage, all cut into thin strips, are added as liberally as the yogurt sauce, with hot chilli flakes as an extra.

In sum, during the four-decade-long experiment of a state separated in two and subject to opposing political systems, West Germany saw an immense pluralization of taste, a complex pattern of numerous lifestyles and habits which no longer strictly corresponded to social groups. While catching up after the deprivations, sacrifices and hardships – real and perceived – of the first half of the century, West Germans eagerly embraced many new elements from outside Germany, first on paper, then on their plates, even if some were adapted versions. It might be said that this urge was also rooted in a widespread reluctance to face their own identity; to acknowledge local products and traditions that were perceived as tainted with the horrors and guilt of recent history. Mozzarella and pizza, doner kebabs and hamburgers seemed lighter in every respect. Just as the Berlin Wall came down, West Germans started to face the fact that their country was neither Mediterranean nor part of the United States. East Germans' love of *Kasslerrolle*, boiled eggs in mustard sauce and potato dumplings might have looked old-fashioned in comparison, but in fact it pointed to the next major trend: regionality.

Soluna bakery, summer 2012.

TWELVE

Spaghetti and *Rouladen*:
Regionality in a Globalized World, Reunified Germany since 1990

The gigantic experiment that subjected the Germans to two completely different cultural spheres added yet another layer to the country's foodways, although one that took a while to bond with the existing complexities. Since the Berlin Wall went up in 1961, East and West Germany had increasingly grown apart. A GDR journalist in an interview in 2010 remembered that when she was allowed to attend the Berlinale film festival in West Berlin in 1988, she thought it all very impersonal and formal compared to film festivals in Moscow. Since she didn't have West German currency and hadn't been invited to any of the official parties, she had to diplomatically beg the press office for meal tickets and felt very much excluded: 'West Berlin was a foreign city.'[1] Half of Germany had shot full throttle in one direction, searching for the new, whereas the other side had been forced, at least officially, to look in the opposite direction, stay closer to home and thereby safeguard more traditional ways. When the two sides finally became familiar with each other once again and got used to their new oneness from widely diverging perspectives, their combined experiences made them astonishingly well equipped for the 'thinking global, acting local' trend of the twenty-first century; the philosophy of being open to new things while remaining true to one's own identity.

Since then interest in regional food products and cuisines has grown simultaneously with the acceptance of foodstuffs imported from all over the world. You could call it a new balance, or a move away from dogmatism. Bread is a good example of this. Heavy, dark bread baked from scratch has almost turned into a luxury product, whereas light wheat bread from industrial production is ubiquitous and affordable. However, unlike in English-speaking countries, in Germany sourdough is still taken for granted. A new generation of artisanal bakers feels completely free from any political or philosophical mission in their creations, picking up on worldwide traditions in a multicultural way. Similar to the Weichardts spearheading the return to *Vollkornbrot* in the late 1970s, Peter Klann has been the pioneer of this next step in the history of bread in Germany since the early 2000s. On the shelves of his Soluna bakery in the Kreuzberg district of Berlin, rustic round rye loaves called *Rundling* sit next to Swabian *Dinkelseelen*, large breadsticks made from spelt and sprinkled with salt and caraway seeds, English scones and *petits pains obscures* with bay leaves from Provence. These new bakers are open to any inspiration and taste, yet are very much focused on their local customers.

Similarly EU legislation, while often accused of furthering uniformity on its citizens' plates, also offers bureaucratic structures to protect regional foodstuffs with an entire framework of geographical indications. This mostly takes the form of the protected geographical indication (PGI), which stipulates processing according to traditional recipes, but not the local origin of the raw material. So far it has been granted to *Dresdner Christstollen, Halberstädter Würstchen, Swabian Spätzle, Holsteiner Katenschinken, Spreewaldgurken, Lübecker Marzipan, Nürnberger Lebkuchen,* some beer varieties and many other products. A whole list of natural mineral waters, four types of cheeses (*Allgäuer Emmentaler, Allgäuer Bergkäse, Altenburger Ziegenkäse* and *Odenwälder Frühstückskäse*) and two varieties of moorland sheep carry the PDO seal (protected designation of origin) under which all the ingredients and the whole production process are tied to a place and traditional methods.[2] As we have seen, some of these foodstuffs have been associated with a certain place for centuries, such as Nuremberg gingerbread or Lübeck marzipan. For others their regionality only emerged in contrast to a larger or even global context. In some cases, whole regions reinvented themselves based on a small number of selected products. Regionality is a notoriously difficult notion to pin down. It is often linked to the idea of sustainability, implying rural origins (such as in *Landmilch* or *Landmetzgerei*, country milk, country butcher) or short distances between producer and consumer. It is however rarely consistently defined and often plays on buyers' desires. Economic, socio-cultural and ecological factors exploit the longing for harmony, cosiness, a sense of belonging and identity.[3]

Not long after reunification, nostalgia for the GDR past set in among east Germans, dubbed *Ostalgie*. East Germans rarely long for the GDR as such to rematerialize, but for some of the familiar shapes, looks and tastes of their home country. As certain brands vanished they came to symbolize the loss of an entire world, and a whole range of cookbooks is dedicated to recipes presented as being specific to GDR cuisine. In 2003 the film *Goodbye Lenin*, the highly original story of a family living in a small flat in East Berlin's Karl Marx Allee at the time of the fall of the Berlin Wall, focused on this dilemma, featuring above all *Spreewaldgurken*, pickles from the Spreewald region southeast of Berlin, but also packaged food such as Mocca-Fix Gold coffee. In 1989 the East German food industry was faced with the sudden collapse of their home market as well as the no less abrupt loss of socialist export markets. Monetary union in July 1990 was the final blow, exposing them to competition with the Western food industry. Many East German companies were forced to close down or sell out and Westernize their products. Nowadays, some people favour east German food products for nostalgic reasons and others want to contribute to economic stabilization in the east, while many perceive them as regional and therefore more authentic. In some cases products have been revived; others survive as real success stories (such as *Rotkäppchen* sparkling wine or *Hallorenkugeln*, sweets from one of the oldest German chocolate factories in Halle/Saale), while still others continue as regional products (such as mustard from Bautzen/Saxony). Building on its long history, the east German food retail group Konsum was revived and restyled in Dresden, and in 2008 expanded across the former border into Nuremberg and Erlangen.

All over Germany regional cuisines are being reinterpreted at home and in restaurant kitchens. In 2009 three-quarters of the respondents to a survey declared regional cooking styles to be important, up from two-thirds in 2003. Almost every second household declared that they served traditional fare such as Spätzle, *Semmelknödel* (bread dumplings), schnitzel, *Eintopf* stews or *Labskaus* (a northern German dish based on salted meat, potatoes, beetroot and pickled herring) at least once a week. But 13 per cent also said that they experimented with more exotic recipes.[4] Ethnic restaurants and foodstuffs from around the world experienced a real boom, be it Thai restaurants or the virtually omnipresent sushi. When in 1987 EU law forced Germany to open its market to foreign beer even if it was not brewed according to the strict old *Reinheitsgebot*, using other ingredients than water, hops, yeast and malt, domestic brewers felt threatened. Today beer from all over the world is mingling happily on the shelves with that of small local producers, some of them organic, and huge brands without any problem. This inclusive openness is characteristic of contemporary German food-ways. While artisanal cheese producers increasingly explore the notion of terroir in the form of solid milk beyond the *lac concretum* of Tacitus' times, the dairy industry's big players export ever larger amounts of German cheese to Russia and Japan (although the main export market for the German dairy industry is Italy, followed by the Netherlands and France).

The language on menus shows the same mix of curiosity and quiet self-confidence, as witnessed by the menus of the new Hotel Adlon. Lorenz Adlon's masterwork escaped the Allied bombings of 1940 to '45, but burned down in May 1945 under mysterious circumstances. The sur-viving wing first continued as a hotel, then became a dormitory for apprentices in the 1970s, and in 1984 was finally torn down. In the 1950s Hedda Adlon, Louis Adlon's second wife and widow, sold her option for purchase and the name to the Kempinski hotel group. After reuni-fication it was rebuilt on exactly the same spot and modelled on its first incarnation, albeit with one more floor. When it opened in 1997, it looked just as pompous as the original did. Today menus from the Lorenz Adlon restaurant are notable for mentioning the products' origins. The dishes are described in much greater detail than a century before. Occa-sionally French terms are used, and headings (*Crustacés et Poissons*) are generally bilingual. Some riddles remain for the untrained Adlon guest: *confiert, Loup de mer, petits pois à la française*. This could be seen as a tribute to the Escoffier legend; the Adlon past is rooted in a time when French ruled supreme in ambitious kitchens.

Back in 1903, in the years immediately before the first Adlon opened, Ernst Lössnitzer's *Speisekarte* Germanizing booklet tackled what he called the usual objections to German terminology. French expressions suppos-edly were more distinguished: the higher art of cooking, after all, was and had always been French (a belief that of course is revealed to be nonsense when you examine it closely), and the technical terminology therefore had to be French. He then listed arguments in favour of Germanizing: German people had started to feel like good Germans and had been 'clean-ing up' their language in all areas, he wrote. The mixing up of all kinds of languages was not only tasteless, it also corrupted comprehensibility – menus were written for guests, not experts. To the present day French and other foreign terms on menus often reflect chefs demonstrating professional expertise, using a *Fachsprache*, a specialist language, and thus excluding ordinary people and exploiting the insecure. *Consommé* is an example of this, also quoted by Lössnitzer. But many of the words he complained about and wanted translated have definitely become naturalized (*Aroma, Bonbon, Champignons, Estragon, Sauce*). Others have indeed been replaced by German words, for instance *assaisonnieren*, to season (although *gratinieren* lives happily next to its German equivalent *überbacken*). But altogether, although the linguistic Germanizing movement of a century and more ago was in many cases exaggerated and arguably contributed indirectly to the rise of fascist thinking, it certainly did not try to construct an alternate reality the way the Nazis did with their propaganda and comprehensive, all-encompassing dictatorship. Today German on the menu has the opposite effect, leaving more choice to the guest, and thus provides the basis for an ongoing search for the culinary reality of a distinctive German cuisine. As chefs are ready to interpret old recipes with new ingredients and vice versa, Germans are ready to adopt new words. Common sense has thankfully prevailed over fundamentalism.

In 2009 a court ruling put an end to the CMA (Centrale Marketing-Gesellschaft der deutschen Agrarwirtschaft), a quango promoting German agricultural products. Its financing through compulsory contributions by producers was declared illegal under European law, and producers complained about the agency's inefficiency. Meanwhile the similarly structured German wine institute was also the subject of legal attacks, but survived them, successfully reinvented itself and is now flourishing. Vineyards represent less than 1 per cent of Germany's agricultural area, but are of entirely disproportional cultural impact. German wines have seen a real revolution in quality and reputation since 2000, overcoming the stigma of their nationality as well as the 1960s' industrialization of erstwhile successes like *Liebfraumilch*. A new generation of professionally trained winegrowers is well connected in the international wine world, able to focus on *terroir*, the wines' origin in the vineyard, and in many cases converting to organic methods.

For agriculture in general the same trend exists, albeit in a considerably less pronounced form. In unfavourable areas such as the low mountain ranges, steep valleys or pastoral mountain regions, agriculture tends to be on the retreat, and as Germany is no exception to the general trend towards concentration, the number of farms on the 17 million hectares presently under cultivation is declining. Although slightly more farms are run as a part-time job than as a main business, the former cultivate less than one-quarter of all used land. The most successful farms combine production with processing and distribution, selling their own bread, cheese, meat and other products at farm shops or farmers' markets and taking in holiday-makers for *Urlaub auf dem Bauernhof*, holidays on the farm. About one-third of the total agricultural area is grassland and a very small area is covered with orchards (mainly apples, followed by sweet and sour cherries, plums and pears) and vineyards, but the bulk is cultivated as fields. Of these grain makes up more than half the total, with wheat dominating, followed by barley, rye and oats. Besides these, maize, rapeseed, sugar beet and potatoes are produced. The production of strawberries, the second most important fruit crop behind apples, increased by more than two-thirds between 1999 and 2005, and surveys show that in spite of year-round imports, domestic consumption still follows the German season. Likewise the importance (and diversity) of domestically grown vegetables is on the rise. Cabbage in all its varieties is followed by asparagus (for which the area under cultivation doubled between 1995 and 2005), lettuce, carrots, onions, and to a lesser degree green peas, green beans, spinach and radishes. Trade structures have been changing too: wholesale markets of fruit and vegetables today only serve the restaurant trade, hospitals, and small retailers (in Berlin, for instance, they only reach about 15 per cent of the population), as large discounters and supermarkets all buy directly from producers.[5]

Meat production in Germany concentrates on pigs (EU number one) and cattle (EU number two behind France), although poultry is increasing, representing more than 15 per cent of all slaughtered meat in 2004. More than half of all pigs are kept on farms in Lower Saxony and North-Rhine Westphalia, a tendency that started over a century ago due to the proximity of shipping ports for imported feed and for the export of the meat, as well as to the markets on Rhine and in the Ruhr region. The related problems (pollution with excrement, the high risk of pests and diseases) are augmented by the fact that industrial poultry farming tends to be in the same areas. Dairy farming is less concentrated and still mostly situated in areas with limited value for other crops, that is the marshes on the Northern and Baltic Sea, the lower mountain ranges and the foothills of the Alps. The EU milk quota system (which EU officials plan to abolish in 2015) stunted the growth of dairy farms. The number of dairy cows decreased further by more than one-fifth between 1995 and 2005, while yields per animal rose significantly, from an average of 5,320 litres per cow per year in 1995 to 6,840 litres in 2009. The abolition of state regulations for regional milk deliveries in 1970 led to the concentration of dairies, reflecting the worldwide trend. Milk is transported over ever larger distances: the number of dairies in West Germany went down from 2,758 in 1960 to just 196 in 2009. That year, the five largest German dairies processed about half of all German milk, up from less than one-quarter in 1996.[6]

One of the driving factors behind this development is the major food retailers. In 1998 the five leading retailers (and the trend is towards further supranational concentration) represented 64 per cent of all food sales in Germany. This requires large amounts of standardized products of reliable quality at prices that are as low as possible. Unsurprisingly retailers' idea of quality isn't necessarily the same as consumers', as the example of ESL (extended shelf life) milk shows. First introduced in German stores in 2008, its treatment often places it nearer in taste to UHT milk, in particular towards the end of its shelf life. However, it is legally labelled as fresh milk, with the addition of *länger haltbar*, or 'keeps longer', as opposed to conventionally pasteurized milk now labelled *traditionell hergestellt*, 'traditionally produced'. The latter has almost disappeared from discount stores' shelves.

As in earlier centuries, worries about food security continue to influence Germans' shopping and eating habits. Food often makes it into the mass media in the form of scares and scandals. Salmonella, campylobacter, E. coli and listeria all have to be reported to the relevant authorities. As in other industrialized countries, the contamination potential in large-scale production units, along with the ever increasing miles that foods travel and their ever longer shelf lives, certainly creates risks on a scale that was hitherto unknown. But looked at rationally and put into a larger perspective, most of these scares and scandals seem at least somewhat overblown when set against the actual (minimal or non-existent) casualties. Although no one issue caused as many casualties as the deadly Spanish cooking oil scandal in 1981 or the Italian red wine poisoned with methyl alcohol in 1986, food scandals in Germany spread an atmosphere of fear and disgust in consumers that borders on the superstitious. In most cases buying patterns change for only a brief period, or until the next problem flares up; a pattern of ritualized emotional response. However, the outbreak of bovine spongiform encephalopathy (BSE) in Germany led to a substantial agricultural crisis and considerably strengthened the green movement.

The first report about BSE in the United Kingdom reached Germany in November 1987. In 1990 a German health inspector came across the first indications of the disease in Germany, but lost her job when she reported her findings to the public. In 1997 pre-emptive culling took place, with government officials insisting that Germany was BSE-free and at no risk. In November 2000, however, the German government had to admit the existence of the first official BSE case in Germany. A total ban of meat and bonemeal for animal feed followed, as well as nation-wide tests of all animals slaughtered at under 24 months of age. One-third of all Germans reduced their beef consumption significantly at the time; one-quarter even renounced it completely.[7] In 2007 the official statistics declared four BSE cases, a significant drop from the 125 cases reported in 2001. So far it seems that there has not been a single BSE-related human casualty in Germany, whereas 176 casualties have been reported in the UK.[8]

The BSE crisis led to a fundamental rethinking and restructuring of agricultural policy and consumer protection, instigated by the Green Party's push for transparency and organic agriculture. Organic grocers, farm shops and supermarkets flourished and have since become much more mainstream. In 2010 every fifth German bought organic food, women more frequently than men. In 2011 organic products repre-sented 3.7 per cent of all food retail sales, while the area organically farmed in Germany almost tripled from 2.1 per cent in 1996 to 6.1 per cent in 2011, over 1 million hectares. However, that isn't even close to the 20 per cent set as a goal in 2002 by the Green Party. Today 7.5 per cent of all farms work according to organic principles. On average their yields are much lower than those of conventional farms, but since they realize significantly higher prices, the results in financial terms are about equal. Two-thirds of all Germans are familiar with the *Bio-Siegel*, the European organic food label for foodstuffs produced according to the EU-Eco-regulation. With €73.60 spent on organic food per head in 2010, Germany is seventh in Europe (behind Switzerland, Denmark, Luxemburg, Austria, Liechtenstein and Sweden), the EU aver-age being €32.20, compared with €64.30 in the U.S.[9] Farmers' markets, farm shops and organic stores are mostly used by households with above average income.

Germans mostly buy their food in supermarkets, followed by dis-count stores and special grocery stores. Although food discount stores' sales have stagnated during the last years, during the last decades they have been extremely successful. This can be traced back to the early 1960s, when the brothers Karl and Theo Albrecht redesigned their family's small grocery store in Essen and built it into a chain of food discount stores which would eventually grow into the worldwide operating company of today. By cutting their range down to the fastest-selling items and doing away with any frills in their bare neon-lit shops where products were sold directly from pallets, they were able to undercut regular supermarkets and suggest to consumers that the lowest possible prices were to be found in their stores. This proved an almost magical formula and the ALDI chain soon covered all of Germany. Their methods remain much the same to this day and have been widely copied by their competitors. Whereas until the 1980s their main customer group was among those with lower budgets, they have since become accepted by a larger range of social groups and expanded their range to include fresh food and organic produce (an attempt not to lose market share to the popular new organic supermarkets).

Overall taste is the criteria most often given for what Germans buy (over 75 per cent), followed by freshness, shelf life, health and seasonality, with price in the midfield, closely followed by organic certification.[10] Dietary choices and restrictions, such as eating no meat, no wheat or no dairy products, seem to be on the rise and may often have physiological reasons, but could also be interpreted psychologically, as a reaction to the overwhelming and sometimes confusing choice of foodstuffs on retailers' shelves. Critics repeatedly point out that organic food and farming chase a utopian and romantically idealized notion of nature similar to the life reform movement's rejection of industrialization, sharing its longing for a return to a 'original' and 'natural' diet that in fact never existed. They stress the fact that present-day quality control of food only became possible through modern mass production and that most familiar foodstuffs deemed natural are in fact shaped by human intervention, such as eggs, milk or grain, all originally serving other purposes in nature than feeding mankind. On the other hand, the critics tend to play down the long-term environmental effects of the use of chemical fertilizer and pesticides, as well as the health implications of industrial scale animal husbandry. Official policy tries to integrate environmental, social and economic interests to secure farmers' long-term survival.

Since 2008 the *Verbraucherinformationsgesetz*, or consumer information law, aims for a higher transparency for all food on the shelf. Genetically engineered food is a much discussed and very controversial topic in Germany, where the first experimental plantings have only recently been allowed. However, additives from genetically engineered soybeans, mostly imported from the United States, are being used in all kinds of food, and they do not always have to be declared on the label. Every second German (and in particular the better educated) thinks of genetically modified or irradiated food as more risky than untreated food.[11] Germany ranks second only behind Poland in the numbers of allotments (1.24 million in 2008, in comparison with 80,000 in the UK and 150,000 in France), and their popularity for food production is increasing once again, particularly among young urban professionals.[12]

Where does all of this leave us with regard to the question posed at the beginning of this book: what is German about the way Germans eat and what they eat? Before I try to answer this, let's look at what they actually consume today. The latest statistics tell us that in general men consume larger quantities of food than women (except for fruit), whereas women tend to make more health-conscious choices. Bread is the most important staple food and together with dairy products the most important energy source. Vegetables and fruit are consumed daily by almost everybody, with quantities slightly higher for women and increasing with age and higher social status. Surprisingly, most fresh fruit is eaten during the winter months. Although Frederick the Great, the potato promoter, remains an important historical character, Germans now eat less than 100 g of potatoes per day (and much of that in processed form such as french fries), but the old eat more. Butter is favoured on bread over margarine, and for both fats quantities increase with age, but decrease overall with higher social status. One-fifth of the substantial quantities of dairy products consumed today is made up by quark and cheese (slightly more than 40 g per day), and whereas the overall amount of food decreases with age, more cheese and quark is eaten. Germans clearly don't go to work on an egg: on average they eat much less than one egg per day. Predictably men devour about twice as much meat and related products as women (160 g versus 80 g on average per day), but statistically they consume fewer processed meat products such as sausages and hamburgers the higher their social status. Fish is much less popular than meat in general, but is consumed more frequently with higher social status, although almost every fifth German doesn't eat it at all. More than half of all Germans reject offal. Soups and stews become much more popular with increasing age, whereas the popularity of tomato ketchup and other condiments as well as sweets declines with age – with the exception of jam, of which the elderly eat more than younger people, who in turn eat far more savoury snack foods such as crisps and popcorn.

As for drinks, coffee is by far the most popular hot beverage, with less than one-fifth rejecting it completely. On average most Germans drink either less than a cup daily or more than two, with men around 40 topping the chart with more than half a litre daily. Women drink much larger quantities of herbal tea than men, who prefer soft drinks (of which general consumption decreases with higher social standing). Men drink on average almost four times as much alcohol as women, and clearly prefer beer, whereas women are undecided in this respect. Spirits play a very minor role and are mostly consumed by men of lower social standing. Men drink most when they are young (fourteen- to eighteen-year-olds consume one glass of alcoholic beverages daily on average, mostly bingeing on the weekend) whereas women's consumption peaks when they are over 50. For both men and women, wine and sparkling wine become more popular with age, whereas alcopops and cocktails are almost exclusively drunk by those under 25. With higher social standing, women on average drink larger quantities (in the form of wine), whereas for men they stay about the same, but less of it is consumed in the form of beer. Smoking and alcohol consumption frequently go together.[13]

Compared to surveys taken in the mid-1980s, fat and alcohol consumption in general have decreased. In spite of this officials are still not entirely happy with the state of national nutrition (will they ever be?), although Germans clearly tend to eat more lightly and healthily than they did a generation ago. American fast-food chains in Germany originally presented their restaurants as they did in the u.s., as affordable family restaurants and an alternative to bourgeois rituals. However in the 1990s they were increasingly seen as ecologically, nutritionally and culturally unsound, even disastrously so. In recent years many have tried – with considerable success – to change their reputation by offering more healthy options, redesigning their outlets and working intensively to change their public image. At the other end of the scale, the German section of the Slow Food movement celebrated its twentieth anniversary in 2012 and has taken serious efforts to emancipate itself from its image of being an elitist foodie club and to present itself as a politically responsible, more inclusive and active movement.

It is telling that food surveys typically don't include the very young, the very elderly, non-German speakers and the homeless, but it is difficult to judge if this is because these groups are deemed too marginal or if other reasons are responsible for their exclusion. In fact, as average life expectancy is increasing, food in elderly people's homes and hospitals represents a growing challenge. It is often declared bland or unsuitable. In a similar vein, although one-fifth of all food in Germany is ultimately thrown away, according to estimates (comparable to other highly industrialized countries such as the UK), this is no guarantee that everybody is eating well or even sufficiently. According to a survey taken in 2012 and initiated by the German government, two-thirds of that waste occurs in private households, whereas food banks, intending to help those in need, focus on the 17 per cent lost in retail and the catering sector. Modelled on the New Yorker City Harvest, the *Berliner Tafel* was founded in 1993. This charity project (whose example has been followed nationwide) collects up to 660 tons of surplus and leftover food monthly from retailers and the restaurant trade, and redistributes it to those in need, be they homeless, jobless, elderly or single parents with low income or other serious problems.

On average the amount of food Germans consume exceeds their actual needs. Five per cent of all adults are on a diet to lose weight. Based on a national food survey taken in 2008, two-thirds of all men and about every second woman are overweight or obese, with weights generally decreasing with better education and higher incomes, but increasing with age. More than three-quarters of all children are of normal weight, with less than one-fifth overweight, but almost one-tenth of all young girls (between the ages of fourteen and seventeen) are underweight, pointing to serious eating disorders. According to a national time study, as early as between the ages of ten and fourteen, girls contribute fifteen minutes more time to household tasks than boys, and for fifteen- to twenty-year-olds this gap grows to 30 minutes. But it is striking that under-twenties in general spent less time preparing meals in 2001 than a decade earlier. They tend to use the kitchen in a much more multifunctional way. Overall women are still mainly responsible for household chores, although they spend nineteen minutes less on preparing meals than a decade earlier, while men dedicate fourteen minutes more per day to household chores, including cooking and shopping. However, this change is due to a small group who invest more time than the rest. Even when both partners work full time, women invest more time in the home.

Every third father says he would like to have more time with his family, but in reality traditional gender-specific patterns tend to re-emerge with the first child, and men tend to work longer the more children there are in the family.[14]

Contrary to the old cliché which has Germans only eating to survive, never truly savouring their meals like their French neighbours, eating well came top of the list in a survey taken in 2004 that asked what people would be willing to spend money on (followed by housing, travelling and clothing).[15] In 2008 Germans used 12.4 per cent of their disposable income to buy food and non-alcoholic drinks (slightly less than the French, but about double that of Americans), which translates into €214 on average per household and month. An additional €85 per household was spent monthly on eating out, of which €57 ended up in restaurants, cafés and the like.[16] Statistics also show that the average time spent eating actually increased during the decade following reunification, from 1 hour 22 minutes daily to 1 hour 43 minutes, and the largest part of this increase was spent eating at home.

At a quick glance one might think that Christianity's traditional cultural influence on everyday life is waning. Churches tend to be empty, Christmas is highly commercialized and the popularity of eastern philosophies is rising, as witnessed by the success of yoga schools. Less than 60 per cent of all Germans are legally registered as Christian. However, long-established patterns persist and include the wide acceptance of alcoholic beverages and the ideal of communal meals, as well as Sundays' special status as a quiet day of rest with longer and more elaborate meals. At weekends Germans enjoy their food on average for over two hours per day. The traditional meal pattern persists, with two-thirds having breakfast between six and nine o'clock, lunch between noon and two o'clock, and dinner between six and eight o'clock at night. In families with both parents working, the main meal shifts to the evening, as not even one-fifth eat their midday meal in a canteen at work or school.

Especially when personal finances are tight, many Germans tend to cook themselves instead of buying convenience food or ready meals. Two-thirds of all women and less than one-third of all men pronounce their cooking skills to be very good or good. Women acquire them primarily from their mothers while men are mostly self-taught, with both groups mentioning cookbooks third, and TV, magazines and other media ranging fifth for women, sixth for men.[17] TV cooking shows, popular since the mid-1990s, could of course be seen as the ultimate incarnation of the ancient Roman formula of *panem et circenses*, bread and circuses to keep the populace happy. Formats such as *Ready, Steady, Cook*/*Kochduell* or *Hell's Kitchen*/*TeufelsKüche* have been imported from Britain (as is common for many kinds of TV show); others were developed in Germany, and some successful TV hosts use cooking as a background to present and interview guests. Chefs have seen a significant social repositioning since the 1990s, and for ambitious restaurant chefs, a successful marketing campaign now seems to include books and a TV show as a matter of course.

How does all this translate into actual food on the plate? A survey taken in 2007 (on fourteen- to 60-year-olds) produced the following list of the most popular dishes eaten by Germans, in decreasing order:[18]

Spaghetti bolognese
Spaghetti with tomato sauce
Schnitzel
Pizza
Rouladen (beef roulades)
Asparagus
Sauerbraten
Lasagna
Steak
Nudelauflauf (pasta dish casserole in the style of macaroni
and cheese)
Kohlrouladen (braised cabbage roulades with a minced meat
stuffing)
Fish
Kasslerbraten (brined and smoked pork roast)
Spinach
Königsberger Klopse (meatballs in a white sauce flavoured with
lemon, capers, and herring or anchovies)
Grünkohl (curly kale) with meat and potatoes

This, finally, brings us back to the argument I made right at the beginning of this book: German food today reflects the manifold influences we have seen accumulating through history extremely well. It is a mix of regional and global, homely and elegant, traditional and modern, with vegetables and meat almost evenly represented. The long-standing culinary connection with the Romans and with Italy is as obvious as the heritage of French influence. Sweet-and-sour *Sauerbraten* represents medieval times. The old love of pork persists, but American steak has also become a regular on German plates reflecting the post-Second World War Americanism of West Germany. Old religious rules are reflected in the listing of vegetables and fish. *Kasslerbraten* reminds us not only of Celtic salt pork, but of more recent East German preferences. Not on the list, because they are regarded as dessert rather than main courses, are the contemporary forms of the Neolithic gruel with which we started our time travel: *Milchreis*, rice pudding, and *Griesspudding*, semolina pudding, are German comfort foods. They bring back childhood memories to most Germans, but also, as we have seen, go back much further, connecting them to the earliest layers of our culinary fabric. The remarkable thing is that no single period seems to stand out in particular, at least from the culinary point of view: Germans have achieved a notable balance. One could even say, serenity.

Furthermore, if we had similar lists for individual regions of Germany, another important characteristic of German foodways would emerge even more clearly: there is no such thing as a national dish or cuisine in Germany. As I argued at the beginning, the openness to all kinds of influences, combined with the prevailing decentralized political and economic structures, has led to great diversity. Germans love their sausages, but there are any number of different kinds from different regions, after which they continue to be named. The general knowledge about this diversity today on the one hand reinforces curiosity and receptivity, but on the other makes people even more aware of specifically regional food choices.

Recently a historian has drawn a picture of each German as five persons in one, and I think this description perfectly illustrates German foodways.[19] First of all, they are all from a certain village or town, let's say Nuremberg, and identify themselves with local foodstuffs such as *Nürnberger Rostbratwurst*. On the next level is the state, in this case Bavaria, although I'd argue for an in-between level of region: a Nuremberger is first Franconian, favouring for instance a milder kind of sauerkraut, flavoured with caraway seeds with his or her roast sausages, then Bavarian. He or she will be out in a beer garden as soon as weather permits, with a large mug of lager that will taste much less bitter than any comparable beer in the north of Germany. While travelling abroad, our Nuremberger will be German, often rapidly longing for sourdough bread with some rye in it. However, beyond that, he or she will also identify themselves

With the Markthalle Neun project, one of the old covered markets has seen a
glorious revival featuring a farmers' market on Fridays and Saturdays as well as a
street food market on Thursday, with additional special themes on Sundays.

as European, for instance in India missing morning coffee or tea with
milk, or bread and butter. Finally, most Germans also feel themselves to
be citizens of the world. The longing for familiar food that tastes of
home does not exclude enjoying Turkish *köfte* or meatballs, Vietnamese
pho or noodle soup or any other food, be it at an ethnic restaurant, at
home or in the country of its origin. All these identities are layers that build
upon and intertwine with each other and therefore none is felt to be a
contradiction of any of the others, although they might often appear to
be when seen from outside. This is underlined by the fact that the Green
Party nowadays is an accepted fact of German political life and not a
counter-movement, like its life-reform precursor.

It now remains to pose the question of where German food might
go from here; what will the next layer be? The signs are pointing in different directions: Asian food beyond sushi is certainly on the up, as is
Turkish refined cuisine beyond doner kebabs. On a different level, affordable, healthy and sustainable, combining locally grown with imported
from afar, might sound like yet another utopian concept. But these are
factors that a growing number of German consumers deem important
and are actively looking for in their food choices. If this seems far too

sensible and sober, after our culinary grand tour through German history we know that one thing does not necessarily exclude the other: our Nuremberger from above might eat sauerkraut today and sushi tomorrow, but also healthy organically grown salad one day and junky french fries and a big fat grilled shank of pork the next. That's contemporary German.

References

ONE: From Gruel to Sourdough Bread

1 Oliver E. Craig et al., 'Ancient Lipids Reveal Continuity in Culinary Practices across the Transition to Agriculture in Northern Europe', *Proceedings of the National Academy of Sciences of the United States of America*, published online before print 24 October 2011, www.pnas.org.
2 Colin Tudge, *Neanderthals, Bandits and Farmers: How Agriculture Really Began* (New Haven, CT, 1998), p. 4.
3 W. Tegel et al., 'Early Neolithic Water Wells Reveal the World's Oldest Wood Architecture', *plos one*, VII/12 (2012).
4 Ruth Bollongino, 'Boeuf oriental: Die Herkunft unserer Hausrinder aus genetischer Sicht', *Journal Culinaire: Kultur und Wissenschaft des Essens*, 14 (2012), pp. 100–3.
5 Museum für Vor- und Frühgeschichte, Berlin.
6 M. Salque et al., 'Earliest Evidence for Cheese Making in the Sixth Millennium BC in Northern Europe', *Nature*, XDXCIII/522–45 (2012), at www.nature.com.

TWO: Fresh Meat and *Lac Concretum*

1 Cornelius Tacitus, *Agricola* and *Germania*, trans. Anthony R. Birley (Oxford, 1999), p. 49.
2 L. Annaeus Seneca, *De Providentia*, IV 14, my trans.

THREE: Christianity, Social Stratification and Medicine

1 Jan Keupp, '"Der Tisch hat manche Herrlichkeit": Tafelfreuden im Mittelalter', *Mitteilungen der Deutschen Gesellschaft für Archäologie im Mittelalter und der Neuzeit*, 19 (2007), pp. 51–2.
2 Ekkehard IV, *St Galler Klostergeschichten*, trans. Hans F. Haefele, 4th edn (Darmstadt, 2002), p. 45.
3 Gerd Althoff, 'Der frieden-, bündnis- und gemeinschaftsstiftende Charakter des Mahles im frühen Mittelalter', in *Essen und Trinken in Mittelalter und*

Neuzeit, ed. Irmgard Bitsch, Trude Ehlert and Xenja von Ertzdorff (Sigmaringen, 1987), pp. 13–25.

4 Edith Ennen, *Frauen im Mittelalter*, 2nd edn (München, 1985), pp. 85–9, and Diedrich Saalfeld, 'Wandlungen der bäuerlichen Konsumgewohnheiten vom Mittelalter zur Neuzeit', in *Essen und Trinken in Mittelalter und Neuzeit*, ed. Bitsch, Ehlert and von Ertzdorff, p. 66.

5 C. M. Woolgar, 'Feasting and Fasting: Food and Taste in Europe in the Middle Ages', in *Food: The History of Taste*, ed. Paul Freedman (London, 2007), p. 165.

6 Léon Levillain, *Examen critique des chartes mérovingiennes et carolingiennes de l'abbaye de Corbie* (Paris, 1902), p. 198, at http://ia600302.us.archive.org.

7 Johanna Maria van Winter, 'Kochen und Essen im Mittelalter', in *Mensch und Umwelt im Mittelalter*, 3rd edn, ed. Bernd Herrmann (Stuttgart, 1987), pp. 88–100.

8 André Miquel, 'L'Europe occidentale dans la relation arabe d'Ibrahim b. Ya'qub (xe siècle)', *Annales. Economies, Sociétés, Civilisations*, 5 (1966), pp. 1048–64, at www.persee.fr.

9 Jacques Le Goff, *Kultur des europäischen Mittelalters* (München, 1970), p. 351.

10 Karl-Ernst Behre, 'Die Ernährung im Mittelalter', in *Mensch und Umwelt im Mittelalter*, ed. Hermann, pp. 75–87.

11 'Carolingian Culture at Reichenau and St Gall', www.stgallplan.org, accessed 24 August 2012; Walter Janssen, 'Mittelalterliche Gartenkultur. Nahrung und Rekreation', in *Mensch und Umwelt im Mittelalter*, ed. Hermann, pp. 224–43.

12 Ekkehard iv, *St Galler Klostergeschichten*, pp. 171–3.

13 Ennen, *Frauen im Mittelalter*, p. 85.

14 Harry Kühnel, ed., *Alltag im Spätmittelalter*, 3rd edn (Graz, 1986), pp. 200–01.

15 Jörg Jarnut, 'Konsumvorschriften im Früh- und Hochmittelalter', in *Haushalt und Familie in Mittelalter und früher Neuzeit. Vorträge eines interdisziplinären Symposions vom 6.–9. Juni 1990 an der Rheinischen Friedrich-Wilhelms-Universität Bonn*, ed. Trude Ehlert (Sigmaringen, 1991), pp. 120–22.

16 Ekkehard iv, *St Galler Klostergeschichten*, pp. 209–15.

FOUR: Luxurious Feasts and Terrible Famine

1 'Tannhäuser – Tischzucht', in *Höfische Tischzuchten*, ed. Thomas Perry Thornton (Berlin, 1957), p. 43.

2 Otto Borst, *Alltagsleben im Mittelalter* (Frankfurt am Main, 1983), p. 326.

3 Hermann Boettcher, *Neue Halberstädter Chronik von der Gründung des Bistums i.J. 804 bis zur Gegenwart* (Halberstadt, 1913), p. 78, my trans.

4 Hugo von Trimberg, *Der Renner*, ed. Gustav Ehrismann (Tübingen, 1909, repr. Berlin, 1970), p. 31.

5 Jan Keupp, '"Der Tisch hat manche Herrlichkeit": Tafelfreuden im Mittelalter', *Mitteilungen der Deutschen Gesellschaft für Archäologie im Mittelalter und der Neuzeit*, 19 (2007), pp. 53.

6 Joachim Bumke, *Höfische Kultur: Literatur und Gesellschaft im hohen Mittelalter*, 5th edn (München, 2005), p. 261.

7 Joachim Bumke, ed., *Parzival/Wolfram von Eschenbach: Auf Grundlage der Handschrift D* (Tübingen, 2008), p. 259.

8 Wolfgang Spiewok, 'Wolfram von Eschenbach, Maître Queux aus Visages de Janus ou Faim et Abondance dans le *Parzival* de Wolfram von Eschenbach', in *Banquets et Manières de Table au Moyen Âge*, ed. Centre Universitaire d'Etudes et de Recherches Médiévales d'Aix, 38 (1996), pp. 481–92.

9 Sieglinde Hartmann, 'Vom 'vrâz' zum Parnass: Ein mentalitätsgeschichtlicher Versuch über die Bedeutung der Kochkunst in Mittelalter und früher Neuzeit', in *Essen und Trinken in Mittelalter und Neuzeit*, ed. Irmgard Bitsch, Trude Ehlert and Xenja von Ertzdorff (Sigmaringen, 1987), pp. 117–25.

10 'Tannhäuser – Tischzucht', pp. 38–45.

11 Bartholomäus Anglicus, *On the Properties of Things*, trans. John Trevisa (Oxford, 1975), I, pp. 330–31.

12 Bartholomäus Anglicus, in *Handbuch der europäischen Wirtschafts- und Sozialgeschichte*, ed. Hermann Kellenbenz, II (Stuttgart, 1980), p. 549.

13 *Prümer Urbar*, in Siegfried Epperlein, *Bäuerliches Leben im Mittelalter: Schriftquellen und Bildzeugnisse* (Köln, 2003), p. 34.

14 Richard Hoffmann, 'Environmental Change and the Culture of Common Carp in Medieval Europe', *Guelph Ichthyology: Reviews, North America*, 3 (2005), pp. 57–85, at http://journal.lib.uoguelph.ca.

15 Jacques Le Goff, *Kultur des europäischen Mittelalters* (München, 1970), p. 411, and David R. Montgomery, *Dirt: The Erosion of Civilizations* (Chicago, IL, 2007), p. 91.

16 *Bremisches Urkundenbuch,* in Epperlein, *Bäuerliches Leben im Mittelalter: Schriftquellen und Bildzeugnisse*, p. 32.

17 *Annales Pegavienses*, in Epperlein, *Bäuerliches Leben im Mittelalter*, p. 32.

18 Ken Albala, *Eating Right in the Renaissance* (Berkeley, CA, 2002), p. 281.

19 Ulf Dirlmeier, 'Zu den Lebensbedingungen in der mittelalterlichen Stadt: Trinkwasserversorgung und Abfallbeseitigung', in *Mensch und Umwelt im Mittelalter*, 3rd edn, ed. Bernd Herrmann (Stuttgart, 1987), pp. 150–59.

20 Felix Grüttner, *Geschichte der Fleischversorgung in Deutschland* (Braunschweig, 1938), p. 22.

21 Augustinus Nentewitz, *Warhafftige Beschreibung der langen Bratwurst als auch der acht grossen Strützel* (Königsberg, 1650).

22 Joh. Gottlieb von Eckhard, *Vollständige Esperimental Oekonomie* (1754), in Grüttner, *Geschichte der Fleischversorgung*, p. 101.

23 Dietrich Denecke, 'Strasse und Weg im Mittelalter als Lebensraum und Vermittler zwischen entfernten Orten', in *Mensch und Umwelt im Mittelalter*, ed. Hermann, pp. 207–23.

24 Godfrey of Bouillon's letter to Pope Paschal II on the first crusade, in *Fighting Words: Competing Voices from the Crusades*, ed. Andrew Holt and James Muldoon (Oxford, 2008), p. 211.

25 Melitta Weiss-Adamson, 'Baby-food in the Middle Ages', in *Nurture: Proceedings of the Oxford Symposium on Food and Cookery 2003*, ed. Richard Hosking (Bristol, 2004), pp. 1–11.

26 Melitta Weiss-Amer, 'Die "Physica" Hildegards von Bingen als Quelle für das "Kochbuch Meister Eberhards"', *Sudhoffs Archiv*, LXXVI/1 (Stuttgart, 1992), pp. 87–96.

27 Melitta Weiss Adamson, ed., *Regional Cuisines of Medieval Europe: A Book of Essays* (New York, 2002), pp. 162–3.

28 Melitta Weiss Adamson, *Daz buoch von guoter spise (The Book of Good Food): A Study Edition, and English Translation of the Oldest German Cookbook* (Krems, 2000), p. 103.

29 Melitta Weiss Adamson, *Medieval Dietetics: Food and Drink in Regimen Sanitatis: Literature from 800 to 1400* (Frankfurt am Main, 1995), pp. 203–4; Johanna Maria van Winter, 'Interregional Influences in Medieval Cooking', in *Food in the Middle Ages: A Book of Essays*, ed. Adamson (New York, 1995), pp. 45–59; Constance B. Hieatt, 'Sorting through the Titles of Medieval Dishes: What Is, or Is Not, a "Blanc manger"', in *Food in the Middle Ages: A Book of Essays*, ed. Adamson, pp. 25–43; Rudolf Grewe and Constance B. Hieatt, eds, *Libellus de arte coquinaria: An Early Northern Cookery Book* (Tempe, AZ, 2001), pp. 3, 93, 104.

30 Ibid.

31 Hans Wiswe, 'Ein mittelniederdeutsches Kochbuch des 15. Jahrhunderts', *Braunschweigisches Jahrbuch*, 37 (Braunschweig, 1956), pp. 19–55.

32 Grewe and Hieatt, eds, *Libellus*, p. 43.

33 *Annales Colmarienses maiores*, in Epperlein, *Bäuerliches Leben im Mittelalter*, p. 110.

34 For an excellent analysis of the Great Famine, see William Chester Jordan, *The Great Famine: Northern Europe in the Early Fourteenth Century* (Princeton, NJ, 1996), on whom I rely here (following quotes pp. 20, 25).

35 Siegrid Düll, ed., *Die Inschriften der Stadt Oppenheim* (Wiesbaden, 1984), p. 7.

FIVE: *Butterbrot* and Saffron

1 Ulf Dirlmeier and Gerhard Fouquet, 'Ernährung und Konsumgewohnheiten im spätmittelalterlichen Deutschland', in *Geschichte und Wissenschaft im Unterricht*, ed. H. Boockmann, J. Rohlfes and W. Schulze, 7 (1993), pp. 511, 516 and 519; Günter Wiegelmann, 'Butterbrot und Butterkonservierung im Hanseraum', in *Nahrung und Tischkultur im Hanseraum*, ed. Günter Wiegelmann and Ruth-E. Mohrmann (Münster, 1996), pp. 463–99; Günter Wiegelmann, 'Introduction', in *Nahrung und Tischkultur im Hanseraum*, pp. 9–21.

2 Volker Henn, 'Der hansische Handel mit Nahrungsmitteln', in *Nahrung und Tischkultur im Hanseraum*, ed. Wiegelmann and Mohrmann, pp. 23–48.

3 Detlev Ellmers, 'Die Verlagerung des Fernhandels vom öffentlichen Ufermarkt in die privaten Häuser der Kaufleute', *Lübecker Schriften zur Archäologie und Kulturgeschichte*, 20 (1990), pp. 101–18.

4 Bruno Kuske, 'Der Kölner Fischhandel vom 14.–17. Jahrhundert', in *Westdeutsche Zeitschrift für Geschichte und Kunst*, ed. H. Graeven and J. Hansen (Trier, 1905), pp. 227–313.

5 Philip de Souza, *Seafaring and Civilization: Maritime Perspectives on World History* (London, 2002), pp. 70–73.

6 Michel Balard, 'Epices et condiments dans quelques livres de cuisine allemands (xive–xvie siècles)', in *Du manuscrit à la table: Essais sur la cuisine au Moyen Age et répertoire des manuscrits médiévaux contenant des recettes culinaires,* ed. Carole Lambert (Montréal, 1992), pp. 193–201; Bruno Laurioux, 'De l'usage des épices dans l'alimentation médiévale', *Médiévales*, 5 (1983), pp. 15–31, at www.persee.fr, and Anna C. Johnson, *Peasant Life in Germany* (New York, 1858), p. 316.

7 Trude Ehlert, ed., *Maister Hannsen des von Wirtenberg Koch* (Frankfurt am Main, 1460, repr. 1996).

8 Luise Bardenhewer, *Der Safranhandel im Mittelalter*, diss. (Bonn, 1914) and M. Kronfeld, *Geschichte des Safrans und seiner Cultur in Europa* (Vienna, 1892).

9 Franz Irsigler, *Die wirtschaftliche Stellung der Stadt Köln im 14. und 15. Jahrhundert: Strukturanalyse einer spätmittelalterlichen Exportgewerbe-und Fernhandelstadt* (Wiesbaden, 1979), and 'Ein grossbürgerlicher Kölner Haushalt am Ende des 14. Jahrhunderts', in *Festschrift Matthias Zender: Studien zu Volkskultur, Sprache und Landesgeschichte*, ed. Edith Ennen and Günter Wiegelmann, 2 (1972), pp. 635–68.

10 Dirlmeier and Fouquet, 'Ernährung und Konsumgewohnheiten im spätmittelalterlichen Deutschland', p. 520.

11 Gerhard Wahle, *Reineke Fuchs: Das mittelniederdeutsche Tierepos Reynke de Vos, Lübeck, 1498, nach der Ausgabe Prien/Leitzmann, Halle/Saale, 1960 ins Neuhochdeutsche übertragen* (Stuttgart, 2000), p. 120, my trans.

12 Ludwig Haenselmann, ed., *Henning Brandis' Diarium: Hildesheimsche Geschichten aus den Jahren 1471–1528* (Hildesheim, 1896), pp. 136–7.

13 For 2006, www.destatis.de, accessed 16 June 2011.

14 Franz Irsigler, '"Ind machden alle lant beirs voll": Zur Diffusion des Hopfenbierkonsums im westlichen Hanseraum', in *Nahrung und Tischkultur im Hanseraum*, ed. Wiegelmann and Mohrmann, pp. 377–97.

15 Helmut Müller, 'Weinbau und Weinkonsum in Westfalen', in *Nahrung und Tischkultur im Hanseraum*, ed. Wiegelmann and Mohrmann, pp. 399–428.

16 Fritz Schumann, 'Rebsorten und Weinarten im mittelalterlichen Deutschland', in *Weinwirtschaft im Mittelalter: Zur Verbreitung, Regionalisierung und wirtschaftlichen Nutzung einer Sonderkultur aus der Römerzeit*, ed. Christhard Schrenk and Hubert Weckbach (Heilbronn, 1997), pp. 221–54 (including Hildegard quote); Hans Hartmeyer, *Der Weinhandel im Gebiete der Hanse im Mittelalter*, diss. (Jena, 1905) and Wilhelm Loose, ed., *Anton Tuchers Haushaltbuch* (Stuttgart, 1877), pp. 203–4.

17 Siegfried Epperlein, *Bäuerliches Leben im Mittelalter: Schriftquellen und Bildzeugnisse* (Köln, 2003), pp. 107–08.

18 Henn, 'Der hansische Handel mit Nahrungsmitteln', pp. 40–44, and Hartmeyer, *Der Weinhandel im Gebiete der Hanse im Mittelalter*.

19 Epperlein, *Bäuerliches Leben im Mittelalter*, p. 110.

20 Wilhelm Abel, *Einige Bemerkungen zum Land-Stadtproblem im Spätmittelalter* (Göttingen, 1976), p. 28; data source Bundesverband der deutschen

Fleischwarenindustrie eV (National Association of German Meat Industry) www.bvdf.de, accessed 16 June 2011.

21 Wilhelm Abel, *Stufen der Ernährung: Eine historische Skizze* (Göttingen, 1981), p. 11.

22 Heinz Wiese, 'Die Fleischversorgung der nordwesteuropäischen Grossstädte vom xv. bis xix. Jahrhundert unter besonderer Berücksichtigung des interterritorialen Rinderhandels', *Jahrbücher für Nationalökonomik und Statistik*, ed. Friedrich Lütge and Erich Preiser, 179 (Stuttgart, 1966), pp. 125–39.

23 Quoted in Bruno Laurioux, *Manger au Moyen Âge: Pratiques et discours alimentaires en Europe au xive et xve siècle* (Paris, 2002), p. 17.

24 Craig R. Thompson, ed., *Collected Works of Erasmus*, vol. xxxix: *Colloquies* (Toronto, 1997), pp. 368–80.

25 Terence Scully, *Art of Cookery in the Middle Ages* (Woodbridge, 1995), p. 233.

26 Gerhard Schapper, *Die Hofordnung von 1470 und die Verwaltung am Berliner Hofe zur Zeit Kurfürst Albrechts, im historischen Zusammenhang betrachtet* (Leipzig, 1912), pp. 41–2.

27 Melitta Weiss-Adamson, ed., *Regional Cuisines of Medieval Europe: A Book of Essays* (New York, 2002), pp. 156–7.

28 Bruno Laurioux, *Une Histoire Culinaire du Moyen Âge* (Paris, 2005), pp. 57–68.

six: German Food Writing

1 Franz Irsigler, *Die wirtschaftliche Stellung der Stadt Köln im 14. und 15. Jahrhundert: Strukturanalyse einer spätmittelalterlichen Exportgewerbe-und Fernhandelstadt* (Wiesbaden, 1979), pp. 663–4.

2 Père Louis Thomassin, *Traité des jeûnes de l'Eglise*, 2nd edn (1693), p. 297 (my thanks to Ken Albala and David Sutton).

3 Jean-Louis Flandrin, 'Le goût et la nécessité: sur l'usage des graisses dans les cuisines d' Europe occidentale (xive–xviiie siècle)', *Annales. Économies, Sociétés, Civilisations*, 2 (1983), p. 390.

4 Konrad Bedal, 'Alte Feuerstätten im Bauernhaus Nordbayerns', in *Mitteilungen der Deutschen Gesellschaft für Archäologie des Mittelalters und der Neuzeit*, ed. Matthias Untermann, Ulrich Klein and Michaela Jansen, 19 (2007), pp. 11–24.

5 Barbara Krug-Richter, 'Alltag und Fest: Nahrungsgewohnheiten im Magdalenenhospital in Münster 1558 bis 1635', in *Haushalt und Familie in Mittelalter und früher Neuzeit: Vorträge eines interdisziplinären Symposions vom 6.–9. Juni 1990 an der Rheinischen Friedrich-Wilhelms-Universität Bonn*, ed. Trude Ehlert (Sigmaringen, 1991), pp. 71–90.

6 Gerhard Fouquet, ed., *Goldene Speisen in den Maien – Das Kochbuch des Augsburger Zunftbürgermeisters Ulrich Schwarz* (St Katharinen, 2000).

7 Hugo Stopp, ed., *Das Kochbuch der Sabine Welserin* (Heidelberg, 1980), at www.uni-giessen.de, recipes 43 and 89.

8 Marx Rumpolt, *Ein new Kochbuch*, ed. Manfred Lemmer [1581] (facs., Leipzig, 1977), p. 41.

9 Ibid., p. cxliiiiv.

10 J. A. Massard, '300 Jahre Kartoffel in Luxemburg', in *Lëtzebuerger Journal* (2009), at http://massard.info.

11 Constance B. Hieatt, 'Sorting through the Titles of Medieval Dishes: What Is, or Is Not, a "Blanc manger"', in *Food in the Middle Ages: A Book of Essays*, ed. Melitta Weiss-Adamson (New York, 1995), pp. 25–43.

12 Rudolf Grewe and Constance B. Hieatt, ed., *Libellus de arte coquinaria: An Early Northern Cookery Book* (Tempe, AZ, 2001), p. 71.

13 Sebastian Münster's *Cosmographia universa*, first published in Basel 1541, the first travel guide, done with a team of authors and based on extensive travels and the latest scientific knowledge.

14 This different attitude to wine drinking between French and Germans turns up again and again, for instance in Honoré de Balzac's *Le Cousin Pons*, where Germans are said to have the 'absorbency of sponges or sand, but harmonious, without the French shouting'.

SEVEN: Coffee, Sugar and Potatoes

1 Adelheid Schleitz, 'Die Bäckerinnung und die Brotbank von Weida', in *Von Brotbänken, Erdäpfeln und Brauhäusern. Thüringer Hefte für Volkskunde*, ed. Gudrun Braune and Peter Fauser, 13 (2006), pp. 99–102.

2 Friederich Karl Freiher von Moser, *Fabeln* (Mannheim, 1786), p. 119, my trans.

3 'Gewohnt, gethan' (1813), in *Gesamtwerke* I (1827), p. 126, my trans.

4 *Traité des Jardins*, 3rd edn (Paris, 1789).

5 Hans J. Teuteberg and Günter Wiegelmann, *Unsere tägliche Kost: Geschichte und regionale Prägung* (Münster, 1986), p. 341, and Sidney W. Mintz, *Sweetness and Power: The Place of Sugar in Modern History* (New York, 1985), p. 143.

6 Karl-Peter Ellerbrock, *Geschichte der deutschen Nahrungs- und Genussmittelindustrie 1750–1914* (Stuttgart, 1993), pp. 199–204.

7 Amaranthes, ed., *Frauenzimmer-Lexicon* (Leipzig, 1715), pp. 483 and 1979.

8 Johann Ernst Marbach, *Beschreibung des . . . Städtleins Schöneck*, I (Schneeberg, 1761), pp. 17–18.

9 Carl Wilhelm Ernst Putsche, *Versuch einer Monographie oder ausführliche Beschreibung der Kartoffeln . . .* (Weimar, 1819).

10 Sylk Schneider, 'Die Geschichte der Kartoffel und des Klosses in Thüringen, insbesondere im Herzogtum Sachsen-Weimar', in *Von Brotbänken, Erdäpfeln und Brauhäusern*, ed. Braune and Fauser, pp. 82–93.

11 Walter Achilles, *Deutsche Agrargeschichte im Zeitalter der Reformen und der Industrialisierung* (Stuttgart, 1993), p. 77.

12 Ibid., p. 69.

13 Hans J. Teuteberg and Günter Wiegelmann, *Der Wandel der Nahrungsgewohnheiten unter dem Einfluss der Industrialisierung* (Göttingen, 1972), p. 266.

14 Ellerbrock, *Geschichte der deutschen Nahrungs- und Genussmittelindustrie 1750–1914*, pp. 60–85.

15 Karl Friedrich von Rumohr, *Geist der Kochkunst* (Heidelberg, 1994), p. 221.

16 Ellerbrock, *Geschichte der deutschen Nahrungs- und Genussmittelindustrie 1750–1914*, pp. 139–47.

17 Teuteberg and Wiegelmann, *Wandel*, pp. 243–5 and 254–6.

EIGHT: Potatoes without Salt and Soup Kitchens

1 Hans J. Teuteberg and Günter Wiegelmann, *Unsere tägliche Kost: Geschichte und regionale Prägung* (Münster, 1986), p. 118.

2 Jürgen Kuczynski, *Darstellung der Lage der Arbeiter in Deutschland von 1789 bis 1849* (Berlin, 1961), pp. 308–21.

3 Anna C. Johnson, *Peasant Life in Germany* (New York, 1858), p. 249.

4 Michael Grüttner, 'Alkoholkonsum in der Arbeiterschaft 1871–1939', in *Haushalt und Verbrauch in historischer Perspektive: Zum Wandel des privaten Verbrauchs in Deutschland im 19. und 20. Jahrhundert*, ed. Toni Pierenkemper (St Katharinen, 1987), pp. 229–73, and Ulla Heise, *Kaffee und Kaffeehaus: Eine Bohne macht Geschichte* (Leipzig, 1996), pp. 128–9.

5 Werner K. Blessing, '"Theuerungsexcesse" im vorrevolutionären Kontext – Getreidetumult und Bierkrawall im späten Vormärz', in *Arbeiterexistenz im 19. Jahrhundert*, ed. Werner Conze (Stuttgart, 1981), pp. 356–84.

6 *Neue Lausizische Monatsschrift* (Görlitz, 1805), pp. 193–211.

7 Walter F. Willcox, *International Migrations*, I (New York, 1929), pp. 114–22 and 178; Heike Paul, 'Tasting America: Food, Race, and Anti-American Sentiments in Nineteenth-century German-American Writing', in *Eating Culture: The Poetics and Politics of Food*, ed. Tobias Döring, Markus Heide and Susanne Mühleisen (Heidelberg, 2003), pp. 109–32; and Johnson, *Peasant Life in Germany*, pp. 389–90.

8 Rupert Busche, *Beiträge zur Schiffshygiene* (Eisfeld i. Thür., 1939).

9 Jane Ziegelman, *97 Orchard: An Edible History of Five Immigrant Families in One New York Tenement* (New York, 2010), pp. 1–45.

10 Carl Voit, ed., *Untersuchung der Kost in einigen öffentlichen Anstalten für Aerzte und Verwaltungsbeamte* (München, 1877), pp. 142–52.

11 Ulrike Thoms, *Anstaltskost im Rationalisierungsprozess: Die Ernährung in Krankenhäusern und Gefängnissen im 18. und 19. Jahrhundert* (Stuttgart, 2005), and Wilhelm Schumburg, *Hygiene der Einzelernährung und Massenernährung* (Leipzig, 1913), pp. 405–73.

12 Werner Friedrich Kümmel, 'Tafelmusik aus medizin- und musikhistorischer Sicht', in *Ernährung und Ernährungslehre im 19. Jahrhundert*, ed. Edith Heischkel-Artelt (Göttingen, 1976), pp. 386–407.

13 *Pickled Herring and Pumpkin Pie: A Nineteenth-century Cookbook for German Immigrants to America* [1897] (Madison, WI, 2003).

14 Rudolf Weinhold, 'Speisemeidung als Mittel soziokultureller Identifikation: das Exempel Pferdefleisch', in *Essen und kulturelle Identität*, ed. Hans J. Teuteberg, Gerhard Neumann and Alois Wierlacher (Berlin, 1997), pp. 403–14.

NINE: Stock Cubes and Baking Powder

1 Nikolaus Mani, 'Die wissenschaftliche Ernährungslehre im 19. Jahrhundert', in *Ernährung und Ernährungslehre im 19. Jahrhundert*, ed. Edith Heischkel-Artelt (Göttingen, 1976), pp. 22–75.

2 Günther Klaus Judel, 'Die Geschichte von Liebigs Fleischextrakt: Zur populärsten Erfindung des berühmten Chemikers', *Spiegel der Forschung*, 20 (2003), pp. 6–17; Hans Jürgen Teuteberg, Karl-Peter Ellerbrock, Uwe Spiekermann, Ulrike Thoms and Angela Zatsch, *Die Rolle des Fleischextrakts für die Ernährungswissenschaften und den Aufstieg der Suppenindustrie* (Stuttgart, 1990).

3 Bernward Selter, 'Der "satte" Verbraucher: Idole des Ernährungsverhaltens zwischen Hunger und Überfluss 1890–1970', in *Bilderwelt des Alltags: Werbung in der Konsumgesellschaft des 19. und 20. Jahrhunderts*, ed. Peter Borscheid and Clemens Wischermann (Stuttgart, 1995), pp. 190–221.

4 Paul Degener, *Zur Frage der Jam- und Marmelade-Industrie, sowie des Zuckerverbrauchs in England* (Berlin, 1899).

5 Sibylle Meyer, *Das Theater mit der Hausarbeit: Bürgerliche Repräsentation in der Familie der wilhelminischen Zeit* (Frankfurt, 1982), pp. 139–40, and *Die Salicylsäure als Conservirmittel für Consumartikel*, ed. Chemische Fabrik von Heyden (Radebeul-Dresden, 1896).

6 Hans Jürgen Teuteberg, 'Anfänge des modernen Milchzeitalters', in Hans J. Teuteberg and Günter Wiegelmann, *Unsere tägliche Kost: Geschichte und regionale Prägung* (Münster, 1986), pp. 163–84.

7 Wilhelm Schumburg, *Hygiene der Einzelernährung und Massenernährung* (Leipzig, 1913).

8 Hans Jürgen Teuteberg, 'Wie ernährten sich Arbeiter im Kaiserreich?', in *Arbeiterexistenz im 19. Jahrhundert*, ed. Werner Conze (Stuttgart, 1981), pp. 57–73.

9 Reinhard Spree, 'Zu den Veränderungen der Volksgesundheit zwischen 1870 und 1913 und ihren Determinanten in Deutschland (vor allem in Preussen)', in *Arbeiterexistenz im 19. Jahrhundert*, ed. Conze, pp. 235–73, and Klaus Tenfelde, 'Klassenspezifische Konsummuster im Deutschen Kaiserreich', in *Europäische Konsumgeschichte: Zur Gesellschafts- und Kulturgeschichte des Konsums (18. bis 20. Jahrhundert)*, ed. Hannes Siegrist, Hartmut Kaelble and Jürgen Kocka (Frankfurt, 1997), pp. 245–66.

10 Alfred Grotjahn, *Über Wandlungen in der Volksernährung* (Leipzig, 1902).

11 Meyer, *Das Theater mit der Hausarbeit*, pp. 131–3.

12 Karl-Peter Ellerbrock, 'Lebensmittelqualität vor dem Ersten Weltkrieg: Industrielle Produktion und staatliche Gesundheitpolitik', in *Durchbruch zum modernen Massenkonsum: Lebensmittelmärkte und Lebensmittelqualität im Städtewachstum des Industriezeitalters*, ed. Hans J. Teuteberg (Münster, 1987), pp. 127–88, and Degener, *Zur Frage der Jam- und Marmelade-Industrie*, p. 15.

13 Adelheid von Saldern, *Häuserleben: Zur Geschichte städtischen Arbeiterwohnens vom Kaiserreich bis heute* (Bonn, 1995), p. 42.

14 *Berlin und seine Bauten*, II, publ. Architekten-Verein zu Berlin (Berlin, 1896), pp. 563–77, and Peter Lummel, 'Berlins nimmersatter "Riesenbauch":

Ausbau der Lebensmittelversorgung einer werdenden Millionenmetropole', in *Die Revolution am Esstisch: Neue Studien zur Nahrungskultur im 19./20. Jahrhundert*, ed. Hans J. Teuteberg (Stuttgart, 2004), pp. 84–100.

15 Sabine Dittler, 'Milch für Berlin – Die Versorgung einer Metropole', in *Die Milch: Geschichte und Zukunft eines Lebensmittels*, ed. Helmut Ottenjann (Cloppenburg, 1996), pp. 243–51.

16 Maria von Treskow, *Berliner Kochbuch: aus alten Familienrezepten* (Weingarten, 1987), p. 21.

17 David R. Montgomery, *Dirt: The Erosion of Civilizations* (Chicago, IL, 2007) p. 110.

18 Joachim Drews, *Die Nazi-Bohne* (Münster, 2004).

19 Christiane Lamberty, *Reklame in Deutschland 1890–1914* (Berlin, 2000), pp. 50–51 and 153–4, and Dirk Reinhardt 'Beten oder Bummeln? Der Kampf um die Schaufensterfreiheit', in *Bilderwelt des Alltags*, ed. Borscheid and Wischermann, pp. 116–25.

20 William Medlicott, *The Congress of Berlin and After* (London, 1938), pp. 115–16.

21 Renate Petras, *Das Café Bauer in Berlin* (Berlin, 1994), pp. 33–62.

22 Jürgen Weisser, *Zwischen Lustgarten und Lunapark: Der Volksgarten in Nymphenburg (1890–1916) und die Entwicklung der kommerziellen Belustigungsgärten* (München, 1998), pp. 188–98.

23 Sussan Milantchi Ameri, 'Die deutschnationale Sprachbewegung im Wilhelminischen Reich', in *German Life and Civilization*, 5 (New York, 1991), p. 4.

24 'Phases of Foreign Life', *New York Times*, 11 May 1884. I'm grateful to Keith Arbour for this.

25 Kirsten Schlegel-Matthies, *'Im Haus und am Herd': Der Wandel des Hausfrauenbildes und der Hausarbeit 1880–1930* (Stuttgart, 1995).

26 Gunilla-Friederike Budde, 'Des Haushalts "schönster Schmuck": Die Hausfrau als Konsumexpertin des deutschen und englischen Bürgertums im 19. und frühen 20. Jahrhunderts', in *Europäische Konsumgeschichte*, ed. Siegrist, Kaelble and Kocka, pp. 411–40.

27 Oscar Stillich, *Die Lage der weiblichen Dienstboten in Berlin* (Berlin, 1902).

28 Hiltraud Schmidt-Waldherr, 'Rationalisierung der Hausarbeit in den zwanziger Jahren', in *Arbeitsplatz Haushalt*, ed. Gerda Tornieporth (Berlin, 1988), pp. 32–52.

29 Fritz Kalle, *Ueber Volksernährung und Haushaltungsschulen als Mittel zur Verbesserung derselben* (Wiesbaden, 1891), p. 29.

30 Michael Klein, Aschinger-Konzern (Landesarchiv Berlin A Rep. 225 Findbuch), www.landesarchiv-berlin.de, accessed 18 December 2011, and Keith R. Allen, *Hungrige Metropole: Essen, Wohlfahrt und Kommerz in Berlin* (Hamburg, 2002), pp. 95–113.

31 Paul Göhre, *Drei Monate Fabrikarbeiter und Handwerksbursche* (Leipzig, 1891).

32 Anton Delbrück, *Hygiene des Alkoholismus* (Leipzig, 1913), pp. 479–569; James S. Roberts, 'Drink and Working Class Living Standards in Late 19th Century Germany', in *Arbeiterexistenz im 19. Jahrhundert*, ed. Conze, pp. 74–91; Elisabeth Meyer-Renschhausen (with Albert Wirz), *Der Streit um den*

heissen Brei: Zu Ökologie und Geschlecht einer Kulturanthropologie der Ernährung (Herbolzheim, 2002), pp. 63–89; and Michael Grüttner, 'Alkoholkonsum in der Arbeiterschaft 1871–1939', in *Haushalt und Verbrauch in historischer Perspektive: Zum Wandel des privaten Verbrauchs in Deutschland im 19. und 20. Jahrhundert*, ed. Toni Pierenkemper (St Katharinen, 1987), pp. 229–81.

33 Ulrike Thoms, 'Essen in der Arbeitswelt: Das betriebliche Kantinenwesen seit seiner Entstehung um 1850', in *Die Revolution am Esstisch*, ed. Teuteberg, pp. 203–18.

34 Lothar Machtan and René Ott, '"Batzebier!" Überlegungen zur sozialen Protestbewegung in den Jahren nach der Reichsgründung am Beispiel der süddeutschen Bierkrawalle vom Frühjahr 1873', in *Sozialer Protest: Studien zu traditioneller Resistenz und kollektiver Gewalt in Deutschland vom Vormärz bis zur Reichsgründung*, ed. Heinrich Volkmann and Jürgen Bergmann (Opladen, 1984), pp. 128–66; Thomas Lindenberger, 'Die Fleischrevolte am Wedding. Lebensmittelversorgung und Politik in Berlin am Vorabend des Ersten Weltkriegs' and Christoph Nonn, 'Fleischteuerungsprotest und Parteipolitik im Rheinland und im Reich 1905–1914', both in *Der Kampf um das tägliche Brot: Nahrungsmangel, Versorgungspolitik und Protest 1770–1990*, ed. Manfred Gailus and Heinrich Volkmann (Opladen, 1994), pp. 282–304, 305–15.

35 Cornelia Kemp, 'Vom Schokoladenverkäufer zum Bajazzo – Die Anfänge der Münzautomaten-Herstellung in Deutschland', in *Wenn der Groschen fällt . . . Münzautomaten – gestern und heute*, ed. Cornelia Kemp and Ulrike Gierlinger (München, 1988), pp. 10–24.

36 Heinrich Tappe, 'Der Genuss, die Wirkung und ihr Bild: Werte, Konventionen und Motive gesellschaftlichen Alkoholgebrauchs im Spiegel der Werbung', in *Bilderwelt des Alltags*, ed. Borscheid and Wischermann, pp. 222–41.

37 Sabine Merta, '"Weg mit dem Fett": Wege und Irrwege zur "schlanken Linie": Der Kampf gegen die Korpulenz als Phänomen der Moderne', in *Die Revolution am Esstisch*, ed. Teuteberg, pp. 263–81.

38 Agathe Haggenmiller, *Die Wörishofer Küche* (Wörishofen, 1897).

TEN: Hope and Hunger

1 Horace Cornelius Peterson, *Propaganda for War: The Campaign Against American Neutrality, 1914–1917* (Port Washington, NY, 1968), p. 83.

2 Frank Trentmann, 'Coping with Shortage: The Problem of Food Security and Global Visions of Coordination, *c.* 1890s–1950', in *Food and Conflict in Europe in the Age of the Two World Wars*, ed. Frank Trentmann and Flemming Just (Houndmills, 2006), p. 15.

3 August Skalweit, *Die deutsche Kriegsernährungswirtschaft* (Stuttgart, 1927), p. 32.

4 I am grateful to Len Fisher for clarifying this.

5 Wilhelm Schumburg, *Hygiene der Einzelernährung und Massenernährung* (Leipzig, 1913), p. 426.

6 Anne Roerkohl, *Hungerblockade und Heimatfront: Die kommunale Lebensmittelversorgung in Westfalen während des Ersten Weltkriegs* (Stuttgart, 1991), p. 126.

7 Bernward Selter, 'Der "satte" Verbraucher: Idole des Ernährungsverhaltens zwischen Hunger und Überfluss 1890–1970', in *Bilderwelt des Alltags: Werbung in der Konsumgesellschaft des 19. und 20. Jahrhunderts*, ed. Peter Borscheid and Clemens Wischermann (Stuttgart, 1995), pp. 190–221.

8 Ute Daniel, *Arbeiterfrauen in der Kriegsgesellschaft: Beruf, Familie und Politik im Ersten Weltkrieg* (Göttingen, 1989), p. 214, and Roerkohl, *Hungerblockade und Heimatfront*, p. 320.

9 Skalweit, *Die deutsche Kriegsernährungswirtschaft*, pp. 120–33, and Roerkohl, *Hungerblockade und Heimatfront*, p. 262.

10 Daniel, *Arbeiterfrauen in der Kriegsgesellschaft*, p. 224, and Roerkohl, *Hungerblockade und Heimatfront*, p. 315.

11 Paul C. Vincent, *The Politics of Hunger: The Allied Blockade of Germany, 1915–1919* (Athens, OH, 1985), pp. 9–12.

12 Ibid., p. 168.

13 Ibid., pp. 150, 156, 160–65.

14 Keith R. Allen, *Hungrige Metropole: Essen, Wohlfahrt und Kommerz in Berlin* (Hamburg, 2002), pp. 83–94.

15 Vincent, *The Politics of Hunger*, p. 136.

16 Andrea Lefèvre, 'Lebensmittelunruhen in Berlin 1920–1923', in *Der Kampf um das tägliche Brot: Nahrungsmangel, Versorgungspolitik und Protest 1770–1990*, ed. Manfred Gailus and Heinrich Volkmann (Opladen, 1994), pp. 346–60.

17 Café Reimann in Hans-Christian Täubrich, *Zu Gast im alten Berlin*, 2nd edn (München, 1990), p. 201.

18 This is based on the brochure Kempinski published on the occasion of Haus Vaterland's tenth anniversary; other sources mention 1913 and 2,500 seats. See also Elfi Pracht, *M. Kempinski & Co* (Berlin, 1994), pp. 72–9.

19 Mary Nolan, *Visions of Modernity: American Business and the Modernization of Germany* (New York, 1994), p. 213.

20 Jan Grossarth in *Frankfurter Allgemeine Zeitung*, 36, 8 September 2013, p. 10.

21 Hans Dittmer, *Deutschland erweitert seinen Nahrungsraum durch Landeskulturmassnahmen* (Berlin, 1941).

22 Fritz Blaich, *Wirtschaft und Rüstung im 'Dritten Reich'* (Düsseldorf, 1987), pp. 30–32.

23 Uwe Spiekermann, 'Vollkorn für die Führer', in *Zeitschrift für Sozialgeschichte des 20. und 21. Jahrhunderts*, ed. Angelika Ebbinghaus, 1 (2001), pp. 91–128, and 'Brown Bread for Victory: German and British Wholemeal Politics in the Inter-war Period', in *Food and Conflict in Europe in the Age of the Two World Wars*, ed. Trentmann and Just, pp. 143–71.

24 *Deutsche Kriegsfibel* (1936–40), my trans.

25 Arnulf Huegel, *Kriegsernährungswirtschaft Deutschlands während des Ersten und Zweiten Weltkriegs im Vergleich* (Konstanz, 2003), p. 287.

26 Hartmut Berghoff, 'Enticement and Deprivation: The Regulation of Consumption on Pre-War Nazi Germany', in *The Politics of Consumption:*

Material Culture and Citizenship in Europe and America, ed. Martin Daunton and Matthew Hilton (Oxford, 2001), pp. 165–84; Blaich, *Wirtschaft und Rüstung im 'Dritten Reich'*; Henry Notaker, 'Cookery and Ideology in the Third Reich', *Food & History*, 1 (2008), pp. 67–82; and Nancy R. Reagin, *Sweeping the German Nation: Domesticity and National Identity in Germany, 1870–1945* (Cambridge, 2007), p. 119.

27 *Die Kunst zu werben: Das Jahrhundert der Reklame*, ed. Susanne Bäumler (Köln, 1996), p. 363; Joachim Drews, *Die Nazi-Bohne* (Münster, 2004), p. 118; 'Verordnung über die Herstellung von Sahne', in *Deutscher Reichsanzeiger*, 250 (25 October 1938 – I am grateful to Wolfram Eberhard for his help in procuring this); Gustavo Corni and Horst Gies, *Brot, Butter, Kanonen: Die Ernährungswirtschaft in Deutschland unter der Diktatur Hitlers* (Berlin, 1997), p. 482; *Die Macht der Hausfrau: Eine ernährungswirtschaftliche Fibel für den Verbraucher*, ed. Liane Haskarl (Kiel, 1952), p. 16; and Richard Grunberger, *A Social History of the Third Reich* (London, 1971), p. 207.

28 Ibid., p. 210, albeit quoting *marmalade* and *cottage cheese* instead of jam and quark, undoubtedly translating *Marmelade* and *Quark*.

29 Grunberger, *A Social History of the Third Reich*, p. 211, and Reagin, *Sweeping the German Nation*, pp. 144–5, 158, 175.

30 Ibid., p. 172.

31 Berghoff, 'Enticement and Deprivation', pp. 169–70; Grunberger, *A Social History of the Third Reich*, p. 208; and Blaich, *Wirtschaft und Rüstung im 'Dritten Reich'*, pp. 96–7.

32 Margarete Adelung, *Der 'Kampf dem Verderb' im Haushalt mit sparsamen Mitteln*, diss. (München, 1940); Berghoff, 'Enticement and Deprivation', pp. 177–8; Margarete Dörr, *'Wer die Zeit nicht miterlebt hat . . .': Frauenerfahrungen im Zweiten Weltkrieg und in den Jahren danach*, II (Frankfurt, 1998), p. 24, and Grunberger, *A Social History of the Third Reich*, pp. 203–5.

33 Peter von Polenz, 'Fremdwort und Lehnwort, sprachwissenschaftlich betrachtet', in *Fremdwort-Diskussion*, ed. Peter Braun (München, 1979), p. 11.

34 'Erlass des Reichsministers für Wissenschaft, Erziehung und Volksbildung', *Deutsche Wissenschaft, Erziehung und Volksbildung*, 6 (1940), p. 534.

35 Michael Townson, *Mother-tongue and Fatherland: Language and Politics in German* (Manchester, 1992), pp. 121, 145.

36 Lizzie Collingham, *The Taste of War: World War Two and the Battle for Food* (London, 2011), pp. 370–73, and Roger Moorhouse, *Berlin at War: Life and Death in Hitler's Capital, 1939–45* (London, 2010), pp. 127, 233, 238.

37 Hubert Schmitz, *Die Bewirtschaftung der Nahrungsmittel und Verbrauchsgüter, 1939–1950* (Essen, 1956).

38 Dörr, *'Wer die Zeit nicht miterlebt hat . . .'*, p. 20; Götz Aly, *Hitlers Volksstaat: Raub, Rassenkrieg und nationaler Sozialismus* (Frankfurt, 2005), pp. 93–206; and Heinrich Böll, *Briefe aus dem Krieg 1939–1945* (Köln, 2001).

39 Ulrich Kluge, *Agrarwirtschaft und ländliche Gesellschaft im 20. Jahrhundert* (München, 2005), p. 34.

40 Mogens R. Nissen, 'Danish Food Production in the German War Economy', in *Food and Conflict in Europe in the Age of the Two World Wars*, ed. Trentmann and Just, pp. 172–92.

41 Moorhouse, *Berlin at War*, p. 97.

42 Ibid., p. 99.

43 Herbert Obenaus, 'Hunger und Überleben in den nationalsozialistischen Konzentrationslagern (1938–1945)', in *Der Kampf um das tägliche Brot*, ed. Gailus and Volkmann, pp. 361–76, and Primo Levi, *If This is a Man*, trans. Stuart Woolf (London, 1966), pp. 83–5.

44 Ulrich Kluge, 'Kriegs- und Mangelernährung im Nationalsozialismus', in *Beiträge zur historischen Sozialkunde*, 2 (1985), pp. 67–73, Dörr, '*Wer die Zeit nicht miterlebt hat . . .*', p. 29.

45 Herbert Gierschke, *Zur Problematik der Nahrungsversorgung in Krisenzeiten*, diss. (Hohenheim, 1963), examining the question of food supplies in times of crises, the author cites the First World War as a negative model to learn from for the future and the Second World War as a positive model. His analytical words and numbers are an example of how a so-called scientific approach makes horror palatable.

46 Dörr, '*Wer die Zeit nicht miterlebt hat . . .*', p. 37.

47 Ibid., pp. 39–40, my trans.

48 Alois Wierlacher, *Vom Essen in der deutschen Literatur* (Stuttgart, 1987), pp. 65–8.

49 Dörr, '*Wer die Zeit nicht miterlebt hat . . .*', p. 30; Victor Gollancz, *In Darkest Germany* (London, 1947), pp. 27–9; and Sibylle Meyer and Eva Schulze, *Wie wir das alles geschafft haben: Alleinstehende Frauen berichten über ihr Leben nach 1945* (Munich, 1988), p. 191.

50 Gollancz, *In Darkest Germany*, p. 13.

51 Dörr, '*Wer die Zeit nicht miterlebt hat . . .*', p. 19, and Arnold Sywottek, 'From Starvation to Excess? Trends in the Consumer Society from the 1940s to the 1970s', in *The Miracle Years: A Cultural History of West Germany, 1949–1968*, ed. Hanna Schissler (Princeton, NJ, 2001), pp. 341–58.

52 Allen, *Hungrige Metropole*, pp. 95–113, and Pracht, *M. Kempinski & Co.*, pp. 102–66.

53 Dörr, '*Wer die Zeit nicht miterlebt hat . . .*', p. 39.

54 Wolfgang Protzner, 'Vom Hungerwinter', in *Vom Hungerwinter zum Schlaraffenland: Aspekte einer Kulturgeschichte des Essens in der Bundesrepublik Deutschland*, ed. Wolfgang Protzner (Wiesbaden, 1987), pp. 11–30.

55 Meyer and Schulze, *Wie wir das alles geschafft haben*, p. 132.

56 Annette Kaminsky, 'Ungleichheit in der SBZ/DDR am Beispiel des Konsums: Versandhandel, Intershop und Delikat', in *Soziale Ungleichheit in der DDR*, ed. Lothar Mertens (Berlin, 2002), pp. 57–79.

57 Ursula Neeb, *Wasserhäuschen: Eine Frankfurter Institution* (Frankfurt, 2005).

58 Uwe Timm, *The Invention of Curried Sausage*, trans. Leila Vennewitz (New York, 1995).

ELEVEN: *Kasslerrollen* and *Toast Hawaii*

1 Ina Merkel, *Utopie und Bedürfnis: Die Geschichte der Konsumkultur in der DDR* (Köln, 1999), pp. 172–5, and Mary Fulbrook, *The People's State: East German Society from Hitler to Honecker* (New Haven, CT, 2005), p. 282.

2 Jutta Voigt, *Der Geschmack des Ostens: Vom Essen, Trinken und Leben in der DDR* (Berlin, 2008), p. 29.

3 Philipp Heldmann, 'Negotiating Consumption in a Dictatorship: Consumption Politics in the GDR in the 1950s and 1960s', in *The Politics of Consumption: Material Culture and Citizenship in Europe and America*, ed. Martin Daunton and Matthew Hilton (Oxford, 2001), pp. 185–202; Merkel, *Utopie und Bedürfnis*, pp. 48–65 and pp. 270–77; and Voigt, *Der Geschmack des Ostens*, p. 198.

4 Heldmann, 'Negotiating Consumption in a Dictatorship', p. 201. From 1979 East Germans weren't allowed to directly spend their West German currency at Intershops, but had to swap DM for *Forum Schecks* issued by the GDR state bank.

5 Annette Kaminsky, 'Ungleichheit in der SBZ/DDR am Beispiel des Konsums: Versandhandel, Intershop und Delikat', in *Soziale Ungleichheit in der DDR: Zu einem tabuisierten Strukturmerkmal der sed-Diktatur*, ed. Lothar Mertens (Berlin, 2002), pp. 57–79.

6 Voigt, *Der Geschmack des Ostens*, p. 43.

7 Kaminsky, 'Ungleichheit in der SBZ/DDR am Beispiel des Konsums', p. 74.

8 Christoph Klessmann and Georg Wagner, ed., *Das gespaltene Land: Leben in Deutschland 1945–1990: Texte und Dokumente zur Sozialgeschichte* (München, 1993), pp. 378–79, and Voigt, *Der Geschmack des Ostens*, p. 197.

9 Ulf Dirlmeier et al., *Kleine deutsche Geschichte* (Stuttgart, 2006), p. 451.

10 Fulbrook, *The People's State*, p. 42; Voigt, *Der Geschmack des Ostens*, p. 101; and Heinrich-Karl Gräfe, *Richtige Ernährung – gesunde Menschen: Nahrungsbedarf, Ernährungsweise und Kostpläne unter verschiedenen Lebens- und Arbeitsbedingungen* (Leipzig, 1967).

11 Fulbrook, *The People's State*, p. 159, and Klessmann and Wagner, ed., *Das gespaltene Land*, pp. 459–60.

12 Patrice G. Poutrus, *Die Erfindung des Goldbroilers: Über den Zusammenhang zwischen Herrschaftssicherung und Konsumentwicklung in der DDR* (Köln, 2002).

13 Ursula Winnington, *Ein Leib- und Magenbuch: Kulinarische Notizen* (Berlin, 1981).

14 'Bienen vom Grill', *Der Spiegel*, 47 (1982), pp. 270–73.

15 Manfred Otto, *Gastronomische Entdeckungen* (Berlin, 1984).

16 Merkel, *Utopie und Bedürfnis*, p. 171.

17 Hans-Hermann Hertle and Stefan Wolle, *Damals in der DDR: Der Alltag im Arbeiter- und Bauernstaat* (München, 2004), pp. 163–6.

18 Kurt Drummer, *Kochkunst aus dem Fernsehstudio* (Leipzig, n.d. [1968]), pp. 178–210.

19 Karin Weiss and Mike Dennis, eds, *Erfolg in der Nische? Die Vietnamesen in*

der DDR *und in Ostdeutschland* (Münster, 2005).

20 Michael Wildt, *Am Beginn der 'Konsumgesellschaft'* (Hamburg, 1994), p. 33.

21 Michael Wildt, 'Abschied von der "Fresswelle" oder: die Pluralisierung des Geschmacks: Essen in der Bundesrepublik Deutschland der fünfziger Jahre', in *Kulturthema Essen*, ed. Alois Wierlacher, Gerhard Neumann and Hans Jürgen Teuteberg (Berlin, 1993), p. 224.

22 Harald Winkel, 'Vom Gourmand zum Gourmet', in *Vom Hungerwinter zum Schlaraffenland: Aspekte einer Kulturgeschichte des Essens in der Bundesrepublik Deutschland*, ed. Wolfgang Protzner (Wiesbaden, 1987), p. 35.

23 Ursula Heinzelmann, *Food Culture in Germany* (Westport, CT, 2008), p. 36, and Wildt, *Am Beginn der 'Konsumgesellschaft'*, p. 381.

24 Ibid., pp. 79–81.

25 Ibid., p. 67.

26 Ibid., pp. 214–39.

27 Klessmann and Wagner, ed., *Das gespaltene Land*, p. 337.

28 Wildt, *Am Beginn der 'Konsumgesellschaft'*, pp. 121, 182.

29 Silvia Becker, *Kochsendungen in der Bundesrepublik Deutschland und in der* DDR: *Clemens Wilmenrods 'Bitte in zehn Minuten zu Tisch' und Kurt Drummers 'Der Fernsehkoch empfiehlt' im Vergleich* (Hamburg, 2010).

30 Klessmann and Wagner, ed., *Das gespaltene Land*, p. 186, my trans.

31 H. Kraut and W. Wirths, ed., *Mehr Wissen um Ernährung* (Frankfurt am Main, 1955), pp. 89–93.

32 Irmgard Schön, 'Wandlungen in den Verzehrsgewohnheiten bei Fleisch von 1945 bis zur Gegenwart', in *Vom Hungerwinter zum Schlaraffenland*, ed. Protzner, p. 109.

33 Otto Neuloh and Hans-Jürgen Teuteberg, *Ernährungsfehlverhalten im Wohlstand: Ergebnisse einer empirisch-soziologischen Untersuchung in heutigen Familienhaushalten* (Paderborn, 1979), pp. 115, 140, 196, 208.

34 *Statistisches Jahrbuch der Bundesrepublik Deutschland 1979* (1980), p. 435, at www.tiefkuehlkost.de, and *Statistisches Jahrbuch der Bundesrepublik Deutschland 1990* (1991), p. 488.

35 Klessmann and Wagner, ed., *Das gespaltene Land*, p. 278, and Helge Pross, *Die Wirklichkeit der Hausfrau* (Reinbek, 1976), pp. 107–8.

36 Frank Grube and Gerhard Richter, *Das Wirtschaftswunder: Unser Weg in den Wohlstand* (Hamburg, 1983), p. 102.

37 Klessmann and Wagner, ed., *Das gespaltene Land*, pp. 194, 250–52, 183.

38 Ulrich Kluge, *Agrarwirtschaft und ländliche Gesellschaft im 20. Jahrhundert* (München, 2005), p. 45.

39 Günter Wallraff, *13 unerwünschte Reportagen* (Köln, 1969), pp. 18–36, http://de.statista.com, accessed 30 July 2012.

40 Günter Walraff, *Ganz unten* (Köln, 1986), trans. *Lowest of the Low* (London, 1988).

41 Hartmut Heller, '"Kritik an Vorstellungen von der 'frühen bodenständigen Hausmannskos'": Alte und junge Globalisierungstendenzen in der Nahrungslandschaft Franken', in *Ernährung und Raum: Regionale und ethnische Ernährungsweisen in Deutschland*, ed. Kurt Gedrich and Ulrich Oltersdorf (Karlsruhe, 2002), p. 193.

TWELVE: Spaghetti and *Rouladen*

1 Jutta Voigt quoted in *Tagesspiegel*, no. 20523 (2010), p. 54.

2 For an up-to-date list see 'Agriculture and Rural Development: DOOR', http://ec.europa.eu, accessed 12 August 2012.

3 Ulrich Ermann, 'Regional essen? Wert und Authentizität der Regionalität von Nahrungsmitteln', in *Ernährung und Raum: Regionale und ethnische Ernährungsweisen in Deutschland*, ed. Kurt Gedrich and Ulrich Oltersdorf (Karlsruhe, 2002), pp. 121–40.

4 Christine Brombach, 'Essen und Trinken im Familienalltag – eine qualitative Studie: Essen hessische Familien hessische Kost?', in *Ernährung und Raum*, ed. Gedrich and Oltersdorf, pp. 87–99.

5 Statistisches Bundesamt, 'Erzeugung und Verbrauch von Lebensmitteln, Presseexemplar', *Frankfurter Allgemeine Sonntagszeitung*, 11 (2006), p. 44.

6 Werner Klohn, 'Konzentrationsprozesse in der deutschen Ernährungswirtschaft: Ursachen, Verlauf, Auswirkungen', in *Ernährung und Raum*, ed. Gedrich and Oltersdorf, pp. 197–212.

7 Hans J. Teuteberg, *Die Revolution am Esstisch: Neue Studien zur Nahrungskultur im 19./20. Jahrhundert* (Stuttgart, 2004), p. 13.

8 At www.cjd.ed.ac.uk, latest CJD figures accessed 22 August 2012.

9 *Frankfurter Allgemeine Sonntagszeitung* 4 (2010), 'Ökolandbau in Zahlen', at www.oekolandbau.de, and Bund Ökolögische Lebensmittelwirtschaft, 'Die Bio-Branche 2012', at www.boelw.de, both accessed 5 August 2012.

10 Nationale Verzehrsstudie II (Karlsruhe, 2008)

11 Ibid.

12 Anne-Marie Pailhès, 'From the 'Niche Society' to a Retreat from Society: East German Allotments as the Continuation of a Tradition?', in *Remembering the German Democratic Republic: Divided Memory in a United Germany*, ed. David Clarke and Ute Wölfel (Basingtoke, 2011), pp. 131–43.

13 Mensink, 2002, and Nationale Verzehrsstudie II, Karlsruhe: Max-Rubner-Institut, Bundesforschungsinstitut für Ernährung und Lebensmittel (2008), at www.was-esse-ich.de. Twenty-eight per cent of German women and 37 per cent of German men consider that one has the right to smoke. Since 2007 it is generally banned in all public spaces, including on public transportation and in taxis. However, the law concerning restaurants and the catering trade is subject to the jurisdiction of the individual *Länder* (states). Many restaurant and pub owners are lobbying against a total ban, for fear of losing customers, so that a patchwork of different regulations is to be expected, similar to the differing alcohol laws in the United States.

14 Claudia Pinl, 'Wo bleibt die Zeit? Die Zeitbudgeterhebung 2001/02 des Statistischen Bundesamts', in *Aus Politik und Zeitgeschichte*, 31–2 (2004), pp. 19–25.

15 *Frankfurter Allgemeine Sonntagszeitung* 29 (2004).

16 See www.destatis.de, accessed 5 August 2012.

17 Uta Meier, Christine Küster and Uta Zander, 'Alles wie gehabt? – Geschlechtsspezifische Arbeitsteilung und Mahlzeitenmuster im Zeitvergleich', in *Alltag in Deutschland: Forum der Bundesstatistik*,

Statistisches Bundesamt 43 (2004), pp. 114–130, Forsa survey 2010, and Nationale Verzehrsstudie.

18 Podomedi, 'Was essen di Deutschen am liebsten?: Die Hitliste der Lebensgerichte', at www.podomedi.com, accessed 13 August 2012.

19 Steven Ozment, *A Mighty Fortress: A New History of the German People* (New York, 2005), p. 316.

Select Bibliography

Abel, Wilhelm, *Einige Bemerkungen zum Land-Stadtproblem im Spätmittelalter* (Göttingen, 1976)

——, *Stufen der Ernährung: Eine historische Skizze* (Göttingen, 1981)

Achilles, Walter, *Deutsche Agrargeschichte im Zeitalter der Reformen und der Industrialisierung* (Stuttgart, 1993)

Adamson, Melitta Weiss, *Medieval Dietetics: Food and Drink in Regimen Sanitatis: Literature from 800 to 1400* (Frankfurt, 1995)

——, ed., *Regional Cuisines of Medieval Europe: A Book of Essays* (New York, 2002)

——, ed., *Food in the Middle Ages: A Book of Essays* (New York, 1995)

——, *Daz buoch von guoter spise (The Book of Good Food): A Study, Edition, and English Translation of the Oldest German Cookbook* (Krems, 2000)

Albala, Ken, *Eating Right in the Renaissance* (Berkeley, CA, 2002)

Allen, Keith R., *Hungrige Metropole: Essen, Wohlfahrt und Kommerz in Berlin* (Hamburg, 2002)

Aly, Götz, *Hitlers Volksstaat: Raub, Rassenkrieg und nationaler Sozialismus* (Frankfurt, 2005)

Amaranthes, *Nutzbares, galantes und curiöses Frauenzimmer-Lexicon . . .* [1715], ed. Manfred Lemmer (Leipzig, 1980)

Bäumler, Susanne, ed., *Die Kunst zu werben: Das Jahrhundert der Reklame* (Köln, 1996)

Bardenhewer, Luise, *Der Safranhandel im Mittelalter*, diss. (Bonn, 1914)

Barlösius, Eva, *Naturgemässe Lebensführung: Zur Geschichte der Lebensreform um die Jahrhundertwende* (Frankfurt, 1997)

Becker, Silvia, *Kochsendungen in der Bundesrepublik Deutschland und in der DDR: Clemens Wilmenrods 'Bitte in zehn Minuten zu Tisch' und Kurt Drummers 'Der Fernsehkoch empfiehlt' im Vergleich* (Hamburg, 2010)

Bekmann, Johann Christoph, *Historische Beschreibung der Chur und Mark Brandenburg* (Berlin, 1751)

Berg-Ehlers, Luise, and Gotthard Erler, eds, *'Ich bin nicht für halbe Portionen': Essen und Trinken mit Theodor Fontane* (Berlin, 1995)

Berghoff, Hartmut, ed., *Konsumpolitik: Die Regulierung des privaten Verbrauchs im 20. Jahrhundert* (Göttingen, 1999)

Bickel, Walter, *Deutsche Landesküchen* (Leipzig, n.d. [1949])

Bircher, Alice, *Speisezettel und Kochrezepte für diätetische Ernährung*, 2nd edn (Berlin, 1908)

Bitsch, Irmgard, Trude Ehlert und Xenja von Ertzdorff, eds, *Essen und Trinken in Mittelalter und Neuzeit* (Sigmaringen, 1987)

Blaich, Fritz, *Wirtschaft und Rüstung im 'Dritten Reich'* (Düsseldorf, 1987)

Borscheid, Peter, and Clemens Wischermann, eds, *Bilderwelt des Alltags: Werbung in der Konsumgesellschaft des 19. und 20. Jahrhunderts* (Stuttgart, 1995)

Borst, Otto, *Alltagsleben im Mittelalter* (Frankfurt, 1983)

Braune, Gudrun, and Peter Fauser, eds, *Von Brotbänken, Erdäpfeln und Brauhäusern, Thüringer Hefte für Volkskunde*, 13 (2006)

Bumke, Joachim, *Höfische Kultur: Literatur und Gesellschaft im hohen Mittelalter*, 5th edn (München, 2005)

Clarke, David and Ute Wölfel, eds, *Remembering the German Democratic Republic: Divided Memory in a United Germany* (Basingtoke, 2011)

Collingham, Lizzie, *The Taste of War: World War Two and the Battle for Food* (London, 2011)

Conze, Werner, ed., *Arbeiterexistenz im 19. Jahrhundert* (Stuttgart, 1981)

Corni, Gustavo, and Horst Gies, *Brot, Butter, Kanonen: Die Ernährungswirtschaft in Deutschland unter der Diktatur Hitlers* (Berlin, 1997)

Craig, Gordon A., *The Germans* (New York, 1982, 1991)

Curschmann, Fritz, *Hungersnöte im Mittelalter: Ein Beitrag zur deutschen Wirtschaftsgeschichte des 8. bis 13. Jahrhunderts* (Leipzig, 1900)

Daniel, Ute, *Arbeiterfrauen in der Kriegsgesellschaft: Beruf, Familie und Politik im Ersten Weltkrieg* (Göttingen, 1989)

Dapper, Alexandra, *Zu Tisch bei Martin Luther* (Halle, 2008)

Daunton, Martin and Matthew Hilton, eds, *The Politics of Consumption: Material Culture and Citizenship in Europe and America* (Oxford, 2001)

Degener, Paul, *Zur Frage der Jam- und Marmelade-Industrie, sowie des Zuckerverbrauchs in England* (Berlin, 1899)

Delbrück, Anton, *Hygiene des Alkoholismus* (Leipzig, 1913)

Döring, Tobias, Markus Heide and Susanne Mühleisen, eds, *Eating Culture: The Poetics and Politics of Food* (Heidelberg, 2003)

Dörr, Margarete, *'Wer die Zeit nicht miterlebt hat . . .': Frauenerfahrungen im Zweiten Weltkrieg und in den Jahren danach*, II (Frankfurt, 1998)

Drews, Joachim, *Die Nazi-Bohne* (Münster, 2004)

Drummer, Kurt, *Kochkunst aus dem Fernsehstudio* (Leipzig, n.d. [1968])

Dunger, Hermann, ed., *Verdeutschungsbücher des Allgemeinen Deutschen Sprachvereins*, I *Deutsche Speisekarte* (Braunschweig, 1888)

Ekkehard IV, *St Galler Klostergeschichten*, trans. Hans. F. Haefele, 4th edn (Darmstadt, 2002)

Ehlert, Trude, ed., *Haushalt und Familie in Mittelalter und früher Neuzeit: Vorträge eines interdisziplinären Symposions vom 6.–9. Juni 1990 an der Rheinischen Friedrich-Wilhelms-Universität Bonn* (Sigmaringen, 1991)

Ellerbrock, Karl-Peter, *Geschichte der deutschen Nahrungs- und Genussmittelindustrie 1750–1914* (Stuttgart, 1993)

Elsas, M. J., *Umriss einer Geschichte der Preise und Löhne in Deutschland* (Leiden, 1949)

Ennen, Edith, *Frauen im Mittelalter*, 2nd edn (München, 1985)

Epperlein, Siegfried, *Bäuerliches Leben im Mittelalter: Schriftquellen und Bildzeugnisse* (Köln, 2003)

Freedman, Paul, ed., *Food: The History of Taste* (London, 2007)

Fulbrook, Mary, *A Concise History of Germany*, 2nd edn (Cambridge, 2004)

——, *The People's State: East German Society from Hitler to Honecker* (New Haven, CT, 2005)

Gailus, Manfred, and Heinrich Volkmann, eds, *Der Kampf um das tägliche Brot: Nahrungsmangel, Versorgungspolitik und Protest 1770–1990* (Opladen, 1994)

Gedrich, Kurt, and Ulrich Oltersdorf, eds, *Ernährung und Raum: Regionale und ethnische Ernährungsweisen in Deutschland* (Karlsruhe, 2002)

Göhre, Paul, *Drei Monate Fabrikarbeiter und Handwerksbursche* (Leipzig, 1891)

Gollancz, Victor, *In Darkest Germany* (London, 1947)

Gräfe, Heinrich-Karl, *Richtige Ernährung – gesunde Menschen: Nahrungsbedarf, Ernährungsweise und Kostpläne unter verschiedenen Lebens- und Arbeitsbedingungen* (Leipzig, 1967)

Grotjahn, Alfred, *Über Wandlungen in der Volksernährung* (Leipzig, 1902)

Grunberger, Richard, *A Social History of the Third Reich* (London, 1971)

Grüttner, Felix, *Geschichte der Fleischversorgung in Deutschland* (Braunschweig, 1938)

Haberlandt, Friedrich, *Die Sojabohne* (Wien, 1878)

Habs, Robert, and Leopold Rosner, eds, *Appetit-Lexikon* (Vienna, 1894)

Haskarl, Liane, ed., *Die Macht der Hausfrau: Eine ernährungswirtschaftliche Fibel für den Verbraucher* (Kiel, 1952)

Heinzelmann, Ursula, *Food Culture in Germany* (Westport, CT, 2008)

Heischkel-Artelt, Edith, ed., *Ernährung und Ernährungslehre im 19. Jahrhundert* (Göttingen, 1976)

Heise, Ulla, *Kaffee und Kaffeehaus* (Leipzig, 1996)

Henning, Friedrich-Wilhelm, *Deutsche Agrargeschichte des Mittelalters: 9. bis 15. Jahrhundert* (Stuttgart, 1994)

Herrmann, Bernd, ed., *Mensch und Umwelt im Mittelalter*, 3rd edn (Stuttgart, 1987)

Hertle, Hans-Hermann, and Stefan Wolle, *Damals in der DDR: Der Alltag im Arbeiter- und Bauernstaat* (München, 2004)

Huegel, Arnulf, *Kriegsernährungswirtschaft Deutschlands während des Ersten und Zweiten Weltkriegs im Vergleich* (Konstanz, 2003)

Irsigler, Franz, *Die wirtschaftliche Stellung der Stadt Köln im 14. und 15. Jahrhundert: Strukturanalyse einer spätmittelalterlichen Exportgewerbe- und Fernhandelstadt* (Wiesbaden, 1979)

Johnson, Anna C., *Peasant Life in Germany* (New York, 1858)

Jordan, William Chester, *The Great Famine: Northern Europe in the Early Fourteenth Century* (Princeton, NJ, 1996)

Kellenbenz, Hermann, ed., *Handbuch der europäischen Wirtschafts- und Sozialgeschichte* (Stuttgart, 1980)

Kippenberger, Susanne, *Am Tisch: Die kulinarische Bohème oder Die Entdeckung der Lebenslust* (Berlin, 2009)

Kleßmann, Christoph and Georg Wagner, eds, *Das gespaltene Land: Leben in Deutschland 1945-1990: Texte und Dokumente zur Sozialgeschichte* (München, 1993)

Kluge, Ulrich, *Agrarwirtschaft und ländliche Gesellschaft im 20. Jahrhundert* (München, 2005)

Kraut, H. and W. Wirths, eds, *Mehr Wissen um Ernährung* (Frankfurt am Main, 1955)

Kronfeld, M. *Geschichte des Safrans und seiner Cultur in Europa* (Vienna, 1892)

Kuczynski, Jürgen, *Darstellung der Lage der Arbeiter in Deutschland von 1789 bis 1849* (Berlin, 1961)

Kühnel, Harry, ed., *Alltag im Spätmittelalter*, 3rd edn (Graz, 1986)

Lamberty, Christiane, *Reklame in Deutschland 1890–1914* (Berlin, 2000)

Laurioux, Bruno, *Une Histoire Culinaire du Moyen Âge* (Paris, 2005)

——, *Manger au Moyen Âge: Pratiques et discours alimentaires en Europe au xive et xve siècle* (Paris, 2002)

Levi, Primo, *If This is a Man*, trans. Stuart Woolf (London, 1966)

Lössnitzer, Ernst, *Verdeutschungs-Wörterbuch der Fachsprache der Kochkunst und Küche*, 2nd edn (Dresden, 1903)

Lüning, Jens, Albrecht Jockenhövel, Helmut Bender and Torsten Capelle, *Deutsche Agrargeschichte Vor- und Frühgeschichte* (Stuttgart, 1997)

MacDonogh, Giles, *Berlin* (London, 1997)

Marperger, Paul Jacob, *Vollständiges Küch- und Keller-Dictionarium* (Hamburg, 1716)

Mensink, Gert, *Was essen wir heute? Ernährungsverhalten in Deutschland* (Berlin, 2002)

Merkel, Ina, *Utopie und Bedürfnis: Die Geschichte der Konsumkultur in der DDR* (Köln, 1999)

Meyer, Sibylle, *Das Theater mit der Hausarbeit: Bürgerliche Repräsentation in der Familie der wilhelminischen Zeit* (Frankfurt, 1982)

——, and Eva Schulze, *Wie wir das alles geschafft haben: Alleinstehende Frauen berichten über ihr Leben nach 1945* (München, 1988)

Meyer-Renschhausen, Elisabeth (with Albert Wirz), *Der Streit um den heissen Brei: Zu Ökologie und Geschlecht einer Kulturanthropologie der Ernährung* (Herbolzheim, 2002)

Moorhouse, Roger, *Berlin at War: Life and Death in Hitler's Capital, 1939–45* (London, 2010)

Nolan, Mary, *Visions of Modernity: American Business and the Modernization of Germany* (New York, 1994)

Otto, Manfred, *Gastronomische Entdeckungen* (Berlin, 1984)

Ozment, Steven, *A Mighty Fortress: A New History of the German People* (New York, 2005)

Petras, Renate, *Das Café Bauer in Berlin* (Berlin, 1994)

Pierenkemper, Toni, ed., *Haushalt und Verbrauch in historischer Perspektive: Zum Wandel des privaten Verbrauchs in Deutschland im 19. und 20. Jahrhundert* (St Katharinen, 1987)

Poutrus, Patrice G., *Die Erfindung des Goldbroilers: Über den Zusammenhang zwischen Herrschaftssicherung und Konsumentwicklung in der DDR* (Köln, 2002)

Pracht, Elfi, *M. Kempinski & Co* (Berlin, 1994)

Pross, Helge, *Die Wirklichkeit der Hausfrau* (Reinbek, 1976)

Protzner, Wolfgang, ed., *Vom Hungerwinter zum Schlaraffenland: Aspekte einer Kulturgeschichte des Essens in der Bundesrepublik Deutschland* (Wiesbaden, 1987)

Putsche, Carl Wilhelm Ernst, *Versuch einer Monographie oder ausführliche Beschreibung der Kartoffeln . . .* (Weimar, 1819)

Reagin, Nancy R., *Sweeping the German Nation: Domesticity and National Identity in Germany, 1870–1945* (Cambridge, 2007)

Roerkohl, Anne, *Hungerblockade und Heimatfront: Die kommunale Lebensmittelversorgung in Westfalen während des Ersten Weltkriegs* (Stuttgart, 1991)

Saldern, Adelheid von, *Häuserleben: Zur Geschichte städtischen Arbeiterwohnens vom Kaiserreich bis heute* (Bonn, 1995)

Schissler, Hanna, ed., *The Miracle Years: A Cultural History of West Germany, 1949–1968* (Princeton, NJ, 2001)

Schlegel-Matthies, Kirsten, *'Im Haus und am Herd': Der Wandel des Hausfrauenbildes und der Hausarbeit 1880–1930* (Stuttgart, 1995)

Schönfeldt, Sybil Gräfin, *Sonderappell* (München, 2002)

Schumburg, Wilhelm, *Hygiene der Einzelernährung und Massenernährung* (Leipzig, 1913)

Scully, Terence, *Art of Cookery in the Middle Ages* (Woodbridge, 1995)

Siegrist, Hannes, Hartmut Kaelble and Jürgen Kocka, eds, *Europäische Konsumgeschichte: Zur Gesellschafts- und Kulturgeschichte des Konsums (18. bis 20. Jahrhundert)* (Frankfurt, 1997)

Skalweit, August, *Die deutsche Kriegsernährungswirtschaft* (Stuttgart, 1927)

Stillich, Oscar, *Die Lage der weiblichen Dienstboten in Berlin* (Berlin, 1902)

Tacitus, Cornelius, *Agricola* and *Germania*, trans. Anthony R. Birley (Oxford, 1999)

Täubrich, Hans-Christian, *Zu Gast im alten Berlin*, 2nd edn (München, 1990)

Teuteberg, Hans Jürgen, ed., *Durchbruch zum modernen Massenkonsum: Lebensmittelmärkte und Lebensmittelqualität im Städtewachstum des Industriezeitalters* (Münster, 1987)

——, *Die Revolution am Esstisch: Neue Studien zur Nahrungskultur im 19./20. Jahrhundert* (Stuttgart, 2004)

Teuteberg, Hans Jürgen, Gerhard Neumann and Alois Wierlacher, eds, *Essen und kulturelle Identität* (Berlin, 1997)

Teuteberg, Hans J., and Günter Wiegelmann, *Der Wandel der Nahrungsgewohnheiten unter dem Einfluß der Industrialisierung* (Göttingen, 1972)

——, *Unsere tägliche Kost: Geschichte und regionale Prägung* (Münster, 1986)

Thoms, Ulrike, *Anstaltskost im Rationalisierungsprozeß: Die Ernährung in Krankenhäusern und Gefängnissen im 18. und 19. Jahrhundert* (Stuttgart, 2005)

Townson, Michael, *Mother-tongue and Fatherland: Language and Politics in German* (Manchester, 1992)

Trentmann, Frank, and Flemming Just, eds, *Food and Conflict in Europe in the Age of the Two World Wars* (Houndsmills, 2006)

von Treskow, Maria, *Berliner Kochbuch: aus alten Familienrezepten* (Weingarten, 1987)

Tudge, Colin, *Neanderthals, Bandits and Farmers: How Agriculture Really Began* (New Haven, 1998)

Vincent, C. Paul, *The Politics of Hunger: The Allied Blockade of Germany, 1915–1919* (Athens, OH, 1985)

Voigt, Jutta, *Der Geschmack des Ostens: Vom Essen, Trinken und Leben in der DDR* (Berlin, 2008)

Voit, Carl, ed., *Untersuchung der Kost in einigen öffentlichen Anstalten für Aerzte und Verwaltungsbeamte* (München, 1877)

Volkmann, Heinrich and Jürgen Bergmann, eds, *Sozialer Protest: Studien zu traditioneller Resistenz und kollektiver Gewalt in Deutschland vom Vormärz bis zur Reichsgründung* (Opladen, 1984)

Wallraff, Günter, *13 unerwünschte Reportagen* (Köln, 1969)

Weiss, Karin and Mike Dennis, eds, *Erfolg in der Nische? Die Vietnamesen in der DDR und in Ostdeutschland* (Münster, 2005)

Weisser, Jürgen, *Zwischen Lustgarten und Lunapark: Der Volksgarten in Nymphenburg (1890–1916) und die Entwicklung der kommerziellen Belustigungsgärten* (München, 1998)

Wiegelmann, Günter, ed., *Nord-Süd-Unterschiede in der städtischen und ländlichen Kultur Mitteleuropas* (Münster, 1985)

——, *Wandel der Alltagskultur seit dem Mittelalter: Phasen – Epochen – Zäsuren* (Münster, 1987)

——, and Ruth-E. Mohrmann, eds, *Nahrung und Tischkultur im Hanseraum* (Münster, 1996)

Wierlacher, Alois, *Vom Essen in der deutschen Literatur* (Stuttgart, 1987)

——, Gerhard Neumann und Hans Jürgen Teuteberg, eds, *Kulturthema Essen* (Berlin, 1993)

Wildt, Michael, *Am Beginn der 'Konsumgesellschaft'* (Hamburg, 1994)

Willcox, Walter F., *International Migrations*, I (New York, 1929)

Ziegelman, Jane, *97 Orchard: An Edible History of Five Immigrant Families in One New York Tenement* (New York, 2010)

Acknowledgements

How much easier it is to deal with hunger and thirst when one feels surrounded by a group of like-minded people, be they family, friends or colleagues. For this book, many have provided me with food and drink, literally on the plate and in the glass, and in the form of helpful guidance and information. Very special mentions are due to Stefan Abtmeyer, Keith Arbour, Hans Bergemann, Frank Ebbinghaus, Jutta and Wolfram Eberhard, Elisabeth Luard, William Rubel, Sabrina Small, Melitta Weiss-Adamson and Barbara Ketcham Wheaton. They all supported me in the most generous way after Michael Leaman of Reaktion Books trusted me with this task. My grandparents and my parents provided me with the cultural and social background without which this book would have been impossible to write, and Stuart Pigott convinced me I could do it. *Danke.*

Photo Acknowledgements

The author and publishers wish to express their thanks to the below sources of illustrative material and / or permission to reproduce it

Photo Stefan Abtmeyer: pp. 172, 282, 312; from Dr Oetker, *Backbuch* (*c.* 1960s): pp. 110, 2231; photo Konrad Bedal: p. 114; photo Ullstein Bild: p. 175; courtesy Botanical Museum Berlin: p. 140; courtesy Bröhan Museum Berlin: p. 222; courtesy Bundesarchiv: pp. 105 (photo Brodde), 246 (photo Seiler), 259 (Designer Grünwald), 270 (designer Max Eschle), 285 (photo Hans Lachmann), 297 (photo Helmut Schaar); from Leonhart Fuchs, *Kreutterbuch* (Basel, 1543): p. 87; photo Victor Gollancz: p. 284; photo Hanns Hubmann: pp. 280 (top), 287; from Sigrid Jacobeit, *Ill Alltagsgeschichte des deutschen Volkes Bd1* (Berlin: Urania, 1985): pp. 55, 63, 75, 115, 117, 152, 160, 162, 188, 191, 192, 193, 212, 220, 226, 241; from *Catalogue. 2000 Jahre Weinkultur an Mosel-Saar-Ruwer* (Rheinisches Landesmuseum Trier, 1987): pp. 25, 27; photo Vuk D. Karadzic: p. 289; courtesy of Juliusspital: p. 101; courtesy SMBPK Kunstbibliothek Berlin: p. 141; from Bruno Laurioux, *Tafelfreuden im Mittelalter* (Paris: Adam Biró, 1989): pp. 33 (top), 44; photo Jens Rötzsch: p. 306; from Fritz Ruf, ed., *Löffelspeise* (Velbert-Neviges: BeRing, 1989): pp. 13, 153, 168; courtesy LH-Bildarchiv: p. 317; Courtesy Nationalgalerie Berlin: pp. 215, 225; photo courtesy Niederegger GmbH: p. 83; photo Florian Niedermeier: p. 344; courtesy www.stgallplan.org: p. 41; photo Achim Tsutsui: p. 78; courtesy Werner Forman Archive, from *Hildegard von Bingen, Book of Divine Works Part One, Vision Four: Symmetries: World, Body and Soul* (1165): p. 64.

Index